£2.60

POETICAL WORKS

OF

ROBERT BRIDGES

UNIFORM EDITION OF
ROBERT BRIDGES' POETICAL WORKS

In Six Volumes, Small Post 8vo, 6s. each

CONTENTS: VOLUME I, Prometheus the Firegiver—Eros and Psyche—The Growth of Love—Notes. VOLUME II, Shorter Poems—New Poems—Notes. VOLUME III, The First Part of Nero—Achilles in Scyros—Notes. VOLUME IV, Palicio—The Return of Ulysses—Notes. VOLUME V, The Christian Captives—Humours of the Court—Notes. VOLUME VI, The Feast of Bacchus—Second Part of the History of Nero—Notes.

EROS AND PSYCHE

Second edition, 1894, revised and in part rewritten. Ex. fcap 8vo, pp. 178.
10s. 6d. net. *Clarendon Press.*

PLAYS

Crown 4to.   7s. 6d. net each.   *Clarendon Press.*

ii. PALICIO. First edition, 1890. Pp. 34.   iv. CHRISTIAN CAPTIVES. First edition, 1890. Pp. 26.   vi. HUMOURS OF THE COURT. First edition, 1893. Pp. 36.   vii. FEAST OF BACCHUS. First published edition, 1894. Pp. 50. viii. NERO, Part 2. First edition, 1894. Pp. 34.

THE TESTAMENT OF BEAUTY

A Poem in Four Books

1929.   Crown 8vo, pp. 202.   7s. 6d. net; quarter-niger morocco,
12s. 6d. net.   *Clarendon Press.*

1930.   4to, pp. 184.   10s. net.   *Clarendon Press.*

1930.   Med. 8vo, pp. 184.   18s. net.   *Oxford University Press, New York.*

THE SHORTER POEMS OF ROBERT BRIDGES

Enlarged edition, 1931.   Fcap 8vo, pp. 242.   7s. 6d. net.   *Clarendon Press.*

NEW VERSE WRITTEN IN 1921

With the other poems of that year and a few earlier pieces.   1925.
Crown 8vo, pp. 102.   6s. net.   *Clarendon Press.*

DEMETER, A MASK

1905.   Crown 8vo, cloth, 2s. net.   Lyrics and Incidental Music by
W. H. HADOW.   Crown 4to, 2s. 6d. net.   *Clarendon Press.*

BRITANNIA VICTRIX

First edition, 1918.   Crown 8vo, pp. 4.   2s. 6d. net.
Oxford University Press

Charles Furse Pinxit 1893

Robert Bridges
Aug 1912

POETICAL WORKS

OF

ROBERT BRIDGES

*excluding
the eight dramas
& The Testament of Beauty*

LONDON
OXFORD UNIVERSITY PRESS
1936

OXFORD
UNIVERSITY PRESS
AMEN HOUSE, E.C. 4
London Edinburgh Glasgow
New York Toronto Melbourne
Capetown Bombay Calcutta
Madras
HUMPHREY MILFORD
PUBLISHER TO THE
UNIVERSITY

PRINTED IN GREAT BRITAIN

O.S.A.

NOTE
TO SECOND EDITION

THE first edition of this book consisted of the Poems and Masks (as apart from the Dramas) contained in the collected editions of the Poetical Works of Robert Bridges, together with two groups of Later Poems, and Poems in Classical Prosody which were then published or collected for the first time.

To these are now added another piece in Classical Prosody, reprints of two later volumes of verse (*October and other Poems* and *New Verse*), and two pieces hitherto not included in any collection.

A record of the previous publication of the poems will be found in the bibliographical notes prefixed to the various sections of the present book.

The spelling of certain words is not uniform throughout the poems. This is due to observance of the text of the earlier editions of different dates, in the notes to which the author's justification of these peculiarities was given.

CONTENTS

CONTENTS

PROMETHEUS THE FIREGIVER

A Mask in the Greek Manner

PREVIOUS EDITIONS

1. *Private Press of H. Daniel.   Oxford,* 1883.
2. *Chiswick Press.   G. Bell & Sons,* 1884.
3. *Clarendon Press.   Smith, Elder & Co.   Vol. I,* 1898.

ARGUMENT

Prometheus coming on earth to give fire to men appears before the palace of Inachus in Argos on a festival of Zeus. He interrupts the ceremony by announcing fire and persuades Inachus to dare the anger of Zeus and accept the gift. Inachus fetching Argeia his wife from the palace has in turn to quiet her fears. He asks a prophecy of Prometheus who foretells the fate of Io their daughter. Prometheus then setting flame to the altar and writing his own name thereon in the place of Zeus disappears.

The Chorus sing (1) a Hymn to Zeus with the stories of the birth of Zeus and the marriage of Hera with the dances of the Curetes and the Hesperides, (2) their anticipation of fire with an Ode on Wonder, (3) a Tragic Hymn on the lot of man, (4) a Fire-chorus, (5) a final Chorus in praise of Prometheus.

All the characters are good. Prometheus prologizes. He carries a long reed.

DRAMATIS PERSONÆ

PROMETHEUS.
INACHUS.
ARGEIA.
SERVANT.
IO (persona muta).
CHORUS: Youths and maidens of the house of Inachus.

The SCENE is in ARGOS before the palace of Inachus. An altar inscribed to Zeus is at the centre of the stage.

PROMETHEUS
THE FIREGIVER

PROMETHEUS.

From high Olympus and the ætherial courts,
Where mighty Zeus our angry king confirms
The Fates' decrees and bends the wills of the gods,
I come : and on the earth step with glad foot.
  This variegated ocean-floor of the air,
The changeful circle of fair land, that lies
Heaven's dial, sisterly mirror of night and day :
The wide o'er-wandered plain, this nether world
My truant haunt is, when from jealous eyes
I steal, for hither 'tis I steal, and here   10
Unseen repair my joy : yet not unseen
Methinks, nor seen unguessed of him I seek.
Rather by swath or furrow, or where the path
Is walled with corn I am found, by trellised vine
Or olive set in banks or orchard trim :
I watch all toil and tilth, farm, field and fold,
And taste the mortal joy ; since not in heaven
Among our easeful gods hath facile time
A touch so keen, to wake such love of life
As stirs the frail and careful being, who here,   20
The king of sorrows, melancholy man,
Bows at his labour, but in heart erect
A god stands, nor for any gift of god
Would barter his immortal-hearted prime.
  Could I but win this world from Zeus for mine,
With not a god to vex my happy rule,
I would inhabit here and leave high heaven :
So much I love it and its race of men,

Even as he hates them, hates both them, and me
For loving what he hates, and would destroy me,   30
Outcast in the scorn of all his cringing crew,
For daring but to save what he would slay :
And me must first destroy.   Thus he denieth
My heart's wish, thus my counsel sets at naught,
Which him saved once, when all at stake he stood
Uprisen in rebellion to overthrow
The elderseated Titans, for I that day
Gave him the counsels which his foes despised.
Unhappy they, who had still their blissful seats
Preserved and their Olympian majesty,   40
Had they been one with me.   Alas, my kin !
    But he, when he had taken the throne and chained
His foes in wasteful Tartarus, said no more
Where is Prometheus our wise counsellor ?
What saith Prometheus ? tell us, O Prometheus,
What Fate requires ! but waxing confident
And wanton, as a youth first tasting power,
He wrecked the timeless monuments of heaven,
The witness of the wisdom of the gods,
And making all about him new, beyond   50
Determined to destroy the race of men,
And that create afresh or else have none.
    Then his vain mind imagined a device,
And at his bidding all the opposèd winds
Blew, and the scattered clouds and furlèd snows,
From every part of heaven together flying,
He with brute hands in huge disorder heaped :
They with the winds' weight and his angry breath
Were thawed : in cataracts they fell, and earth
In darkness deep and whelmèd tempest lay,   60
Drowned 'neath the waters.   Yet on the mountain-tops
Some few escaped, and some, thus warned by me,
Made shift to live in vessels which outrode
The season and the fury of the flood.

And when his rain was spent and from clear skies
Zeus looking down upon the watery world,
Beheld these few, the remnant of mankind,
Who yet stood up and breathed; he next withdrew
The seeds of fire, that else had still lain hid
In withered branch and the blue flakes of flint   70
For man to exact and use, but these withdrawn,
Man with the brutes degraded would be man
No more; and so the tyrant was content.

But I, despised again, again upheld
The weak, and pitying them sent sweet Hope,
Bearer of dreams, enchantress fond and kind,
From heaven descending on the unhindered rays
Of every star, to cheer with visions fair
Their unamending pains.   And now this day
Behold I come bearing the seal of all   80
Which Hope had promised : for within this reed
A prisoner I bring them stolen from heaven,
The flash of mastering fire, and it have borne
So swift to earth, that when yon noontide sun
Rose from the sea at morning I was by,
And unperceived of Hêlios plunged the point
I' the burning axle, and withdrew a tongue
Of breathing flame, which lives to leap on earth
For man the father of all fire to come.

And hither have I brought it even to Argos   90
Unto king Inachus, him having chosen
Above all mortals to receive my gift :
For he is hopeful, careful, wise, and brave.

He first, when first the floods left bare the land,
Grew warm with enterprise, and gathered men
Together, and disposed their various tasks
For common weal combined ; for soon were seen
The long straight channels dwindling on the plain,
Which slow from stagnant pool and wide morass
The pestilent waters to the rivers bore :   100

Then in the ruined dwellings and old tombs
He dug, unbedding from the wormèd ooze
Vessels and tools of trade and husbandry;
Wherewith, all seasonable works restored,
Oil made he and wine anew, and taught mankind
To live not brutally though without fire,
Tending their flocks and herds and weaving wool,
Living on fruit and milk and shepherds' fare,
Till time should bring back flame to smithy and hearth,
Or Zeus relent.   Now at these gates I stand,   110
At this mid hour, when Inachus comes forth
To offer sacrifice unto his foe.
For never hath his faithful zeal forborne
To pay the power, though hard, that rules the world
The smokeless sacrifice; which first to-day
Shall smoke, and rise at heaven in flame to brave
The baffled god.   See here a servant bears
For the cold altar ceremonial wood:
My shepherd's cloak will serve me for disguise.

SERVANT.

With much toil have I hewn these sapless logs.   120
   Pr. But toil brings health, and health is happiness.
   Serv. Here's one I know not—nay, how came he here
Unseen by me?   I pray thee, stranger, tell me
What wouldst thou at the house of Inachus?
   Pr. Intruders, friend, and travellers have glib tongues,
Silence will question such.
   Serv.   If 'tis a message,
To-day is not thy day—who sent thee hither?
   Pr. The business of my leisure was well guessed:
But he that sent me hither is I that come.
   Serv. I smell the matter—thou wouldst serve the house?
   Pr. 'Twas for that very cause I fled my own.   131
   Serv. From cruelty or fear of punishment?
   Pr. Cruel was my master, for he slew his father.

His punishments thou speakest of are crimes.

    SERV. Thou dost well flying one that slew his father.

    PR. Thy lord, they say, is kind.

    SERV.   Well, thou wilt see.
Thou may'st at once begin—come, give a hand.

    PR. A day of freedom is a day of pleasure:
And what thou doest have I never done,
And understanding not might mar thy work.   140

    SERV. Ay true—there is a right way and a wrong
In laying wood.

    PR.   Then let me see thee lay it:
The sight of a skill'd hand will teach an art.

    SERV. Thou seest this faggot which I now unbind,
How it is packed within.

    PR.   I see the cones
And needles of the fir, which by the wind
In melancholy places ceaselessly
Sighing are strewn upon the tufted floor.

    SERV. These took I from a sheltered bank, whereon
The sun looks down at noon ; for there is need   150
The things be dry. These first I spread ; and then
Small sticks that snap i' the hand.

    PR.   Such are enough
To burden the slow flight of labouring rooks,
When on the leafless tree-tops in young March
Their glossy herds assembling soothe the air
With cries of solemn joy and cawings loud.
And such the long-necked herons will bear to mend
Their airy platform, when the loving spring
Bids them take thought for their expected young.

    SERV. See even so I cross them and cross them so :   160
Larger and by degrees a steady stack
Have built, whereon the heaviest logs may lie :
And all of sun-dried wood : and now 'tis done.

    PR. And now 'tis done, what means it now 'tis done?

    SERV. Well, thus 'tis rightly done : but why 'tis so

I cannot tell, nor any man here knows ;
Save that our master when he sacrificeth,
As thou wilt hear anon, speaketh of fire ;
And fire he saith is good for gods and men ;
And the gods have it and men have it not :   170
And then he prays the gods to send us fire ;
And we, against they send it, must have wood
Laid ready thus as I have shewn thee here.

   PR. To-day he sacrificeth ?

   SERV.   Ay, this noon.

Hark ! hear'st thou not ? they come. The solemn flutes
Warn us away ; we must not here be seen
In these our soilèd habits, yet may stand
Where we may hear and see and not be seen.

                                [Exeunt R.

Enter CHORUS, *and from the palace* INACHUS *bearing cakes : he
comes to stand behind the altar.*

CHORUS.

God of Heaven !
We praise thee, Zeus most high,   180
To whom by eternal Fate was given
The range and rule of the sky ;
When thy lot, first of three
Leapt out, as sages tell,
And won Olympus for thee,
Therein for ever to dwell :
But the next with the barren sea
To grave Poseidôn fell,
And left fierce Hades his doom, to be
The lord and terror of hell.   190
   (2) Thou sittest for aye
Encircled in azure bright,
Regarding the path of the sun by day,
And the changeful moon by night :

Attending with tireless ears
To the song of adoring love,
With which the separate spheres
Are voicèd that turn above:
And all that is hidden under
The clouds thy footing has furl'd   200
Fears the hand that holdeth the thunder,
The eye that looks on the world.

Semichorus of youths.

Of all the isles of the sea
Is Crete most famed in story:
Above all mountains famous to me
Is Ida and crowned with glory.
There guarded of Heaven and Earth
Came Rhea at fall of night
To hide a wondrous birth
From the Sire's unfathering sight.   210
The halls of Cronos rang
With omens of coming ill,
And the mad Curêtes danced and sang
Adown the slopes of the hill.

Then all the peaks of Gnossus kindled red
Beckoning afar unto the sinking sun,
He thro' the vaporous west plunged to his bed,
Sunk, and the day was done.
But they, though he was fled,
Such light still held, as oft   220
Hanging in air aloft,
At eve from shadowed ship
The Egyptian sailor sees:
Or like the twofold tip
That o'er the topmost trees
Flares on Parnassus, and the Theban dames
Quake at the ghostly flames.

Then friendly night arose
To succour Earth, and spread
Her mantle o'er the snows   230
And quenched their rosy red;
But in the east upsprings
Another light on them,
Selêné with white wings
And hueless diadem.
Little could she befriend
Her father's house and state,
Nor her weak beams defend
Hypérion from his fate.
Only where'er she shines,   240
In terror looking forth,
She sees the wailing pines
Stoop to the bitter North:
Or searching twice or thrice
Along the rocky walls,
She marks the columned ice
Of frozen waterfalls:
But still the darkened cave
Grew darker as she shone,
Wherein was Rhea gone   250
Her child to bear and save.

[*They dance.*

Then danced the Dactyls and Curêtes wild,
And drowned with yells the cries of mother and child;
Big-armed Damnámeneus gan prance and shout:
And burly Acmon struck the echoes out:
And Kermis leaped and howled: and Titias pranced
And broad Cyllenus tore the air and danced:
While deep within the shadowed cave at rest
Lay Rhea, with her babe upon her breast.

The Firegiver

If any here there be whose impure hands 260
Among pure hands, or guilty heart among
Our guiltless hearts be stained with blood or wrong,
Let him depart!
   If there be any here in whom high Zeus
Seeing impiety might turn away,
Now from our sacrifice and from his sin
Let him depart!

Semichorus of maidens.

   I have chosen to praise
   Hêra the wife, and bring
   A hymn for the feast on marriage days 270
   To the wife of the gods' king.
   How on her festival
   The gods had loving strife,
   Which should give of them all
   The fairest gift to the wife.
   But Earth said, Fair to see
   Is mine and yields to none,
   I have grown for her joy a sacred tree,
   With apples of gold thereon.

   Then Hêra, when she heard what Earth had given, 280
Smiled for her joy, and longed and came to see:
On dovewings flying from the height of heaven,
   Down to the golden tree:
   As tired birds at even
   Come flying straight to house
   On their accustomed boughs.
   'Twas where, on tortured hands
   Bearing the mighty pole.
   Devoted Atlas stands:
   And round his bowed head roll 290

Day-light and night, and stars unmingled dance,
Nor can he raise his glance.

She saw the rocky coast
Whereon the azured waves
Are laced in foam, or lost
In water-lighted caves ;
The olive island where,
Amid the purple seas,
Night unto Darkness bare
The four Hesperides :   300
And came into the shade
Of Atlas, where she found
The garden Earth had made
And fenced with groves around.
And in the midst it grew
Alone, the priceless stem,
As careful, clear and true
As graving on a gem.
Nature had kissèd Art
And borne a child to stir   310
With jealousy the heart
Of heaven's Artificer.
From crown to swelling root
It mocked the goddess' praise,
The green enamelled sprays,
The emblazoned golden fruit.

[They dance

And 'neath the tree, with hair and zone unbound,
The fair Hesperides aye danced around,
And Ægle danced and sang 'O welcome, Queen !'
And Erytheia sang 'The tree is green !'   320
And Hestia danced and sang 'The fruit is gold !'
And Arethusa sang 'Fair Queen, behold !'
And all joined hands and danced about the tree,
And sang 'O Queen, we dance and sing for thee !'

IN. If there be any here who has complaint
Against our rule or claim or supplication,
Now in the name of Zeus let it appear,
Now let him speak !

Prometheus re-enters.

PR. All hail, most worthy king, such claim have I.

IN. May grace be with thee, stranger; speak thy mind.

PR. To Argos, king of Argos, at thy house   331
I bring long journeying to an end this hour,
Bearing no idle message for thine ears.
For know that far thy fame has reached, and men
That ne'er have seen thee tell that thou art set
Upon the throne of virtue, that goodwill
And love thy servants are, that in thy land
Joy, honour, trust and modesty abide
And drink the air of peace, that kings must see
Thy city, would they know their peoples' good   340
And stablish them therein by wholesome laws.
But one thing mars the tale, for o'er thy lands
Travelling I have not seen from morn till eve,
Either from house or farm or labourer's cot,
In any village, nor this town of Argos
A blue-wreathed smoke arise : the hearths are cold,
This altar cold : I see the wood and cakes
Unbaken—O king, where is the fire ?

IN. If hither, stranger, thou wert come to find
That which thou findest wanting, join with us   350
Now in our sacrifice, take food within,
And having learnt our simple way of life
Return unto thy country whence thou camest.
But hast thou skill or knowledge of this thing,
How best it may be sought, or by what means
Hope to be reached, O speak ! I wait to hear.

PR. There is, O king, fire on the earth this day.

IN. On earth there is fire thou sayest !

PR.   There is fire.

(13)

IN. On earth this day!

PR.   There is fire on earth this day.

IN. This is a sacred place, a solemn hour,   360
Thy speech is earnest: yet even if thou speak truth,
O welcome messenger of happy tidings,
And though I hear aright, yet to believe
Is hard: thou canst not know what words thou speakest
Into what ears: they never heard before
This sound but in old tales of happier times,
In sighs of prayer and faint unhearted hope:
Maybe they heard not rightly, speak again!

  PR. There is, O king, fire on the earth this day.

  IN. Yes, yes, again. Now let sweet Music blab   370
Her secret and give o'er; here is a trumpet
That mocks her method. Yet 'tis but the word.
Maybe thy fire is not the fire I seek;
Maybe though thou didst see it, now 'tis quenched,
Or guarded out of reach: speak yet again
And swear by heaven's truth is there fire or no;
And if there be, what means may make it mine.

  PR. There is, O king, fire on the earth this day:
But not as thou dost seek it to be found.

  IN. How seeking wrongly shall I seek aright?   380

  PR. Thou prayest here to Zeus, and him thou callest
Almighty, knowing he could grant thy prayer:
That if 'twere but his will, the journeying sun
Might drop a spark into thine outstretched hand:
That at his breath the splashing mountain brooks
That fall from Orneæ, and cold Lernè's pool
Would change their element, and their chill streams
Bend in their burning banks a molten flood:
That at his word so many messengers
Would bring thee fire from heaven, that not a hearth 390
In all thy land but straight would have a god
To kneel and fan the flame: and yet to him,
It is to him thou prayest.

In.   Therefore to him.

Pr. Is this thy wisdom, king, to sow thy seed
Year after year in this unsprouting soil?
Hast thou not proved and found the will of Zeus
A barren rock for man with prayer to plough?

In. His anger be averted! we judge not god
Evil, because our wishes please him not.
Oft our shortsighted prayers to heaven ascending   400
Ask there our ruin, and are then denied
In kindness above granting: were 't not so,
Scarce could we pray for fear to pluck our doom
Out of the merciful withholding hands.

Pr. Why then provokest thou such great goodwill
In long denial and kind silence shown?

In. Fie, fie! Thou lackest piety: the god's denial
Being nought but kindness, there is hope that he
Will make that good which is not:—or if indeed
Good be withheld in punishment, 'tis well   410
Still to seek on and pray that god relent.

Pr. O Sire of Argos, Zeus will not relent.

In. Yet fire thou say'st is on the earth this day.

Pr. Not of his knowledge nor his gift, O king.

In. By kindness of what god then has man fire?

Pr. I say but on the earth unknown to Zeus.

In. How boastest thou to know, not of his knowledge?

Pr. I boast not: he that knoweth not may boast.

In. Thy daring words bewilder sense with sound.

Pr. I thought to find thee ripe for daring deeds.   420

In. And what the deed for which I prove unripe?

Pr. To take of heaven's fire.

In.   And were I ripe,
What should I dare, beseech you?

Pr.   The wrath of Zeus.

In. Madman, pretending in one hand to hold
The wrath of god and in the other fire.

Pr. Thou meanest rather holding both in one.

In. Both impious art thou and incredible.

Pr. Yet impious only till thou dost believe.

In. And what believe? Ah, if I could believe!
It was but now thou saidst that there was fire,   430
And I was near believing; I believed:
Now to believe were to be mad as thou.

    Chorus. He may be mad and yet say true—maybe
The heat of prophecy like a strong wine
Shameth his reason with exultant speech.

    Pr. Thou say'st I am mad, and of my sober words
Hast called those impious which thou fearest true,
Those which thou knowest good, incredible.
Consider ere thou judge: be first assured
All is not good for man that seems god's will.   440
See, on thy farming skill, thy country toil
Which bends to aid the willing fruits of earth,
And would promote the seasonable year,
The face of nature is not always kind:
And if thou search the sum of visible being
To find thy blessing featured, 'tis not there:
Her best gifts cannot brim the golden cup
Of expectation which thine eager arms
Lift to her mouthèd horn—what then is this
Whose wide capacity outbids the scale   450
Of prodigal beauty, so that the seeing eye
And hearing ear, retiring unamazed
Within their quiet chambers, sit to feast
With dear imagination, nor look forth
As once they did upon the varying air?
Whence is the fathering of this desire
Which mocks at fated circumstance? nay though
Obstruction lie as cumbrous as the mountains,
Nor thy particular hap hath armed desire
Against the brunt of evil,—yet not for this   460
Faints man's desire: it is the unquenchable
Original cause, the immortal breath of being:

The Firegiver

Nor is there any spirit on Earth astir,
Nor 'neath the airy vault, nor yet beyond
In any dweller in far-reaching space,
Nobler or dearer than the spirit of man:
That spirit which lives in each and will not die,
That wooeth beauty, and for all good things
Urgeth a voice, or in still passion sigheth,
And where he loveth draweth the heart with him.   470
Hast thou not heard him speaking oft and oft,
Prompting thy secret musings and now shooting
His feathered fancies, or in cloudy sleep
Piling his painted dreams?   O hark to him!
For else if folly shut his joyous strength
To mope in her dark prison without praise,
The hidden tears with which he wails his wrong
Will sour the fount of life.   O hark to him!
Him may'st thou trust beyond the things thou seest.
For many things there be upon this earth   480
Unblest and fallen from beauty, to mislead
Man's mind, and in a shadow justify
The evil thoughts and deeds that work his ill;
Fear, hatred, lust and strife, which, if man question
The heavenborn spirit within him, are not there.
Yet are they bold of face, and Zeus himself,
Seeing that Mischief held her head on high,
Lest she should go beyond his power to quell
And draw the inevitable Fate that waits
On utmost ill, himself preventing Fate   490
Hasted to drown the world, and now would crush
Thy little remnant: but among the gods
Is one whose love and courage stir for thee;
Who being of manlike spirit, by many shifts
Has stayed the hand of the enemy, who crieth
Thy world is not destroyed, thy good shall live:
Thou hast more power for good than Zeus for ill,
More courage, justice, more abundant art,

More love, more joy, more reason : though around thee
Rank-rooting evil bloom with poisonous crown,   500
Though wan and dolorous and crooked things
Have made their home with thee, thy good shall live.
Know thy desire : and know that if thou seek it,
And seek, and seek, and fear not, thou shalt find.

    SEM. (*youths*). Is this a god that speaketh thus ?

    SEM. (*maidens*). He speaketh as a man
In love or great affliction yields his soul.

    IN. Thou, whencesoe'er thou comest, whoe'er thou art,
Who breakest on our solemn sacrifice
With solemn words, I pray thee not depart   510
Till thou hast told me more.   This fire I seek
Not for myself, whose thin and silvery hair
Tells that my toilsome age nears to its end,
But for my children and the aftertime,
For great the need thereof, wretched our state ;
Nay, set by what has been, our happiness
Is very want, so that what now is not
Is but the measure of what yet may be.
And first are barest needs, which well I know
Fire would supply, but I have hope beyond,   520
That Nature in recovering her right
Would kinder prove to man who seeks to learn
Her secrets and unfold the cause of life.
So tell me, if thou knowest, what is fire ?
Doth earth contain it ? or, since from the sun
Fire reaches us, since in the glimmering stars
And pallid moon, in lightning, and the glance
Of tracking meteors that at nightfall show
How in the air a thousand sightless things
Travel, and ever on their windswift course   530
Flame when they list and into darkness go,—
Since in all these a fiery nature dwells,
Is fire an airy essence, a thing of heaven,
That could we poise it, were an alien power

To make our wisdom less, our wonder more?

PR. Thy wish to know is good, and happy is he
Who thus from chance and change has launched his mind
To dwell for ever with undisturbèd truth.
This high ambition doth not prompt his hand
To crime, his right and pleasure are not wronged   540
By folly of his fellows, nor his eye
Dimmed by the griefs that move the tears of men.
Son of the earth, and citizen may be
Of Argos or of Athens and her laws,
But still the eternal nature, where he looks,
O'errules him with the laws which laws obey,
And in her heavenly city enrols his heart.

IN. Thus ever have I held of happiness,
The child of heavenly truth, and thus have found it
In prayer and meditation and still thought,   550
And thus my peace of mind based on a floor
That doth not quaver like the joys of sense:
Those I possess enough in seeing my slaves
And citizens enjoy, having myself
Tasted for once and put their sweets away.
But of that heavenly city, of which thou sayest
Her laws o'errule us, have I little learnt,
For when my wandering spirit hath dared alone
The unearthly terror of her voiceless halls,
She hath fallen from delight, and without guide   560
Turned back, and from her errand fled for fear.

PR. Think not that thou canst all things know, nor deem
Such knowledge happiness: the all-knowing Fates
No pleasure have, who sit eternally
Spinning the unnumbered threads that Time hath woven,
And weaves, upgathering in his furthest house
To store from sight; but what 'tis joy to learn
Or use to know, that may'st thou ask of right.

IN. Then tell me, for thou knowest, what is fire?

PR. Know then, O king, that this fair earth of men,   570

The Olympus of the gods, and all the heavens
Are lesser kingdoms of the boundless space
Wherein Fate rules; they have their several times,
Their seasons and the limit of their thrones,
And from the nature of eternal things
Springing, themselves are changed; even as the trees
Or birds or beasts of earth, which now arise
To being, now in turn decay and die.

    The heaven and earth thou seest, for long were held
By Fire, a raging power, to whom the Fates   580
Decreed a slow diminishing old age,
But to his daughter, who is that gentle goddess,
Queen of the clear and azure firmament,
In heaven called Hygra, but by mortals Air,
To her, the child of his slow doting years,
Was given a beauteous youth, not long to outlast
His life, but be the pride of his decay,
And win to gentler sway his lost domains.

    And when the day of time arrived, when Air
Took o'er from her decrepit sire the third   590
Of the Sun's kingdoms, the one-moonèd earth,
Straight came she down to her inheritance.

    Gaze on the sun with thine unshaded eye
And shrink from what she saw.   Forests of fire
Whose waving trunks, sucking their fuel, reared
In branched flame roaring, and their torrid shades
Aye underlit with fire.   The mountains lifted
And fell and followed like a running sea,
And from their swelling flanks spumed froth of fire;
Or, like awakening monsters, mighty mounds   600
Rose on the plain awhile.

    SEM. (*maidens*).   He discovers a foe.
    SEM. (*youths*). An enemy he paints.
    PR.   These all she quenched,
Or charmed their fury into the dens and bowels
Of earth to smoulder, there the vital heat

To hold for her creation, which then—to her aid
Summoning high Reason from his home in heaven,—
She wrought anew upon the temperate lands.

    SEM. (*maidens*). 'Twas well Air won this kingdom of her
        sire.

    SEM. (*youths*). Now say how made she green this home
        of fire.

    PR. The waters first she brought, that in their streams
And pools and seas innumerable things   611
Brought forth, from whence she drew the fertile seeds
Of trees and plants, and last of footed life,
That wandered forth, and roaming to and fro,
The rejoicing earth peopled with living sound.
Reason advised, and Reason praised her toil;
Which when she had done she gave him thanks, and said,
'Fair comrade, since thou praisest what is done,
Grant me this favour ere thou part from me:
Make thou one fair thing for me, which shall suit   620
With what is made, and be the best of all.'
'Twas evening, and that night Reason made man.

    SEM. (*maidens*). Children of Air are we, and live by fire.

    SEM. (*youths*). The sons of Reason dwelling on the
        earth.

    SEM. (*maidens*). Folk of a pleasant kingdom held
        between
Fire's reign of terror and the latter day
When dying, soon in turn his child must die.

    SEM. (*youths*). Having a wise creator, above time
Or youth or change, from whom our kind inherit
The grace and pleasure of the eternal gods.   630

    IN. But how came gods to rule this earth of Air?

    PR. They also were her children who first ruled,
Cronos, Iapetus, Hypérion,
Theia and Rhea, and other mighty names
That are but names—whom Zeus drave out from heaven,
And with his tribe sits on their injured thrones.

In. There is no greater god in heaven than he.

Pr. Nor none more cruel nor more tyrannous.

In. But what can man against the power of god?

Pr. Doth not man strive with him? thyself dost pray.

In. That he may pardon our contrarious deeds.　641

Pr. Alas! alas! what more contrarious deed,
What greater miracle of wrong than this,
That man should know his good and take it not?
To what god wilt thou pray to pardon this?
In vain was reason given, if man therewith
Shame truth, and name it wisdom to cry down
The unschooled promptings of his best desire.
The beasts that have no speech nor argument
Confute him, and the wild hog in the wood　650
That feels his longing, hurries straight thereto,
And will not turn his head.

In.　　　　　　　　How mean'st thou this?

Pr. Thou hast desired the good, and now canst feel
How hard it is to kill the heart's desire.

In. Shall Inachus rise against Zeus, as he
Rose against Cronos and made war in heaven?

Pr. I say not so, yet, if thou didst rebel,
The tongue that counselled Zeus should counsel thee.

Sem. (*maidens*). This is strange counsel.

Sem. (*youths*).　　　　　　　　He is not
A counsellor for gods or men.　660

In. O that I knew where I might counsel find,
That one were sent, nay, were't the least of all
The myriad messengers of heaven, to me!
One that should say 'This morn I stood with Zeus,
He hath heard thy prayer and sent me: ask a boon,
What thing thou wilt, it shall be given thee.'

Pr. What wouldst thou say to such a messenger?

In. No need to ask then what I now might ask,
How 'tis the gods, if they have care for mortals,
Slumber our worst necessities—and the boon,　670

No need to tell him that.

Pr.   Now, king, thou seest
Zeus sends no messenger, but I am here.

In. Thy speech is hard, and even thy kindest words
Unkind.   If fire thou hast, in thee 'tis kind
To proffer it: but thou art more unkind
Yoking heaven's wrath therewith.   Nay, and how knowest
      thou
Zeus will be angry if I take of it?
Thou art a prophet: ay, but of the prophets
Some have been taken in error, and honest time
Has honoured many with forgetfulness.   680
I'll make this proof of thee; Show me thy fire—
Nay, give't me now—if thou be true at all,
Be true so far: for the rest there's none will lose,
Nor blame thee being false—where is thy fire?

Pr. O rather, had it thus been mine to give,
I would have given it thus: not adding aught
Of danger or diminishment or loss;
So strong is my goodwill; nor less than this
My knowledge, but in knowledge all my power.
Yet since wise guidance with a little means   690
Can more than force unminded, I have skill
To conjure evil and outcompass strength.
Now give I thee my best, a little gift
To work a world of wonder; 'tis thine own
Of long desire, and with it I will give
The cunning of invention and all arts
In which thy hand instructed may command,
Interpret, comfort, or ennoble nature;
With all provision that in wisdom is,
And what prevention in foreknowledge lies.   700

In. Great is the gain.

Pr.   O king, the gain is thine,
The penalty I more than share.

In.   Enough,

I take thy gift; nor hast thou stood more firm
To every point of thy strange chequered tale,
Revealing, threatening, offering more and more,
And never all, than I to this resolve.

   Pr. I knew thy heart would fail not at the hour.

   In. Nay, failed I now, what were my years of toil
More than the endurance of a harnessed brute,
Flogged to his daily work, that cannot view   710
The high design to which his labour steps?
And I of all men were dishonoured most
Shrinking in fear, who never shrank from toil,
And found abjuring, thrusting stiffly back,
The very gift for which I stretched my hands.
What though I suffer? are these wintry years
Of growing desolation to be held
As cherishable as the suns of spring?
Nay, only joyful can they be in seeing
Long hopes accomplished, long desires fulfilled.   720
And since thou hast touched ambition on the side
Of nobleness, and stirred my proudest hope,
And wilt fulfil this, shall I count the cost?
Rather decay will triumph, and cold death
Be lapped in glory, seeing strength arise
From weakness, from the tomb go forth a flame.

   Pr. 'Tis well; thou art exalted now, the grace
Becomes thy valiant spirit.

   In.   Lo! on this day
Which hope despaired to see, hope manifests
A vision bright as were the dreams of youth;   730
When life was easy as a sleeper's faith
Who swims in the air and dances on the sea;
When all the good that scarce by toil is won,
Or not at all is won, is as a flower
Growing in plenty to be plucked at will:
Is it a dream again or is it truth,
This vision fair of Greece inhabited?

A fairer sight than all fair Iris sees,
Footing her airy arch of colours spun
From Ida to Olympus, when she stays   740
To look on Greece and thinks the sight is fair ;
Far fairer now, clothed with the works of men.

   Pr. Ay, fairer far : for nature's varied pleasaunce
Without man's life is but a desert wild,
Which most, where most she mocks him, needs his aid.
She knows her silence sweeter when it girds
His murmurous cities, her wide wasteful curves
Larger beside his economic line ;
Or what can add a mystery to the dark,
As doth his measured music when it moves   750
With rhythmic sweetness through the void of night ?
Nay, all her loveliest places are but grounds
Of vantage, where with geometric hand,
True square and careful compass he may come
To plan and plant and spread abroad his towers,
His gardens, temples, palaces and tombs.

   And yet not all thou seest, with trancèd eye
Looking upon the beauty that shall be,
The temple-crownèd heights, the wallèd towns,
Farms and cool summer seats, nor the broad ways   760
That bridge the rivers and subdue the mountains,
Nor all that travels on them, pomp or war
Or needful merchandise, nor all the sails
Piloting over the wind-dappled blue
Of the summer-soothed Ægean, to thy mind
Can picture what shall be : these are the face
And form of beauty, but her heart and life
Shall they be who shall see it, born to shield
A happier birthright with intrepid arms,
To tread down tyranny and fashion forth   770
A virgin wisdom to subdue the world,
To build for passion an eternal song,
To shape her dreams in marble, and so sweet

Their speech, that envious Time hearkening shall stay
In fear to snatch, and hide his rugged hand.
Now is the birthday of thy conquering youth,
O man, and lo ! thy priest and prophet stand
Beside the altar and have blessed the day.

    In. Ay, blessed be this day.   Where is thy fire ?
Or is aught else to do, ere I may take ?   780

    Pr. This was my message, speak and there is fire.

    In. There shall be fire.   Await me here awhile.
I go to acquaint my house, and bring them forth.

                                             [*Exit.*

Chorus.

Hearken, O Argos, hearken !
There will be fire.
And thou, O Earth, give ear !
There will be fire.

    Sem. (*maidens*). Who shall be sent to fetch this fire for
    the king ?

    Sem. (*youths*). Shall we put forth in boats to reap,
And shall the waves for harvest yield   790
The rootless flames that nimbly leap
Upon their ever-shifting field ?

    Sem. (*maidens*). Or we in olive-groves go shake
And beat the fruiting sprays, till all
The silv'ry glitter which they make
Beneath into our baskets fall ?

    Sem. (*youths*). To bind in sheaves and bear away
The white unshafted darts of day ?

    Sem. (*maidens*). And from the shadow one by one
Pick up the playful oes of sun ?   800

    Sem. (*youths*). Or wouldst thou mine a passage deep
Until the darksome fire is found,
Which prisoned long in seething sleep
Vexes the caverns underground ?

    Sem. (*maidens*). Or bid us join our palms perchance,

To cup the slant and chinkèd beam,
Which mounting morn hath sent to dance
Across our chamber while we dream?

    SEM. (*youths*). Say whence and how shall we fetch this
      fire for the king?

Our hope is impatient of vain debating.   810

    SEM. (*maidens*). My heart is stirred at the name of the
        wondrous thing,

And trembles awaiting.

ODE.

A coy inquisitive spirit, the spirit of wonder,
Possesses the child in his cradle, when mortal things
Are new, yet a varied surface and nothing under.
It busies the mind on trifles and toys and brings
Her grasp from nearer to further, from smaller to greater,
And slowly teaches flight to her fledgeling wings.

Where'er she flutters and falls surprises await her:
She soars, and beauty's miracles open in sight,   820
The flowers and trees and beasts of the earth; and later
The skies of day, the moon and the stars of night;
'Neath which she scarcely venturing goes demurely,
With mystery clad, in the awe of depth and height.

O happy for still unconscious, for ah! how surely,
How soon and surely will disenchantment come,
When first to herself she boasts to walk securely,
And drives the master spirit away from his home;

Seeing the marvellous things that make the morning
Are marvels of every-day, familiar, and some   830
Have lost with use, like earthly robes, their adorning,
As earthly joys the charm of a first delight,
And some are fallen from awe to neglect and scorning;
Until—

        O tarry not long, dear needed sprite!

Till thou, though uninvited, with fancy returnest
To hallow beauty and make the dull heart bright:
To inhabit again thy gladdened kingdom in earnest;
Wherein—
        from the smile of beauty afar forecasting
The pleasure of god, thou livest at peace and yearnest
        With wonder everlasting.   840

SECOND PART

Re-enter from the palace INACHUS, *with* ARGEIA *and* IO.

INACHUS.

THAT but a small and easy thing now seems,
Which from my house when I came forth at noon
A dream was and beyond the reach of man.
'Tis now a fancy of the will, a word,
Liberty's lightest prize. Yet still as one
Who loiters on the threshold of delight,
Delaying pleasure for the love of pleasure,
I dally—Come, Argeia, and share my triumph!
And set our daughter by thee; though her eyes
Are young, there are no eyes this day so young   850
As shall forget this day—while one thing more
I ask of thee; this evil, will it light
On me or on my house or on mankind?

  PR. Scarce on mankind, O Inachus, for Zeus
A second time failing will not again
Measure his spite against their better fate.
And now the terror, which awhile o'er Earth
Its black wings spread, shall up to Heaven ascend
And gnaw the tyrant's heart: for there is whispered
A word gone forth to scare the mighty gods;   860
How one must soon be born, and born of men,

Who shall drive out their impious host from heaven,
And from their skyey dwellings rule mankind
In truth and love.   So scarce on man will fall
This evil, nay, nor on thyself, O king;
Thy name shall live an honoured name in Greece.

    In. Then on my house 'twill be.   Know'st thou no more?

    Pr. Know I no more?   Ay, if my purpose fail
'Tis not for lack of knowing: if I suffer,
'Tis not that poisonous fear hath slurred her task,   870
Or let brave resolution walk unarmed.
My ears are callous to the threats of Zeus,
The direful penalties his oath hath laid
On every good that I in heart and hand
Am sworn to accomplish, and for all his threats,
Lest their accomplishment should outrun mine,
Am bound the more.   Nay, nor his evil minions,
Nor force, nor strength, shall bend me to his will.

ARGEIA.

Alas, alas, what heavy words are these,
That in the place of joy forbid your tongue,   880
That cloud and change his face, while desperate sorrow
Sighs in his heart?   I came to share a triumph:
All is dismay and terror.   What is this?

    In. True, wife, I spake of triumph, and I told thee
The winter-withering hope of my whole life
Has flower'd to-day in amaranth: what the hope
Thou knowest, who hast shared; but the condition
I told thee not and thou hast heard: this prophet,
Who comes to bring us fire, hath said that Zeus
Wills not the gift he brings, and will be wroth   890
With us that take it.

    Ar.   O doleful change, I came
In pious purpose, nay, I heard within
The hymn to glorious Zeus: I rose and said,
The mighty god now bends, he thrusts aside

His heavenly supplicants to hear the prayer
Of Inachus his servant; let him hear.
O let him turn away now lest he hear.
Nay, frown not on me; though a woman's voice
That counsels is but heard impatiently,
Yet by thy love, and by the sons I bare thee,　　　900
By this our daughter, our last ripening fruit,
By our long happiness and hope of more,
Hear me and let me speak.
　　IN.　　　　　　　　Well, wife, speak on.
　　AR. Thy voice forbids more than thy words invite:
Yet say whence comes this stranger.　Know'st thou not?
Yet whencesoe'er, if he but wish us well,
He will not bound his kindness in a day.
Do nought in haste.　Send now to Sicyon
And fetch thy son Phorôneus, for his stake
In this is more than thine, and he is wise.　　　910
'Twere well Phorôneus and Ægialeus
Were both here: maybe they would both refuse
The strange conditions which this stranger brings.
Were we not happy too before he came?
Doth he not offer us unhappiness?
Bid him depart, and at some other time,
When you have well considered, then return.
　　IN. 'Tis his conditions that we now shall hear.
　　AR. O hide them yet!　Are there not tales enough
Of what the wrathful gods have wrought on men?　920
Nay, 'twas this very fire thou now wouldst take,
Which vain Salmoneus, son of Æolus,
Made boast to have, and from his rattling car
Threw up at heaven to mock the lightning.　Him
The thunderer stayed not to deride, but sent
One blinding fork, that in the vacant sky
Shook like a serpent's tongue, which is but seen
In memory, and he was not, or for burial
Rode with the ashes of his royal city

Upon the whirlwind of the riven air.   930
And after him his brother Athamas,
King of Orchomenos, in frenzy fell
For Hera's wrath, and raving killed his son;
And would have killed fair Ino, but that she fled
Into the sea, preferring there to woo
The choking waters, rather than that the arm
Which had so oft embraced should do her wrong.
For which old crimes the gods yet unappeased
Demand a sacrifice, and the king's son
Dreads the priest's knife, and all the city mourns.   940
Or shall I say what shameful fury it was
With which Poseidon smote Pasiphaë,
But for neglect of a recorded vow:
Or how Actæon fared of Artemis
When he surprised her, most himself surprised:
And even while he looked his boasted bow
Fell from his hands, and through his veins there ran
A strange oblivious trouble, darkening sense
Till he knew nothing but a hideous fear
Which bade him fly, and faster, as behind   950
He heard his hounds give tongue, that through the wood
Were following, closing, caught him and tore him down.
And many more thus perished in their prime;
Lycaon and his fifty sons, whom Zeus
In their own house spied on, and unawares
Watching at hand, from his disguise arose
And overset the table where they sat
Around their impious feast and slew them all:
Alcyonè and Ceyx, queen and king,
Who for their arrogance were changed to birds: 960
And Cadmus now a serpent, once a king:
And saddest Niobe, whom not the love
Of Leto aught availed, when once her boast
Went out, though all her crime was too much pride
Of heaven's most precious gift, her children fair.

Six daughters had she, and six stalwart sons;
But Leto bade her two destroy the twelve.
And somewhere now, among lone mountain rocks
On Sipylus, where couch the nymphs at night
Who dance all day by Achelous' stream,   970
The once proud mother lies, herself a rock,
And in cold breast broods o'er the goddess' wrong.

    In. Now hush thy fear.   See how thou tremblest still.
Or if thou fear, fear passion; for the freshes
Of tenderness and motherly love will drown
The eye of judgment: yet, since even excess
Of the soft quality fits woman well,
I praise thee; nor would ask thee less to aid
With counsel, than in love to share my choice.
Tho' weak thy hands to poise, thine eye may mark   980
This balance, how the good of all outweighs
The good of one or two, though these be us.
Let not reluctance shame the sacrifice
Which in another thou wert first to praise.

    Ar. Alas for me, for thee and for our children,
Who, being our being, having all our having,
If they fare ill, our pride lies in the dust.

    In. O deem not a man's children are but those
Out of his loins engendered—our spirit's love
Hath such prolific consequence, that Virtue   990
Cometh of ancestry more pure than blood,
And counts her seed as sand upon the shore.
Happy is he whose body's sons proclaim
Their father's honour, but more blest to whom
The world is dutiful, whose children spring
Out of all nations, and whose pride the proud
Rise to regenerate when they call him sire.

    Ar. Thus, husband, ever have I bought and buy
Nobleness cheaply being linked with thee.
Forgive my weakness; see, I now am bold;   1000
Tell me the worst I'll hear and wish 'twere more.

The Firegiver

In. Retire—thy tears perchance may stir again.

Ar. Nay, I am full of wonder and would hear.

Pr. Bid me not tell if ye have fear to hear;
But have no fear.   Knowledge of future things
Can nothing change man's spirit: and though he seem
To aim his passion darkly, like a shaft
Shot toward some fearful sound in thickest night,
He hath an owl's eye, and must blink at day.
The springs of memory, that feed alike   1010
His thought and action, draw from furthest time
Their constant source, and hardly brook constraint
Of actual circumstance, far less attend
On glassed futurity; nay, death itself,
His fate unquestioned, his foretasted pain,
The certainty foreknown of things unknown,
Cannot discourage his habitual being
In its appointed motions, to make waver
His eager hand, nor loosen the desire
Of the most feeble melancholy heart   1020
Even from the unhopefullest of all her dreams.

In. Since then I long to know, now something say
Of what will come to mine when I am gone.

Pr. And let the maid too hear, for 'tis of her
I speak, to tell her whither she should turn
The day ye drive her forth from hearth and home.

In. What say'st thou? drive her out? and we? from
   home?
Banish the comfort of our eyes?   Nay rather
Believe that these obedient hands will tear
The heart out of my breast, ere it do this.   1030

Pr. When her wild cries arouse the house at night,
And, running to her bed, ye see her set
Upright in trancèd sleep, her starting hair
With deathly sweat bedewed, in horror shaking,
Her eyeballs fixed upon the unbodied dark,
Through which a draping mist of luminous gloom

(33)   D

Drifts from her couch away,—when, if asleep,
She walks as if awake, and if awake
Dreams, and as one who nothing hears or sees,
Lives in a sick and frantic mood, whose cause   1040
She understands not or is loth to tell—

Ar. Ah, ah, my child, my child!—Dost thou feel aught?
Speak to me—nay, 'tis nothing—hearken not.

Pr. Ye then distraught with sorrow, neither knowing
Whether to save were best or lose, will seek
Apollo's oracle.

In.   And what the answer?
Will it discover nought to avert this sorrow?

Pr. Or else thy whole race perish root and branch.

In. Alas! alas!

Pr. Yet shall she live though lost; from human form
Changed, that thou wilt not know thy daughter more.   1051

In. Woe, woe! my thought was praying for her death.

Pr. In Hera's temple shall her prison be
At high Mycenæ, till from heaven be sent
Hermes, with song to soothe and sword to slay
The beast whose hundred eyes devour the door.

In. Enough, enough is told, unless indeed,
The beast once slain, thou canst restore our child.

Pr. Nay, with her freedom will her wanderings
Begin.   Come hither, child—nay, let her come: 1060
What words remain to speak will not offend her,
And shall in memory quicken, when she looks
To learn where she should go;—for go she must,
Stung by the venomous fly, whose angry flight
She still will hear about her, till she come
To lay her sevenfold-carried burden down
Upon the Æthiop shore where he shall reign.

In. But say—say first, what form—

Pr.   In snow-white hide
Of those that feel the goad and wear the yoke.   1069

In. Round-hoofed, or such as tread with cloven foot?

(34)

PR. Wide-horned, large-eyed, broad-fronted, and the feet
Cloven which carry her to her far goal.

IN. Will that of all these evils be the term?

PR. Ay, but the journey first which she must learn.
Hear now, my child; the day when thou art free,
Leaving the lion-gate, descend and strike
The Trêtan road to Nemea, skirting wide
The unhunted forest o'er the watered plain
To walled Cleônæ, whence the traversed stream
To Corinth guides: there enter not, but pass   1080
To narrow Isthmus, where Poseidon won
A country from Apollo, and through the town
Of Crommyon, till along the robber's road
Pacing, thy left eye meet the westering sun
O'er Geraneia, and thou reach the hill
Of Megara, where Car thy brother's babe
In time shall rule; next past Eleusis climb
Stony Panactum and the pine-clad slopes
Of Phyle; shun the left-hand way, and keep
The rocks; the second day thy feet shall tread   1090
The plains of Græa, whence the roadway serves
Aulis and Mycalessus to the point
Of vext Euripus: fear not then the stream,
Nor scenting think to taste, but plunging in
Breast its salt current to the further shore.
For on this island mayst thou lose awhile
Thy maddening pest, and rest and pasture find,
And from the heafs of bold Macistus see
The country left and sought: but when thou feel
Thy torment urge, move down, recross the flood,   1100
And west by Harma's fencèd gap arrive
At seven-gated Thebes: thy friendly goddess
Ongan Athenè has her seat without.

CHOR. Now if she may not stay thy toilsome destined
    steps,
I pray that she may slay for thee the maddening fly.

Pr. Keep not her sanctuary long, but seek
Bœotian Ascra, where the Muses' fount,
Famed Aganippè, wells : Ocalea
Pass, and Tilphusa's northern steeps descend
By Alalcomenæ, the goddess' town.   1110
Guard now the lake's low shore, till thou have crossed
Hyrcana and Cephissus, the last streams
Which feed its reedy pools, when thou shalt come
Between two mountains that enclose the way
By peakèd Abæ to Hyampolis.
The right-hand path that thither parts the vale
Opes to Cyrtonè and the Locrian lands ;
Toward Elateia thou, where o'er the marsh
A path with stones is laid ; and thence beyond
To Thronium, Tarphè, and Thermopylæ,   1120
Where rocky Lamia views the Maliac gulf.

Chor. If further she should go, will she not see
That other Argos, the Dodonian land ?

Pr. Crossing the Phthian hills thou next shalt reach
Pharsalus, and Olympus' peakèd snows
Shall guide thee o'er the green Pelasgic plains
For many a day, but to Argissa come
Let old Peneius thy slow pilot be
Through Tempè, till they turn upon his left
Crowning the wooded slopes with splendours bare.   1130
Thence issuing forth on the Pierian shore
Northward of Ossa thou shalt touch the lands
Of Macedon.

Chor.   Alas, we wish thee speed,
But bid thee here farewell ; for out of Greece
Thou goest 'mongst the folk whose chattering speech
Is like the voice of birds, nor home again
Wilt thou return.

Pr.   Thy way along the coast
Lies till it southward turn, when thou shalt seek
Where wide on Strymon's plain the hindered flood

Spreads like a lake; thy course to his oppose　　　1140
And face him to the mountain whence he comes:
Which doubled, Thrace receives thee: barbarous names
Of mountain, town and river, and a people
Strange to thine eyes and ears, the Agathyrsi,
Of pictured skins, who owe no marriage law,
And o'er whose gay-spun garments sprent with gold
Their hanging hair is blue.　Their torrent swim
That measures Europe in two parts, and go
Eastward along the sea, to mount the lands
Beyond man's dwelling, and the rising steeps　　　1150
That face the sun untrodden and unnamed.—
　Know to earth's verge remote thou then art come,
The Scythian tract and wilderness forlorn,
Through whose rude rocks and frosty silences
No path shall guide thee then, nor my words now.
There as thou toilest o'er the treacherous snows,
A sound then thou shalt hear to stop thy breath,
And prick thy trembling ears; a far-off cry,
Whose throat seems the white mountain and its passion
The woe of earth.　Flee not, nor turn not back:　　　1160
Let thine ears drink and guide thine eyes to see
That sight whose terrors shall assuage thy terror,
Whose pain shall kill thy pain.　Stretched on the rock,
Naked to scorching sun, to pinching frost,
To wind and storm and beaks of wingèd fiends
From year to year he lies.　Refrain to ask
His name and crime—nay, haply when thou see him
Thou wilt remember—'tis thy tyrant's foe,
Man's friend, who pays his chosen penalty.
Draw near, my child, for he will know thy need,　　　1170
And point from land to land thy further path.

Chorus.

　O miserable man, hear now the worst.
O weak and tearful race,

Born to unhappiness, see now thy cause
Doomed and accurst !

It surely were enough, the bad and good
Together mingled, against chance and ill
To strive, and prospering by turns,
Now these, now those, now folly and now skill,
Alike by means well understood   1180
Or 'gainst all likelihood ;
Loveliness slaving to the unlovely will
That overrides the right and laughs at law.

But always all in awe
And imminent dread :
Because there is no mischief thought or said,
Imaginable or unguessed,
But it may come to be ; nor home of rest,
Nor hour secure : but anywhere,
At any moment ; in the air,   1190
Or on the earth or sea,
Or in the fair
And tender body itself it lurks, creeps in,
Or seizes suddenly,
Torturing, burning, withering, devouring,
Shaking, destroying ; till tormented life
Sides with the slayer, not to be,
And from the cruel strife
Falls to fate overpowering.

Or if some patient heart,   1200
In toilsome steps of duty tread apart,
Thinking to win her peace within herself,
And thus awhile succeed :
She must see others bleed,
At others' misery moan,
And learn the common suffering is her own,
From which it is no freedom to be freed :

Nay, Nature, her best nurse,
Is tender but to breed a finer sense,
Which she may easier wound, with smart the worse   1210
And torture more intense.

     And no strength for thee but the thought of duty,
Nor any solace but the love of beauty.
O Right's toil unrewarded!
O Love's prize unaccorded!

     I say this might suffice,
O tearful and unstable
And miserable man,
Were 't but from day to day
Thy miserable lot,   1220
This might suffice, I say,
To term thee miserable.
But thou of all thine ills too must take thought,
Must grow familiar till no curse astound thee,
With tears recall the past,
With tears the times forecast;
With tears, with tears thou hast
The scapeless net spread in thy sight around thee.

     How then support thy fate,
O miserable man, if this befall,   1230
That he who loves thee and would aid thee, daring
To raise an arm for thy deliverance,
Must for his courage suffer worse than all?

     In. Bravest deliverer, for thy prophecy
Has torn the veil which hid thee from my eyes,
If thyself art that spirit, of whom some things
Were darkly spoken,—nor can I doubt thou art,
Being that the heaven its fire withholds not from thee
Nor time his secrets,—tell me now thy name,
That I may praise thee rightly; and my late   1240

Unwitting words pardon thou, and these who still
In blinded wonder kneel not to thy love.

PR. Speak not of love.   See, I am moved with hate,
And fiercest anger, which will sometimes spur
The heart to extremity, till it forget
That there is any joy save furious war.
Nay, were there now another deed to do,
Which more could hurt our enemy than this,
Which here I stand to venture, here would I leave thee
Conspiring at his altar, and fly off   1250
To plunge the branding terror in his soul.
But now the rising passion of my will
Already jars his reaching sense, already
From heaven he bids his minion Hermes forth
To bring his only rebel to his feet.
Therefore no more delay, the time is short.

IN. I take, I take.   'Tis but for thee to give.

PR. O heavenly fire, life's life, the eye of day,
Whose nimble waves upon the starry night
Of boundless ether love to play,   1260
Carrying commands to every gliding sprite
To feed all things with colour, from the ray
Of thy bright-glancing, white
And silver-spinning light :
Unweaving its thin tissue for the bow
Of Iris, separating countless hues
Of various splendour for the grateful flowers
To crown the hasting hours,
Changing their special garlands as they choose.

O spirit of rage and might,   1270
Who canst unchain the links of winter stark,
And bid earth's stubborn metals flow like oil,
Her porphyrous heart-veins boil ;
Whose arrows pierce the cloudy shields of dark ;
Let now this flame, which did to life awaken

(40)

Beyond the cold dew-gathering veils of morn,
And thence by me was taken,
And in this reed was borne,
A smothered theft and gift to man below,
Here with my breath revive,   1280
Restore thy lapsèd realm, and be the sire
Of many an earthly fire.

   O flame, flame bright and live,
Appear upon the altar as I blow.

   CHOR. 'Twas in the marish reed.
See to his mouth he sets its hollow flute
And breathes therein with heed,
As one who from a pipe with breathings mute
Will music's voice evoke.—
See, the curl of a cloud.   1290
   IN. The smoke, the smoke!
   SEMICHORUS. Thin clouds mounting higher.
   IN. 'Tis smoke, the smoke of fire.
   SEMICHORUS. Thick they come and thicker,
      Quick arise and quicker,
      Higher still and higher.
      Their wreaths the wood enfold.
      —I see a spot of gold.
      They spring from a spot of gold,
      Red gold, deep among   1300
      The leaves : a golden tongue.
      O behold, behold,
      Dancing tongues of gold,
      That leaping aloft flicker,
      Higher still and higher.
      IN. 'Tis fire, the flame of fire!
      SEMICHORUS. The blue smoke overhead
Is turned to angry red.
The fire, the fire, it stirs.
Hark, a crackling sound,   1310

As when all around
Ripened pods of furze
Split in the parching sun
Their dry caps one by one,
And shed their seeds on the ground.
—Ah! what clouds arise.
Away! O come away.
The wind-wafted smoke,
Blowing all astray,
Blinds and pricks my eyes.
Ah! I choke, I choke.
—All the midst is rent:
See, the twigs are all
By the flaming spent
White and gold, and fall.
How they writhe, resist,
Blacken, flake, and twist,
Snap in gold and fall.
—See the stars that mount,
Momentary bright
Flitting specks of light
More than eye can count.
Insects of the air,
As in summer night
Show a fire in flying
Flickering here and there,
Waving past and dying.
—Look, a common cone
Of the mountain pine
Solid gold is grown;
Till its scales outshine,
Standing each alone
In the spiral rows
Of their fair design,
All the brightest shows
Of the sun's decline.

*[PROMETHEUS,
after writing his
name on the al-
tar, goes out un-
observed.]*

1330

1340

—Hark, there came a hiss,
Like a startled snake
Sliding through the brake.
Oh, and what is this?   1350
Smaller flames that flee
Sidelong from the tree,
Hark, they hiss, they hiss.
—How the gay flames flicker,
Spurting, dancing, leaping
Quicker yet and quicker,
Higher yet and higher,
—Flaming, flaring, fuming,
Cracking, crackling, creeping,
Hissing and consuming: 1360
Mighty is the fire.

IN. Stay, stay, cease your rejoicings.   Where is he,
The prophet,—nay, what say I,—the god, the giver?
   CHOR. He is not here—he is gone.
   IN.   Search, search around.
Search all, search well.
   CHOR.   He is gone,—he is not here.
   IN. The palace gate lies open: go, Argeia,
Maybe he went within: go seek him there.
                                        [*Exit* AR.
Look down the sea road, down the country road:
Follow him if ye see him.
   CHOR.   ·   He is not there.
   IN. Strain, strain your eyes: look well: search everywhere.
Look townwards—is he there?
   Part of CHORUS *returning.*   He is not there.—   1371
   Other part returning. He is not there.
                  Argeia re-entering.
   AR.   He is not there.

   CHOR. O see!
   CHOR.   See where?

                    (43)

CHOR.   See on the altar—see !

CHOR. What see ye on the altar?

CHOR.   Here in front
Words newly writ.

CHOR.   What words?

CHOR.   A name—

IN.   Ay true—
There is the name.   How like a child was I,
That I must wait till these dumb letters gave
The shape and soul to knowledge : when the god
Stood here so self-revealed to ears and eyes
That, 'tis a god I said, yet wavering still,   1380
Doubting what god,—and now, who else but he?
I knew him, yet not well; I knew him not :
Prometheus—ay, Prometheus.   Know ye, my children,
This name we see was writ by him we seek.
'Tis his own name, his own heart-stirring name,
Feared and revered among the immortal gods :
Divine Prometheus : see how here the large
Cadmeian characters run, scoring out
The hated title of his ancient foe,—
To Zeus 'twas made,—and now 'tis to Prometheus—   1390
Writ with the charrèd reed—theft upon theft.
He hath stolen from Zeus his altar, and with his fire
Hath lit our sacrifice unto himself.
Ió Prometheus, friend and firegiver,
For good or ill thy thefts and gifts are ours.
We worshipped thee unknowing.

CHOR.   But now where is he?

IN. No need to search—we shall not see him more.
We look in vain.   The high gods when they choose
Put on and off the solid visible shape
Which more deceives our hasty sense, than when   1400
Seeing them not we judge they stand aloof.
And he, he now is gone ; his work is done :
'Tis ours to see it be not done in vain.

CHOR. What is to do? speak, bid, command, we fly.

IN. Go some and fetch more wood to feed the fire;
And some into the city to proclaim
That fire is ours : and send out messengers
To Corinth, Sicyon, Megara and Athens
And to Mycenæ, telling we have fire :
And bid that in the temples they prepare   1410
Their altars, and send hither careful men
To learn of me what things the time requires.

                        [*Exit part of* CHORUS.

The rest remain to end our feast; and now
Seeing this altar is no more to Zeus,
But shall for ever be with smouldering heat
Fed for the god who first set fire thereon,
Change ye your hymns, which in the praise of Zeus
Ye came to sing, and change the prayer for fire
Which ye were wont to raise, to high thanksgiving,
Praising aloud the giver and his gift.   1420

    Part of CHORUS.   Now our happy feast hath ending,
           While the sun in heaven descending
           Sees us gathered round a light
           Born to cheer his vacant night.
           Praising him to-day who came
           Bearing far his heavenly flame :
           Came to crown our king's desire
           With his gift of golden fire.

SEMICHORUS. My heart, my heart is freed.
Now can I sing.   I loose a shaft from my bow,   1430
A song from my heart to heaven, and watch it speed.
It revels in the air, and straight to its goal doth go.
   I have no fear . I praise distinguishing duly :
I praise the love that I love and I worship truly.
Goodness I praise, not might,
Nor more will I speak of wrong,

But of lovingkindness and right ;
And the god of my love shall rejoice at the sound of my song.
   I praise him whom I have seen :
As a man he is beautiful, blending prime and youth,   1440
Of gentle and lovely mien,
With the step and the eyes of truth,
As a god,—O were I a god, but thus to be man !
As a god, I set him above
The rest of the gods ; for his gifts are pledges of love,
The words of his mouth rare and precious,
His eyes' glance and the smile of his lips are love.
   He is the one
Alone of all the gods,
Of righteous Themis the lofty-spirited son,   1450
Who hates the wrongs they have done.
He is the one I adore.
For if there be love in heaven with evil to cope,—
And he promised us more and more,—
For what may we not hope ?

ODE.

   My soul is drunk with joy, her new desire
In far forbidden places wanders away.
Her hopes with free bright-coloured wings of fire
Upon the gloom of thought
Are sailing out.   1460
Awhile they rise, awhile to rest they softly fall,
Like butterflies, that flit
Across the mountains, or upon a wall
Winking their idle fans at pleasure sit.

    O my vague desires !
Ye lambent flames of the soul, her offspring fires :
That are my soul herself in pangs sublime
Rising and flying to heaven before her time :

(46)

The Firegiver

What doth tempt you forth
To melt in the south or shiver in the frosty north?   1470
What seek ye or find ye in your random flying,
For ever soaring aloft, soaring and dying?
    Joy, the joy of flight;
They hide in the sun, they flare and dance in the night.
Gone up, gone out of sight—and ever again
Follow fresh tongues of fire, fresh pangs of pain.
    Ah! could I control
These vague desires, these leaping flames of the soul:
Could I but quench the fire, ah! could I stay
My soul that flieth, alas, and dieth away!   1480

[Enter other part of CHORUS.

Part of CHOR. Here is wood to feed the fire—
Never let its flames expire.
Sing ye still while we advance
Round the fire in measured dance,
While the sun in heaven descending
Sees our happy feast have ending.
Weave ye still your joyous song,
While we bear the wood along.

SEMICHORUS. But O return,
Return, thou flower of the gods!   1490
Remember the limbs that toil and the hearts that yearn,
Remember, and soon return!
To prosper with peace and skill
Our hands in the works of pleasure, beauty and use.
Return, and be for us still
Our shield from the anger of Zeus.
    And he, if he raise his arm in anger to smite thee,
    And think for the good thou hast done with pain to requite
        thee,
Vengeance I heard thee tell,
And the curse I take for my own,   1500
That his place is prepared in hell,

(47)

And a greater than he shall hurl him down from his throne.
    Down, down from his throne!
For the god who shall rule mankind from the deathless
    skies
By mercy and truth shall be known,
In love and peace shall arise.
For him,—if again I hear him thunder above,
O then, if I crouch or start,
I will press thy lovingkindness more to my heart,
Remember the words of thy mouth rare and precious,   1510
Thy heart of hearts and gifts of divine love.

DEMETER

A Mask

"Dreams & the light imaginings of men"

WRITTEN FOR THE LADIES AT

SOMERVILLE COLLEGE

& ACTED BY THEM

AT THE INAUGURATION OF THEIR NEW BUILDING

IN 1904

PREVIOUS EDITION

Oxford: at the Clarendon Press, 1905

E

ARGUMENT OF THE PLAY

The scene is in the flowery valley below Enna. Hades prologizes, and tells how he has come with consent of Zeus to carry off Persephone to be his queen. The Chorus of Ocean nymphs entering praise Sicily and the spring. Persephone enters with Athena and Artemis to gather flowers for the festival of Zeus. Persephone being left alone is carried off by Hades.

In the second act, which is ten days later, the Chorus deplore the loss of Persephone. Demeter entering upbraids them in a choric scene and describes her search for Persephone until she learnt her fate from Helios. Afterwards she describes her plan for compelling Zeus to restore her. Hermes brings from Zeus a command to Demeter that she shall return to Olympus. She sends defiance to Zeus, and the Chorus end the scene by vowing to win Poseidon to aid Demeter.

In the third act, which is a year later, the Chorus, who have been summoned by Demeter to witness the restoration of Persephone, lament Demeter's anger. Demeter narrates the Eleusinian episode of her wanderings, until Hermes enters leading Persephone. After their greeting Demeter hears from Hermes the terms of Persephone's restoration; she is reconciled thereto by Persephone, and invites her to Eleusis. The Chorus sing and crown Persephone with flowers.

DRAMATIS PERSONÆ

HADES. ⎫	*ARTEMIS.* ⎫
DEMETER. ⎭	*HERMES.* ⎭
PERSEPHONE.	*Chorus of*
ATHENA.	*OCEANIDES.*

DEMETER

HADES.

I AM the King of Hell, nor prone to vex
Eternal destiny with weak complaint;
Nor when I took my kingdom did I mourn
My lot, from heav'n expell'd, deny'd to enjoy
Its radiant revelry and ambrosial feast,
Nor blamed our mighty Sisters, that not one
Would share my empire in the shades of night.

But when a younger race of gods arose,
And Zeus set many sons on heav'nly seats,
And many daughters dower'd with new domain,   10
And year by year were multiply'd on earth
Their temples and their statu'd sanctities,
Mirrors of man's ideas that grow apace,
Yea, since man's mind was one with my desire
That Hell should have a queen,—for heav'n hath queens
Many, nor on all earth reigns any king
In unkind isolation like to me,—
I claimed from Zeus that of the fair immortals
One should be given to mè to grace my throne.

Willing he was, and quick to praise my rule,   20
And of mere justice thère had granted me
Whome'er I chose : but 'Brother mine,' he said,
'Great as my power among the gods, this thing
I cannot compass, that a child of mine,
Who once hath tasted of celestial life,
Should all forgo, and destitute of bliss
Descend into the shades, albeit to sit
An equal on thy throne.   Take whom thou wilt;

But by triumphant force persuade, as erst
I conquer'd heav'n.' Said I 'My heart is set :   30
I take Demeter's child Persephone ;
Dost thou consent?' Whereto he gave his nod.
And I am come to-day with hidden powers,
Ev'n unto Enna's fair Sicilian field,
To rob her from the earth.   'Tis here she wanders
With all her train : nor is this flow'ry vale
Fairer among the fairest vales of earth,
Nor any flower within this flow'ry vale
Fair above other flowers, as she is fairest
Among immortal goddesses, the daughter   40
Of gentle-eyed Demeter ; and her passion
Is for the flowers, and every tenderness
That I have long'd for in my fierce abodes.
But she hath always in attendant guard
The dancing nymphs of Ocean, and to-day
The wise Athena and chaste Artemis
Indulge her girlish fancy, gathering flowers
To deck the banner of my golden brother,
Whose thought they guess not, tho' their presence here
Affront his will and mine.   If once alone   50
I spy her, I can snatch her swiftly down ;
And after shall find favour for my fault,
When I by gentle means have won her love.
   I hear their music now.   Hither they come :
I'll to my ambush in the rocky cave.   [*Exit.*

Demeter

ACT I

Enter Chorus of Oceanides, with baskets.

OCEANIDES.

Gay and lovely is earth, man's decorate dwelling ;
With fresh beauty ever varying hour to hour.
As now bathed in azure joy she awakeneth
With bright morn to the sun's life-giving effluence,
Or sunk into solemn darkness aneath the stars   60
In mysterious awe slumbereth out the night,
Then from darkness again plunging again to day ;
Like dolphins in a swift herd that accompany
Poseidon's chariot whén he rebukes the waves.
But no country to mè 'neath the enarching air
Is fair as Sicily's flowery fruitful isle :
Always lovely, whether winter adorn the hills
With his silvery snow, or generous summer
Outpour her heavy gold on the river-valleys.
Her rare beauty giveth gaiety unto man,   70
    A delite dear to immortals.

2

And one season of all chiefly deliteth us,
When fair Spring is afield.   O happy is the Spring !
Now birds early arouse their pretty minstreling ;
Now down its rocky hill murmureth ev'ry rill ;
Now all bursteth anew, wantoning in the dew
Their bells of bonny blue, their chalices honey'd.
Unkind frost is away ; now sunny is the day ;
Now man thinketh aright, Life it is all delite.
Now maids playfully dance o'er enamel'd meadows,   80
And with goldy blossom deck forehead and bosom ;
While old Pan rollicketh thro' the budding shadows,
Voicing his merry reed, laughing aloud to lead
    The echoes madly rejoicing.

3

We be Océanids, Persephone's lovers,
Who all came hurrying joyfully from the sea
Ere daybreak to obey her belovèd summons.
At her fancy to pluck these violets, lilies,
Windflow'rs and daffodils, all for a festival
Whereat shé will adorn Zeuses honour'd banner.   90
And with Persephone there cometh Artemis
And grave Pallas . . . Hilloo! already they approach!
Haste, haste! stoop to gather! seem busy ev'ryone!
Crowd all your wicker arcs with the meadow-lilies;
Lest our disreverenc'd deity should rebuke
        The divine children of Ocean.

[*Enter* ATHENA, PERSEPHONE, *and* ARTEMIS.   *Persephone has
        a basket half fill'd with gather'd flowers.*]

ATHENA.

These then are Enna's flowery fields, and here
In midmost isle the garden of thy choice?

PERSEPHONE.

Is not all as I promist?   Feel ye not
Your earthborn ecstasy concenter'd here?   100
Tell me, Athena, of thy wisdom, whénce
Cometh this joy of earth, this penetrant
Palpitant exultation so unlike
The balanc't calm of high Olympian state?
Is 't in the air, the tinted atmosphere
Whose gauzy veil, thrown on the hills, will paint
Their features, changing with the gradual day,
Rosy or azure, clouded now, and now
Again afire?   Or is it that the sun's
Electric beams—which shot in circling fans   110
Whirl all things with them—as they strike the earth
Excite her yearning heart, till stir'd beneath

The rocks and silent plains, she cannot hold
Her fond desires, but sends them bursting forth
In scents and colour'd blossoms of the spring?—
Breathes it not in the flowers?

ATH.   Fair are the flowers,
Dear child; and yet to me far lovelier
Than all their beauty is thy love for them.
Whate'er I love, I contemplate my love
More than the object, and am so rejoic'd.   120
For life is one, and like a level sea
Life's flood of joy. Thou wond'rest at the flowers,
But I would teach thee wonder of thy wonder:
Would shew thee beauty in the desert-sand,
The worth of things unreckt of, and the truth
That thy desire and love may spring of evil
And ugliness, and that Earth's ecstasy
May dwell in darkness also, in sorrow and tears.

PER. I'd not believe it: why then should we pluck
The flowers and not the stalks without the flowers?   130
Or do thy stones breathe scent? Would not men laugh
To see the banner of almighty Zeus
Adorn'd with ragged roots and straws?—Dear Artemis,
How lovest thou the flowers?

ARTEMIS.

                          I'll love them better
Ever for thy sake, Cora; but for me
The joy of Earth is in the breath of life
And animal motions: nor are flowery sweets
Dear as the scent of life. This petal'd cup,
What is it by the wild fawn's liquid eye
Eloquent as love-music 'neath the moon?   140
Nay, not a flower in all thy garden here,
Nor wer't a thousand-thousand-fold enhanc't
In every charm, but thou wouldst turn from it
To view the antler'd stag, that in the glade

(55)

With the coy gaze of his majestic fear
Faced thee a moment ere he turn'd to fly.

PER. But why, then, hunt and kill what thou so lovest?

AR. Dost thou not pluck thy flowers?

PER.   'Tis not the same.
Thy victims fly for life : they pant, they scream.

AR. Were they not mortal, sweet, I coud not kill them.
They kill each other in their lust for life ;   151
Nay, cruelly persecute their blemisht kin :
And they that thus are exiled from the herd
Slink heart-brok'n to sepulchral solitudes,
Defenceless and dishonour'd ; there to fall
Prey to the hungry glutton of the cave,
Or stand in mute pain lingering, till they drop
In their last lair upon the ancestral bones.

PER. What is it that offends me?

ATH.   'Tis Pity, child,
The mortal thought that clouds the brow of man   160
With dark reserve, or poisoning all delite
Drives him upon his knees in tearful prayer
To avert his momentary qualms : till Zeus
At his reiterated plaint grows wrath,
And burdens with fresh curse the curse of care.
And they that haunt with men are apt to take
Infection of his mind : thy mighty mother
Leans to his tenderness.

PER.   How should man, dwelling
On earth that is so gay, himself be sad?
Is not earth gay? Look on the sea, the sky,   170
The flowers!

ATH.   'Tis sad to him because 'tis gay.—
For whether he consider how the flowers,
—Thy miracles of beauty above praise,—
Are wither'd in the moment of their glory,
So that of all the mounting summer's wealth
The show is chang'd each day, and each day dies,

(56)

Of no more count in Nature's estimate
Than crowded bubbles of the fighting foam:
Or whether 'tis the sea, whose azure waves
Play'd in the same infinity of motion   180
Ages ere he beheld it, and will play
For ages after him;—alike 'tis sad
To read how beauty dies and he must die.

    PER. Were I a man, I would not worship thee,
Thou cold essential wisdom.   If, as thou say'st,
Thought makes men sorrowful, why help his thought
To quench enjoyment, who might else as I
Revel among bright things, and feast his sense
With beauty well-discern'd?   Nay, why came ye
To share my pastime?   Ye love not the flowers.   190

    ATH. Indeed I love thee, child; and love thy flowers,—
Nor less for loving wisely.   All emotions,
Whether of gods or men, all loves and passions,
Are of two kinds; they are either inform'd by wisdom,
To reason obedient,—or they are unconducted,
Flames of the burning life.   The brutes of earth
And Pan their master know these last; the first
Are seen in me: betwixt the extremes there lie
Innumerable alloys and all of evil.

    PER. Nay, and I guess your purpose with me well: 200
I am a child, and ye would nurse me up
A pupil in your school.   I know ye twain
Of all the immortals are at one in this;
Ye wage of cold disdain a bitter feud
With Aphrodite, and ye fear for me,
Lest she should draw me to her wanton way.
Fear not: my party is taken.   Hark! I'll tell
What I have chosen, what mankind shall hold
Devote and consecrate to me on earth:
It is the flowers: but only among the flowers   210
Those that men love for beauty, scent, or hue,
Having no other uses: I have found

Demeter, my good mother, heeds them not.—
She loves vines, olives, orchards, 'the rich leas
Of wheat, rye, barley, vetches, oats, and peas,'
But for the idle flowers she hath little care :
She will resign them willingly.   And think not,
Thou wise Athena, I shall go unhonour'd,
Or rank a meaner goddess unto man.
His spirit setteth beauty before wisdom,   220
Pleasures above necessities, and thus
He ever adoreth flowers.   Nor this I guess
Where rich men only and superfluous kings
Around their palaces reform the land
To terraces and level lawns, whereon
Appointed slaves are told, to tend and feed
Lilies and roses and all rarest plants
Fetch'd from all lands ; that they—these lordly men—
'Twixt flaunting avenues and wafted odours
May pace in indolence : this is their bliss ;   230
This first they do : and after, it may be,
Within their garden set their academe :—
But in the poorest villages, around
The meanest cottage, where no other solace
Comforts the eye, some simple gaiety
Of flowers in tended garden is seen ; some pinks,
Tulips, or crocuses that edge the path ;
Where oft at eve the grateful labourer
Sits in his jasmin'd porch, and takes the sun :
And even the children, that half-naked go,   240
Have posies in their hands, and of themselves
Will choose a queen in whom to honour Spring,
Dancing before her garlanded with may.
The cowslip makes them truant, they forget
The hour of hunger and their homely feast
So they may cull the delicate primrose,
Sealing their birthright with the touch of beauty ;
With unconsider'd hecatombs assuring

Their dim sense of immortal mystery.—
Yea, rich and poor, from cradle unto grave   250
All men shall love me, shall adore my name,
And heap my everlasting shrine with flowers.

    ATH. Thou sayest rightly thou art a child.   May Zeus
Give thee a better province than thy thought.

                              [Music heard.

    AR. Listen! the nymphs are dancing.   Let us go!

                              [They move off.

Come, Cora; wilt thou learn a hunting dance?
I'll teach thee.

    PER.   Can I learn thy hunter-step
Without thy bare legs and well-buskin'd feet?

    AR. Give me thy hand.

    PER.   Stay! stay! I have left my flowers.
I follow.   *[Exeunt Athena and Artemis.*

             [Persephone returning to right slowly.

They understand not—Now, praise be to Zeus,   261
That, tho' I sprang not from his head, I know
Something that Pallas knows not.

*[She has come to where her basket lies. In stooping towards it she kneels
to pluck a flower: and then comes to sit on a bank with the basket
in hand on her knees, facing the audience.]*

          Thou tiny flower!
          Art thou not wise?
Who taught thee else, thou frail anemone,
Thy starry notion, thy wind-wavering motion,
Thy complex of chaste beauty, unimagin'd
Till thou art seen?—And how so wisely, thou,
Indifferent to the number of thy rays,   270
While others are so strict? This six-leaved tulip,
—He would not risk a seventh for all his worth,—
He thought to attain unique magnificence
By sheer simplicity—a pointed oval
Bare on a stalk erect: and yet, grown old
He will his young idea quite abandon,

In his dishevel'd fury wantoning
Beyond belief . . . Some are four-leaved : this poppy
Will have but four.   He, like a hurried thief,
Stuffs his rich silks into too small a bag—   280
I think he watch'd a summer-butterfly
Creep out all crumpled from his winter-case,
Trusting the sun to smooth his tender tissue
And sleek the velvet of his painted wings :—
And so doth he.—Between such different schemes,
Such widely varied loveliness, how choose ?
Yet loving all, one should be most belov'd,
Most intimately mine ; to mortal men
My emblem : tho' I never find in one
The sum of all distinctions.—Rose were best :   290
But she is passion's darling, and unkind
To handle—set her by.—Choosing for odour,
The violet were mine—men call her modest,
Because she hides, and when in company
Lacks manner and the assertive style of worth :—
While this narcissus here scorns modesty,
Will stand up what she is, tho' something prim :
Her scent, a saturation of one tone,
Like her plain symmetry, leaves nought to fancy :—
Whereas this iris,—she outvieth man's   300
Excellent artistry ; elaboration
Confounded with simplicity, till none
Can tell which sprang of which.   Coud I but find
A scented iris, I should be content :
Yet men would call me proud : Iris is Pride.—
To-day I'll favour thee, sweet violet ;
Thou canst live in my bosom.   I'll not wrong thee
Wearing thee in Olympus.—Help ! help ! Ay me !

[*Persephone rises to her feet, and amidst a contrivance of confused
    darkness Hades is seen rushing from behind.   He seizes her and
    drags her backward.   Her basket is thrown up and the flowers
    scattered.*]

A C T   II

CHORUS.

I (a)

Bright day succeedeth unto day—
   Night to pensive night—   310
   With his towering ray
   Of all-fathering light—
   With the solemn trance
   Of her starry dance.—

   Nought is new or strange
   In the eternal change.—

   As the light clouds fly
   O'er the tree-tops high,
   So the days go by.—

   Ripples that arrive   320
   On the sunny shore,
   Dying to their live
   Music evermore.—

   Like pearls on a thread,—
   Like notes of a song,—
   Like the measur'd tread
   Of a dancing throng.—

(β)

Ocëanides are we,
   Nereids of the foam,
   But we left the sea   330
   On the earth to roam
   With the fairest Queen
   That the world hath seen.—

Why amidst our play
Was she sped away?—

Over hill and plain
We have sought in vain;
She comes not again.—

Not the Naiads knew
On their dewy lawns :—   340
Not the laughing crew
Of the leaping Fauns.—

Now, since she is gone,
All our dance is slow,
All our joy is done,
And our song is woe.—

II

Saw ye the mighty Mother, where she went
    Searching the land?
Nor night nor day resting from her lament,
    With smoky torch in hand.   350
Her godhead in the passion of a sorrow spent
Which not her mind coud suffer, nor heart withstand?—

2

Enlanguor'd like a fasting lioness,
    That prowls around
Robb'd of her whelps, in fury comfortless
    Until her lost be found :
Implacable and terrible in her wild distress;
And thro' the affrighted country her roars resound.—

3

But lo! what form is there?   Thine eyes awaken!
    See! see! O say,   360
Is not that she, the furious, the forsaken?
    She cometh, lo! this way;
Her golden-rippling hair upon her shoulders shaken,
And all her visage troubled with deep dismay.

DEMETER (entering).

Here is the hateful spot, the hollow rock
Whence the fierce ravisher sprang forth—
            (seeing the nymphs) Ah! ye!
I know you well: ye are the nymphs of Ocean.
Ye, graceful as your watery names
And idle as the mimic flames
That skip upon his briny floor,   370
When the hot sun smiteth thereo'er;
Why did ye leave your native waves?
Did false Poseidon, to my hurt
Leagued with my foe, bid you desert
Your opalescent pearly caves,
Your dances on the shelly strand?

    CH. Poseidon gave us no command,
Lady; it was thy child Persephone,
Whose beauty drew us from the sea.

    DEM. Ill company ye lent, ill-fated guards!   380
How was she stolen from your distracted eyes?

    CH. There, where thou standest now, stood she com-
        panion'd
By wise Athena and bright Artemis.
We in flower-gathering dance and idle song
Were wander'd off apart; we fear'd no wrong.

    DEM. In heav'n I heard her cry: ye nothing heard?

    CH. We heard no cry—How coudst thou hear in
        heaven?
Ask us not óf her:—we have nought to tell.—

    DEM. I seek not knowledge óf you, for I know.

    CH. Thou knowest? Ah, mighty Queen, deign then to tell
If thou hast found her. Tell us—tell us—tell!   391

    DEM. Oh, there are calls that love can hear,
That strike not on the outward ear.
None heard save I: but with a dart
Of lightning-pain it pierc'd my heart,

That call for aid, that cry of fear.
It echo'd from the mountain-steeps
Down to the dark of Ocean-deeps;
O'er all the isle, from ev'ry hill
It pierc'd my heart and echoes still,   400
      Ay me! Ay me!
   Ch. Where is she, O mighty Queen?—Tell us—O tell!—
   Dem. Swift unto earth, in frenzy led
By Cora's cry, from heav'n I sped.
Immortal terror froze my mind:
I fear'd, ev'n as I yearn'd to find
My child, my joy, faln from my care
Wrong'd or distresst, I knew not where,
      Cora, my Cora!
Nor thought I whither first to fly,   410
Answ'ring the appeal of that wild cry:
But still it drew me till I came
To Enna, calling still her name,
      Cora, my Cora!
   Ch. If thou hast found her, tell us, Queen, O tell!
   Dem. Nine days I wander'd o'er the land.
From Enna to the eastern strand
I sought, and when the first night came
I lit my torch in Etna's flame.
But neither 'mid the chestnut woods   420
That rustle o'er his stony floods;
Nor yet at daybreak on the meads
Where bountiful Symaethus leads
His chaunting boatmen to the main;
Nor where the road on Hybla's plain
Is skirted by the spacious corn;
Nor where embattled Syracuse
With lustrous temple fronts the morn;
Nor yet by dolphin'd Arethuse;
Nor when I crossed Anapus wide,   430
Where Cyane, his reedy bride,

Uprushing from her crystal well,
Doth not his cold embrace repel;
Nor yet by western Eryx, where
Gay Aphrodite high in air
Beams gladness from her marble chair;
Nor 'mong the mountains that enfold
Panormos in her shell of gold,
Found I my Cora: no reply
Came to my call, my helpless cry,   440
       Cora, my Cora!
  CH. Hast thou not found her, then? Tell us—O tell!
  DEM. What wonder that I never found
Her whom I sought on mortal ground,
When she—(now will ye understand?)—
Dwelt in the land that is no land,
The fruitless and unseason'd plain
Where all lost things are found again ;
Where man's distract imaginings
Head-downward hang on bat-like wings,   450
'Mid mummied hopes, sleep-walking cares,
Crest-faln illusions and despairs,
The tortur'd memories of crime,
The outcasts of forgotten time?
  CH. Where is she, Queen?—where?—where?
  DEM.   Nor had I known,
Had not himself high Helios seen and told me.
  CH. Alas! Alas! we cannot understand—
We pray, dear Queen, may great Zeus comfort thee.
  DEM. Yea, pray to Zeus; but pray ye for yourselves,
That he have pity on you, for there is need.   460
Or let Zeus hear a strange, unwonted prayer
That in his peril he will aid himself;
For I have said, nor coud his Stygian oath
Add any sanction to a mother's word,
That, if he give not back my daughter to me,
Him will I slay, and lock his pining ghost

In sleepy prisons of unhallowing hell.

CH. (*aside*). Alas ! alas ! she is distraught with grief.—
What comfort can we make?—How reason with her?—   469
(*to* D.) This coud not be, great Queen.   How coud it be
That Zeus should be destroy'd, or thou destroy him ?

DEM. Yea, and you too : so make your prayer betimes.

CH. We pray thee, Lady, sit thou on this bank
And we will bring thee food ; or if thou thirst,
Water.   We know too in what cooling caves
The sly Fauns have bestow'd their skins of wine.

DEM. Ye simple creatures, I need not these things,
And stand above your pity.   Think ye me
A woman of the earth derang'd with grief?
Nay, nay : but I have pity on your pity,   480
And for your kindness I will ease the trouble
Wherewith it wounds your gentleness : attend !
Ye see this jewel here, that from my neck
Hangs by this golden chain.
                      [*They crowd near to see.*
                  Look, 'tis a picture,
'Tis of Persephone.

CH.   How ?—Is that she ?—
A crown she weareth.—She was never wont
Thus . . .—nor her robe thus—and her countenance
Hath not the smile which drew us from the sea.

DEM. Daedalus cut it, in the year he made
The Zibian Aphrodite, and Hephaestus   490
O'erlookt and praised the work.   I treasure it
Beyond all other jewels that I have,
And on this chain I guard it.   Say now : think ye
It cannot fall loose until every link
Of all the chain be broken, or if one
Break, will it fall ?

CH.   Surely if one break, Lady,
The chain is broken and the jewel falls.

DEM. 'Tis so.   Now hearken diligently.   All life
Is as this chain, and Zeus is as the jewel.

The universal life dwells first in the Earth,   500
The stones and soil; therefrom the plants and trees
Exhale their being; and on them the brutes
Feeding elaborate their sentient life,
And from these twain mankind; and in mankind
A spirit lastly is form'd of subtler sort
Whereon the high gods live, sustain'd thereby,
And feeding on it, as plants on the soil,
Or animals on plants. Now see! I hold,
As well ye know, one whole link of this chain:
If I should kill the plants, must not man perish?   510
And if he perish, then the gods must die.
    Ch. If this were so, thou wouldst destroy thyself.
    Dem. And therefore Zeus will not believe my word.
    Ch. Nor we believe thee, Lady: it cannot be
That thou shouldst seek to mend a private fortune
By universal ruin, and restore
Thy daughter by destruction of thyself.
    Dem. Ye are not mothers, or ye would not wonder.
In me, who hold from great all-mother Rhea
Heritage of essential motherhood,   520
Ye would look rather for unbounded passion.
Coud I, the tenderness of Nature's heart,
Exist, were I unheedful to protect
From wrong and ill the being that I gave,
The unweeting passions that I fondly nurtured
To hopes of glory, the young confidence
In growing happiness?   Shall I throw by
As self-delusion the supreme ambition,
Which I encourag'd till parental fondness
Bore the prophetic blessing, on whose truth   530
My spirit throve?   Oh never! nay, nay, nay!
That were the one disaster, and if aid
I cannot, I can mightily avenge.
On irremediable wrong I shrink not
To pile immortal ruin, there to lie

As trophies on a carven tomb : nor less
For that no memory of my deed survive,
Nor any eye to see, nor tongue to tell.

    CH. So vast injustice, Lady, were not good.

    DEM. To you I seem unjust involving man.   540

    CH. Why should man suffer in thy feud with Zeus ?

    DEM. Let Zeus relent. There is no other way.

I will destroy the seeds of plant and tree :
Vineyard and orchard, oliveyard and cornland
Shall all withhold their fruits, and in their stead
Shall flourish the gay blooms that Cora loved.
There shall be dearth, and yet so gay the dearth
That all the land shall look in holiday
With mockery of foison ; every field
With splendour aflame. For wheat the useless poppy   550
In sheeted scarlet; and for barley and oats
The blue and yellow weeds that mock men's toil,
Centaury and marigold in chequer'd plots :
Where seed is sown, or none, shall dandelions
And wretched ragwort vie, orchis and iris
And garish daisy, and for every flower
That in this vale she pluckt, shall spring a thousand.
Where'er she stept anemones shall crowd,
And the sweet violet. These things shall ye see.
—But I behold him whom I came to meet,   560
Hermes :—he, be he laden howsoe'er,
Will heavier-laden to his lord return.

HERMES (*entering*).

Mighty Demeter, Mother of the seasons,
Bountiful all-sustainer, fairest daughter
Of arch-ancestral Rhea,—to thee Zeus sendeth
Kindly message. He grieves seeing thy godhead
Offended wrongly at eternal justice,
'Gainst destiny ordain'd idly revolting.

Ever will he, thy brother, honour thee
And willingly aid thee; but since now thy daughter   570
Is raised to a place on the tripartite throne,
He finds thee honour'd duly and not injur'd.
Wherefore he bids thee now lament no more,
But with thy presence grace the courts of heav'n.

   Dem. Bright Hermes, Argus-slayer, born of Maia,
Who bearest empty words, the mask of war,
To Zeus make thine own words, that thou hast found me
Offended,—that I still lament my daughter,
Nor heed his summons to the courts of heav'n.

   Her. Giv'st thou me nought but these relentless words?

   Dem. I send not words, nor dost thou carry deeds.   581
But know, since heav'n denies my claim, I take
Earth for my battle-field.   Curse and defiance
Shall shake his throne, and, readier then for justice,
Zeus will enquire my terms : thou, on that day,
Remember them; that he shall bid thee lead
Persephone from Hades by the hand,
And on this spot, whence she was stol'n, restore her
Into mine arms.   Execute that; and praise
Shall rise from earth and peace return to heav'n.   590

   Her. How dare I carry unto Zeus thy threats?

   Dem. Approach him with a gift : this little wallet.
                       [*Giving a little bag of seeds.*
I will not see thee again until the day
Thou lead my daughter hither thro' the gates of Hell.   [*Going.*

   Her. Ah ! mighty Queen, the lightness of thy gift
Is greater burden than thy weighty words.
                    [*Exeunt severally r. and l.*

CHORUS.

(1) Sisters ! what have we heard !
    Our fair Persephone, the flower of the earth,
    By Hades stolen away, his queen to be.
(*others*) Alas !—alas !—ay me !   600

(2) And great Demeter's bold relentless word
    To Hermes given,
    Threatening mankind with dearth.
(*others*) Ay me! alas! alas!—
(3 *or* 1) She in her sorrow strong
    Fears not to impeach the King of Heaven,
    And combat wrong with wrong.—
(*others confusedly*) What can we do?—Alas!—
    Back to our ocean-haunts return
    To weep and mourn.—   610
    What use to mourn?—
    Nay, nay!—Away with sorrow:
    Let us forget to-day
    And look for joy to-morrow:—
[(1) Nay, nay! hearken to me!]
    Nay, how forget that on us too,—
    Yea, on us all
    The curse will fall.—
[(1) Hearken! I say!]
    What can we do? Alas! alas!   620
(1) Hearken! There's nought so light,
    Nothing of weight so small,
    But that in even balance 'twill avail
    Wholly to turn the scale.
    Let us our feeble force unite,
    And giving voice to tears,
    Assail Poseidon's ears;
    Rob pleasure from his days,
    Darken with sorrow all his ways,
    Until his shifty mind   630
    Become to pity inclined,
    And 'gainst his brother turn.
(*others*) 'Tis well, thou sayest well.
(2) Yea; for if Zeus should learn
    That earth and sea were both combined
    Against his cruel intent,

Sooner will he relent.

(*others*) 'Tis well—we do it—'tis well.—

(1) Come let us vow.   Vow all with one accord
    To harden every heart   640
    Till we have won Poseidon to our part.

(*all*) We vow—we do it—we vow.

(1) Till we have conquer'd heav'n's almighty lord
    And seen Persephone restored.

(*all*) We vow—we vow.

(1) Come then all ; and, as ye go,
    Begin the song of woe.

Song.

Close up, bright flow'rs, and hang the head,
    Ye beauties of the plain,
The Queen of Spring is with the dead,   650
    Ye deck the earth in vain.
From your deserted vale we fly,
    And where the salt waves mourn
Our song shall swell their burd'ning sigh
    Until sweet joy return.

A C T   III

CHORUS.

Song.

Lo where the virgin veilèd in airy beams,
All-holy Morn, in splendor awakening,
    Heav'n's gate hath unbarrèd, the golden
      Aerial lattices set open.

With music endeth night's prisoning terror,   660
With flow'ry incense : Haste to salute the sun,
    That for the day's chase, like a huntsman,
      With flashing arms cometh o'er the mountain.

Inter se. That were a song for Artemis—I have heard
Men thus salute the rising sun in spring—
—See, we have wreaths enough and garlands plenty
To hide our lov'd Persephone from sight
If she should come.— But think you she will come ?—
If one might trust the heavens, it is a morn
Promising happiness—'Tis like the day   670
That brought us all our grief a year ago.—

ODE.

O that the earth, or only this fair isle wer' ours
    Amid the ocean's blue billows,
With flow'ry woodland, stately mountain and valley,
    Cascading and lilied river ;
Nor ever a mortal envious, laborious,
    By anguish or dull care opprest,
Should come polluting with remorseful countenance
    Our haunt of easy gaiety.
For us the grassy slopes, the country's airiness,   680
    The lofty whispering forest,
Where rapturously Philomel invoketh the night
    And million eager throats the morn ;
With doves at evening softly cooing, and mellow
    Cadences of the dewy thrush.
We love the gentle deer, the nimble antelope ;
    Mice love we and springing squirrels ;
To watch the gaudy flies visit the blooms, to hear
    On ev'ry mead the grasshopper.
All thro' the spring-tide, thro' the indolent summer,   690
    (If only this fair isle wer' ours)
Here might we dwell, forgetful of the weedy caves
    Beneath the ocean's blue billows.

Enter Demeter.

Ch. Hail, mighty Mother !—Welcome, great Demeter !—
(1) This day bring joy to thee, and peace to man !

DEM. I welcome you, my loving true allies,
And thank you, who for me your gentle tempers
Have stiffen'd in rebellion, and so long
Harass'd the foe.   Here on this field of flowers
I have bid you share my victory or defeat.   700
For Hermes hath this day command from Zeus
To lead our lost Persephone from Hell,
Hither whence she was stolen.—And yet, alas !
Tho' Zeus is won, some secret power thwarts me ;
All is not won : a cloud is o'er my spirit.
Wherefore not yet I boast, nor will rejoice
Till mine eyes see her, and my arms enfold her,
And breast to breast we meet in fond embrace.

CH. Well hast thou fought, great goddess, so to wrest
Zeus from his word.   We thank thee, call'd to share   710
Thy triumph, and rejoice.   Yet O, we pray,
Make thou this day a day of peace for man !
Even if Persephone be not restored,
Whether Aidoneus hold her or release,
Relent thou.—Stay thine anger, mighty goddess ;
Nor with thy hateful famine slay mankind.

DEM. Say not that word 'relent' lest Hades hear !
CH. Consider rather if mankind should hear.
DEM. Do ye love man ?
CH.   We have seen his sorrows, Lady . . .
DEM. And what can ye have seen that I know not ?—
His sorrow ?—Ah my sorrow !—and ye bid   721
Me to relent ; whose deeds of fond compassion
Have in this year of agony built up
A story for all time that shall go wand'ring
Further than I have wander'd ;—whereto all ears
Shall hearken ever, as ye will hearken now.

CH. Happy are we, who first shall hear the tale
From thine own lips, and tell it to the sea.
DEM. Attend then while I tell.—
—Parting from Hermes hence, anger'd at heart,   730

(73)

Self-exiled from the heav'ns, forgone, alone,
My anguish fasten'd on me, as I went
Wandering an alien in the haunts of men.
To screen my woe I put my godhead off,
Taking the likeness of a worthy dame,
A woman of the people well in years ;
Till going unobserv'd, it irked me soon
To be unoccupy'd save by my grief,
While men might find distraction for their sorrows
In useful toil.   Then, of my pity rather   740
Than hope to find their simple cure my own,
I took resolve to share and serve their needs,
And be as one of them.

  Cн.   Ah, mighty goddess,
Coudst thou so put thy dignities away,
And suffer the familiar brunt of men?

  Dem. In all things even as they.—And sitting down
One evening at Eleusis, by the well
Under an olive-tree, likening myself
Outwardly to some kindly-hearted matron,
Whose wisdom and experience are of worth   750
Either where childhood clamorously speaks
The engrossing charge of Aphrodite's gifts,
Or merry maidens in wide-echoing halls
Want sober governance ;—to me, as there
I sat, the daughters of King Keleos came,
Tall noble damsels, as kings' daughters are,
And, marking me a stranger, they drew from me
A tale told so engagingly, that they
Grew fain to find employment for my skill ;
—As men devise in mutual recompense,   760
Hoping the main advantage for themselves ;—
And so they bad me follow, and I enter'd
The palace of King Keleos, and received
There on my knees the youngest of the house,
A babe, to nurse him as a mother would :

And in that menial service I was proud
To outrun duty and trust : and there I liv'd
Disguised among the maidens many months.
    CH. Often as have our guesses aim'd, dear Lady,
Where thou didst hide thyself, oft as we wonder'd   770
What chosen work was thine, none ever thought
That thou didst deign to tend a mortal babe.
    DEM. What life I led shall be for men to tell.
But for this babe, the nursling of my sorrow,
Whose peevish cry was my consoling care,
How much I came to love him ye shall hear.
    CH. What was he named, Lady?
    DEM.   Demophoön.
Yea, ye shall hear how much I came to love him.
For in his small epitome I read
The trouble of mankind ; in him I saw   780
The hero's helplessness, the countless perils
In ambush of life's promise, the desire
Blind and instinctive, and the will perverse.
His petty needs were man's necessities ;
In him I nurst all mortal natur', embrac'd
With whole affection to my breast, and lull'd
Wailing humanity upon my knee.
    CH. We see thou wilt not now destroy mankind.
    DEM. What I coud do to save man was my thought.
And, since my love was center'd in the boy,   790
My thought was first for him, to rescue him ;
That, thro' my providence, he ne'er should know
Suffering, nor disease, nor fear of death.
Therefore I fed him on immortal food,
And should have gain'd my wish, so well he throve,
But by ill-chance it hapt, once, as I held him
Bathed in the fire at midnight (as was my wont),—
His mother stole upon us, and ascare
At the strange sight, screaming in loud dismay
Compel'd me to unmask, and leave for ever   800

The halls of Keleos, and my work undone.

    CH. 'Twas pity that she came!—Didst thou not grieve to lose
The small Demophoön?—Coudst thou not save him?

    DEM. I had been blinded.   Think ye for yourselves . . .
What vantage were it to mankind at large
That one should be immortal,—if all beside
Must die and suffer misery as before?

    CH. Nay, truly.   And great envy borne to one
So favour'd might have more embitter'd all.

    DEM. I had been foolish.   My sojourn with men   810
Had warpt my mind with mortal tenderness.
So, questioning myself what real gift
I might bestow on man to help his state,
I saw that sorrow was his life-companion,
To be embrac't bravely, not weakly shun'd:
That as by toil man winneth happiness,
Thro' tribulation he must come to peace.
How to make sorrow his friend then,—this my task.
Here was a mystery . . . and how persuade
This thorny truth? . . . Ye do not hearken me.   820

    CH. Yea, honour'd goddess, yea, we hearken still:
Stint not thy tale.

    DEM.   Ye might not understand.
My tale to you must be a tale of deeds—
How first I bade King Keleos build for me
A temple in Eleusis, and ordain'd
My worship, and the mysteries of my thought;
Where in the sorrow that I underwent
Man's state is pattern'd; and in picture shewn
The way of his salvation. . . . Now with me
—Here is a matter grateful to your ears—   830
Your lov'd Persephone hath equal honour,
And in the spring her festival of flowers:
And if she should return . . .   *[Listening.*
                Ah! hark! what hear I?

CH. We hear no sound.

DEM.   Hush ye! Hermes: he comes.

CH. What hearest thou?

DEM.   Hermes; and not alone.
She is there.   'Tis she: I have won.

CH.   Where? where?

DEM. (*aside*). Ah! can it be that out of sorrow's night,
From tears, from yearning pain, from long despair,
Into joy's sunlight I shall come again?—
Aside! stand ye aside!   840

Enter Hermes leading Persephone.

HER. Mighty Demeter, lo! I execute
The will of Zeus and here restore thy daughter.

DEM. I have won.

PER. Sweet Mother, thy embrace is as the welcome
Of all the earth, thy kiss the breath of life.

DEM. Ah! but to me, Cora!   Thy voice again . . .
My tongue is trammel'd with excess of joy.

PER. Arise, my nymphs, my Oceanides!
My Nereids all, arise! and welcome me!
Put off your strange solemnity! arise!   850

CH. Welcome! all welcome, fair Persephone!
(1) We came to welcome thee, but fell abash'd
Seeing thy purple robe and crystal crown.

PER. Arise and serve my pleasure as of yore.

DEM. And thou too doff thy strange solemnity,
That all may see thee as thou art, my Cora,
Restor'd and ever mine.   Put off thy crown!

PER. Awhile! dear Mother—what thou say'st is true;
I am restor'd to thee, and evermore
Shall be restor'd.   Yet am I none the less   860
Evermore Queen of Hades: and 'tis meet
I wear the crown, the symbol of my reign.

DEM. What words are these, my Cora!   Evermore
Restor'd to me thou say'st . . . 'tis well—but then

(77)

Evermore Queen of Hades . . . what is this?
I had a dark foreboding till I saw thee ;
Alas, alas! it lives again : destroy it!
Solve me this riddle quickly, if thou mayest.

  PER. Let Hermes speak, nor fear thou. All is well.

  HER. Divine Demeter, thou hast won thy will, 870
And the command of Zeus have I obey'd.
Thy daughter is restor'd, and evermore
Shall be restor'd to thee as on this day.
But Hades holding to his bride, the Fates
Were kind also to him, that she should be
His queen in Hades as thy child on earth.
Yearly, as spring-tide cometh, she is thine
While flowers bloom and all the land is gay ;
But when thy corn is gather'd, and the fields
Are bare, and earth withdraws her budding life 880
From the sharp bite of winter's angry fang,
Yearly will she return and hold her throne
With great Aidoneus and the living dead :
And she hath eaten with him of such fruit
As holds her his true bride for evermore.

  DEM. Alas! alas !

  PER. Rejoice, dear Mother. Let not vain lament
Trouble our joy this day, nor idle tears.

  DEM. Alas ! from my own deed my trouble comes :
He gave thee of the fruit which I had curs'd : 890
I made the poison that enchanted thee.

  PER. Repent not in thy triumph, but rejoice,
Who hast thy will in all, as I have mine.

  DEM. I have but half my will, how hast thou more ?

  PER. It was my childish fancy (thou rememb'rest),
I would be goddess of the flowers : I thought
That men should innocently honour me
With bloodless sacrifice and spring-tide joy.
Now Fate, that look'd contrary, hath fulfill'd
My project with mysterious efficacy : 900

And as a plant that yearly dieth down
When summer is o'er, and hideth in the earth,
Nor showeth promise in its wither'd leaves
That it shall reawaken and put forth
Its blossoms any more to deck the spring;
So I, the mutual symbol of my choice,
Shall die with winter, and with spring revive.
How without winter coud I have my spring?
How come to resurrection without death?
Lo thus our joyful meeting of to-day,   910
Born of our separation, shall renew
Its annual ecstasy, by grief refresht:
And no more pall than doth the joy of spring
Yearly returning to the hearts of men.
See then the accomplishment of all my hope:
Rejoice, and think not to put off my crown.

    DEM. What hast thou seen below to reconcile thee
To the dark moiety of thy strange fate?

    PER. Where have I been, mother? what have I seen?
The downward pathway to the gates of death: 920
The skeleton of earthly being, stript
Of all disguise: the sudden void of night:
The spectral records of unwholesome fear:—
Why was it given to me to see these things?
The ruin'd godheads, disesteem'd, condemn'd
To toil of deathless mockery: conquerors
In the reverse of glory, doom'd to rule
The multitudinous army of their crimes:
The naked retribution of all wrong:—
Why was it given to me to see such things?   930

    DEM. Not without terror, as I think, thou speakest,
Nor as one reconcil'd to brook return.

    PER. But since I have seen these things, with salt and fire
My spirit is purged, and by this crystal crown
Terror is tamed within me. If my words
Seem'd to be tinged with terror, 'twas because

I knew one hour of terror (on the day
That took me hence) and with that memory
Colour'd my speech, using the terms which paint
The blindfold fears of men, who little reckon   940
How they by holy innocence and love,
By reverence and gentle lives may win
A title to the fair Elysian fields,
Where the good spirits dwell in ease and light
And entertainment of those fair desires
That made earth beautiful . . . brave souls that spent
Their lives for liberty and truth, grave seers
Whose vision conquer'd darkness, pious poets
Whose words have won Apollo's deathless praise,
Who all escape Hell's mysteries, nor come nigh   950
The Cave of Cacophysia.

    DEM.   Mysteries !
What mysteries are these? and what the Cave?

    PER. The mysteries of evil, and the cave
Of blackness that obscures them.   Even in hell
The worst is hidden, and unfructuous night
Stifles her essence in her truthless heart.

    DEM. What is the arch-falsity?   I seek to know
The mystery of evil.   Hast thou seen it?

    PER. I have seen it.   Coud I truly rule my kingdom
Not having seen it?

    DEM.   Tell me what it is.   960

    PER. 'Tis not that I forget it; tho' the thought
Is banisht from me.   But 'tis like a dream
Whose sense is an impression lacking words.

    DEM. If it would pain thee telling . . .

    PER.   Nay, but surely
The words of gods and men are names of things
And thoughts accustom'd : but of things unknown
And unimagin'd are no words at all.

    DEM. And yet will words sometimes outrun the thought.

    PER. What can be spoken is nothing : 'twere a path

That leading t'ward some prospect ne'er arrived. 970
   DEM. The more thou holdest back, the more I long.
   PER. The outward aspect only mocks my words.
   DEM. Yet what is outward easy is to tell.
   PER. Something is possible. This cavern lies
In very midmost of deep-hollow'd hell.
O'er its torn mouth the black Plutonic rock
Is split in sharp disorder'd pinnacles
And broken ledges, whereon sit, like apes
Upon a wither'd tree, the hideous sins
Of all the world : once having seen within 980
The magnetism is heavy on them, and they crawl
Palsied with filthy thought upon the peaks ;
Or, squatting thro' long ages, have become
Rooted like plants into the griping clefts :
And there they pullulate, and moan, and strew
The rock with fragments of their mildew'd growth.
   DEM. Cora, my child ! and hast thou seen these things !
   PER. Nay but the outward aspect, figur'd thus
In mere material loathsomeness, is nought
Beside the mystery that is hid within. 990
   DEM. Search thou for words, I pray, somewhat to tell.
   PER. Are there not matters past the thought of men
Or gods to know ?
   DEM.   Thou meanest wherefore things
Should be at all ? Or, if they be, why thus,
As hot, cold, hard and soft : and wherefore Zeus
Had but two brothers ; why the stars of heaven
Are so innumerable, constellated
Just as they are ; or why this Sicily
Should be three-corner'd ? Yes, thou sayest well,
Why things are as they are, nor gods nor men 1000
Can know. We say that Fate appointed thus,
And are content.—
   PER. Suppose, dear Mother, there wer' a temple in
   heaven,

Which, dedicated to the unknown Cause
And worship of the unseen, had power to draw
All that was worthy and good within its gate :
And that the spirits who enter'd there became
Not only purified and comforted,
But that the mysteries of the shrine were such,
That the initiated bathed in light   1010
Of infinite intelligence, and saw
The meaning and the reason of all things,
All at a glance distinctly, and perceived
The origin of all things to be good,
And the énd good, and that what appears as evil
Is as a film of dust, that faln thereon,
May,—at one stroke of the hand,—
Be brush'd away, and show the good beneath,
Solid and fair and shining : If moreover
This blessèd vision were of so great power 1020
That none coud e'er forget it or relapse
To doubtful ignorance :—I say, dear Mother,
Suppose that there were such a temple in heaven.

 Dem. O child, my child ! that were a temple indeed.
'Tis such a temple as man needs on earth ;
A holy shrine that makes no pact with sin,
A worthy shrine to draw the worthy and good,
A shrine of wisdom trifling not with folly,
A shrine of beauty, where the initiated
Drank love and light. . . . Strange thou shouldst speak of it.
I have inaugurated such a temple   1031
These last days in Eleusis, have ordain'd
These very mysteries !—Strange thou speakest of it.
But by what path return we to the Cave
Of Cacophysia ?

 Per.   By this path, dear Mother.
The Cave of Cacophysia is in all things
T'ward evil, as that temple were t'ward good.
I enter'd in. Outside the darkness was

But as accumulated sunlessness;
Within 'twas positive as light itself,   1040
A blackness that extinguish'd : Yet I knew,
For Hades told me, that I was to see ;
And so I waited, till a forking flash
Of sudden lightning dazzlingly reveal'd
All at a glance. As on a pitchy night
The warder of some high acropolis
Looks down into the dark, and suddenly
Sees all the city with its roofs and streets,
Houses and walls, clear as in summer noon,
And ere he think of it, 'tis dark again,—   1050
So I saw all within the Cave, and held
The vision, 'twas so burnt upon my sense.

   DEM. What saw'st thou, child? what saw'st thou?
   PER.   Nay, the things
Not to be told, because there are no words
Of gods or men to paint the inscrutable
And full initiation of hell.—I saw
The meaning and the reason of all things,
All at a glance, and in that glance perceiv'd
The origin of all things to be evil,
And the énd evil : that what seems as good   1060
Is as a bloom of gold that spread thereo'er
May, by one stroke of the hand,
Be brush'd away, and leave the ill beneath
Solid and foul and black. . . .
   DEM.   Now tell me, child,
If Hades love thee, that he sent thee thither.
   PER. He said it coud not harm me : and I think
It hath not.   [*Going up to Demeter, who kisses her.*
   DEM.   Nay it hath not, . . . and I kncw
The power of evil is no power at all
Against eternal good. 'Tis fire on water,
As darkness against sunlight, like a dream   1070
To waken'd will. Foolish was I to fear

That aught coud hurt thee, Cora. But to-day
Speak we no more. . . . This mystery of Hell
Will do me service : I'll not tell thee now :
But sure it is that Fate o'erruleth all
For good or ill : and we (no more than men)
Have power to oppose, nor any will nor choice
Beyond such wisdom as a fisher hath
Who driven by sudden gale far out to sea
Handles his fragile boat safe thro' the waves,   1080
Making what harbour the wild storm allows.

    To-day hard-featured and inscrutable Fate
Stands to mine eyes reveal'd, nor frowns upon me.
I thought to find thee as I knew thee, and fear'd
Only to find thee sorrowful : I find thee
Far other than thou wert, nor hurt by Hell.
I thought I must console thee, but 'tis thou
Playest the comforter : I thought to teach thee,
And had prepared my lesson, word by word ;
But thou art still beyond me. One thing only   1090
Of all my predetermin'd plan endures :
My purpose was to bid thee to Eleusis
For thy spring festival, which three days hence
Inaugurates my temple. Thou wilt come ?

    Per. I come. And art thou reconcil'd, dear Mother ?

    Dem. Joy and surprise make tempest in my mind ;
When their bright stir is o'er, there will be peace.
But ere we leave this flowery field, the scene
Of strange and beauteous memories evermore,
I thank thee, Hermes, for thy willing service.   1100

    Per. I thank thee, son of Maia, and bid farewell.

    Her. Have thy joy now, great Mother ; and have thou joy,
Fairest Persephone, Queen of the Spring.

Demeter

CHORUS.

Fair Persephone, garlands we bring thee,
Flow'rs and spring-tide welcome sing thee.
    Hades held thee not,
    Darkness quell'd thee not.
Gay and joyful welcome !
Welcome, Queen, evermore.
    Earth shall own thee,   1110
    Thy nymphs crown thee,
Garland thee and crown thee,
Crown thee Queen evermore.

EROS & PSYCHE

*A narrative Poem
in twelve measures*

THE STORY DONE INTO ENGLISH

FROM THE LATIN

OF

APULEIUS

L'anima semplicetta che sa nulla.

*O lateſt born, O lovelieſt vision far
Of all Olympus' faded hierarchy.*

PREVIOUS EDITIONS

1. *Chiswick Press for Bell & Sons.* 1885.
2. *Do. do. revised.* 1894.
3. *Smith, Elder & Co. Vol. I.* 1898.

FIRST QUARTER

SPRING

PSÝCHE'S EARTHLY PARENTAGE · WORSHIPPED BY
MEN · & PERSECUTED BY APHRODITE · SHE IS
LOVED & CARRIED OFF BY EROS

MARCH

I

In midmost length of hundred-citied Crete,
The land that cradl'd Zeus, of old renown,
Where grave Demeter nurseried her wheat,
And Minos fashion'd law, ere he went down
To judge the quaking hordes of Hell's domain,
There dwelt a King on the Omphalian plain
Eastward of Ida, in a little town.

2

Three daughters had this King, of whom my tale
Time hath preserved, that loveth to despise
The wealth which men misdeem of much avail,
Their glories for themselves that they devise;
For clerkly is he, old hard-featured Time,
And poets' fabl'd song and lovers' rhyme
He storeth on his shelves to please his eyes.

3

These three princesses all were fairest fair:
And of the elder twain 'tis truth to say
That if they stood not high above compare,
Yet in their prime they bore the palm away;
Outwards of loveliness; but Nature's mood,
Gracious to make, had grudgingly endued
And marr'd by gifting ill the beauteous clay.

4

And being in honour they were well content
To feed on lovers' looks and courtly smiles,
To hang their necks with jewel'd ornament,
And gold, that vanity in vain beguiles,
And live in gaze, and take their praise for due,
To be the fairest maidens then to view
Within the shores of Greece and all her isles.

5

But of that youngest one, the third princess,
There is no likeness; since she was as far
From pictured beauty as is ugliness,
Though on the side where heavenly wonders are,
Ideals out of being and above,
Which music worshippeth, but if love love,
'Tis, as the poet saith, to love a star.

6

Her vision rather drave from passion's heart
What earthly soil it had afore possest;
Since to man's purer unsubstantial part
The brightness of her presence was addrest:
And such as mock'd at God, when once they saw
Her heavenly glance, were humbl'd, and in awe
Of things unseen, return'd to praise the Best.

March

And so before her, wheresoe'er she went,
Hushing the crowd a thrilling whisper ran,
And silent heads were reverently bent;
Till from the people the belief began
That Love's own mother had come down on earth,
Sweet Cytherea, or of mortal birth
A greater Goddess was vouchsaf't to man.

Then Aphrodite's statue in its place
Stood without worshippers; if Cretans pray'd
For beauty or for children, love or grace,
The prayer and vow were offer'd to the maid;
Unto the maid their hymns of praise were sung,
Their victims bled for her, for her they hung
Garland and golden gift, and none forbade.

And thence opinion spread beyond the shores,
From isle to isle the wonder flew, it came
Across the Ægæan on a thousand oars,
Athens and Smyrna caught the virgin's fame;
And East or West, where'er the tale had been,
The adoration of the foam-born queen
Fell to neglect, and men forgot her name.

No longer to high Paphos now 'twas sail'd;
The fragrant altar by the Graces served
At Cnidus was forsaken; pilgrims fail'd
The rocky island to her name reserved,
Proud Ephyra, and Meropis renown'd;
'Twas all for Crete her votaries were bound,
And to the Cretan maid her worship swerved.

11

Which when in heaven great Aphrodite saw,
Who is the breather of the year's bright morn,
Fount of desire and beauty without flaw,
Herself the life that doth the world adorn;
Seeing that without her generative might
Nothing can spring upon the shores of light,
Nor any bud of joy or love be born;

12

She, when she saw the insult, did not hide
Her indignation, that a mortal frail
With her eterne divinity had vied,
Her fair Hellenic empire to assail,
For which she had fled the doom of Ninus old,
And left her wanton images unsoul'd
In Babylon and Zidon soon to fail.

13

'Not long,' she cried, 'shall that poor girl of Crete
God it in my despite; for I will bring
Such mischief on the sickly counterfeit
As soon shall cure her tribe of worshipping:
Her beauty will I mock with loathèd lust,
Bow down her dainty spirit to the dust,
And leave her long alive to feel the sting.'

14

With that she calls to her her comely boy,
The limber scion of the God of War,
The fruit adulterous, which for man's annoy
To that fierce partner Cytherea bore,
Eros, the ever young, who only grew
In mischief, and was Cupid named anew
In westering aftertime of latin lore.

March

15

What the first dawn of manhood is, the hour
When beauty, from its fleshy bud unpent,
Flaunts like the corol of a summer flower,
As if all life were for that ornament,
Such Eros seemed in years, a trifler gay,
The prodigal of an immortal day
For ever spending, and yet never spent.

16

His skin is brilliant with the nimble flood
Of ichor, that comes dancing from his heart,
Lively as fire, and redder than the blood,
And maketh in his eyes small flashes dart,
And curleth his hair golden, and distilleth
Honey on his tongue, and all his body filleth
With wanton lightsomeness in every part.

17

Naked he goeth, but with sprightly wings
Red, iridescent, are his shoulders fledged.
A bow his weapon, which he deftly strings,
And little arrows barb'd and keenly edged;
And these he shooteth true ; but else the youth
For all his seeming recketh naught of truth,
But most deceiveth where he most is pledged.

18

'Tis he that maketh in men's heart a strife
Between remorseful reason and desire,
Till with life lost they lose the love of life,
And by their own hands wretchedly expire;
Or slain in bloody rivalries they miss
Even the short embracement of their bliss,
His smile of fury and his kiss of fire.

19

He makes the strong man weak, the weak man wild;
Ruins great business and purpose high;
Brings down the wise to folly reconciled,
And martial captains on their knees to sigh:
He changeth dynasties, and on the head
Of duteous heroes, who for honour bled,
Smircheth the laurel that can never die.

20

Him then she call'd, and gravely kissing told
The great dishonour to her godhead done;
And how, if he from that in heaven would hold,
On earth he must maintain it as her son;
The rather that his weapons were most fit,
As was his skill ordain'd to champion it;
And flattering thus his ready zeal she won.

21

Whereon she quickly led him down on earth,
And show'd him PSYCHE, thus the maid was named;
Whom when she show'd, but coud not hide her worth,
She grew with envy tenfold more enflamed.
'But if,' she cried, 'thou smite her as I bid,
Soon shall our glory of this affront be rid,
And she and all her likes for ever shamed.

22

'Make her to love the loathliest, basest wretch,
Deform'd in body, and of moonstruck mind,
A hideous brute and vicious, born to fetch
Anger from dogs and cursing from the blind.
And let her passion for the monster be
As shameless and detestable as he
Is most extreme and vile of humankind.'

March

Which said, when he agreed, she spake no more,
But left him to his task, and took her way
Beside the ripples of the shell-strewn shore,
The southward stretching margin of a bay,
Whose sandy curves she pass'd, and taking stand
Upon its taper horn of furthest land,
Lookt left and right to rise and set of day.

24

Fair was the sight; for now, though full an hour
The sun had sunk, she saw the evening light
In shifting colour to the zenith tower,
And grow more gorgeous ever and more bright.
Bathed in the warm and comfortable glow,
The fair delighted queen forgot her woe,
And watch'd the unwonted pageant of the night.

25

Broad and low down, where late the sun had been
A wealth of orange-gold was thickly shed,
Fading above into a field of green,
Like apples ere they ripen into red,
Then to the height a variable hue
Of rose and pink and crimson freak'd with blue,
And olive-border'd clouds o'er lilac led.

26

High in the opposèd west the wondering moon
All silvery green in flying green was fleec't;
And round the blazing South the splendour soon
Caught all the heaven, and ran to North and East;
And Aphrodite knew the thing was wrought
By cunning of Poseidon, and she thought
She would go see with whom he kept his feast.

Swift to her wish came swimming on the waves
His lovely ocean nymphs, her guides to be,
The Nereids all, who live among the caves
And valleys of the deep, Cymodocè,
Agavè, blue-eyed Hallia and Nesæa,
Speio, and Thoë, Glaucè and Actæa,
Iaira, Melitè and Amphinomè,

28

Apseudès and Nemertès, Callianassa,
Cymothoë, Thaleia, Limnorrhea,
Clymenè, Ianeira and Ianassa,
Doris and Panopè and Galatea,
Dynamenè, Dexamenè and Maira,
Ferusa, Doto, Proto, Callianeira,
Amphithoë, Oreithuia and Amathea.

29

And after them sad Melicertes drave
His chariot, that with swift unfellied wheel,
By his two dolphins drawn along the wave,
Flew as they plunged, yet did not dip nor reel,
But like a plough that shears the heavy land
Stood on the flood, and back on either hand
O'erturn'd the briny furrow with its keel.

30

Behind came Tritons, that their conches blew,
Greenbearded, tail'd like fish, all sleek and stark;
And hippocampi tamed, a bristly crew,
The browzers of old Proteus' weedy park,
Whose chiefer Mermen brought a shell for boat,
And balancing its hollow fan afloat,
Push'd it to shore and bade the queen embark:

31

And then the goddess stept upon the shell
Which took her weight; and others threw a train
Of soft silk o'er her, that unfurl'd to swell
In sails, at breath of flying Zephyrs twain;
And all her way with foam in laughter strewn,
With stir of music and of conches blown,
Was Aphrodite launch'd upon the main.

APRIL

I

But fairest Psyche still in favour rose,
Nor knew the jealous power against her sworn :
And more her beauty now surpass't her foe's,
Since 'twas transfigured by the spirit forlorn,
That writeth, to the perfecting of grace,
Immortal question in a mortal face,
The vague desire whereunto man is born.

2

Already in good time her sisters both,
Whose honest charms were never famed as hers,
With princes of the isle had plighted troth,
And gone to rule their foreign courtiers ;
But she, exalted evermore beyond
Their loveliness, made yet no lover fond,
And gain'd but number to her worshippers.

H

3

To joy in others' joy had been her lot,
And now that that was gone she wept to see
How her transcendent beauty overshot
The common aim of all felicity.
For love she sigh'd; and had some peasant rude
For true love's sake in simple passion woo'd,
Then Psyche had not scorn'd his wife to be.

4

For what is Beauty, if it doth not fire
The loving answer of an eager soul?
Since 'tis the native food of man's desire,
And doth to good our varying world control;
Which, when it was not, was for Beauty's sake
Desired and made by Love, who still doth make
A beauteous path thereon to Beauty's goal.

5

Should all men by some hateful venom die,
The pity were that o'er the unpeopl'd sphere
The sun would still bedeck the evening sky
And the unimaginable hues appear,
With none to mark the rose and gold and green;
That Spring should walk the earth, and nothing seen
Of her fresh delicacy year by year.

6

And if some beauteous things,—whose heavenly worth
And function overpass our mortal sense,—
Lie waste and unregarded on the earth
By reason of our gross intelligence,
These are not vain, because in nature's scheme
It lives that we shall grow from dream to dream
In time to gather an enchantment thence.

7

Even as we see the fairest works of men
Awhile neglected, and the makers die;
But Truth comes weeping to their graves, and then
Their fames victoriously mounting high
Do battle with the regnant names of eld,
To win their seats; as when the Gods rebel'd
Against their sires and drave them from the sky.

8

But to be praised for beauty and denied
The meed of beauty, this was yet unknown:
The best and bravest men have ever vied
To win the fairest women for their own.
   Thus Psyche spake, or reason'd in her mind,
Disconsolate; and with self-pity pined,
In the deserted halls wandering alone.

9

And grievèd grew the King to see her woe:
And blaming first the gods for her disease,
He purposed to their oracle to go
To question how he might their wrath appease,
Or, if that might not be, the worst to hear,—
Which is the last poor hope of them that fear.—
   So he took his ship upon the northern seas,

10

And journeying to the shrine of Delphi went,
The temple of Apollo Pythian,
Where when the god he question'd if 'twas meant
That Psyche should be wed, and to what man,
The tripod shook, and o'er the vaporous well
The chanting Pythoness gave oracle,
And thus in priestly verse the sentence ran:

11

High on the topmost rock with funeral feast
Convey and leave the maid, nor look to find
A mortal husband, but a savage beast,
The viperous scourge of gods and humankind;
Who shames and vexes all, and as he flies
With sword and fire, Zeus trembles in the skies,
And groans arise from souls to hell consign'd.

12

With which reply the King return'd full sad :
For though he nothing more might understand,
Yet in the bitter bidding that he had
No man made question of the plain command,
That he must sacrifice the tender flower
Of his own blood to a demonian power,
Upon the rocky mount with his own hand.

13

Some said that she to Talos was devote,
The metal giant, who with mile-long stride
Cover'd the isle, walking around by rote
Thrice every day at his appointed tide ;
Who shepherded the sea-goats on the coast,
And, as he past, caught up and live would roast,
Pressing them to his burning ribs and side :

14

Whose head was made of fine gold-beaten work
Of silver pure his arms and gleaming chest,
Thence of green-bloomèd bronze far as the fork,
Of iron weather-rusted all the rest.
One single vein he had, which running down
From head to foot was open in his crown,
And closèd by a nail ; such was this pest.

15

A little while they spent in sad delay,
Then order'd, as the oracle had said,
The cold feast and funereal display
Wherewith the fated bridal should be sped:
And their black pageantry and vain despairing
When Psyche saw, and for herself preparing
The hopeless ceremonial of the dead,

16

Then spake she to the King and said 'O Sire,
Why wilt thou veil those venerable eyes
With piteous tears, which must of me require
More tears again than for myself arise?
Then, on the day my beauty first o'erstept
Its mortal place it had been well to have wept;
But now the fault beyond our ruing lies.

17

'As to be worship'd was my whole undoing,
So my submission must the forfeit pay:
And welcome were the morning of my wooing,
Tho' after it should dawn no other day.
Up to the mountain! for I hear the voice
Of my belovèd on the winds, *Rejoice,*
Arise, my love, my fair one, and come away!'

18

With such distemper'd speech, that little cheer'd
Her mourning house, she went to choose with care
The raiment for her day of wedlock weird,
Her body as for burial to prepare;
But laved with bridal water, from the stream
Where Hera bathed; for still her fate supreme
Was doubtful, whether Love or Death it were:

19

Love that is made of joy, and Death of fear :
Nay, but not these held Psyche in suspense ;
Hers was the hope that following by the bier
Boweth its head beneath the dark immense :
Her fear the dread of life that turns to hide
Its tragic tears, what hour the happy bride
Ventures for love her maiden innocence.

20

They set on high upon the bridal wain
Her bed for bier, and yet no corpse thereon ;
But like as when unto a warrior slain
And not brought home the ceremonies done
Are empty, for afar his body brave
Lies lost, deep buried by the wandering wave
Or 'neath the foes his fury fell upon,—

21

So was her hearse : and with it went afore,
Singing the solemn dirge that moves to tears,
The singers ; and behind, clad as for war,
The King uncrown'd among his mournful peers,
All 'neath their armour robed in linen white ;
And in their left were shields, and in their right
Torches they bore aloft instead of spears.

22

And next the virgin tribe in white forth sail'd,
With wreaths of dittany ; and 'midst them there
Went Psyche, all in lily-whiteness veil'd,
The white Quince-blossom chapleting her hair :
And last the common folk, a weeping crowd,
Far as the city-gates with wailings loud
Follow'd the sad procession in despair.

23

Thus forth and up the mount they went, until
The funeral chariot must be left behind,
Since road was none for steepness of the hill;
And slowly by the narrow path they wind:
All afternoon their white and scatter'd file
Toil'd on distinct, ascending many a mile
Over the long brown slopes and crags unkind.

24

But ere unto the snowy peak they came
Of that stormshapen pyramid so high,
'Twas evening, and with footsteps slow and lame
They gather'd up their lagging company:
And then her sire, even as Apollo bade,
Set on the topmost rock the hapless maid,
With trembling hands and melancholy cry.

25

And now the sun was sunk; only the peak
Flash'd like a jewel in the deepening blue:
And from the shade beneath none dared to speak,
But all look'd up, where glorified anew
Psyche sat islanded in living day.
Breathless they watcht her, till the last red ray
Fled from her lifted arm that waved adieu.

26

There left they her, turning with sad farewells
To haste their homeward course, as best they might:
But night was crowding up the barren fells,
And hid full soon their rocky path from sight;
And each unto his stumbling foot to hold
His torch was fain, for o'er the moon was roll'd
A mighty cloud from heaven, to blot her light.

27

And thro' the darkness for long while was seen
That armour'd train with waving fires to thread
Downwards, by pass, defile, and black ravine,
Each leading on the way that he was led.
Slowly they gain'd the plain, and one by one
Into the shadows of the woods were gone,
Or in the clinging mists were quench'd and fled.

28

But unto Psyche, pondering o'er her doom
In tearful silence on her stony chair,
A Zephyr straying out of heaven's wide room
Rush'd down, and gathering round her unaware
Fill'd with his breath her vesture and her veil;
And like a ship, that crowding all her sail
Leans to accompany the tranquil air,

29

She yielded, and was borne with swimming brain
And airy joy, along the mountain side,
Till, hid from earth by ridging summits twain,
They came upon a valley deep and wide;
Where the strong Zephyr with his burden sank,
And laid her down upon a grassy bank,
'Mong thyme and violets and daisies pied.

30

And straight upon the touch of that sweet bed
Both woe and wonder melted fast away:
And sleep with gentle stress her sense o'erspread,
Gathering as darkness doth on drooping day:
And nestling to the ground, she slowly drew
Her wearied limbs together, and, ere she knew,
Wrapt in forgetfulness and slumber lay.

MAY

1

AFTER long sleep when Psyche first awoke
Among the grasses 'neath the open skies,
And heard the mounting larks, whose carol spoke
Delighted invitation to arise,
She lay as one who after many a league
Hath slept off memory with his long fatigue,
And waking knows not in what place he lies:

2

Anon her quickening thought took up its task,
And all came back as it had happ'd o'ernight;
The sad procession of the wedding mask,
The melancholy toiling up the height,
The solitary rock where she was left;
And thence in dark and airy waftage reft,
How on the flowers she had been disburden'd light.

3

Thereafter she would rise and see what place
That voyage had its haven in, and found
She stood upon a little hill, whose base
Shelved off into the valley all around;
And all round that the steep cliffs rose away,
Save on one side where to the break of day
The widening dale withdrew in falling ground.

4

There, out from over sea, and scarce so high
As she, the sun above his watery blaze
Upbroke the grey dome of the morning sky,
And struck the island with his level rays ;
Sifting his gold thro' lazy mists, that still
Climb'd on the shadowy roots of every hill,
And in the tree-tops breathed their silvery haze.

5

At hand on either side there was a wood ;
And on the upward lawn, that sloped between,
Not many paces back a temple stood,
By even steps ascending from the green ;
With shaft and pediment of marble made,
It fill'd the passage of the rising glade,
And there withstay'd the sun in dazzling sheen.

6

Too fair for human art, so Psyche thought,
It might the fancy of some god rejoice ;
Like to those halls which lame Hephæstos wrought,
Original, for each god to his choice,
In high Olympus ; where his matchless lyre
Apollo wakes, and the responsive choir
Of Muses sing alternate with sweet voice.

7

Wondering she drew anigh, and in a while
Went up the steps as she would entrance win,
And faced her shadow 'neath the peristyle
Upon the golden gate, whose flanges twin—
As there she stood, irresolute at heart
To try—swung to her of themselves apart ;
Whereat she past between and stood within.

May

8

A foursquare court it was with marble floor'd,
Embay'd about with pillar'd porticoes,
That echo'd in a somnolent accord
The music of a fountain, which arose
Sparkling in air, and splashing in its tank;
Whose wanton babble, as it swell'd or sank,
Gave idle voice to silence and repose.

9

Thro' doors beneath the further colonnade,
Like a deep cup's reflected glooms of gold,
The inner rooms glow'd with inviting shade:
And, standing in the court, she might behold
Cedar, and silk, and silver; and that all
The pargeting of ceiling and of wall
Was fresco'd o'er with figures manifold.

10

Then making bold to go within, she heard
Murmur of gentle welcome in her ear;
And seeing none that coud have spoken word,
She waited: when again **Lady, draw near;
Enter!** was cried; and now more voices came
From all the air around calling her name,
And bidding her rejoice and have no fear.

11

And one, if she would rest, would show her bed,
Pillow'd for sleep, with fragrant linen fine;
One, were she hungry, had a table spread
Like as the high gods have it when they dine:
Or, would she bathe, were those would heat the bath;
The joyous cries contending in her path,
Psyche, they said, **What wilt thou? all is thine.**

12

Then Psyche would have thank'd their service true,
But that she fear'd her echoing words might scare
Those sightless tongues ; and well by dream she knew
The voices of the messengers of prayer,
Which fly upon the gods' commandment, when
They answer the supreme desires of men,
Or for a while in pity hush their care.

13

'Twas fancy's consummation, and because
She would do joy no curious despite,
She made no wonder how the wonder was ;
Only concern'd to take her full delight.
So to the bath,—what luxury could be
Better enhanced by eyeless ministry ?—
She follows with the voices that invite.

14

There being deliciously refresht, from soil
Of earth made pure by water, fire, and air,
They clad her in soft robes of Asian toil,
Scented, that in her queenly wardrobe were ;
And led her forth to dine, and all around
Sang as they served, the while a choral sound
Of strings unseen and reeds the burden bare.

15

P athetic strains and passionate they wove,
U rgent in ecstasies of heavenly sense ;
R esponsive rivalries, that, while they strove
C ombined in full harmonious suspense,
E ntrancing wild desire, then fell at last
L ull'd in soft closes, and with gay contrast
L aunch'd forth their fresh unwearied excellence.

May

Now Psyche, when her twofold feast was o'er,
Would feed her eye ; and choosing for her guide
A low-voiced singer, bade her come explore
The wondrous house ; until on every side
As surfeited with beauty, and seeing nought
But what was rich and fair beyond her thought,
And all her own, thus to the voice she cried:

17

' Am I indeed a goddess, or is this
But to be dead : and through the gates of death
Passing unwittingly doth man not miss
Body nor memory nor living breath;
Nor by demerits of his deeds is cast,
But, paid with the desire he holdeth fast,
Is holp with all his heart imagineth ? '

18

But her for all reply the wandering tongue
Call'd to the chamber where her bed was laid
With flower'd broideries of linen hung:
And round the walls in painting were portray'd
Love's victories over the gods renown'd.
Ares and Aphrodite here lay bound
In the fine net that dark Hephæstus made:

19

Here Zeus, in likeness of a tawny bull,
Stoop'd on the Cretan shore his mighty knee,
While off his back Europa beautiful
Stept pale against the blue Carpathian sea;
And here Apollo, as he caught amazed
Daphne, for lo ! her hands shot forth upraised
In leaves, her feet were rooted like a tree:

20

Here Dionysos, springing from his car
At sight of Ariadne; here uplept
Adonis to the chase, breaking the bar
Of Aphrodite's arm for love who wept:
He spear in hand, with leashèd dogs at strain;
A marvellous work.   But Psyche soon grown fain
Of rest, betook her to her bed and slept.

21

Nor long had slept, when at a sudden stir
She woke; and one, that thro' the dark made way,
Drew near, and stood beside; and over her
The curtain rustl'd.   Trembling now she lay,
Fainting with terror: till upon her face
A kiss, and with two gentle arms' embrace,
A voice that call'd her name in loving play.

22

Though for the darkness she coud nothing see,
She wish'd not then for what the night denied:
This was the lover she had lack'd, and she,
Loving his loving, was his willing bride.
O'erjoy'd she slept again, o'erjoy'd awoke
At break of morn upon her love to look;
When lo! his empty place lay by her side.

23

So all that day she spent in company
Of the soft voices; and Of right, they said,
Art thou our Lady now.   Be happily
Thy bridal morrow by thy serbants sped.
But she but long'd for night, if that might bring
Her lover back; and he on secret wing
Came with the dark, and in the darkness fled.

24

And this was all her life ; for every night
He came, and though his name she never learn'd,
Nor was his image yielded to her sight
At morn or eve, she neither look'd nor yearn'd
Beyond her happiness : and custom brought
An ease to pleasure ; nor would Psyche's thought
Have ever to her earthly home return'd,

25

But that one night he said ' Psyche, my soul,
Sad danger threatens us : thy sisters twain
Come to the mountain top, whence I thee stole,
And thou wilt hear their voices thence complain.
Answer them not : for it must end our love
If they should hear or spy thee from above.'
And Psyche said ' Their cry shall be in vain.'

26

But being again alone, she thought 'twas hard
On her own blood ; and blamed her joy as thief
Of theirs, her comfort which their comfort barr'd ;
When she their care might be their care's relief.
All day she brooded on her father's woe,
And when at night her lover kisst her, lo !
Her tender face was wet with tears of grief.

27

Then question'd why she wept, she all confest ;
And begg'd of him she might but once go nigh
To set her sire's and sisters' fears at rest ;
Till he for pity coud not but comply :
' Only if they should ask thee of thy love
Discover nothing to their ears above.'
And Psyche said ' In vain shall be their cry.'

28

And yet with day no sooner was alone,
Than she for loneliness her promise rued:
That having so much pleasure for her own,
'Twas all unshared and spent in solitude.
And when at night her love flew to his place,
More than afore she shamed his fond embrace,
And piteously with tears her plaint renew'd.

29

The more he now denied, the more she wept;
Nor would in anywise be comforted,
Unless her sisters, on the Zephyr swept,
Should in those halls be one day bathed and fed,
And see themselves the palace where she reign'd.
And he, by force of tears at last constrain'd,
Granted her wish unwillingly, and said:

30

' Much to our peril hast thou won thy will;
Thy sisters' love, seeing thee honour'd so,
Will sour to envy, and with jealous skill
Will pry to learn the thing that none may know.
Answer not, nor inquire; for know that I
The day thou seest my face far hence shall fly,
And thou anew to bitterest fate must go.'

31

But Psyche said, ' Thy love is more than life ;
To have thee leaveth nothing to be won:
For should the noonday prove me to be wife
Even of the beauteous Eros, who is son
Of Cypris, I coud never love thee more.'
Whereat he fondly kisst her o'er and o'er,
And peace was 'twixt them till the night was done.

SECOND QUARTER

SUMMER

PSYCHE'S SISTERS · SNARING HER TO DES-
TRUCTION · ARE THEMSELVES DESTROYED

JUNE

1

And truly need there was to the old King
For consolation : since the mournful day
Of Psyche's fate he took no comforting,
But only for a speedy death would pray ;
And on his head his hair grew silver-white.
—Such on life's topmost bough is sorrow's blight,
When the stout heart is cankering to decay.

2

Which when his daughters learnt, they both were quick
Comfort and solace to their sire to lend.
But as not seldom they who nurse the sick
Will take the malady from them they tend,
So happ'd it now ; for they who fail'd to cheer
Grew sad themselves, and in that palace drear
Increased the evil that they came to mend.

3

And them the unhappy father sent to seek
Where Psyche had been left, if they might find
What monster held her on the savage peak;
Or if she there had died of hunger pined,
And, by wild eagles stript, her scatter'd bones
Might still be gather'd from the barren stones;
Or if her fate had left no trace behind.

4

So just upon this time her sisters both
Climb'd on the cliff that hung o'er Psyche's vale;
And finding there no sign, to leave were loth
Ere well assured she lurk'd not within hail.
So calling loud her name, 'Psyche!' they cried,
'Psyche, O Psyche!' and when none replied
They sank upon the rocks to weep and wail.

5

But Psyche heard their voices where she sat,
And summoning the Zephyr bade him fleet
Those mourners down unto the grassy plat
'Midst of her garden, where she had her seat.
Then from the dizzy steep the wondering pair
Came swiftly sinking on his buoyant air,
And stood upon the terrace at her feet.

6

Upsprang she then, and kiss'd them and embraced,
And said 'Lo, here am I, I whom ye mourn.
I am not dead, nor tortured, nor disgraced,
But blest above all days since I was born:
Wherefore be glad. Enter my home and see
How little cause has been to grieve for me,
And my desertion on the rocks forlorn.'

7

So entering by the golden gate, or e'er
The marvel of their hither flight had waned,
Fresh wonder took them now, for everywhere
Their eyes that lit on beauty were enchain'd ;
And Psyche's airy service, as she bade,
Perform'd its magic office, and display'd
The riches of the palace where she reign'd.

8

And through the perfumed chambers they were led,
And bathed therein ; and after, set to sup,
Were upon dreamlike delicacies fed,
And wine more precious than its golden cup.
Till seeing nothing lack'd and naught was theirs,
Their happiness fell from them unawares,
And bitter envy in their hearts sprang up.

9

At last one said ' Psyche, since not alone
Thou livest here in joy, as well we wot,
Who is the man who should these wonders own,
Or god, I say, and still appeareth not ?
What is his name ?   What rank and guise hath he,
Whom winds and spirits serve, who honoureth thee
Above all others in thy blissful lot ? '

10

But Psyche when that wistful speech she heard
Was ware of all her spouse had warn'd her of :
And uttering a disingenuous word,
Said ' A youth yet unbearded is my love ;
He goeth hunting on the plains to-day,
And with his dogs hath wander'd far away ;
And not till eve can he return above.'

11

Then fearing to be nearer plied, she rose
And brought her richest jewels one by one,
Bidding them choose and take whate'er they chose ;
And beckoning the Zephyr spake anon
That he should waft her sisters to the peak ;
The which he did, and, ere they more coud speak,
They rose on high, and in the wind were gone.

12

Nor till again they came upon the road,
Which from the mountain shoulder o'er the plain
Led to the city of their sire's abode,
Found they their tongues, though full of high disdain
Their hearts were, but kept silence, till the strength
Of pride and envious hatred burst at length
In voice, and thus the elder gan complain :

13

'Cruel and unjust fortune ! that of three
Sisters, whose being from one fountain well'd,
Exalts the last so high from her degree,
And leaves the first to be so far excel'd.
My husband is a poor and niggard churl
To him, whoe'er he be, that loves the girl.
Oh ! in what godlike state her house is held !'

14

'Ay,' said the other, 'to a gouty loon
Am I not wedded ? Lo ! thy hurt is mine :
But never call me woman more, if soon
I cannot lure her from her height divine.
Nay, she shall need her cunning wit to save
The wealth of which so grudgingly she gave ;
Wherefore thy hand and heart with me combine.

(116)

15

'She but received us out of pride, to show
Her state, well deeming that her happiness
Was little worth while there was none to know;
So is our lot uninjured if none guess.
Reveal we nothing therefore, but the while
Together scheme this wanton to beguile,
And bring her boasting godhead to distress.'

16

So fresh disordering their dress and hair,
With loud lament they to their sire return,
Telling they found not Psyche anywhere,
And of her sure mischance could nothing learn:
And with that lie the wounded man they slew,
Hiding the saving truth which well they knew;
Nor did his piteous grief their heart concern.

17

Meanwhile her unknown lover did not cease
To warn poor Psyche how her sisters plan'd
To undermine her love and joy and peace;
And urged how well she might their wiles withstand,
By keeping them from her delight aloof:
For better is security than proof,
And malice held afar than near at hand.

18

'And, dearest wife,' he said, 'since 'tis not long
Ere one will come to share thy secrecy,
And be thy babe and mine; let nothing wrong
The happy months of thy maternity.
If thou keep trust, then shalt thou see thy child
A god; but if to pry thou be beguiled,
The lot of both is death and misery.'

19

Then Psyche's simple heart was fill'd with joy,
And counting to herself the months and days,
Look'd for the time, when she should bear a boy
To be her growing stay and godlike praise.
And 'O be sure,' she said, 'be sure, my pride
Having so rich a promise cannot slide,
Even if my love coud fail which thee obeys.'

20

And so most happily her life went by,
In thoughts of love dear to her new estate ;
Until at length the evil day drew nigh,
When now her sisters, joined in jealous hate,
Set forth again, and plotted by the way
How they might best allure her to betray
Her secret ; with what lie their angle bait.

21

That night her husband spake to her, and said
'Psyche, thy sisters come : and when they climb
The peak they will not tarry to be sped
Down by the Zephyr, as that other time,
But winging to the wind will cast themselves
Out in the air, and on the rocky shelves
Be dasht, and pay the penalty of crime.

22

'So let it be, and so shall we be saved.'
Which meditated vengeance of his fear
When Psyche heard, now for their life she craved,
Whose mere distress erewhile had toucht her near.
Around her lover's neck her arms she threw,
And pleaded for them by her faith so true,
Although they went on doom in judgment clear.

23

In terror of bloodguiltiness she now
Forgot all other danger ; she adjured ;
Or using playfulness deep sobs would plow
Her soft entreaties, not to be endured :
Till he at last was fain once more to grant
The service of the Zephyr, to enchant
That wicked couple from their fate assured.

24

So ere 'twas noon were noises at the door
Of knocking loud and voices high in glee ;
Such as within that vale never before
Had been, and now seem'd most unmeet to be.
And Psyche blush'd, though being alone, and rose
To meet her sisters and herself unclose
The gate that made them of her palace free.

25

Fondly she kiss'd them, and with kindly cheer
Sought to amuse ; and they with outward smile
O'ermask'd their hate, and called her sweet and dear,
Finding affection easy to beguile :
And all was smooth, until at last one said
' Tell us, I pray, to whom 'tis thou art wed ;
'Mong gods or men, what is his rank and style ?

26

' Thou canst not think to hide the truth from us,
Who knew thy peevish sorrows when a maid,
And see thee now so glad and rapturous,
As changed from what thou wert as light from shade ;
Thy jewels, too, the palace of a king,
Nor least the serviceable spiriting,
By everything thy secret is betray'd :

27

'And yet thou talkest of thy wondrous man
No more than if his face thou didst not know.'
At which incontinently she began,
Forgetful of her word a month ago,
Answering 'A merchant rich, of middle age,
My husband is ; and o'er his features sage
His temples are already touch'd with snow.

28

'But 'gainst his wish since hither ye were brought
'Twere best depart.'   Then her accustom'd spell
Sped them upon the summit quick as thought ;
And being alone her doing pleased her well :
So was she vext to find her love at night
More sad than ever, of her sisters' spite
Speaking as one that coud the end foretell.

29

'And ere long,' said he, 'they will spy again :
Let them be dash'd upon the rocks and die ;
'Tis they must come to death or thou to pain,
To separation, Psyche, thou and I ;
Nay, and our babe to ill.   I therefore crave
Thou wilt not even once more these vipers save,
Nor to thy love his only boon deny.'

30

But Psyche would not think her sisters' crime
So gross and strange, nor coud her danger see ;
Since 'twere so easy, if at any time
They show'd the venom of their hearts, that she
Should fan them off upon the willing gust.
So she refused, and claiming truer trust,
Would in no wise unto their death agree.

JULY

1

'What think you, sister:' thus one envious fiend
To other spake upon their homeward route,
'What of the story that our wit hath glean'd
Of this mysterious lover, who can shoot
In thirty days from beardless youth to prime,
With wisdom in his face before his time,
And snowy locks upon his head to boot?'

2

'Ay,' said the other, 'true, she lied not well;
And thence I gather knows no more than we:
For surely 'tis a spirit insensible
To whom she is wedded, one she cannot see.
'Tis that I fear; for if 'tis so, her child
Will be a god, and she a goddess styled,
Which, though I die to let it, shall not be.

3

'Lament we thus no longer. Come, consult
What may be done.' And home they came at night,
Yet not to rest, but of their plots occult
Sat whispering on their beds; and ere 'twas light
Resolving on the deed coud not defer;
But roused the sleeping house with sudden stir,
And sallied forth alone to work their spite.

4

And with the noon were climb'd upon the peak,
And swam down on the Zephyr as before;
But now with piercing cry and doleful shriek
They force their entrance through the golden door,
Feigning the urgency of bitter truth;
Such as deforms a friendly face with ruth,
When kindness may not hide ill tidings more.

5

Then Psyche when she heard their wailful din,
And saw their countenances wan and worn
With travel, vigil, and disfiguring sin,
Their hair dishevel'd and their habits torn,
For trembling scarce coud ask what ill had hapt;
And they alert with joy to see her trapt,
Launch'd forth amain, and on their drift were borne.

6

'O Psyche, happiest certainly and blest
Up to this hour,' they said, 'thou surely wert,
Being of thy fearful peril unpossest;
Which now we would not tell but to avert.
But we in solemn truth thy spouse have found
To be the dragon of this mountain ground,
Who holds thee here to work thy shame and hurt.

7

'As yesternight we rode upon the wind
He issued to pursue us from the wood;
We saw his back, that through the tree-tops finn'd,
His fiery eyes glared from their wrinkl'd hood.
Lo, now betimes the oracle, which said
How to the savage beast thou shouldst be wed,
Is plainly for thy safety understood.

'Long time hath he been known to all that dwell
Upon the plain; but now his secret lair
Have we discover'd, which none else coud tell:
Though many women fallen in his snare
Hath he enchanted; who, tradition saith,
Taste love awhile, ere to their cruel death
They pass in turn upon the summits bare.

9

'Fly with us while thou may'st: no more delay;
Renounce the spells of this accursed vale.
We come to save thee, but we dare not stay;
Among these sightless spirits our senses quail.
Fly with us, fly!' Then Psyche, for her soul
Was soft and simple, lost her self-control,
And, thinking only of the horrid tale,

10

'Dear sisters,' said she, and her sobbing speech
Was broken by her terror, 'it is true
That much hath hapt to stablish what ye teach;
For ne'er hath it been granted me to view
My husband; and, for aught I know, he may
Be even that cruel dragon, which ye say
Peer'd at you from the forest to pursue.

11

''Tis sure that scarcely can I win his grace
To see you here; and still he mischief vows
If ever I should ask to see his face,
Which, coming in the dark, he ne'er allows.
Therefore, if ye can help, of pity show,
Since doubt I must, how I may come to know
What kind of spirit it is that is my spouse.'

12

Then to her cue the younger was afore :
'Hide thou a razor,' cried she, 'near thy bed ;
And have a lamp prepared, but whelm thereo'er
Some cover, that no light be from it shed.
And when securely in first sleep he lies,
Look on him well, and ere he can arise,
Gashing his throat, cut off his hideous head.'

13

Which both persuading, off they flew content,
Divining that whate'er she was forbid
Was by her lover for her safety meant,
Which only coud be sure while he was hid.
But Psyche, to that miserable deed
Being now already in her mind agreed,
Wander'd alone, and knew not what she did.

14

Now she would trust her lover, now in turn
Made question of his bidding as unjust ;
But thirsting curiosity to learn
His secret overcame her simple trust,
O'ercame her spoken troth, o'ercame her fear ;
And she prepared, as now the hour drew near,
The mean contrivances, nor felt disgust.

15

She set the lamp beneath a chair, and cloked
Thickly its rebel lustre from the eye :
And laid the knife, to mortal keenness stroked,
Within her reach, where she was wont to lie :
And took her place full early ; but her heart
Beat fast, and stay'd her breath with sudden start,
Feeling her lover's arm laid fond thereby.

16

But when at last he slept, then she arose,
All faint and tremulous : and though it be
That wrong betrayeth innocence with shews
Of novelty, its guilt from shame to free,
Yet 'twas for shame her hand so strangely shook
That held the steel, and from the cloke that took
The lamp, and raised it o'er the bed to see.

17

She had some fear she might not well discern
By that small flame a monster in the gloom ;
When lo ! the air about her seem'd to burn,
And bright celestial radiance fill'd the room.
Too plainly O she saw, O fair to see !
Eros, 'twas Eros' self, her lover, he,
The God of love, reveal'd in deathless bloom.

18

Her fainting strength forsook her ; on her knees
Down by the bed she sank ; the shameless knife
Fell flashing, and her heart took thought to seize
Its desperate haft, and end her wicked life.
Yet coud she not her loving eyes withdraw
From her fair sleeping lover, whom she saw
Only to know she was no more his wife.

19

O treasure of all treasures, late her own !
O loss above all losses, lost for aye !
Since there was no repentance coud atone
For her dishonour, nor her fate withstay.
But yet 'twas joy to have her love in sight ;
And, to the rapture yielding while she might,
She gazed upon his body where he lay.

20

Above all mortal beauty, as was hers,
She saw a rival; but if passion's heart
Be rightly read by subtle questioners,
It owns a wanton and a gentler part.
And Psyche wonder'd, noting every sign
By which the immortal God, her spouse divine,
Betray'd the image of our earthly art;

21

His thickly curling hair, his ruddy cheeks,
And pouting lips, his soft and dimpl'd chin,
The full and cushion'd eye, that idly speaks
Of self-content and vanity within,
The forward, froward ear, and smooth to touch
His body sleek, but rounded overmuch
For dignity of mind and pride akin.

22

She noted that the small irradiant wings,
That from his shoulders lay along at rest,
Were yet disturb'd with airy quiverings,
As if some wakeful spirit his blood possest;
She feared he was awaking, but they kept
Their sweet commotion still, and still he slept,
And still she gazed with never-tiring zest.

23

And now the colour of her pride and joy
Outflush'd the hue of Eros; she, so cold,
To have fired the passion of the heartless boy,
Whom none in heaven or earth were found to hold!
Psyche, the earthborn, to be prized above
The heavenly Graces by the God of love,
And worship by his wantonness untold!

24

Nay, for that very thing she loved him more,
More than herself her sweet self's complement:
Until the sight of him again upbore
Her courage, and renew'd her vigour spent.
And looking now around, she first espied
Where at the bed's foot, cast in haste aside,
Lay his full quiver, and his bow unbent.

25

One of those darts, of which she had heard so oft,
She took to try if 'twas so very keen;
And held its point against her finger soft
So gently, that to touch it scarce was seen;
Yet was she sharply prickt, and felt the fire
Run through her veins; and now a strange desire
Troubl'd her heart, which ne'er before had been:

6

Straight sprang she to her lover on the bed,
And kisst his cheek, and was not satisfied:
When, O the lamp, held ill-balanced o'erhead,
One drop of burning oil spill'd from its side
On Eros' naked shoulder as he slept,
Who waken'd by the sudden smart uplept
Upon the floor, and all the mischief eyed.

27

With nervous speed he seized his bow, and past
Out of the guilty chamber at a bound;
But Psyche, following his flight as fast,
Caught him, and crying threw her arms around:
Till coming to the court he rose in air;
And she, close clinging in her last despair,
Was dragg'd, and then lost hold and fell to ground.

28

Wailing she fell ; but he, upon the roof
Staying his feet, awhile his flight delay'd :
And turning to her as he stood aloof
Beside a cypress, whose profoundest shade
Drank the reflections of the dreamy night
In its stiff pinnacle, the nimble light
Of million stars upon his body play'd :

29

'O simple-hearted Psyche,' thus he spake,
And she upraised her piteous eyes and hands,
'O simple-hearted Psyche, for thy sake
I dared to break my mother's stern commands ;
And gave thee godlike marriage in the place
Of vilest shame ; and, not to hurt thy grace,
Spared thee my arrows, which no heart withstands.

30

'But thou, for doubt I was some evil beast,
Hast mock'd the warnings of my love, to spy
Upon my secret, which concern'd thee least,
Seeing that thy joy was never touch'd thereby.
By faithless prying thou hast work'd thy fall,
And, even as I foretold thee, losest all
For looking on thy happiness too nigh :

31

'Which loss may be thine ample punishment.
But to those fiends, by whom thou wert misled,
Go tell each one in turn that I have sent
This message, that I love her in thy stead ;
And bid them by their love haste hither soon.'
Whereat he fled ; and Psyche in a swoon
Fell back upon the marble floor as dead.

AUGUST

1

When from the lowest ebbing of her blood
The fluttering pulses thrill'd and swell'd again,
Her stricken heart recovering force to flood
With life the sunken conduits of her brain,
Then Psyche, where she had fallen, numb and cold
Arose, but scarce her quaking sense control'd,
Seeing the couch where she that night had lain.

2

The level sunbeams search'd the grassy ground
For diamond dewdrops.   Ah! was this the place?
Where was the court, her home? she look'd around
And question'd with her memory for a space.
There was the cypress, there the well-known wood,
That wall'd the spot : 'twas here her palace stood,
As surely as 'twas vanish'd without trace.

3

Was all a dream ?   To think that all was dreamt
Were now the happier thought ;   but arguing o'er
That dream it was, she fell from her attempt,
Feeling the wifely burden that she bore.
Nay, true, 'twas true.   She had had all and lost ;
The joy, the reckless wrong, the heavy cost
Were hers, the dead end now, and woe in store.

(129)   K

4

What to be done? Fainting and shelterless
Upon the mountain it were death to bide:
And harbour knew she none, where her distress
Might comfort find, or love's dishonour hide;
Nor felt she any dread like that of home:
Yet forth she must, albeit to rove and roam
An outcast o'er the country far and wide.

5

Anon she marvel'd noting from the vale
A path lead downward to the plain below,
Crossing the very site, whereon the pale
Of all her joy had stood few hours ago;
A run of mountain beasts, that keep their track
Through generations, and for ages back
Had trod the self-same footing to and fro.

6

That would she try: so forth she took her way,
Turning her face from the dishonour'd dell,
Adown the broadening eastward lawns, which lay
In gentle slant, till suddenly they fell
In sheer cliff; whence the path that went around,
Clomb by the bluffs, or e'er it downward wound
Beneath that precipice impassable.

7

There once she turn'd, and gazing up the slope
She bid the scene of all her joy adieu;
'Ay, and farewell,' she cried, 'farewell to hope,
Since there is none will rescue me anew,
Who have kill'd God's perfection with a doubt.'
Which said, she took the path that led about,
And hid the upland pleasance from her view.

8

But soon it left her, entering 'neath the shade
Of cedar old and russeted tall pine,
Whose mighty tops, seen from the thorny glade,
Belted the hills about; and now no sign
Had she to guide her, save the slow descent.
But swiftly o'er the springy floor she went,
And drew the odorous air like draughts of wine.

9

Then next she past a forest thick and dark
With heavy ilexes and platanes high,
And came to long lush grass; and now coud mark
By many a token that the plain was nigh.
When lo! a river: to whose brink at last
Being come, upon the bank her limbs she cast,
And through her sad tears watch'd the stream go by.

10

And now the thought came o'er her that in death
There was a cure for sorrow, that before
Her eyes ran Lethe, she might take one breath
Of water and be freed for evermore.
Leaning to look into her tomb, thereon
She saw the horror of her image wan,
And up she rose at height to leap from shore.

11

When suddenly a mighty voice, that fell
With fury on her ears, their sense to scare,
That bounding from the tree trunks like the yell
Of hundred brazen trumpets, cried 'Forbear!
Forbear, fond maid, that froward step to take,
For life can cure the ills that love may make;
But for the harm of death is no repair.'

12

Then looking up she saw an uncouth form
Perch'd on the further bank, whose parted lips
Volley'd their friendly warning in a storm :
A man he might have been, but for the tips
Of horns appearing from his shaggy head,
For o'er his matted beard his face was red,
And all his shape was manlike to the hips.

13

In forehead low, keen eye, and nostril flat
He bore the human grace in mean degree,
But, set beneath his body squat and fat,
Legs like a goat's, and from the hairy knee
The shank fell spare ; and, though crosswise he put
His limbs in easeful posture, for the foot
The beast's divided hoof was plain to see.

14

Him then she knew the mighty choric God,
The great hill-haunting and tree-loving Pan ;
Whom Zeus had laught to see when first he trod
Olympus, neither god nor beast nor man :
Who every rocky peak and snowy crest
Of the Aspran mountains for his own possest,
And all their alps with bacchic rout o'erran :

15

Whom, when his pipe he plays on loud and sweet,
And o'er the fitted reeds his moist lip flees,
Around in measured step with nimble feet
Water-nymphs dance and Hamadryades :
And all the woodland's airy folk, who shun
Man's presence, to his frolic pastime run
From their perennial wells and sacred trees.

16

Now on his knee his pipe laid by, he spoke
With flippant tongue, wounding unwittingly
The heart he sought to cheer with jest and joke.
' And what hast thou to do with misery,'
He said, ' who hast such beauty as might gain
The love of Eros ?   Cast away thy pain,
And give thy soul to mirth and jollity.

17

' Thy mortal life is but a brittle vase,
But as thee list with wine or tears to fill ;
For all the drops therein are Ohs and Ahs
Of joy or grief according to thy will ;
And wouldst thou learn of me my merry way,
I'd teach thee change thy lover every day,
And prize the cup that thou wert fain to spill.

18

' Nay, if thou plunge thou shalt not drown nor sink,
For I will to thee o'er the stream afloat,
And bear thee safe ; and O I know a drink
For care, that makes sweet music in the throat.
Come live with me, my love ; I'll cure thy chance :
For I can laugh and quaff, and pipe and dance,
Swim like a fish, and caper like a goat.'

19

Speaking, his brute divinity explored
The secret of her silence ; and old Pan
Grew kind and told her of a shallow ford
Where lower down the stream o'er pebbles ran,
And one might pass at ease with ankles dry :
Whither she went, and crossing o'er thereby,
Her lonely wanderings through the isle began.

20

But none coud tell, no, nor herself had told
Where food she found, or shelter through the land
By day or night; until by fate control'd
She came by steep ways to the southern strand,
Where, sacred to the Twins and Britomart,
Pent in its rocky theatre apart,
A little town stood on the level sand.

21

'Twas where her younger sister's husband reign'd :
And Psyche to the palace gate drew near,
Helplessly still by Eros' hest constrain'd,
And knocking begg'd to see her sister dear;
But when in state stepp'd down that haughty queen,
And saw the wan face spent with tears and teen,
She smiled, and said ' Psyche, what dost thou here ?'

22

Then Psyche told how, having well employ'd
Their means, and done their bidding not amiss,
Looking on him her hand would have destroy'd,
'Twas Eros ; whom in love leaning to kiss,
Even as she kisst, a drop of burning oil
Fall'n from the lamp had served her scheme to foil,
Discovering her in vision of her bliss ;

23

Wherewith the god stung, like a startled bird
Arose in air, and she fell back in swoon ;
' But ere he parted,' said she, ' he confer'd
On thee the irrecoverable boon
By prying lost to me : *Go tell*, he said,
Thy sister that I love her in thy stead,
And bid her by her love haste hither soon.'

24

Which when that heart of malice heard, it took
The jealous fancy of her silly lust :
And pitilessly with triumphant look
She drank the flattery, and gave full trust ;
And leaving Psyche ere she more coud tell,
Ran off to bid her spouse for aye farewell,
And in his ear this ready lie she thrust :

25

' My dearest sister Psyche, she whose fate
We mourn'd, hath reappear'd alive and hale,
But brings sad news ; my father dies : full late
These tidings come, but love may yet avail ;
Let me be gone.'   And stealing blind consent,
Forth on that well-remember'd road she went,
And climb'd upon the peak above the dale.

26

There on the topmost rock, where Psyche first
Had by her weeping sire been left to die,
She stood a moment, in her hope accurst
Being happy ; and the cliffs took up her cry
With chuckling mockery from her tongue above,
Zephyr, sweet Zephyr, waft me to my love !
When off she lept upon his wings to fly.

27

But as a dead stone, from a height let fall,
Silent and straight is gather'd by the force
Of earth's vast mass upon its weight so small,
In speed increasing as it nears its source
Of motion—by which law all things soe'er
Are clutch'd and dragg'd and held—so fell she there,
Like a dead stone, down in her headlong course.

The disregardful silence heard her strike
Upon the solid crags ; her dismal shriek
Rang on the rocks and died out laughter-like
Along the vale in hurried trebles weak ;
And soon upon her, from their skiey haunt
Fell to their feast the great birds bald and gaunt
And gorged on her fair flesh with bloody beak.

29

But Psyche, when her sister was gone forth,
Went out again her wandering way to take :
And following a stream that led her north,
After some days she pass'd the Corian Lake,
Whereby Athena's temple stands, and he
Who traverses the isle from sea to sea
May by the plain his shortest journey make :

30

Till on the northern coast arrived she came
Upon a city built about a port,
The which she knew, soon as she heard the name,
Was where her elder sister had her court ;
To whom, as Eros had commanded her,
She now in turn became the messenger
Of vengeful punishment, that fell not short :

31

For she too hearing gan her heart exalt,
Nor pity felt for Psyche's tears and moans,
But, fellow'd with that other in her fault,
Follow'd her to her fate upon the stones ;
And from the peak leaping like her below
The self-same way unto the self-same woe,
Lay dasht to death upon her sister's bones.

THIRD QUARTER

AUTUMN

SEPTEMBER

1

On the Hellenic board of Crete's fair isle,
Westward of Drepanon, along a reach
Which massy Cyamum for many a mile
Jutting to sea delivers from the breach
Of North and East,—returning to embay
The favour'd shore—an ancient city lay,
Aptera, which is *Wingless* in our speech.

2

And hence the name ; that here in rocky cove,
Thence called Museion, was the trial waged
What day the Sirens with the Muses strove,
By jealous Hera in that war engaged :
Wherein the daughters of Mnemosynè
O'ercame the chauntresses who vex'd the sea,
Nor vengeance spared them by their pride enraged.

3

For those strange creatures, who with women's words
And wiles made ravenous prey of passers-by,
Were throated with the liquid pipe of birds :
Of love they sang ; and none, who sail'd anigh
Through the grey hazes of the cyanine sea,
Had wit the whirlpool of that song to flee,
Nor fear'd the talon hook'd and feather'd thigh.

4

But them the singers of the gods o'ercame,
And pluck'd them of their plumage, where in fright
They vainly flutter'd off to hide their shame,
Upon two rocks that lie within the bight,
Under the headland, barren and alone ;
Which, being with the scatter'd feathers strewn,
Were by the folk named Leukæ, which is *White*.

5

Thereon about this time the snowy gull,
Minion of Aphrodite, being come,
Plumed himself, standing on the sea-wrack dull,
That drifted from the foot of Cyamum ;
And 'twas his thought, that had the goddess learnt
The tale of Psyche loved and Eros burnt,
She ne'er so long had kept aloof and dumb.

6

Wherefore that duteous gossip of Love's queen
Devised that he the messenger would be ;
And rising from the rock, he skim'd between
The chasing waves—such grace have none but he ;—
Into the middle deep then down he dived,
And rowing with his glistening wings arrived
At Aphrodite's bower beneath the sea.

7

The eddies from his silver pinions swirl'd
The crimson, green, and yellow floss, that grew
About the caves, and at his passing curl'd
Its graceful silk, and gently waved anew:
Till, oaring here and there, the queen he found
Stray'd from her haunt unto a sandy ground,
Dappl'd with eye-rings in the sunlight blue.

8

She, as he came upon her from above,
With Hora play'd; Hora, her herald fair,
That lays the soft necessity of Love
On maidens' eyelids, and with tender care
Marketh the hour, as in all works is fit:
And happy they in love who time outwit,
Fondly constrainèd in her season rare.

9

But he with garrulous and laughing tongue
Broke up his news; how Eros, fallen sick,
Lay tossing on his bed, to frenzy stung
By such a burn as did but barely prick:
A little bleb, no bigger than a pease,
Upon his shoulder 'twas, that kill'd his ease,
Fever'd his heart, and made his breathing thick.

10

' For which disaster hath he not been seen
This many a day at all in any place:
And thou, dear mistress,' piped he, 'hast not been
Thyself amongst us now a dreary space:
The pining mortals suffer from a dearth
Of love; and for this sadness of the earth
Thy family is darken'd with disgrace.

11

'Now on the secret paths of dale and wood,
Where lovers walk'd are lovers none to find:
And friends, besworn to equal brotherhood,
Forget their faith, and part with words unkind:
In the first moon thy honey-bond is loath'd:
And I coud tell even of the new-betroth'd
That fly o'ersea, and leave their loves behind.

12

'Summer is over, but the merry pipe,
That wont to cheer the harvesting, is mute:
And in the vineyards, where the grape is ripe,
No voice is heard of them that take the fruit.
No workman singeth at eve nor maiden danceth:
All joy is dead, and as the year advanceth
The signs of woe increase on man and brute.

13

''Tis plain that if thy pleasure longer pause,
Thy mighty rule on earth hath seen its day:
The race must come to perish, and no cause
But that thou sittest with thy nymphs at play,
While on a Cretan hill thy truant boy
Hath with his pretty mistress turn'd to toy,
And less for pain than love pineth away.'

14

'Ha! Mistress!' cried she; 'Hath my beardless son
Been hunting for himself his lovely game?
Some young Orestiad hath his fancy won?
Some Naiad? say; or is a Grace his flame?
Or maybe Muse, and then 'tis Erato,
The trifling wanton. Tell me, if thou know,
Woman or goddess is she? and her name.'

(140)

15

Then said the snowy gull, 'O heavenly queen,
What is my knowledge, who am but a bird?
Yet is she only mortal, as I ween,
And namèd Psyche, if I rightly heard.'—
But Aphrodite's look daunted his cheer,
Ascare he fled away, screaming in fear,
To see what wrath his simple tale had stirr'd.

16

He flasht his pens, and sweeping widely round
Tower'd to air; so swift in all his way,
That whence he dived he there again was found
As soon as if he had but dipt for prey:
And now, or e'er he join'd his wailful flock,
Once more he stood upon the Sirens' rock,
And preen'd his ruffl'd quills for fresh display.

17

But as ill tidings will their truth assure
Without more witness than their fatal sense,
So, since was nothing bitterer to endure,
The injured goddess guess'd the full offence:
And doubted only whether first to smite
Or Psyche for her new presumptuous flight,
Or Eros for his disobedience.

18

But full of anger to her son she went,
And found him in his golden chamber laid;
And with him sweet Euphrosynè, attent
Upon his murmur'd wants, aye as he bade
Shifted the pillows with each fretful whim;
But scornfully his mother look'd at him,
And reckless of his pain gan thus upbraid:

19

'O worthy deeds, I say, and true to blood,
The crown and pledge of promise! thou that wast
In estimation my perpetual bud,
Now fruiting thus untimely to my cost;
Backsliding from commandment, ay, and worse,
With bliss to favour one I bade thee curse,
And save the life I left with thee for lost!

20

'Thou too to burn with love, and love of her
Whom I did hate; and to thy bed to take
My rival, that my trusted officer
Might of mine enemy my daughter make!
Dost thou then think my love for thee so fond,
And miserably doting, that the bond
By such dishonour strainèd will not break?

21

'Or that I cannot bear another son
As good as thou; or, if I choose not bear,
Not beg as good a lusty boy of one
Of all my nymphs,—and some have boys to spare,—
Whom I might train, to whom thine arms made o'er
Should do me kinder service than before,
To smite my foes and keep my honour fair?

22

'For thou hast ever mockt me, and beguiled
In amours strange my God, thy valiant sire:
And having smirch'd our fame while yet a child
Wilt further foul it now with earthly fire.
But I—do as thou may—have vow'd to kill
Thy fancied girl, whether thou love her still,
Or of her silly charms already tire.

23

' Tell me but where she hides.'   And Eros now,
Proud in his woe, boasted his happy theft :
Confessing he had loved her well, and how
By her own doing she was lost and left ;
And homeless in such sorrow as outwent
The utmost pain of other punishment,
Was wandering of his love and favour reft.

24

By which was Cypris gladden'd, not appeased,
But hid her joy and spake no more her threat :
And left with face like one that much displeased
Hath yet betray'd that he can wrong forget.
   When lo ! as swiftly she came stepping down
From her fair house into the heavenly town
The Kronian sisters on the way she met ;

25

Hera, the Wife of Zeus, her placid front
Dark with the shadow of his troubl'd reign,
And tall Demeter, who with men once wont,
Holding the high Olympians in disdain
For Persephassa's rape ; which now forgiven,
She had return'd unto the courts of Heaven,
And 'mong the immortals liv'd at peace again :

26

Whose smile told Aphrodite that they knew
The meaning of her visit ; and a flush
Of anger answer'd them, while hot she grew.
But Hera laugh'd outright : ' Why thou dost blush !
Now see we modest manners on my life !
And all thy little son has got a wife
Can make the crimson to thy forehead rush.

27

'Didst think he, whom thou madest passion's prince,
No privy dart then for himself would poise?
Nay, by the cuckoo on my sceptre, since
'Twas love that made thee mother of his joys,
Art thou the foremost to his favour bound;
As thou shouldst be the last to think to sound
The heart, and least of all thy wanton boy's.'

28

But her Demeter, on whose stalwart arm
She lean'd, took up: 'If thou wilt hark to me,
This Psyche,' said she, 'hath the heavenly charm,
And will become immortal.   And maybe
To marry with a woman is as well
As wed a god and live below in Hell:
As 'twas my lot in child of mine to see.'

29

Which things they both said, fearing in their hearts
That savage Eros, if they mockt his case,
Would kill their peace with his revengeful darts,
And bring them haply to a worse disgrace:
But Aphrodite, saying 'Good! my dames;
Behind this smoke I see the spite that flames,'
Left them, and on her journey went apace.

30

For having purposed she would hold no truce
With Psyche or her son, 'twas in her mind
To go forthwith unto the throne of Zeus,
And beg that Hermes might be sent to find
The wanderer; and secure that in such quest
He would not fail, she ponder'd but how best
She might inflict her vengeance long-design'd.

OCTOBER

1

HEAVY meanwhile at heart, with bruisèd feet
Was Psyche wandering many nights and days
Upon the paths of hundred-citied Crete,
And chose to step the most deserted ways;
Being least unhappy when she went unseen;
Since else her secret sorrow had no screen
From the plain question of men's idle gaze.

2

Yet wheresoe'er she went one hope she had;
Like mortal mourners, who 'gainst reason strong
Hope to be unexpectedly made glad
With sight of their dead friends, so much they long;
So she for him, whom loss a thousandfold
Endear'd and made desired; nor coud she hold
He would not turn and quite forgive her wrong.

3

Wherefore her eager eyes in every place
Lookt for her lover; and 'twixt hope and fear
She follow'd oft afar some form of grace,
In pain alike to lose or venture near.
And still this thought cheer'd her fatigue, that he,
Or on some hill, or by some brook or tree,
But waited for her coming to appear.

4

And then for comfort many an old love-crost
And doleful ditty would she gently sing,
Writ by sad poets of a lover lost,
Now sounding sweeter for her sorrowing:
Echo, sweet Echo, watching up on high,
Say hast thou seen to-day my love go by,
Or where thou sittest by thy mossy spring?

5

Or say ye nymphs, that from the crystal rills,
When ye have bathed your limbs from morn till eve,
Flying at midnight to the bare-topt hills,
Beneath the stars your mazy dances weave,
Say, my deserter whom ye well may know
By his small wings, his quiver, and his bow,
Say, have ye seen my love, whose loss I grieve?

6

Till climb'd one evening on a rocky steep
Above the plain of Cisamos, that lay,
Robb'd of its golden harvest, in the deep
Mountainous shadows of the dying day,
She saw a temple, whose tall columns fair
Recall'd her home; and 'O if thou be there,
My love,' she cried, 'fly not again away.'

7

Swiftly she ran, and entering by the door
She stood alone within an empty fane
Of great Demeter: and, behold, the floor
Was litter'd with thank-offerings of grain,
With wheat and barley-sheaves together heapt
In holy harvest-home of them that reapt
The goddess plenteous gifts upon the plain;

8

And on the tithe the tackle of the tithe
Thrown by in such confusion, as are laid
Upon the swath sickle, and hook, and scythe,
When midday drives the reapers to the shade.
And Psyche, since had come no priestess there
To trim the temple, in her pious care
Forgat herself, and lent her duteous aid.

9

She drew the offerings from the midst aside,
And piled the sheaves at every pillar's base ;
And sweeping therebetween a passage wide,
Made clear of corn and chaff the temple space :
As countrymen who bring their wheat to mart,
Set out their show along the walls apart
By their allotted stations, each in place ;

10

Thus she, and felt no weariness,—such strength
Hath duty to support our feeble frame,—
Till all was set in order, and at length
Up to the threshold of the shrine she came :
When lo ! before her face with friendly smile,
Tall as a pillar of the peristyle,
The goddess stood reveal'd, and call'd her name.

11

'Unhappy Psyche,' said she, 'know'st thou not
How Aphrodite to thy hurt is sworn ?
And thou, thy peril and her wrath forgot,
Spendest thy thought my temple to adorn.
Take better heed !'—And Psyche, at the voice
Even of so little comfort, gan rejoice,
And at her feet pour'd out this prayer forlorn.

12

'O Gracious giver of the golden grain,
Hide me, I pray thee, from her wrath unkind;
For who can pity as canst thou my pain,
Who wert thyself a wanderer, vex'd in mind
For loss of thy dear Corè once, whenas,
Ravisht to hell by fierce Agesilas,
Thou soughtest her on earth and coudst not find.

13

'How coud thy feet bear thee to western night,
And where swart Libyans watch the sacred tree,
And thrice to ford o'er Achelous bright,
And all the streams of beauteous Sicily?
And thrice to Enna cam'st thou, thrice, they tell,
Satest athirst by Callichorus' well,
Nor tookest of the spring to comfort thee.

14

'By that remember'd anguish of thine heart,
Lady, have pity even on me, and show
Where I may find my love; and take my part
For peace, I pray, against my cruel foe:
Or if thou canst not from her anger shield,
Here let me lie among the sheaves conceal'd
Such time till forth I may in safety go.'

15

Demeter answer'd, 'Nay, though thou constrain
My favour with thy plea, my help must still
Be hidden, else I work for thee in vain
To thwart my mighty sister in her will.
Thou must fly hence: Yet though I not oppose,
Less will I aid her; and if now I close
My temple doors to thee, take it not ill.'

(148)

16

Then Psyche's hope founder'd; as when a ship,
The morrow of the gale can hardly ride
The swollen seas, fetching a deeper dip
At every wave, and through her gaping side
And o'er her shattered bulwark ever drinks,
Till plunging in the watery wild she sinks,
To scoop her grave beneath the crushing tide:

17

So with each word her broken spirit drank
Its doom; and overwhelm'd with deep despair
She turn'd away, and coming forth she sank
Silently weeping on the temple stair,
In midmost night, forspent with long turmoil:
But sleep, the gracious pursuivant of toil,
Came swiftly down, and nursed away her care.

18

And when the sun awaked her with his beams
She found new hope, that still her sorrow's cure
Lay with the gods, who in her morning dreams
Had sent her comfort in a vision sure;
Wherein the Cretan-born, almightiest god,
Cloud-gathering Zeus himself had seem'd to nod,
And bid her with good heart her woes endure.

19

So coming that same day unto a shrine
Of Hera, she took courage and went in:
And like to one that to the cell divine
For favour ventures or a suit to win,
She drew anigh the altar, from her face
Wiping the tears, ere to the heavenly grace,
As thus she pray'd, she would her prayer begin.

20

'Most honour'd Lady, who from ancient doom
Wert made heaven's wife, and art on earth besought
With gracious happiness of all to whom
Thy holy wedlock hath my burden brought,
Save me from Aphrodite's fell pursuit,
And guard unto the birth Love's hapless fruit,
Which she for cruel spite would bring to nought.

21

'As once from her thou wert not shamed to take
Her beauty's zone, thy beauty to enhance;
For which again Zeus loved thee, to forsake
His warlike ire in faithful dalliance;
Show me what means may win my Love to me,
Or how that I may come, if so may be,
Within the favour of his countenance.

22

'If there be any place for tears or prayer,
If there be need for succour in distress,
Now is the very hour of all despair,
Here is the heart of grief and bitterness.
Motherly pity, bend thy face and grant
One beam of ruth to thy poor suppliant,
Nor turn me from thine altar comfortless.'

23

Even as she pray'd a cloud spread through the cell,
And 'mid the wreathings of the vapour dim
The goddess grew in glory visible,
Like some barbaric queen in festal trim;
Such the attire and ornaments she wore,
When o'er the forgèd threshold of the floor
Of Zeus's house she stept to visit him.

(150)

24

From either ear, ring'd to its piercèd lobe
A triple jewel hung, with gold enchas't;
And o'er her breasts her wide ambrosial robe
With many a shining golden clasp was brac't;
The flowering on its smooth embroider'd lawn
Gather'd to colour where the zone was drawn
In fringe of golden tassels at her waist.

25

Her curling hair with plaited braid and brail,
Pendant or loop'd about her head divine,
Lay hidden half beneath a golden veil,
Bright as the rippling ocean in sunshine:
And on the ground, flashing whene'er she stept,
Beneath her feet the dazzling lightnings lept
From the gold network of her sandals fine.

26

Thus Hera stood in royal guise bedeckt
Before poor Psyche on the stair that knelt,
Whose new-nursed hope at that display was checkt
And all her happier thoughts gan fade and melt.
She saw no kindness in such haughty mien,
And venturing not to look upon the queen,
Bow'd down in woe to hear her sentence dealt.

27

And thus the goddess spake, 'In vain thou suest,
Most miserable Psyche; though my heart
Be full of hate for her whose hate thou ruest,
And pride and pity move me to thy part:
Yet not till Zeus make known his will, coud I,
Least of the blameless gods that dwell on high,
Assist thee, wert thou worthier than thou art.

28

' But know if Eros love thee, that thy hopes
Should rest on him ; and I would bid thee go
Where in his mother's house apart he mopes
Grieving for loss of thee in secret woe :
For should he take thee back, there is no power
In earth or heaven will hurt thee from that hour,
Nay, not if Zeus himself should prove thy foe.'

29

Thus saying she was gone, and Psyche now
Surprised by comfort rose and went her way,
Resolved in heart, and only wondering how
'Twas possible to come where Eros lay ;
Since that her feet, however she might roam,
Coud never travel to the heavenly home
Of Love, beyond the bounds of mortal day :

30

Yet must she come to him.   And now 'twas proved
How that to Lovers, as is told in song,
Seeking the way no place is far removed ;
Nor is there any obstacle so strong,
Nor bar so fix'd that it can hinder them :
And how to reach heaven's gate by stratagem
Vex'd not the venturous heart of Psyche long.

31

To face her enemy might well avail :
Wherefore to Cypris' shrine her steps she bent,
Hoping the goddess in her hate might hale
Her body to the skies for punishment,
Whate'er to be ; yet now her fiercest wrath
Seem'd happiest fortune, seeing 'twas the path
Whereby alone unto her love she went.

NOVEMBER

1

But Aphrodite to the house of Zeus
Being bound, bade beckon out her milkwhite steeds,
Four doves, that ready to her royal use
In golden cages stood and peck'd the seeds:
Best of the nimble air's high-sailing folk
That wore with pride the marking of her yoke,
And cooed in envy of her gentle needs.

2

These drew in turn her chariot, when in state
Along the heaven with all her train she fared;
And oft in journeying to the skiey gate
Of Zeus's palace high their flight had dared,
Which darkest vapour and thick glooms enshroud
Above all else in the perpetual cloud,
Wherethro' to mount again they stood prepared,

3

Sleeking their feathers, by her shining car;
  The same Hephæstos wrought for her, when he,
Bruised in his hideous fall from heaven afar,
Was nursed by Thetis, and Eurynomè,
The daughter of the ever-refluent main;
With whom he dwelt till he grew sound again,
Down in a hollow cave beside the sea:

(153)

4

And them for kindness done was prompt to serve,
Forging them brooches rich in make and mode,
Earrings, and supple chains of jointed curve,
And other trinkets, while he there abode:
And none of gods or men knew of his home,
But they two only; and the salt sea-foam
To and fro past his cavern ever flow'd.

5

'Twas then he wrought this work within the cave,
Emboss'd with rich design, a moonèd car;
And when return'd to heaven to Venus gave,
In form imagined like her crescent star;
Which circling nearest earth, maketh at night
To wakeful mortal men shadow and light
Alone of all the stars in heaven that are.

6

Two slender wheels it had, with fretted tires
Of biting adamant, to take firm hold
Of cloud or ether; and their whirling fires
Threw off the air in halo where they roll'd:
And either nave that round the axle turn'd
A ruby was, whose steady crimson burn'd
Betwixt the twin speed-mingling fans of gold.

7

Thereon the naked goddess mounting, shook
The reins; whereat the doves their wings outspread,
And rising high their flight to heaven they took:
And all the birds, that in those courts were bred,
Of her broad eaves the nested families,
Sparrows and swallows, join'd their companies
Awhile and twitter'd to her overhead.

8

But onward she with fading tracks of flame
Sped swiftly, till she reacht her journey's end:
And when within the house of Zeus she came,
She pray'd the Sire of Heaven that he would lend
Hermes, the Argus-slayer, for her hest;
And he being granted her at her request,
She went forthwith to seek him and to send.

9

Who happ'd within the palace then to wait
Upon the almighty pleasure; and her tale
Was quickly told, and he made answer straight
That he would find the truant without fail;
Asking the goddess by what signs her slave
Might best be known, and what the price she gave
For capture, or admitted for the bail.

10

All which he took his silver stile to write
In letters large upon a waxèd board;
Her age and name, her colour, face and height,
Her home, and parentage, and the reward:
And then read o'er as 'twas to be proclaim'd.
And she took oath to give the price she named,
Without demur, when Psyche was restored.

11

Then on his head he closely set his cap
With earèd wings erect, and o'er his knee
He cross'd each foot in turn to prove the strap
That bound his wingèd sandals, and shook free
His chlamys, and gat up, and in his hand
Taking his fair white-ribbon'd herald's wand,
Lept forth on air, accoutred cap-a-pè.

12

And piloting along the mid-day sky,
Held southward, till the narrow map of Crete
Lay like a fleck in azure 'neath his eye;
When down he came, and as an eagle fleet
Drops in some combe, then checks his headlong stoop
With wide-flung wing, wheeling in level swoop
To strike the bleating quarry with his feet,

13

Thus he alighted; and in every town
In all the isle before the close of day
Had cried the message, which he carried down,
Of Psyche, Aphrodite's runaway;
That whosoever found the same and caught,
And by such time unto her temple brought,
To him the goddess would this guerdon pay:

14

SIX HONIED KISSES FROM HER ROSY MOUTH
WOULD CYTHEREA GIVE, AND ONE BESIDE
TO QUENCH AT HEART FOR AYE LOVE'S MORTAL DROUTH:
BUT UNTO HIM THAT HID HER, WOE BETIDE!
Which now was on all tongues, and Psyche's name
Herself o'erheard, or ever nigh she came
To Aphrodite's temple where she hied.

15

When since she found her way to heaven was safe,
She only wisht to make it soon and sure;
Nor fear'd to meet the goddess in her chafe,
So she her self-surrender might secure,
And not be given of other for the price;
Nor was there need of any artifice
Her once resplendent beauty to obscure.

16

For now so changed she was by heavy woe,
That for the little likeness that she bore
To her description she was fear'd to go
Within the fane; and when she stood before
The priestess, scarce coud she with oath persuade
That she was Psyche, the renownèd maid,
Whom men had left the temple to adore.

17

But when to Hermes she was shown and given,
He took no doubt, but eager to be quit,
And proud of speed, return'd with her to heaven,
And left her with the proclamation writ,
Hung at her neck, the board with letters large,
At Aphrodite's gate with those in charge;
And up whence first he came made haste to flit.

18

But hapless Psyche fell, for so it chanced,
To moody SYNETHEA'S care, the one
Of Aphrodite's train whom she advanced
To try the work abandon'd by her son.
Who by perpetual presence made ill end
Of good or bad; though she coud both amend,
And merit praise for work by her begun.

19

But she to better thought her heart had shut,
And proved she had a spite beyond compare:
Nor coud the keenest taunts her anger glut,
Which she when sour'd was never wont to spare:
And now she mock'd at Psyche's shame and grief,
As only she might do, and to her chief
Along the courtyard dragg'd her by the hair.

20

Nor now was Aphrodite kinder grown:
Having her hated rival in her power,
She laught for joy, and in triumphant tone
Bade her a merry welcome to her bower:
''Tis fit indeed daughters-in-law should wait
Upon their mothers; but thou comest late,
Psyche; I lookt for thee before this hour.

21

'And yet,' thus gave she rein to jeer and gibe,
'Forgive me if I held thee negligent,
Or if accustom'd vanity ascribe
An honour to myself that was not meant.
Thy lover is it, who so dearly prized
The pretty soul, then left her and despised?
To him more like thy heavenward steps were bent:

22

'Nor without reason: Zeus, I tell thee, swoon'd
To hear the story of the drop of oil,
The revelation and the ghastly wound:
My merriment is but my fear's recoil.
But if my son was unkind, thou shalt see
How kind a goddess can his mother be
To bring thy tainted honour clear of soil.'

23

And so, to match her promise with her mirth,
Two of her ministers she call'd in ken,
That work the melancholy of the earth;
Merimna that with care perplexes, when
The hearts of mortals have the gods forgot,
And Lypè, that her sorrow spares them not,
When mortals have forgot their fellow men.

(158)

24

These, like twin sharks that in a fair ship's wake
Swim constant, showing 'bove the water blue
Their shearing fins, and hasty ravin make
Of overthrow or offal, so these two
On Aphrodite's passing follow hard;
And now she offer'd to their glut's regard
Sweet Psyche, with command their wont to do.

25

But in what secret chamber their foul task
These soul-tormentors plied, or what their skill,
Pity of tender nature may not ask,
Nor poet stain his rhyme with such an ill.
But they at last themselves turn'd from their rack,
Weary of cruelty, and led her back,
Saying that further torture were to kill.

26

Then when the goddess saw her, more she mockt
'Art thou the woman of the earth,' she said,
'That hast in sorceries mine Eros lockt,
And stood thyself for worship in my stead?
Looking that I should pity thee, or care
For what illicit offspring thou may'st bear;
Or let thee to that god my son be wed?

27

'I know thy trick; and thou art one of them
Who steal love's favour in the gentle way,
Wearing submission for a diadem,
Patience and suffering for thy rich array:
Thou wilt be modest, kind, implicit, so
To rest thy wily spirit out of show
That it may leap the livelier into play:

28

'Devout at doing nothing, if so be
The grace become thee well; but active yet
Above all others be there none to see
Thy business, and thine eager face asweat.
Lo! I will prove thy talent: thou may'st live,
And all that thou desirest will I give,
If thou perform the task which I shall set.'

29

She took her then aside, and bade her heed
A heap of grains piled high upon the floor,
Millet and mustard, hemp and poppy seed,
And fern-bloom's undistinguishable spore,
All kinds of pulse, of grasses, and of spice,
Clover and linseed, rape, and corn, and rice,
Dodder, and sesame, and many more.

30

'Sort me these seeds' she said; 'it now is night,
I will return at morning; if I find
That thou hast separated all aright,
Each grain from other grain after its kind,
And set them in unmingl'd heaps apart,
Then shall thy wish be granted to thine heart.'
Whereat she turn'd, and closed the door behind.

FOURTH QUARTER

WINTER

DECEMBER

1

A SINGLE lamp there stood beside the heap,
And shed thereon its mocking golden light;
Such as might tempt the weary eye to sleep
Rather than prick the nerve of taskèd sight.
Yet Psyche, not to fail for lack of zeal,
With good will sat her down to her ordeal,
Sorting the larger seeds as best she might.

2

When lo! upon the wall, a shadow past
Of doubtful shape, across the chamber dim
Moving with speed : and seeing nought that cast
The shade, she bent her down the flame to trim ;
And there the beast itself, a little ant,
Climb'd up in compass of the lustre scant,
Upon the bowl of oil ran round the rim.

M

3

Smiling to see the creature of her fear
So dwarf'd by truth, she watcht him where he crept,
For mere distraction telling in his ear
What straits she then was in, and telling wept.
Whereat he stood and trim'd his horns ; but ere
Her tale was done resumed his manner scare,
Ran down, and on his way in darkness kept.

4

But she intent drew forth with dextrous hand
The larger seeds, or push'd the smaller back,
Or light from heavy with her breathing fan'd.
When suddenly she saw the floor grow black,
And troops of ants, flowing in noiseless train,
Moved to the hill of seeds, as o'er a plain
Armies approach a city for attack ;

5

And gathering on the grain, began to strive
With grappling horns : and each from out the heap
His burden drew, and all their motion live
Struggled and slid upon the surface steep.
And Psyche wonder'd, watching them, to find
The creatures separated kind from kind :
Till dizzied with the sight she fell asleep.

6

And when she woke 'twas with the morning sound
Of Aphrodite's anger at the door,
Whom high amaze stay'd backward, as she found
Her foe asleep with all her trouble o'er :
And round the room beheld, in order due,
The piles arranged distinct and sorted true,
Grain with grain, seed with seed, and spore with spore.

December

She fiercely cried 'Thou shalt not thus escape;
For to this marvel dar'st thou not pretend.
There is but one that coud this order shape,
Demeter,—but I knew her not thy friend.
Therefore another trial will I set,
In which she cannot aid thee nor abet,
But thou thyself must bring it fair to end.'

Thereon she sped her to the bounds of Thrace,
And set her by a river deep and wide,
And said 'To east beyond this stream, a race
Of golden-fleecèd sheep at pasture bide.
Go seek them out; and this thy task, to pull
But one lock for me of their precious wool,
And give it in my hands at eventide:

'This do and thou shalt have thy heart's desire.'
Which said, she fled and left her by the stream:
And Psyche then, with courage still entire,
Had plunged therein; but now of great esteem
Her life she rated, while it lent a spell
Wherein she yet might hope to quit her well,
And in one winning all her woes redeem.

10

There as she stood in doubt, a fluting voice
Rose from the flood, 'Psyche, be not afraid
To hear a reed give tongue, for 'twas of choice
That I from mortal flesh a plant was made.
My name is Syrinx; once from mighty Pan
Into the drowning river as I ran,
A fearful prayer my steps for ever stay'd.

11

'But by that change in many climes I live;
And Pan, my lover, who to me alone
Is true and does me honour, I forgive—
Nor if I speak in sorrow is't my own:
Rather for thee my voice I now uplift
To warn thee plunge not in the river swift,
Nor seek the golden sheep to men unknown.

12

'If thou should cross the stream, which may not be,
Thou coudst not climb upon the hanging rocks,
Nor ever, as the goddess bade thee, see
The pasture of the yellow-fleecèd flocks:
Or if thou coud, their herded horns would gore
And slay thee on the crags, or thrust thee o'er
Ere thou coudst rob them of their golden locks.

13

'The goddess means thy death.   But I can show
How thy obedience yet may thwart her will.
At noon the golden flocks descend below,
Leaving the scented herbage of the hill,
And where the shelving banks to shallows fall,
Drink at the rippling water one and all,
Nor back return till they have drawn their fill.

14

'I will command a thornbush, that it stoop
Over some ram that steppeth by in peace.
And him in all its prickles firmly coop,
Making thee seizure of his golden fleece;
So without peril of his angry horns
Shalt thou be quit: for he upon the thorns
Must leave his ransom ere he win release.'

December

15

Then Psyche thankt her for her kind befriending,
And hid among the rushes looking east;
And when noon came she saw the flock descending
Out of the hills; and lo! one golden beast
Caught in a thornbush; and the mighty brute
Struggl'd and tore it from its twisted root
Into the stream, or e'er he was releas't.

And when they water'd were and gone, the breeze
Floated the freighted thorn where Psyche lay:
Whence she unhook'd the golden wool at ease,
And back to heaven for passage swift gan pray.
And Hermes, who was sent to be her guide
Ifso she lived, came down at eventide,
And bore her thither ere the close of day.

17

But when the goddess saw the locks of gold
Held to her hands, her heart with wrath o'erran:
'Most desperate thou, and by abetting bold,
That dost outwit me, prove thee as I can.
Yet this work is not thine: there is but one
Of all the gods who coud the thing have done.
Hast thou a friend too in the lusty Pan?

'I'll give thee trial where he cannot aid.'
 Which said, she led her to a torrid land,
Level and black, but not with flood or shade,
For nothing coud the mighty heat withstand,
Which aye from morn till eve the naked sun
Pour'd on that plain, where never foot had run,
Nor any herb sprung on its molten sand.

19

Far off a gloomy mountain rose alone :
And Aphrodite, thither pointing, said
'There lies thy task.   Out of the topmost stone
Of yonder hill upwells a fountain head.
Take thou this goblet ; brimming must thou bring
Its cup with water from that sacred spring,
If ever to my son thou wouldst be wed.'

20

Saying, she gave into her hands a bowl
Cut of one crystal, open, broad and fair ;
And bade her at all hazard keep it whole,
For heaven held nought beside so fine or rare.
Then was she gone ; and Psyche on the plain
Now doubted if she ever should regain
The love of Eros, strove she howsoe'er.

21

Yet as a helmsman, at the word to tack,
Swiftly without a thought puts down his helm,
So Psyche turn'd to tread that desert black,
Since was no fear that coud her heart o'erwhelm ;
Nor knew she that she went the fount to seek
Of cold Cocytus, springing to the peak,
Secretly from his source in Pluto's realm.

22

All night and day she journey'd, and at last
Come to the rock gazed up in vain around :
Nothing she saw but precipices vast
O'er ruined scarps, with rugged ridges crown'd :
And creeping to a cleft to rest in shade,
Or e'er the desperate venture she assay'd,
She fell asleep upon the stony ground.

December

A dream came to her, thus : she stood alone
Within her palace in the high ravine ;
Where nought but she was changed, but she to stone.
Worshippers throng'd the court, and still were seen
Folk flying from the peak, who, ever more
Flying and flying, lighted on the floor,
Hail! cried they, *wife of Eros, adorèd queen!*

24

A hurtling of the battl'd air disturb'd
Her sunken sense, and waked her eyes to meet
The kingly bird of Zeus, himself that curb'd
His swooping course, alighting at her feet ;
With motion gentle, his far-darting eye
In kindness dim'd upon her, he drew nigh,
And thus in words unveil'd her foe's deceit :

25

' In vain, poor Psyche, hast thou hither striven
Across the fiery plain toiling so well ;
Cruelly to destruction art thou driven
By her, whose hate thou canst not quit nor quell.
No mortal foot may scale this horrid mount,
And those black waters of its topmost fount
Are guarded by the hornèd snakes of hell.

26

' Its little rill is an upleaping jet
Of cold Cocytus, which for ever licks
Earth's base, and when with Acheron 'tis met,
Its waters with that other cannot mix,
Which holds the elemental air dissolved ;
But with it in its ceaseless course revolved
Issues unmingl'd in the lake of Styx.

27

'The souls of murderers, in guise of fish,
Scream as they swim therein and wail for cold,
Their times of woe determined by the wish
Of them they murder'd on the earth of old :
Whom each five years they see, whene'er they make
Their passage to the Acherusian lake,
And there release may win from pains condoled.

28

'For if the pitying ear of them they slew
Be haply piercèd by their voices spare,
Then are they freed from pain ; as are some few;
But, for the most, again they forward fare
To Tartarus obscene, and outcast thence
Are hurried back into the cold intense,
And with new company their torments share.

29

'Its biting lymph may not be touch'd of man
Or god, unless the Fates have so ordain'd ;
Nor coud I in thy favour break the ban,
Nor pass the dragons that thereby are chain'd,
Didst thou not bear the sacred cup of Zeus ;
Which, for thy peril lent, shall turn to use,
And truly do the service which it feign'd.'

30

Thus as he spake, his talons made he ring
Around the crystal bowl, and soaring high
Descended as from heaven upon the spring :
Nor dared the hornèd snakes of hell deny
The minister of Zeus, that bore his cup,
To fill it with their trusted water up,
Thence to the King of heaven therewith to fly.

December

31

But he to Psyche bent his gracious speed,
And bidding her to mount his feather'd back
Bore her aloft as once young Ganymede;
Nor ever made his steady flight to slack,
Ere that he set her down beside her goal,
And gave into her hands the crystal bowl
Unspill'd, o'erbrimming with the water black.

JANUARY

1

But Eros now recover'd from his hurt,
Felt other pangs; for who would not relent
Weighing the small crime and unmatch'd desert
Of Psyche with her cruel punishment?
And shamed he grew to be so near allied
To her, who by her taunts awoke his pride,
As his compassion by her spite unspent.

2

Which Aphrodite seeing, wax'd more firm
That he should never meet with Psyche more;
And had in thought already set the term
To their communion with that trial sore,
Which sent her forth upon a quest accurst,
And not to be accomplisht, that of thirst
She there might perish on hell's torrid shore.

(169)

3

And now it chanced that she had called her son
Into her presence-chamber, to unfold
Psyche's destruction, that her fate might stun
What love remained by duty uncontrol'd;
And he to hide his tears' rebellious storm
Was fled; when in his place another form
Rose 'neath the golden lintel; and behold

4

Psyche herself, in slow and balanced strain,
Poising the crystal bowl with fearful heed,
Her eyes at watch upon the steadied plane,
And whole soul gather'd in the single deed.
Onward she came, and stooping to the floor
Set down the cup unspill'd and brimming o'er
At Aphrodite's feet, and rose up freed.

5

Surprise o'ercame the goddess, and she too
Stood like a statue, but with passion pale:
Till, when her victim nothing spake, she threw
Some kindness in her voice, and bade her hail;
But in the smiling judge 'twas plain to see—
Saying 'What water bringst thou here to me?'—
That justice over hate should not prevail.

6

Then Psyche said 'This is the biting flood
Of black Cocytus, silver'd with the gleam
Of souls, that guilty of another's blood
Are pent therein, and as they swim they scream.
The hornèd snakes of hell, upon the mount
Enchain'd, for ever guard the livid fount:
And but the Fates can grant to touch the stream.'

7

'Wherefore,' the goddess cried, ''tis plain that none
But one I wot of coud this thing have wrought.
That which another doth may well be done,
Nor thou the nearer to my promise brought.
Thou buildest on a hope to be destroy'd,
If thou accept conditions, and avoid
Thy parcel, nor thyself accomplish aught.

8

'Was it not kindness in me, being averse
To all thy wish, to yield me thus to grant
Thy heart's desire,—and nothing loathe I worse,—
If thou wouldst only work as well as want?
See, now I will not yet be all denial,
But offer thee one last determining trial;
And let it be a mutual covenant:

9

'This box,' and in her hands she took a pyx
Square-cut, of dark obsidian's rarest green,
'Take; and therewith beyond Tartarean Styx
Go thou, and entering Hades' house obscene,
Say to Persephonè, *If 'tis thy will*
To shew me so much favour, prithee fill
This little vase with beauty for Love's queen.

10

'*She begs but what shall well o'erlast a day;*
For of her own was much of late outspent
In nursing of her son, in bed who lay
Wounded by me, who for the gift am sent.
Then bring me what she gives, and with all speed;
For truth to say I stand, thou seest, in need
Of some such charm in my disparagement.

(171)

11

'If thou return to me with that acquist,
Having thyself the journey made, I swear
That day to give thee whatsoe'er thou list,
An be it my son.   Now, Psyche, wilt thou dare?'
And Psyche said 'If this thou truly mean,
I will go down to Tartarus obscene,
And beg of Hades' queen thy beauty there.

12

'Show me the way.'   But Aphrodite said,
'That may'st thou find.   Yet I will place thee whence
A way there is : mortals have on it sped ;
Ay, and return'd thereby : so let us hence.'
Then swift to earth her willing prey she bore,
And left her on the wide Laconian shore,
Alone, at midnight, in the darkness dense.

13

'Twas winter ; and as shivering Psyche sat
Waiting for morn, she question'd in her mind
What place the goddess meant, arrived whereat
She might descend to hell, or how should find
The way which Gods to living men deny.
'No Orpheus, nay, nor Hercules am I,'
Said she, 'to loosen where the great Gods bind.'

14

And when at length the long-delaying dawn
Broke on the peaks of huge Taÿgetus,
And Psyche through the skirts of dark withdrawn
Look'd on that promontory mountainous,
And saw high-crested Taleton in snow,
Her heart sank, and she wept with head bent low
The malice of her foe dispiteous.

15

And seeing near at hand an ancient tower,
Deserted now, but once a hold of men,
She came thereto, and, though 'twas all her power,
Mounted its steep unbroken stair again.
'Surely,' she said, for now a second time
She thought to die—'this little height I climb
Will prove my shortest road to Pluto's den.

16

'Hence must I come to Tartarus; once there
Turn as I may,' and straight to death had sprung;
When in the mossy tower the imprison'd air
Was shaken, and the hoary stones gave tongue,
'Stand firm! Stand firm!' that rugged voice outcried;
'Of such as choose despondency for guide
Hast thou not heard what bitterest fate is sung?

17

'Hearken; for I the road and means can teach
How thou may'st come to hell and yet escape.
And first must thou, that upper gate to reach,
Along these seagirt hills thy journey shape,
To where the land in sea dips furthest South
At Tænarus and Hades' earthly mouth,
Hard by Poseidon's temple at the cape.

18

'Thereby may one descend: but they that make
That passage down must go provided well.
So take in either hand a honey-cake
Of pearlèd barley mix'd with hydromel;
And in thy mouth two doits, first having bound
The pyx beneath thy robe enwrap'd around:
Thus set thou forth; and mark what more I tell.

19

'When thou hast gone alone some half thy road
Thou wilt o'ertake a lame outwearied ass ;
And one that beats him, tottering 'neath his load
Of loosely bundl'd wood, will cry *Alas ;*
Help me, kind friend, my faggots to adjust !
But thou that silly cripple's words mistrust ;
'Tis planted for thy death.   Note it and pass.

20

'And when thy road the Stygian river joins,
Where woolly Charon ferries o'er the dead,
He will demand his fare : one of thy coins
Force with thy tongue between thy teeth, thy head
Offering instead of hand to give the doit.
His fingers in this custom are adroit,
And thine must not set down the barleybread.

21

Then in his crazy bark as, ferrying o'er
The stream, thou sittest, one that seems to float
Rather than swim, midway 'twixt shore and shore,
Will stretch his fleshless hand upon the boat,
And beg thee of thy pity take him in.
Shut thy soft ear unto his clamour thin,
Nor for a phantom deed thyself devote.

22

' Next, on the further bank when thou art stept,
Three wizen'd women weaving at the woof
Will stop, and pray thee in their art adept
To free their tangl'd threads.   Hold thou aloof ;
For this and other traps thy foe hath plan'd
To make thee drop the cakes out of thy hand,
Putting thy prudence to perpetual proof.

23

'For by one cake thou comest into Hell,
And by one cake departest; since the hound
That guards the gate is ever pleasèd well
To taste man's meal, or sweeten'd grain unground.
Cast him a cake; for that thou may'st go free
Even to the mansion of Persephonè,
Withouten stay or peril, safe and sound.

24

'She will receive thee kindly; thou decline
Her courtesies, and make the floor thy seat;
Refusing what is offer'd, food or wine;
Save only beg a crust of bread to eat.
Then tell thy mission, and her present take;
Which when thou hast, set forth with pyx and cake,
One in each hand, while yet thou may'st retreat.

25

'Giving thy second cake to Cerberus,
The coin to Charon, and that way whereby
Thou camest following, thou comest thus
To see again the starry choir on high.
But guard thou well the pyx, nor once uplift
The lid to look on Persephassa's gift;
Else 'tis in vain I bid thee now not die.'

26

Then Psyche thank'd the tower, and stoopt her
mouth
To kiss the stones upon his rampart hoary;
And coming down his stair went hasting south,
Along the steep Tænarian promontory;
And found the cave and temple by the cape,
And took the cakes and coins, and made escape
Beneath the earth, according to his story.

27

And overtook the ass, but lent no aid;
And offer'd Charon with her teeth his fee;
And pass'd the floating ghost, in vain who pray'd;
And turned her back upon the weavers three;
And threw the honey-cake to that hell-hound
Three-headed Cerberus; and safe and sound,
Came to the mansion of Persephonè.

28

Kindly received, she courtesy declined:
Sat on the ground; ate not, save where she lay,
A crust of bread; reveal'd the goddess' mind;
The gift took; and return'd upon her way:
Gave Cerberus his cake, Charon his fare,
And saw through Hell's mouth to the purple air
And one by one the keen stars melt in day.

29

Awhile from so long journeying in the shades
Resting at Tænarus she came to know
How, up the eastern coast some forty stades,
There stood a temple of her goddess foe.
There would she make her offering, there reclaim
The prize, which now 'twas happiness to name,
The joy that should redeem all passèd woe.

30

And wending by the sunny shore at noon,
She with her pyx, and wondering what it hid,
Of what kind, what the fashion of the boon
Coud be, that she to look on was forbid,—
Alas for Innocence so hard to teach!—
At fancy's prick she sat her on the beach,
And to content desire lifted the lid.

She saw within nothing : But o'er her sight
That looked on nothing gan a darkness creep.
A cloudy poison, mix'd of Stygian night,
Rapt her to deadly and infernal sleep.
Backward she fell, like one when all is o'er,
And lay outstretch'd, as lies upon the shore
A drown'd corpse cast up by the murmuring deep.

FEBRUARY

1

WHILE Eros in his chamber hid his tears,
Mourning the loss of Psyche and her fate,
The rumour of her safety reacht his ears
And how she came to Aphrodite's gate :
Whereat with hope return'd his hardihood,
And secretly he purposed while he coud
Himself to save her from the goddess' hate.

2

Then learning what he might and guessing more,
His ready wit came soon to understand
The journey to the far Laconian shore ;
Whither to fly and seek his love he plan'd :
And making good escape in dark of night,
Ere the sun crost his true meridian flight
He by Teuthronè struck the southern strand.

3

There as it chanct he found that snowy bird
Of Crete, that late made mischief with his queen,
And now along the cliffs with wings unstir'd
Sail'd, and that morn had cross'd the sea between :
Whom as he past he hail'd, and question'd thus,
'O snowy gull, if thou from Tænarus
Be come, say, hast thou there my Psyche seen ?'

4

The gull replied 'Thy Psyche have I seen ;
Walking beside the sea she joy'th to bear
A pyx of dark obsidian's rarest green,
Wherein she gazeth on her features fair.
She is not hence by now six miles at most.'
Then Eros bade him speed, and down the coast
Held on his passage through the buoyant air.

5

With eager eye he search'd the salty marge,
Boding all mischief from his mother's glee ;
And wondering of her wiles, and what the charge
Shut in the dark obsidian pyx might be.
And lo ! at last, outstretch'd beside the rocks,
Psyche as lifeless ; and the open box
Laid with the weedy refuse of the sea.

6

He guess'd all, flew down, and beside her knelt,
With both his hands stroking her temples wan ;
And for the poison with his fingers felt,
And drew it gently from her ; and anon
She slowly from those Stygian fumes was freed ;
Which he with magic handling and good heed
Replaced in pyx, and shut the lid thereon.

7

'O Psyche,' thus, and kissing her he cried,
'O simple-hearted Psyche, once again
Hast thou thy foolish longing gratified,
A second time hath prying been thy bane.
But lo! I, love, am come, for I am thine:
Nor ever more shall any fate malign,
Or spite of goddess smite our love in twain.

8

'Let now that I have saved thee twice outweigh
The once that I deserted thee: and thou
Hast much obey'd for once to disobey,
And wilt no more my bidding disallow.
Take up thy pyx; to Aphrodite go,
And claim the promise of thy mighty foe;
Maybe that she will grant it to thee now.

9

'If she should yet refuse, despair not yet!'
Then Psyche, when she felt his arms restore
Their old embrace, and as their bodies met,
Knew the great joy that grief is pardon'd for;
And how it doth first ecstasy excel,
When love well-known, long-lost, and mournèd well
In long days of no hope, comes home once more.

10

But Eros leaping up with purpose keen
Into the air, as only love can fly,
Bore her to heaven, and setting her unseen
At Aphrodite's golden gate,—whereby
They came as night was close on twilight dim,—
There left, and bidding her say nought of him
Went onward to the house of Zeus most high.

11

Where winning audience of the heavenly sire,
Who well disposed to him was used to be,
He told the story of his strong desire;
And boldly begg'd that Zeus would grant his plea
That he might have sweet Psyche for his wife,
And she be dower'd with immortal life,
Since she was worthy, by his firm decree.

12

And great Zeus smiled; and at the smile of Zeus
All heaven was glad, and on the earth below
Was calm and peace awhile and sorrow's truce:
The sun shone forth and smote the winter snow,
The flowërs sprang, the birds gan sing and pair,
And mortals, as they drew the brighten'd air,
Marvel'd, and quite forgot their common woe.

13

Yet gave the Thunderer not his full consent
Without some words: 'At length is come the day,'
Thus spake he, 'when for all thy youth misspent,
Thy mischief-making and thy wanton play
Thou art upgrown to taste the sweet and sour:
Good shall it work upon thee: from this hour
Look we for better things.   And this I say,

14

'That since thy birth, which all we took for bliss,
Thou hast but mock'd us; and no less on me
Hast brought disfavour and contempt, ywiss,
Than others that have had to do with thee:
Till only such as vow'd themselves aloof
From thee and thine were held in good approof;
And few there were, who thus of shame went free.

(180)

15

'That punishment is shapen as reward
Is like thy fortune : but our good estate
We honour, while we sit to be adored :
And thus 'twas written in the book of Fate.
Not for thy pleasure, but the general weal
Grant I the grace for which thou here dost kneel;
And that which I determine shall not wait.'

16

So wingèd Hermes through the heaven he sped,
To warn the high celestials to his hall,
Where they should Psyche see with Eros wed,
And keep the day with feast ambrosial.
And Hermes, flying through the skiey ways
Of high Olympus, spread sweet Psyche's praise,
And bade the mighty gods obey his call

17

Then all the Kronian gods and goddesses
Assembl'd at his cry,—and now 'twas known
Why Zeus had smiled,—the lesser majesties
Attending them before his royal throne.
Athena, mistress good of them that know,
Came, and Apollo, warder off of woe,
Who had to Psyche's sire her fate foreshown;

18

Demeter, giver of the golden corn,
Fair Hebe, honour'd at her Attic shrine,
And Artemis with hunting spear and horn,
And Dionysos, planter of the vine,
With old Poseidon from the barren sea,
And Leto, and the lame Hephæstos, he
Himself who built those halls with skill divine.

19

And ruddy Pan with many a quip and quirk
Air'd 'mong those lofty gods his mirth illbred,
Bearing a mighty bowl of cretan work :
Stern Arês, with his crisp hair helmeted,
Came, and retirèd Hestia, and the god
Hermes, with wingèd cap and ribbon'd rod,
By whom the company was heralded.

20

And Hera sat by Zeus, and all around
The Muses, that of learning make their choice ;
Who, when Apollo struck his strings to sound,
Sang in alternate music with sweet voice :
And righteous Themis, and the Graces three
Ushering the anger'd Aphrodite ; she
Alone of all were there might not rejoice

21

But ere they sat to feast, Zeus bade them fill
The cup ambrosial of immortal life,
And said ' If Psyche drink,—and 'tis my will,—
There is an end of this unhappy strife.
Nor can the goddess, whose mislike had birth
From too great honour paid the bride on earth,
Forbid her any more for Eros' wife.'

22

Then Aphrodite said 'So let it be.'
And Psyche was brought in, with such a flush
Of joy upon her face, as there to see
Was fairer to love's eye than beauty's blush.
And then she drank the eternal wine, whose draught
Can Terror cease : which flesh hath never quafft,
Nor doth it flow from grape that mortals crush.

23

And next stood Eros forth, and took her hand,
And kisst her happy face before them all :
And Zeus proclaim'd them married, and outban'd
From heaven whoever should that word miscall.
And then all sat to feast, and one by one
Pledged Psyche ere they drank and cried *Well done !*
And merry laughter rang throughout the hall.

24

So thus was Eros unto Psyche wed,
The heavenly bridegroom to his earthly bride,
Who won his love, in simple maidenhead :
And by her love herself she glorified,
And him from wanton wildness disinclined ;
Since in his love for her he came to find
A joy unknown through all Olympus wide.

25

And Psyche for her fall was quite forgiven,
Since 'gainst herself when tempted to rebel,
By others' malice on her ruin driven,
Only of sweet simplicity she fell:—
Wherein who fall may fall unto the skies ;—
And being foolish she was yet most wise,
And took her trials patiently and well.

26

And Aphrodite since her full defeat
Is kinder and less jealous than before,
And smiling on them both, calls Psyche sweet ;
But thinks her son less manly than of yore :
Though still she holds his arm of some renown,
When he goes smiting mortals up and down,
Piercing their marrow with his weapons sore.

So now in steadfast love and happy state
They hold for aye their mansion in the sky,
And send down heavenly peace on those who mate,
In virgin love, to find their joy thereby:
Whom gently Eros shooteth, and apart
Keepeth for them from all his sheaf that dart
Which Psyche in his chamber pickt to try.

28

Now in that same month Psyche bare a child,
Who straight in heaven was namèd Hedonè
In mortal tongues by other letters styled;
Whom all to love, however named, agree:
Whom in our noble English JOY we call,
And honour them among us most of all,
Whose happy children are as fair as she.

29

ENVOY

IT IS MY PRAYER THAT SHE MAY SMILE ON ALL
WHO READ MY TALE AS SHE HATH SMILED ON ME.

THE GROWTH OF LOVE

PREVIOUS EDITIONS

1. *XXIV Sonnets.*   *Ed. Bumpus,* 1876.
2. *LXXIX Sonnets.*   *Daniel Press,* 1889.
   This edition was copied in America.
3. *Do.   do.   Black letter.*   1890.
4. *LXIX Sonnets.   Smith, Elder & Co.   Vol. I,* 1898.

THE GROWTH
OF LOVE

THEY that in play can do the thing they would,
   Having an instinct throned in reason's place,
—And every perfect action hath the grace
Of indolence or thoughtless hardihood—
These are the best: yet be there workmen good
Who lose in earnestness control of face,
Or reckon means, and rapt in effort base
Reach to their end by steps well understood.

   Me whom thou sawest of late strive with the pains
Of one who spends his strength to rule his nerve,
—Even as a painter breathlessly who strains
His scarcely moving hand lest it should swerve—
Behold me, now that I have cast my chains,
Master of the art which for thy sake I serve.

2

FOR thou art mine : and now I am ashamed
To have usèd means to win so pure acquist,
And of my trembling fear that might have misst
Thro' very care the gold at which I aim'd ;
And am as happy but to hear thee named,
As are those gentle souls by angels kisst
In pictures seen leaving their marble cist
To go before the throne of grace unblamed.

Nor surer am I water hath the skill
To quench my thirst, or that my strength is freed
In delicate ordination as I will,
Than that to be myself is all I need
For thee to be most mine : so I stand still,
And save to taste my joy no more take heed.

3

THE whole world now is but the minister
Of thee to me : I see no other scheme
But universal love, from timeless dream
Waking to thee his joy's interpreter.
I walk around and in the fields confer
Of love at large with tree and flower and stream,
And list the lark descant upon my theme,
Heaven's musical accepted worshipper.

Thy smile outfaceth ill : and that old feud
'Twixt things and me is quash'd in our new truce ;
And nature now dearly with thee endued
No more in shame ponders her old excuse,
But quite forgets her frowns and antics rude,
So kindly hath she grown to her new use.

4

THE very names of things belov'd are dear,
And sounds will gather beauty from their sense,
As many a face thro' love's long residence
Groweth to fair instead of plain and sere:
But when I say thy name it hath no peer,
And I suppose fortune determined thence
Her dower, that such beauty's excellence
Should have a perfect title for the ear.

Thus may I think the adopting Muses chose
Their sons by name, knowing none would be heard
Or writ so oft in all the world as those,—
Dan Chaucer, mighty Shakespeare, then for third
The classic Milton, and to us arose
Shelley with liquid music in the word.

5

THE poets were good teachers, for they taught
Earth had this joy; but that 'twould ever be
That fortune should be perfected in me,
My heart of hope dared not engage the thought.
So I stood low, and now but to be caught
By any self-styled lords of the age with thee
Vexes my modesty, lest they should see
I hold them owls and peacocks, things of nought.

And when we sit alone, and as I please
I taste thy love's full smile, and can enstate
The pleasure of my kingly heart at ease,
My thought swims like a ship, that with the weight
Of her rich burden sleeps on the infinite seas
Becalm'd, and cannot stir her golden freight.

6

WHILE yet we wait for spring, and from the dry
And blackening east that so embitters March,
Well-housed must watch grey fields and meadows parch,
And driven dust and withering snowflake fly;
Already in glimpses of the tarnish'd sky
The sun is warm and beckons to the larch,
And where the covert hazels interarch
Their tassell'd twigs, fair beds of primrose lie.

Beneath the crisp and wintry carpet hid
A million buds but stay their blossoming;
And trustful birds have built their nests amid
The shuddering boughs, and only wait to sing
Till one soft shower from the south shall bid,
And hither tempt the pilgrim steps of spring.

7

IN thee my spring of life hath bid the while
A rose unfold beyond the summer's best,
The mystery of joy made manifest
In love's self-answering and awakening smile;
Whereby the lips in wonder reconcile
Passion with peace, and show desire at rest,—
A grace of silence by the Greek unguesst,
That bloom'd to immortalize the Tuscan style:

When first the angel-song that faith hath ken'd
Fancy pourtray'd, above recorded oath
Of Israel's God, or light of poem pen'd;
The very countenance of plighted troth
'Twixt heaven and earth, where in one moment blend
The hope of one and happiness of both.

8

FOR beauty being the best of all we know
Sums up the unsearchable and secret aims
Of nature, and on joys whose earthly names
Were never told can form and sense bestow;
And man hath sped his instinct to outgo
The step of science; and against her shames
Imagination stakes out heavenly claims,
Building a tower above the head of woe.

Nor is there fairer work for beauty found
Than that she win in nature her release
From all the woes that in the world abound:
Nay with his sorrow may his love increase,
If from man's greater need beauty redound,
And claim his tears for homage of his peace.

9

THUS to thy beauty doth my fond heart look,
That late dismay'd her faithless faith forbore;
And wins again her love lost in the lore
Of schools and script of many a learned book:
For thou what ruthless death untimely took
Shalt now in better brotherhood restore,
And save my batter'd ship that far from shore
High on the dismal deep in tempest shook.

So in despite of sorrow lately learn'd
I still hold true to truth since thou art true,
Nor wail the woe which thou to joy hast turn'd:
Nor come the heavenly sun and bathing blue
To my life's need more splendid and unearn'd
Than hath thy gift outmatch'd desire and due.

10

WINTER was not unkind because uncouth ;
His prison'd time made me a closer guest,
And gave thy graciousness a warmer zest,
Biting all else with keen and angry tooth :
And bravelier the triumphant blood of youth
Mantling thy cheek its happy home possest,
And sterner sport by day put strength to test,
And custom's feast at night gave tongue to truth.

Or say hath flaunting summer a device
To match our midnight revelry, that rang
With steel and flame along the snow-girt ice ?
Or when we hark't to nightingales that sang
On dewy eves in spring, did they entice
To gentler love than winter's icy fang ?

11

THERE's many a would-be poet at this hour,
Rhymes of a love that he hath never woo'd,
And o'er his lamplit desk in solitude
Deems that he sitteth in the Muses' bower :
And some the flames of earthly love devour,
Who have taken no kiss of Nature, nor renew'd
In the world's wilderness with heavenly food
The sickly body of their perishing power.

So none of all our company, I boast,
But now would mock my penning, coud they see
How down the right it maps a jagged coast ;
Seeing they hold the manlier praise to be
Strong hand and will, and the heart best when most
'Tis sober, simple, true, and fancy-free.

12

How coud I quarrel or blame you, most dear,
Who all thy virtues gavest and kept back none;
Kindness and gentleness, truth without peer,
And beauty that my fancy fed upon?
　　Now not my life's contrition for my fault
Can blot that day, nor work me recompence,
Tho' I might worthily thy worth exalt,
Making thee long amends for short offence.

　　For surely nowhere, love, if not in thee
Are grace and truth and beauty to be found;
And all my praise of these can only be
A praise of thee, howe'er by thee disown'd:
　　While still thou must be mine tho' far removed,
And I for one offence no more beloved.

13

Now since to me altho' by thee refused
The world is left, I shall find pleasure still;
The art that most I have loved but little used
Will yield a world of fancies at my will:
　　And tho' where'er thou goest it is from me,
I where I go thee in my heart must bear;
And what thou wert that wilt thou ever be,
My choice, my best, my loved, and only fair.

　　Farewell, yet think not such farewell a change
From tenderness, tho' once to meet or part
But on short absence so coud sense derange
That tears have graced the greeting of my heart;
　　They were proud drops and had my leave to fall,
Not on thy pity for my pain to call.

14

WHEN sometimes in an ancient house where state
From noble ancestry is handed on,
We see but desolation thro' the gate,
And richest heirlooms all to ruin gone;
    Because maybe some fancied shame or fear,
Bred of disease or melancholy fate,
Hath driven the owner from his rightful sphere
To wander nameless save to pity or hate:

    What is the wreck of all he hath in fief,
When he that hath is wrecking? nought is fine
Unto the sick, nor doth it burden grief
That the house perish when the soul doth pine.
    Thus I my state despise, slain by a sting
So slight 'twould not have hurt a meaner thing.

15

WHO builds a ship must first lay down the keel
    Of health, whereto the ribs of mirth are wed:
And knit, with beams and knees of strength, a bed
For decks of purity, her floor and ceil.
Upon her masts, Adventure, Pride, and Zeal,
To fortune's wind the sails of purpose spread:
And at the prow make figured maidenhead
O'erride the seas and answer to the wheel.

    And let him deep in memory's hold have stor'd
Water of Helicon: and let him fit
The needle that doth true with heaven accord:
Then bid her crew, love, diligence and wit
With justice, courage, temperance come aboard,
And at her helm the master reason sit.

16

THIS world is unto God a work of art,
Of which the unaccomplish'd heavenly plan
Is hid in life within the creature's heart,
And for perfection looketh unto man.
　　Ah me! those thousand ages: with what slow
Pains and persistence were his idols made,
Destroy'd and made, ere ever he coud know
The mighty mother must be so obey'd.

　　For lack of knowledge and thro' little skill
His childish mimicry outwent his aim;
His effort shaped the genius of his will;
Till thro' distinction and revolt he came,
True to his simple terms of good and ill,
Seeking the face of Beauty without blame.

17

SAY who be these light-bearded, sunburnt faces
In negligent and travel-stain'd array,
That in the city of Dante come to-day,
Haughtily visiting her holy places?
O these be noble men that hide their graces,
True England's blood, her ancient glory's stay,
By tales of fame diverted on their way
Home from the rule of oriental races.

　　Life-trifling lions these, of gentle eyes
And motion delicate, but swift to fire
For honour, passionate where duty lies,
Most loved and loving: and they quickly tire
Of Florence, that she one day more denies
The embrace of wife and son, of sister or sire.

(195)

18

WHERE San Miniato's convent from the sun
At forenoon overlooks the city of flowers
I sat, and gazing on her domes and towers
Call'd up her famous children one by one:
And three who all the rest had far outdone,
Mild Giotto first, who stole the morning hours,
I saw, and god-like Buonarroti's powers,
And Dante, gravest poet, her much-wrong'd son.

Is all this glory, I said, another's praise?
Are these heroic triumphs things of old,
And do I dead upon the living gaze?
Or rather doth the mind, that can behold
The wondrous beauty of the works and days,
Create the image that her thoughts enfold?

19

REJOICE, ye dead, where'er your spirits dwell,
Rejoice that yet on earth your fame is bright;
And that your names, remember'd day and night,
Live on the lips of those that love you well.
'Tis ye that conquer'd have the powers of hell,
Each with the special grace of your delight:
Ye are the world's creators, and thro' might
Of everlasting love ye did excel.

Now ye are starry names, above the storm
And war of Time and nature's endless wrong
Ye flit, in pictured truth and peaceful form,
Wing'd with bright music and melodious song,—
The flaming flowers of heaven, making May-dance
In dear Imagination's rich pleasance.

The Growth of Love

20

THE world still goeth about to shew and hide,
Befool'd of all opinion, fond of fame :
But he that can do well taketh no pride,
And see'th his error, undisturb'd by shame :
   So poor 's the best that longest life can do,
The most so little, diligently done ;
So mighty is the beauty that doth woo,
So vast the joy that love from love hath won.

   God's love to win is easy, for He loveth
Desire's fair attitude, nor strictly weighs
The broken thing, but all alike approveth
Which love hath aim'd at Him : that is heaven's praise:
   And if we look for any praise on earth,
'Tis in man's love : all else is nothing worth.

21

O FLESH and blood, comrade to tragic pain
And clownish merriment ; whose sense could wake
Sermons in stones, and count death but an ache,
All things as vanity, yet nothing vain :
The world, set in thy heart, thy passionate strain
Reveal'd anew ; but thou for man didst make
Nature twice natural, only to shake
Her kingdom with the creatures of thy brain.

   Lo, Shakespeare, since thy time nature is loth
To yield to art her fair supremacy ;
In conquering one thou hast so enrichèd both.
What shall I say? for God—whose wise decree
Confirmeth all He did by all He doth—
Doubled His whole creation making thee.

22

I WOULD be a bird, and straight on wings I arise,
And carry purpose up to the ends of the air:
In calm and storm my sails I feather, and where
By freezing cliffs the unransom'd wreckage lies:
Or, strutting on hot meridian banks, surprise
The silence: over plains in the moonlight bare
I chase my shadow, and perch where no bird dare
In treetops torn by fiercest winds of the skies.

Poor simple birds, foolish birds! then I cry,
Ye pretty pictures of delight, unstir'd
By the only joy of knowing that ye fly;
Ye are nót what ye are, but rather, sum'd in a word,
The alphabet of a god's idea, and I
Who master it, I am the only bird.

23

O WEARY pilgrims, chanting of your woe,
That turn your eyes to all the peaks that shine,
Hailing in each the citadel divine
The which ye thought to have enter'd long ago;
Until at length your feeble steps and slow
Falter upon the threshold of the shrine,
And your hearts overburden'd doubt in fine
Whether it be Jerusalem or no:

Dishearten'd pilgrims, I am one of you;
For, having worshipp'd many a barren face,
I scarce now greet the goal I journey'd to:
I stand a pagan in the holy place;
Beneath the lamp of truth I am found untrue,
And question with the God that I embrace.

24

SPRING hath her own bright days of calm and peace;
Her melting air, at every breath we draw,
Floods heart with love to praise God's gracious law:
But suddenly—so short is pleasure's lease—
The cold returns, the buds from growing cease,
And nature's conquer'd face is full of awe;
As now the trait'rous north with icy flaw
Freezes the dew upon the sick lamb's fleece,

And 'neath the mock sun searching everywhere
Rattles the crispèd leaves with shivering din:
So that the birds are silent with despair
Within the thickets; nor their armour thin
Will gaudy flies adventure in the air,
Nor any lizard sun his spotted skin.

25

NOTHING is joy without thee: I can find
No rapture in the first relays of spring,
In songs of birds, in young buds opening,
Nothing inspiriting and nothing kind;
For lack of thee, who once wert throned behind
All beauty, like a strength where graces cling,—
The jewel and heart of light, which everything
Wrestled in rivalry to hold enshrined.

Ah! since thou'rt fled, and I in each fair sight
The sweet occasion of my joy deplore,
Where shall I seek thee best, or whom invite
Within thy sacred temples and adore?
Who shall fill thought and truth with old delight,
And lead my soul in life as heretofore?

26

THE work is done, and from the fingers fall
The bloodwarm tools that brought the labour thro':
The tasking eye that overrunneth all
Rests, and affirms there is no more to do.
     Now the third joy of making, the sweet flower
Of blessed work, bloometh in godlike spirit;
Which whoso plucketh holdeth for an hour
The shrivelling vanity of mortal merit.

And thou, my perfect work, thou'rt of to-day;
To-morrow a poor and alien thing wilt be,
True only should the swift life stand at stay:
Therefore farewell, nor look to bide with me.
     Go find thy friends, if there be one to love thee:
Casting thee forth, my child, I rise above thee.

27

THE fabled sea-snake, old Leviathan,
Or else what grisly beast of scaly chine
That champ'd the ocean-wrack and swash'd the brine,
Before the new and milder days of man,
Had never rib nor bray nor swindging fan
Like his iron swimmer of the Clyde or Tyne,
Late-born of golden seed to breed a line
Of offspring swifter and more huge of plan.

Straight is her going, for upon the sun
When once she hath look'd, her path and place are plain;
With tireless speed she smiteth one by one
The shuddering seas and foams along the main;
And her eased breath, when her wild race is run,
Roars thro' her nostrils like a hurricane.

28

A THOUSAND times hath in my heart's behoof
My tongue been set his passion to impart;
A thousand times hath my too coward heart
My mouth reclosed and fix'd it to the roof;
Then with such cunning hath it held aloof,
A thousand times kept silence with such art
That words coud do no more: yet on thy part
Hath silence given a thousand times reproof.

I should be bolder, seeing I commend
Love, that my dilatory purpose primes,
But fear lest with my fears my hope should end:
Nay, I would truth deny and burn my rhymes,
Renew my sorrows rather than offend,
A thousand times, and yet a thousand times.

29

I TRAVEL to thee with the sun's first rays,
That lift the dark west and unwrap the night;
I dwell beside thee when he walks the height,
And fondly toward thee at his setting gaze.
I wait upon thy coming, but always—
Dancing to meet my thoughts if they invite—
Thou hast outrun their longing with delight,
And in my solitude dost mock my praise.

Now doth my drop of time transcend the whole:
I see no fame in Khufu's pyramid,
No history where loveless Nile doth roll.
—This is eternal life, which doth forbid
Mortal detraction to the exalted soul,
And from her inward eye all fate hath hid.

30

My lady pleases me and I please her;
This know we both, and I besides know well
Wherefore I love her, and I love to tell
My love, as all my loving songs aver.
But what on her part could the passion stir,
Tho' 'tis more difficult for love to spell,
Yet can I dare divine how this befel,
Nor will her lips deny it if I err.

She loves me first because I love her, then
Loves me for knowing why she should be loved,
And that I love to praise her, loves again.
So from her beauty both our loves are moved,
And by her beauty are sustain'd; nor when
The earth falls from the sun is this disproved.

31

In all things beautiful, I cannot see
Her sit or stand, but love is stir'd anew:
'Tis joy to watch the folds fall as they do,
And all that comes is past expectancy.
If she be silent, silence let it be;
He who would bid her speak might sit and sue
The deep-brow'd Phidian Jove to be untrue
To his two thousand years' solemnity.

Ah, but her launchèd passion, when she sings,
Wins on the hearing like a shapen prow
Borne by the mastery of its urgent wings:
Or if she deign her wisdom, she doth show
She hath the intelligence of heavenly things,
Unsullied by man's mortal overthrow.

32

Thus to be humbled: 'tis that ranging pride
No refuge hath; that in his castle strong
Brave reason sits beleaguer'd, who so long
Kept field, but now must starve where he doth hide;
That industry, who once the foe defied,
Lies slaughter'd in the trenches; that the throng
Of idle fancies pipe their foolish song,
Where late the puissant captains fought and died.

Thus to be humbled: 'tis to be undone;
A forest fell'd; a city razed to ground;
A cloak unsewn, unwoven and unspun
Till not a thread remains that can be wound.
And yet, O lover, thee, the ruin'd one,
Love who hath humbled thus hath also crown'd.

33

I care not if I live, tho' life and breath
Have never been to me so dear and sweet.
I care not if I die, for I coud meet—
Being so happy—happily my death.
I care not if I love; to-day she saith
She loveth, and love's history is complete.
Nor care I if she love me; at her feet
My spirit bows entranced and worshippeth.

I have no care for what was most my care,
But all around me see fresh beauty born,
And common sights grown lovelier than they were:
I dream of love, and in the light of morn
Tremble, beholding all things very fair
And strong with strength that puts my strength to scorn.

34

O my goddess divine sometimes I say :—
Now let this word for ever and all suffice;
Thou art insatiable, and yet not twice
Can even thy lover give his soul away:
And for my acts, that at thy feet I lay;
For never any other, by device
Of wisdom, love or beauty, could entice
My homage to the measure of this day.

    I have no more to give thee: lo, I have sold
My life, have emptied out my heart, and spent
Whate'er I had; till like a beggar, bold
With nought to lose, I laugh and am content.
A beggar kisses thee; nay, love, behold,
I fear not: thou too art in beggarment.

35

ALL earthly beauty hath one cause and proof,
To lead the pilgrim soul to beauty above:
Yet lieth the greater bliss so far aloof,
That few there be are wean'd from earthly love.
    Joy's ladder it is, reaching from home to home,
The best of all the work that all was good;
Whereof 'twas writ the angels aye upclomb,
Down sped, and at the top the Lord God stood.

    But I my time abuse, my eyes by day
Center'd on thee, by night my heart on fire—
Letting my number'd moments run away—
Nor e'en 'twixt night and day to heaven aspire:
    So true it is that what the eye seeth not
But slow is loved, and loved is soon forgot.

36

O MY life's mischief, once my love's delight,
  That drew'st a mortgage on my heart's estate,
Whose baneful clause is never out of date,
Nor can avenging time restore my right:
Whom first to lose sounded that note of spite,
Whereto my doleful days were tuned by fate:
That art the well-loved cause of all my hate,
The sun whose wandering makes my hopeless night:

  Thou being in all my lacking all I lack,
It is thy goodness turns my grace to crime,
Thy fleetness from my goal which holds me back;
Wherefore my feet go out of step with time,
My very grasp of life is old and slack,
And even my passion falters in my rhyme.

37

AT times with hurried hoofs and scattering dust
I race by field or highway, and my horse
Spare not, but urge direct in headlong course
Unto some fair far hill that gain I must:
But near arrived the vision soon mistrust,
Rein in, and stand as one who sees the source
Of strong illusion, shaming thought to force
From off his mind the soil of passion's gust.

  My brow I bare then, and with slacken'd speed
Can view the country pleasant on all sides,
And to kind salutation give good heed:
I ride as one who for his pleasure rides,
And stroke the neck of my delighted steed,
And seek what cheer the village inn provides.

38

An idle June day on the sunny Thames,
Floating or rowing as our fancy led,
Now in the high beams basking as we sped,
Now in green shade gliding by mirror'd stems;
    By lock and weir and isle, and many a spot
Of memoried pleasure, glad with strength and skill,
Friendship, good wine, and mirth, that serve not ill
The heavenly Muse, tho' she requite them not:

    I would have life—thou saidst—all as this day,
Simple enjoyment calm in its excess,
With not a grief to cloud, and not a ray
Of passion overhot my peace to oppress;
With no ambition to reproach delay,
Nor rapture to disturb its happiness.

39

A MAN that sees by chance his picture, made
As once a child he was, handling some toy,
Will gaze to find his spirit within the boy,
Yet hath no secret with the soul pourtray'd:
He cannot think the simple thought which play'd
Upon those features then so frank and coy;
'Tis his, yet oh! not his: and o'er the joy
His fatherly pity bends in tears dismay'd.

    Proud of his prime maybe he stand at best,
And lightly wear his strength, or aim it high,
In knowledge, skill and courage self-possest:—
Yet in the pictured face a charm doth lie,
The one thing lost more worth than all the rest,
Which seeing, he fears to say *This child was I.*

40

TEARS of love, tears of joy and tears of care,
Comforting tears that fell uncomforted,
Tears o'er the new-born, tears beside the dead,
Tears of hope, pride and pity, trust and prayer,
Tears of contrition; all tears whatsoe'er
Of tenderness or kindness had she shed
Who here is pictured, ere upon her head
The fine gold might be turn'd to silver there.

    The smile that charm'd the father hath given place
Unto the furrow'd care wrought by the son;
But virtue hath transform'd all change to grace:
So that I praise the artist, who hath done
A portrait, for my worship, of the face
Won by the heart my father's heart that won.

41

IF I coud but forget and not recall
So well my time of pleasure and of play,
When ancient nature was all new and gay,
Light as the fashion that doth last enthrall,—
Ah mighty nature, when my heart was small,
Nor dream'd what fearful searchings underlay
The flowers and leafy ecstasy of May,
The breathing summer sloth, the scented fall:

    Coud I forget, then were the fight not hard,
Press'd in the mêlée of accursed things,
Having such help in love and such reward:
But that 'tis I who once—'tis this that stings—
Once dwelt within the gate that angels guard,
Where yet I'd be had I but heavenly wings.

42

WHEN I see childhood on the threshold seize
The prize of life from age and likelihood,
I mourn time's change that will not be withstood,
Thinking how Christ said *Be like one of these.*
For in the forest among many trees
Scarce one in all is found that hath made good
The virgin pattern of its slender wood,
That courtesied in joy to every breeze;

But scath'd, but knotted trunks that raise on high
Their arms in stiff contortion, strain'd and bare;
Whose patriarchal crowns in sorrow sigh.
So, little children, ye—nay nay, ye ne'er
From me shall learn how sure the change and nigh,
When ye shall share our strength and mourn to share.

43

WHEN parch'd with thirst, astray on sultry sand
The traveller faints, upon his closing ear
Steals a fantastic music: he may hear
The babbling fountain of his native land.
Before his eyes the vision seems to stand,
Where at its terraced brink the maids appear,
Who fill their deep urns at its waters clear,
And not refuse the help of lover's hand.

O cruel jest—he cries, as some one flings
The sparkling drops in sport or shew of ire—
O shameless, O contempt of holy things.
But never of their wanton play they tire,
As not athirst they sit beside the springs,
While he must quench in death his lost desire.

44

THE image of thy love, rising on dark
And desperate days over my sullen sea,
Wakens again fresh hope and peace in me,
Gleaming above upon my groaning bark.
Whate'er my sorrow be, I then may hark
A loving voice: whate'er my terror be,
This heavenly comfort still I win from thee,
To shine my lodestar that wert once my mark.

Prodigal nature makes us but to taste
One perfect joy, which given she niggard grows;
And lest her precious gift should run to waste,
Adds to its loss a thousand lesser woes:
So to the memory of the gift that graced
Her hand, her graceless hand more grace bestows.

45

IN this neglected, ruin'd edifice
Of works unperfected and broken schemes,
Where is the promise of my early dreams,
The smile of beauty and the pearl of price?
No charm is left now that could once entice
Wind-wavering fortune from her golden streams,
And full in flight decrepit purpose seems,
Trailing the banner of his old device.

Within the house a frore and numbing air
Has chill'd endeavour: sickly memories reign
In every room, and ghosts are on the stair:
And hope behind the dusty window-pane
Watches the days go by, and bow'd with care
Forecasts her last reproach and mortal stain.

46

ONCE I would say, before thy vision came,
My joy, my life, my love, and with some kind
Of knowledge speak, and think I knew my mind
Of heaven and hope, and each word hit its aim.
Whate'er their sounds be, now all mean the same,
Denoting each the fair that none can find;
Or if I say them, 'tis as one long blind
Forgets the sights that he was used to name.

Now if men speak of love, 'tis not my love;
Nor are their hopes nor joys mine, nor their life
Of praise the life that I think honour of:
Nay tho' they turn from house and child and wife
And self, and in the thought of heaven above
Hold, as do I, all mortal things at strife.

47

SINCE then 'tis only pity looking back,
Fear looking forward, and the busy mind
Will in one woeful moment more upwind
Than lifelong years unroll of bitter or black;
What is man's privilege, his hoarding knack
Of memory with foreboding so combined,
Whereby he comes to dream he hath of kind
The perpetuity which all things lack?

Which but to hope is doubtful joy, to have
Being a continuance of what, alas,
We mourn, and scarcely bear with to the grave;
Or something so unknown that it o'erpass
The thought of comfort, and the sense that gave
Cannot consider it thro' any glass.

48

COME gentle sleep, I woo thee : come and take
Not now the child into thine arms, from fright
Composed by drowsy tune and shaded light,
Whom ignorant of thee thou didst nurse and make ;
Nor now the boy, who scorn'd thee for the sake
Of growing knowledge or mysterious night,
Tho' with fatigue thou didst his limbs invite,
And heavily weigh the eyes that would not wake ;

No, nor the man severe, who from his best
Failing, alert fled to thee, that his breath,
Blood, force and fire should come at morn redrest ;
But me, from whom thy comfort tarrieth,
For all my wakeful prayer sent without rest
To thee, O shew and shadow of my death.

49

THE spirit's eager sense for sad or gay
Filleth with what he will our vessel full :
Be joy his bent, he waiteth not joy's day
But like a child at any toy will pull :
If sorrow, he will weep for fancy's sake,
And spoil heaven's plenty with forbidden care.
What fortune most denies we slave to take ;
Nor can fate load us more than we can bear.

Since pleasure with the having disappeareth,
He who hath least in hand hath most at heart,
While he keep hope : as he who alway feareth
A grief that never comes hath yet the smart ;
And heavier far is our self-wrought distress,
For when God sendeth sorrow, it doth bless.

(211)

50

THE world comes not to an end: her city-hives
Swarm with the tokens of a changeless trade,
With rolling wheel, driver and flagging jade,
Rich men and beggars, children, priests and wives.
New homes on old are set, as lives on lives;
Invention with invention overlaid:
But still or tool or toy or book or blade
Shaped for the hand, that holds and toils and strives.

The men to-day toil as their fathers taught,
With little better'd means; for works depend
On works and overlap, and thought on thought:
And thro' all change the smiles of hope amend
The weariest face, the same love changed in nought:
In this thing too the world comes not to an end.

51

O MY uncared-for songs, what are ye worth,
That in my secret book with so much care
I write you, this one here and that one there,
Marking the time and order of your birth?
How, with a fancy so unkind to mirth,
A sense so hard, a style so worn and bare,
Look ye for any welcome anywhere
From any shelf or heart-home on the earth?

Should others ask you this, say then I yearn'd
To write you such as once, when I was young,
Finding I should have loved and thereto turn'd.
'Twere something yet to live again among
The gentle youth beloved, and where I learn'd
My art, be there remember'd for my song.

52

Who takes the census of the living dead,
Ere the day come when memory shall o'ercrowd
The kingdom of their fame, and for that proud
And airy people find no room nor stead?
    Ere hoarding Time, that ever thrusteth back
The fairest treasures of his ancient store,
Better with best confound, so he may pack
His greedy gatherings closer, more and more?

    Let the true Muse rewrite her sullied page,
And purge her story of the men of hate,
That they go dirgeless down to Satan's rage
With all else foul, deform'd and miscreate:
    She hath full toil to keep the names of love
Honour'd on earth, as they are bright above.

53

I heard great Hector sounding war's alarms,
Where thro' the listless ghosts chiding he strode,
As tho' the Greeks besieged his last abode,
And he his Troy's hope still, her king-at-arms.
But on those gentle meads, which Lethe charms
With weary oblivion, his passion glow'd
Like the cold night-worm's candle, and only show'd
Such mimic flame as neither heats nor harms.

    'Twas plain to read, even by those shadows quaint,
How rude catastrophe had dim'd his day,
And blighted all his cheer with stern complaint:
To arms! to arms! what more the voice would say
Was swallow'd in the valleys, and grew faint
Upon the thin air, as he pass'd away.

54

SINCE not the enamour'd sun with glance more fond
Kisses the foliage of his sacred tree,
Than doth my waking thought arise on thee,
Loving none near thee, like thee nor beyond ;
Nay, since I am sworn thy slave, and in the bond
Is writ my promise of eternity ;
Since to such high hope thou'st encouraged me,
That if thou look but from me I despond ;

Since thou'rt my all in all, O think of this :
Think of the dedication of my youth :
Think of my loyalty, my joy, my bliss :
Think of my sorrow, my despair and ruth,
My sheer annihilation if I miss :
Think—if thou shouldst be false—think of thy truth.

55

THESE meagre rhymes, which a returning mood
Sometimes o'errateth, I as oft despise ;
And knowing them illnatured, stiff and rude,
See them as others with contemptuous eyes.
Nay, and I wonder less at God's respect
For man, a minim jot in time and space,
Than at the soaring faith of His elect,
That gift of gifts, the comfort of His grace.

O truth unsearchable, O heavenly love,
Most infinitely tender, so to touch
The work that we can meanly reckon of :
Surely—I say—we are favour'd overmuch.
But of this wonder, what doth most amaze
Is that we know our love is held for praise.

56

BEAUTY sat with me all the summer day,
Awaiting the sure triumph of her eye ;
Nor mark'd I till we parted, how, hard by,
Love in her train stood ready for his prey.
She, as too proud to join herself the fray,
Trusting too much to her divine ally,
When she saw victory tarry, chid him—'Why
Dost thou not at one stroke this rebel slay ? '

Then generous Love, who holds my heart in fee,
Told of our ancient truce : so from the fight
We straight withdrew our forces, all the three.
Baffled but not dishearten'd she took flight
Scheming new tactics : Love came home with me,
And prompts my measured verses as I write.

57

IN autumn moonlight, when the white air wan
Is fragrant in the wake of summer hence,
'Tis sweet to sit entranced, and muse thereon
In melancholy and godlike indolence :
  When the proud spirit, lull'd by mortal prime
To fond pretence of immortality,
Vieweth all moments from the birth of time,
All things whate'er have been or yet shall be.

And like the garden, where the year is spent,
The ruin of old life is full of yearning,
Mingling poetic rapture of lament
With flowers and sunshine of spring's sure returning ;
  Only in visions of the white air wan
By godlike fancy seized and dwelt upon.

58

WHEN first I saw thee, dearest, if I say
The spells that conjure back the hour and place,
And evermore I look upon thy face,
As in the spring of years long pass'd away ;
No fading of thy beauty's rich array,
No detriment of age on thee I trace,
But time's defeat written in spoils of grace,
From rivals robb'd, whom thou didst pity and slay.

So hath thy growth been, thus thy faith is true,
Unchanged in change, still to my growing sense,
To life's desire the same, and nothing new :
But as thou wert in dream and prescience
At love's arising, now thou stand'st to view
In the broad noon of his magnificence.

59

'TWAS on the very day winter took leave
Of those fair fields I love, when to the skies
The fragrant Earth was smiling in surprise
At that her heaven-descended, quick reprieve,
I wander'd forth my sorrow to relieve ;
Yet walk'd amid sweet pleasure in such wise
As Adam went alone in Paradise,
Before God of His pity fashion'd Eve.

And out of tune with all the joy around
I laid me down beneath a flowering tree,
And o'er my senses crept a sleep profound ;
In which it seem'd that thou wert given to me,
Rending my body, where with hurried sound
I feel my heart beat, when I think of thee.

60

Love that I know, love I am wise in, love,
My strength, my pride, my grace, my skill untaught,
My faith here upon earth, my hope above,
My contemplation and perpetual thought :
 The pleasure of my fancy, my heart's fire,
My joy, my peace, my praise, my happy theme,
The aim of all my doing, my desire
Of being, my life by day, by night my dream :

 Love, my sweet melancholy, my distress,
My pain, my doubt, my trouble, my despair,
My only folly and unhappiness,
And in my careless moments still my care :
 O love, sweet love, earthly love, love divine,
Say'st thou to-day, O love, that thou art mine?

61

The dark and serious angel, who so long
Vex'd his immortal strength in charge of me,
Hath smiled for joy and fled in liberty
To take his pastime with the peerless throng.
Oft had I done his noble keeping wrong,
Wounding his heart to wonder what might be
God's purpose in a soul of such degree ;
And there he had left me but for mandate strong.

 But seeing thee with me now, his task at close
He knoweth, and wherefore he was bid to stay,
And work confusion of so many foes :
The thanks that he doth look for, here I pay,
Yet fear some heavenly envy, as he goes
Unto what great reward I cannot say.

(217)

62

I WILL be what God made me, nor protest
Against the bent of genius in my time,
That science of my friends robs all the best,
While I love beauty, and was born to rhyme.
Be they our mighty men, and let me dwell
In shadow among the mighty shades of old,
With love's forsaken palace for my cell;
Whence I look forth and all the world behold,

And say, These better days, in best things worse,
This bastardy of time's magnificence,
Will mend in fashion and throw off the curse,
To crown new love with higher excellence.
Curs'd tho' I be to live my life alone,
My toil is for man's joy, his joy my own.

63

I LIVE on hope and that I think do all
Who come into this world, and since I see
Myself in swim with such good company,
I take my comfort whatsoe'er befall.
I abide and abide, as if more stout and tall
My spirit would grow by waiting like a tree;
And, clear of others' toil, it pleaseth me
In dreams their quick ambition to forestall.

And if thro' careless eagerness I slide
To some accomplishment, I give my voice
Still to desire, and in desire abide.
I have no stake abroad; if I rejoice
In what is done or doing, I confide
Neither to friend nor foe my secret choice.

64

YE blessed saints, that now in heaven enjoy
The purchase of those tears, the world's disdain,
Doth Love still with his war your peace annoy,
Or hath Death freed you from his ancient pain?
    Have ye no springtide, and no burst of May
In flowers and leafy trees, when solemn night
Pants with love-music, and the holy day
Breaks on the ear with songs of heavenly light?

What make ye and what strive for? keep ye thought
Of us, or in new excellence divine
Is old forgot? or do ye count for nought
What the Greek did and what the Florentine?
    We keep your memories well : O in your store
Live not our best joys treasured evermore?

65

AH heavenly joy! But who hath ever heard,
Who hath seen joy, or who shall ever find
Joy's language? There is neither speech nor word;
Nought but itself to teach it to mankind.
    Scarce in our twenty thousand painful days
We may touch something : but there lives—beyond
The best of art, or nature's kindest phase—
The hope whereof our spirit is fain and fond:

The cause of beauty given to man's desires
Writ in the expectancy of starry skies,
The faith which gloweth in our fleeting fires,
The aim of all the good that here we prize;
    Which but to love, pursue and pray for well
Maketh earth heaven, and to forget it, hell.

66

My wearied heart, whenever, after all,
Its loves and yearnings shall be told complete,
When gentle death shall bid it cease to beat,
And from all dear illusions disenthrall:
However then thou shalt appear to call
My fearful heart, since down at others' feet
It bade me kneel so oft, I'll not retreat
From thee, nor fear before thy feet to fall.

And I shall say, ' Receive this loving heart
Which err'd in sorrow only; and in sin
Took no delight; but being forced apart
From thee, without thee hoping thee to win,
Most prized what most thou madest as thou art
On earth, till heaven were open to enter in.'

67

Dreary was winter, wet with changeful sting
Of clinging snowfall and fast-flying frost;
And bitterer northwinds then withheld the spring,
That dallied with her promise till 'twas lost.
    A sunless and half-hearted summer drown'd
The flowers in needful and unwelcom'd rain;
And Autumn with a sad smile fled uncrown'd
From fruitless orchards and unripen'd grain.

But coud the skies of this most desolate year
In its last month learn with our love to glow,
Men yet should rank its cloudless atmosphere
Above the sunsets of five years ago:
    Of my great praise too part should be its own,
Now reckon'd peerless for thy love alone.

68

Away now, lovely Muse, roam and be free :
Our commerce ends for aye, thy task is done :
Tho' to win thee I left all else unwon,
Thou, whom I most have won, art not for me.
My first desire, thou too forgone must be,
Thou too, O much lamented now, tho' none
Will turn to pity thy forsaken son,
Nor thy divine sisters will weep for thee.

None will weep for thee : thou return, O Muse,
To thy Sicilian fields : I once have been
On thy loved hills, and where thou first didst use
Thy sweetly balanced rhyme, O thankless queen,
Have pluck'd and wreath'd thy flowers ; but do thou choose
Some happier brow to wear thy garlands green.

69

Eternal Father, who didst all create,
In whom we live, and to whose bosom move,
To all men be Thy name known, which is Love,
Till its loud praises sound at heaven's high gate.
Perfect Thy kingdom in our passing state,
That here on earth Thou may'st as well approve
Our service, as Thou ownest theirs above,
Whose joy we echo and in pain await.

Grant body and soul each day their daily bread :
And should in spite of grace fresh woe begin,
Even as our anger soon is past and dead
Be Thy remembrance mortal of our sin :
By Thee in paths of peace Thy sheep be led,
And in the vale of terror comforted.

SHORTER POEMS

in Five Books

PREVIOUS EDITIONS

1. *Bks. I–IV. Clarendon Press. Geo. Bell & Sons, Oct. 1890. Reprinted, Nov. 1890, 1891, 1894.*
2. *Bks. I–V. Private Press of H. Daniel. Oxford, 1894.*
3. *Do. do. Clarendon Press. George Bell & Sons, 1896.*
4. *Cheap issue of 3. 1899. Reprinted, 1899.*
5. *Poetical works of R. B. Smith, Elder & Co., 1899, vol. II.*

An account of earlier issues of first four books is given in notes at end of Vol. II of Poetical Works.

SHORTER POEMS

BOOK I

DEDICATED TO H. E. W.

I

ELEGY

CLEAR and gentle stream!
Known and loved so long,
That hast heard the song
And the idle dream
Of my boyish day;
While I once again
Down thy margin stray,
In the selfsame strain
Still my voice is spent,
With my old lament
And my idle dream,
Clear and gentle stream!

Where my old seat was
Here again I sit,
Where the long boughs knit
Over stream and grass
A translucent eaves:

Where back eddies play
Shipwreck with the leaves,
And the proud swans stray,
Sailing one by one
Out of stream and sun,
And the fish lie cool
In their chosen pool.

Many an afternoon
Of the summer day
Dreaming here I lay;
And I know how soon,
Idly at its hour,
First the deep bell hums
From the minster tower,
And then evening comes,
Creeping up the glade,
With her lengthening shade,
And the tardy boon
Of her brightening moon.

Clear and gentle stream !
Ere again I go
Where thou dost not flow,
Well does it beseem
Thee to hear again
Once my youthful song,
That familiar strain
Silent now so long:
Be as I content
With my old lament
And my idle dream,
Clear and gentle stream.

2

ELEGY

THE wood is bare : a river-mist is steeping
　　The trees that winter's chill of life bereaves :
Only their stiffened boughs break silence, weeping
　　　　Over their fallen leaves ;

That lie upon the dank earth brown and rotten,
　　Miry and matted in the soaking wet :
Forgotten with the spring, that is forgotten
　　　　By them that can forget.

Yet it was here we walked when ferns were springing,
　　And through the mossy bank shot bud and blade :—
Here found in summer, when the birds were singing,
　　　　A green and pleasant shade.

'Twas here we loved in sunnier days and greener ;
　　And now, in this disconsolate decay,
I come to see her where I most have seen her,
　　　　And touch the happier day.

For on this path, at every turn and corner,
　　The fancy of her figure on me falls :
Yet walks she with the slow step of a mourner,
　　　　Nor hears my voice that calls.

So through my heart there winds a track of feeling,
　　A path of memory, that is all her own :
Whereto her phantom beauty ever stealing
　　　　Haunts the sad spot alone.

About her steps the trunks are bare, the branches
　　Drip heavy tears upon her downcast head ;
And bleed from unseen wounds that no sun stanches,
　　　　For the year's sun is dead.

And dead leaves wrap the fruits that summer planted:
   And birds that love the South have taken wing.
The wanderer, loitering o'er the scene enchanted,
    Weeps, and despairs of spring.

3

Poor withered rose and dry,
   Skeleton of a rose,
Risen to testify
   To love's sad close:

Treasured for love's sweet sake,
   That of joy past
Thou might'st again awake
   Memory at last.

Yet is thy perfume sweet;
   Thy petals red
Yet tell of summer heat,
   And the gay bed:

Yet, yet recall the glow
   Of the gazing sun,
When at thy bush we two
   Joined hands in one.

But, rose, thou hast not seen,
   Thou hast not wept
The change that passed between,
   Whilst thou hast slept.

To me thou seemest yet
   The dead dream's thrall:
While I live and forget
   Dream, truth and all.

Thou art more fresh than I,
   Rose, sweet and red:
Salt on my pale cheeks lie
   The tears I shed.

4

THE CLIFF-TOP

THE cliff-top has a carpet
 Of lilac, gold and green:
The blue sky bounds the ocean,
 The white clouds scud between.

A flock of gulls are wheeling
 And wailing round my seat;
Above my head the heaven,
 The sea beneath my feet.

THE OCEAN.

Were I a cloud I'd gather
 My skirts up in the air,
And fly I well know whither,
 And rest I well know where.

As pointed the star surely,
 The legend tells of old,
Where the wise kings might offer
 Myrrh, frankincense, and gold;

Above the house I'd hover
 Where dwells my love, and wait
Till haply I might spy her
 Throw back the garden-gate.

There in the summer evening
 I would bedeck the moon;
I would float down and screen her
 From the sun's rays at noon;

And if her flowers should languish,
 Or wither in the drought
Upon her tall white lilies
 I'd pour my heart's blood out:

So if she wore one only,
  And shook not out the rain,
Were I a cloud, O cloudlet,
  I had not lived in vain.

[*A cloud speaks.*

A CLOUD.

But were I thou, O ocean,
  I would not chafe and fret
As thou, because a limit
  To thy desires is set.

I would be blue, and gentle,
  Patient, and calm, and see
If my smiles might not tempt her,
  My love, to come to me.

I'd make my depths transparent,
  And still, that she should lean
O'er the boat's edge to ponder
  The sights that swam between.

I would command strange creatures,
  Of bright hue and quick fin,
To stir the water near her,
  And tempt her bare arm in.

I'd teach her spend the summer
  With me: and I can tell,
That, were I thou, O ocean,
  My love should love me well.

*   *

But on the mad cloud scudded,
  The breeze it blew so stiff;
And the sad ocean bellowed,
  And pounded at the cliff.

5

I HEARD a linnet courting
  His lady in the spring:
His mates were idly sporting,
   Nor stayed to hear him sing
    His song of love.—
I fear my speech distorting
    His tender love.

The phrases of his pleading
  Were full of young delight;
And she that gave him heeding
  Interpreted aright
    His gay, sweet notes,—
So sadly marred in the reading,—
    His tender notes.

And when he ceased, the hearer
  Awaited the refrain,
Till swiftly perching nearer
  He sang his song again,
    His pretty song:—
Would that my verse spake clearer
    His tender song!

Ye happy, airy creatures!
  That in the merry spring
Think not of what misfeatures
  Or cares the year may bring;
    But unto love
Resign your simple natures
    To tender love.

6

DEAR lady, when thou frownest,
    And my true love despisest,
And all thy vows disownest
    That sealed my venture wisest;
I think thy pride's displeasure
Neglects a matchless treasure
Exceeding price and measure.

But when again thou smilest,
    And love for love returnest,
And fear with joy beguilest,
    And takest truth in earnest;
Then, though I sheer adore thee,
The sum of my love for thee
Seems poor, scant, and unworthy.

7

I WILL not let thee go.
Ends all our month-long love in this?
    Can it be summed up so,
    Quit in a single kiss?
    I will not let thee go.

I will not let thee go.
If thy words' breath could scare thy deeds,
    As the soft south can blow
    And toss the feathered seeds,
    Then might I let thee go.

I will not let thee go.
Had not the great sun seen, I might;
    Or were he reckoned slow
    To bring the false to light,
    Then might I let thee go.

I will not let thee go.
The stars that crowd the summer skies
  Have watched us so below
  With all their million eyes,
  I dare not let thee go.

  I will not let thee go.
Have we not chid the changeful moon,
  Now rising late, and now
  Because she set too soon,
  And shall I let thee go?

  I will not let thee go.
Have not the young flowers been content,
  Plucked ere their buds could blow,
  To seal our sacrament?
  I cannot let thee go.

  I will not let thee go.
I hold thee by too many bands:
  Thou sayest farewell, and lo!
  I have thee by the hands,
  And will not let thee go.

8

I FOUND to-day out walking
  The flower my love loves best.
What, when I stooped to pluck it,
  Could dare my hand arrest?

Was it a snake lay curling
  About the root's thick crown?
Or did some hidden bramble
  Tear my hand reaching down?

There was no snake uncurling,
  And no thorn wounded me;
'Twas my heart checked me, sighing
  She is beyond the sea.

9

A POPPY grows upon the shore,
Bursts her twin cup in summer late:
Her leaves are glaucous-green and hoar,
Her petals yellow, delicate.

Oft to her cousins turns her thought,
In wonder if they care that she
Is fed with spray for dew, and caught
By every gale that sweeps the sea.

She has no lovers like the red,
That dances with the noble corn:
Her blossoms on the waves are shed,
Where she stands shivering and forlorn.

10

SOMETIMES when my lady sits by me
My rapture's so great, that I tear
My mind from the thought that she's nigh me,
And strive to forget that she's there.
And sometimes when she is away
Her absence so sorely does try me,
That I shut to my eyes, and assay
To think she is there sitting by me.

II

Long are the hours the sun is above,
But when evening comes I go home to my love.

I'm away the daylight hours and more,
Yet she comes not down to open the door.

She does not meet me upon the stair,—
She sits in my chamber and waits for me there.

As I enter the room she does not move:
I always walk straight up to my love;

And she lets me take my wonted place
At her side, and gaze in her dear dear face.

There as I sit, from her head thrown back
Her hair falls straight in a shadow black.

Aching and hot as my tired eyes be,
She is all that I wish to see.

And in my wearied and toil-dinned ear,
She says all things that I wish to hear.

Dusky and duskier grows the room,
Yet I see her best in the darker gloom.

When the winter eves are early and cold,
The firelight hours are a dream of gold.

And so I sit here night by night,
In rest and enjoyment of love's delight.

But a knock at the door, a step on the stair
Will startle, alas, my love from her chair.

If a stranger comes she will not stay:
At the first alarm she is off and away.

And he wonders, my guest, usurping her throne,
That I sit so much by myself alone.

12

WHO has not walked upon the shore,
And who does not the morning know,
The day the angry gale is o'er,
The hour the wind has ceased to blow?

The horses of the strong south-west
Are pastured round his tropic tent,
Careless how long the ocean's breast
Sob on and sigh for passion spent.

The frightened birds, that fled inland
To house in rock and tower and tree,
Are gathering on the peaceful strand,
To tempt again the sunny sea;

Whereon the timid ships steal out
And laugh to find their foe asleep,
That lately scattered them about,
And drave them to the fold like sheep.

The snow-white clouds he northward chased
Break into phalanx, line, and band:
All one way to the south they haste,
The south, their pleasant fatherland.

From distant hills their shadows creep,
Arrive in turn and mount the lea,
And flit across the downs, and leap
Sheer off the cliff upon the sea;

And sail and sail far out of sight.
But still I watch their fleecy trains,
That piling all the south with light,
Dapple in France the fertile plains.

13

I MADE another song,
In likeness of my love:
And sang it all day long,
Around, beneath, above;
I told my secret out,
That none might be in doubt.

I sang it to the sky,
That veiled his face to hear
How far her azure eye
Outdoes his splendid sphere;
But at her eyelids' name
His white clouds fled for shame.

I told it to the trees,
And to the flowers confest,
And said not one of these
Is like my lily drest;
Nor spathe nor petal dared
Vie with her body bared.

I shouted to the sea,
That set his waves a-prance;
Her floating hair is free,
Free are her feet to dance;
And for thy wrath, I swear
Her frown is more to fear.

And as in happy mood
I walked and sang alone,
At eve beside the wood
I met my love, my own:
And sang to her the song
I had sung all day long.

14

ELEGY

ON A LADY WHOM GRIEF FOR THE DEATH OF HER
BETROTHED KILLED

ASSEMBLE, all ye maidens, at the door,
And all ye loves, assemble; far and wide
Proclaim the bridal, that proclaimed before
Has been deferred to this late eventide:
  For on this night the bride,
  The days of her betrothal over,
  Leaves the parental hearth for evermore;
To-night the bride goes forth to meet her lover.

Reach down the wedding vesture, that has lain
  Yet all unvisited, the silken gown:
Bring out the bracelets, and the golden chain
  Her dearer friends provided: sere and brown
    Bring out the festal crown,
  And set it on her forehead lightly:
  Though it be withered, twine no wreath again;
This only is the crown she can wear rightly.

Cloke her in ermine, for the night is cold,
And wrap her warmly, for the night is long,
In pious hands the flaming torches hold,
While her attendants, chosen from among
  Her faithful virgin throng,
  May lay her in her cedar litter,
  Decking her coverlet with sprigs of gold,
Roses, and lilies white that best befit her.

Sound flute and tabor, that the bridal be
Not without music, nor with these alone;
But let the viol lead the melody,
With lesser intervals, and plaintive moan
      Of sinking semitone ;
    And, all in choir, the virgin voices
  Rest not from singing in skilled harmony
The song that aye the bridegroom's ear rejoices.

Let the priests go before, arrayed in white,
And let the dark-stoled minstrels follow slow,
Next they that bear her, honoured on this night,
And then the maidens, in a double row,
      Each singing soft and low,
    And each on high a torch upstaying :
  Unto her lover lead her forth with light,
With music, and with singing, and with praying.

'Twas at this sheltering hour he nightly came,
And found her trusty window open wide,
And knew the signal of the timorous flame,
That long the restless curtain would not hide
      Her form that stood beside;
    As scarce she dared to be delighted,
  Listening to that sweet tale, that is no shame
To faithful lovers, that their hearts have plighted.

But now for many days the dewy grass
Has shown no markings of his feet at morn :
And watching she has seen no shadow pass
The moonlit walk, and heard no music borne
      Upon her ear forlorn.
    In vain has she looked out to greet him ;
  He has not come, he will not come, alas !
So let us bear her out where she must meet him.

Now to the river bank the priests are come :
The bark is ready to receive its freight :
Let some prepare her place therein, and some
Embark the litter with its slender weight:
     The rest stand by in state,
     And sing her a safe passage over;
   While she is oared across to her new home,
Into the arms of her expectant lover.

And thou, O lover, that art on the watch,
Where, on the banks of the forgetful streams,
The pale indifferent ghosts wander, and snatch
The sweeter moments of their broken dreams,—
     Thou, when the torchlight gleams,
     When thou shalt see the slow procession,
   And when thine ears the fitful music catch,
Rejoice, for thou art near to thy possession.

15

RONDEAU

His poisoned shafts, that fresh he dips
In juice of plants that no bee sips,
He takes, and with his bow renown'd
Goes out upon his hunting ground,
Hanging his quiver at his hips.

He draws them one by one, and clips
Their heads between his finger-tips,
And looses with a twanging sound
       His poisoned shafts.

But if a maiden with her lips
Suck from the wound the blood that drips,
And drink the poison from the wound,
The simple remedy is found
That of their deadly terror strips
       His poisoned shafts.

16

TRIOLET

WHEN first we met we did not guess
That Love would prove so hard a master;
Of more than common friendliness
When first we met we did not guess.
Who could foretell this sore distress,
This irretrievable disaster
When first we met?—We did not guess
That Love would prove so hard a master.

17

TRIOLET

ALL women born are so perverse
No man need boast their love possessing.
If nought seem better, nothing's worse:
All women born are so perverse.
From Adam's wife, that proved a curse
Though God had made her for a blessing,
All women born are so perverse
No man need boast their love possessing.

BOOK II

TO

THE MEMORY OF

G. M. H.

I

MUSE.

WILL Love again awake,
That lies asleep so long?

POET.

O hush! ye tongues that shake
The drowsy night with song.

MUSE.

It is a lady fair
Whom once he deigned to praise,
That at the door doth dare
Her sad complaint to raise.

POET.

She must be fair of face,
As bold of heart she seems,
If she would match her grace
With the delight of dreams.

(242)

Book II

MUSE.

Her beauty would surprise
Gazers on Autumn eves,
Who watched the broad moon rise
Upon the scattered sheaves.

POET.

O sweet must be the voice
He shall descend to hear,
Who doth in Heaven rejoice
His most enchanted ear.

MUSE.

The smile, that rests to play
Upon her lip, foretells
What musical array
Tricks her sweet syllables

POET.

And yet her smiles have danced
In vain, if her discourse
Win not the soul entranced
In divine intercourse.

MUSE.

She will encounter all
This trial without shame,
Her eyes men Beauty call,
And Wisdom is her name.

POET.

Throw back the portals then,
Ye guards, your watch that keep,
Love will awake again
That lay so long asleep.

2

A PASSER-BY

WHITHER, O splendid ship, thy white sails crowding,
  Leaning across the bosom of the urgent West,
That fearest nor sea rising, nor sky clouding,
  Whither away, fair rover, and what thy quest?
  Ah! soon, when Winter has all our vales opprest,
When skies are cold and misty, and hail is hurling,
  Wilt thóu glíde on the blue Pacific, or rest
In a summer haven asleep, thy white sails furling.

I there before thee, in the country that well thou knowest,
  Already arrived am inhaling the odorous air:
I watch thee enter unerringly where thou goest,
  And anchor queen of the strange shipping there,
  Thy sails for awnings spread, thy masts bare;
Nor is aught from the foaming reef to the snow-capped,
    grandest
  Peak, that is over the feathery palms more fair
Than thou, so upright, so stately, and still thou standest.

And yet, O splendid ship, unhailed and nameless,
  I know not if, aiming a fancy, I rightly divine
That thou hast a purpose joyful, a courage blameless,
  Thy port assured in a happier land than mine.
  But for all I have given thee, beauty enough is thine,
As thou, aslant with trim tackle and shrouding,
  From the proud nostril curve of a prow's line
In the offing scatterest foam, thy white sails crowding.

3

LATE SPRING EVENING

I saw the Virgin-mother clad in green,
Walking the sprinkled meadows at sundown;
While yet the moon's cold flame was hung between
The day and night, above the dusky town:
I saw her brighter than the Western gold,
Whereto she faced in splendour to behold.

Her dress was greener than the tenderest leaf
That trembled in the sunset glare aglow:
Herself more delicate than is the brief,
Pink apple-blossom, that May showers lay low,
And more delicious than 's the earliest streak
The blushing rose shows of her crimson cheek.

As if to match the sight that so did please,
A music entered, making passion fain:
Three nightingales sat singing in the trees,
And praised the Goddess for the fallen rain;
Which yet their unseen motions did arouse,
Or parting Zephyrs shook out from the boughs.

And o'er the treetops, scattered in mid air,
The exhausted clouds laden with crimson light
Floated, or seemed to sleep; and, highest there,
One planet broke the lingering ranks of night;
Daring day's company, so he might spy
The Virgin-queen once with his watchful eye.

And when I saw her, then I worshipped her,
And said,—O bounteous Spring, O beauteous Spring,
Mother of all my years, thou who dost stir
My heart to adore thee and my tongue to sing,
Flower of my fruit, of my heart's blood the fire,
Of all my satisfaction the desire !

How art thou every year more beautiful,
Younger for all the winters thou hast cast:
And I, for all my love grows, grow more dull,
Decaying with each season overpast !
In vain to teach him love must man employ thee,
The more he learns the less he can enjoy thee.

4

WOOING

I KNOW not how I came,
New on my knightly journey,
    To win the fairest dame
That graced my maiden tourney.

    Chivalry's lovely prize
With all men's gaze upon her,
    Why did she free her eyes
On me, to do me honour ?

    Ah ! ne'er had I my mind
With such high hope delighted,
    Had she not first inclined,
And with her eyes invited.

    But never doubt I knew,
Having their glance to cheer me,
    Until the day joy grew
Too great, too sure, too near me.

Book II

When hope a fear became,
And passion, grown too tender,
  Now trembled at the shame
Of a despised surrender;

And where my love at first
Saw kindness in her smiling,
  I read her pride, and cursed
The arts of her beguiling.

Till winning less than won,
And liker wooed than wooing,
  Too late I turned undone
Away from my undoing;

And stood beside the door,
Whereto she followed, making
  My hard leave-taking more
Hard by her sweet leave-taking.

Her speech would have betrayed
Her thought, had mine been colder:
  Her eyes' distress had made
A lesser lover bolder.

But no! Fond heart, distrust,
Cried Wisdom, and consider:
  Go free, since go thou must:—
And so farewell I bid her.

And brisk upon my way
I smote the stroke to sever,
  And should have lost that day
My life's delight for ever:

But when I saw her start
And turn aside and tremble;—
  Ah! she was true, her heart
I knew did not dissemble.

5

THERE is a hill beside the silver Thames,
Shady with birch and beech and odorous pine :
And brilliant underfoot with thousand gems
Steeply the thickets to his floods decline.
Straight trees in every place
Their thick tops interlace,
And pendant branches trail their foliage fine
Upon his watery face.

Swift from the sweltering pasturage he flows :
His stream, alert to seek the pleasant shade,
Pictures his gentle purpose, as he goes
Straight to the caverned pool his toil has made.
His winter floods lay bare
The stout roots in the air :
His summer streams are cool, when they have played
Among their fibrous hair.

A rushy island guards the sacred bower,
And hides it from the meadow, where in peace
The lazy cows wrench many a scented flower,
Robbing the golden market of the bees :
And laden barges float
By banks of myosote ;
And scented flag and golden flower-de-lys
Delay the loitering boat.

And on this side the island, where the pool
Eddies away, are tangled mass on mass
The water-weeds, that net the fishes cool,
And scarce allow a narrow stream to pass ;
Where spreading crowfoot mars
The drowning nenuphars,
Waving the tassels of her silken grass
Below her silver stars.

But in the purple pool there nothing grows,
Not the white water-lily spoked with gold;
Though best she loves the hollows, and well knows
On quiet streams her broad shields to unfold:
    Yet should her roots but try
    Within these deeps to lie,
Not her long reaching stalk could ever hold
    Her waxen head so high.

Sometimes an angler comes, and drops his hook
Within its hidden depths, and 'gainst a tree
Leaning his rod, reads in some pleasant book,
Forgetting soon his pride of fishery;
    And dreams, or falls asleep,
    While curious fishes peep
About his nibbled bait, or scornfully
    Dart off and rise and leap.

And sometimes a slow figure 'neath the trees,
In ancient-fashioned smock, with tottering care
Upon a staff propping his weary knees,
May by the pathway of the forest fare:
    As from a buried day
    Across the mind will stray
Some perishing mute shadow,—and unaware
    He passeth on his way.

Else, he that wishes solitude is safe,
Whether he bathe at morning in the stream:
Or lead his love there when the hot hours chafe
The meadows, busy with a blurring steam;
    Or watch, as fades the light,
    The gibbous moon grow bright,
Until her magic rays dance in a dream,
    And glorify the night.

Where is this bower beside the silver Thames?
O pool and flowery thickets, hear my vow!
O trees of freshest foliage and straight stems,
No sharer of my secret I allow:
     Lest ere I come the while
     Strange feet your shades defile;
Or lest the burly oarsman turn his prow
     Within your guardian isle.

6

A WATER-PARTY

LET us, as by this verdant bank we float,
Search down the marge to find some shady pool
Where we may rest awhile and moor our boat,
And bathe our tired limbs in the waters cool.
     Beneath the noonday sun,
     Swiftly, O river, run!

Here is a mirror for Narcissus, see!
I cannot sound it, plumbing with my oar.
Lay the stern in beneath this bowering tree!
Now, stepping on this stump, we are ashore.
     Guard, Hamadryades,
     Our clothes laid by your trees!

How the birds warble in the woods! I pick
The waxen lilies, diving to the root.
But swim not far in the stream, the weeds grow thick,
And hot on the bare head the sunbeams shoot.
     Until our sport be done,
     O merry birds, sing on!

If but to-night the sky be clear, the moon
Will serve us well, for she is near the full.
We shall row safely home; only too soon,—
So pleasant 'tis, whether we float or pull.
     To guide us through the night,
     O summer moon, shine bright!

Book II

THE DOWNS

O BOLD majestic downs, smooth, fair and lonely;
O still solitude, only matched in the skies:
    Perilous in steep places,
    Soft in the level races,
Where sweeping in phantom silence the cloudland flies;
With lovely undulation of fall and rise;
    Entrenched with thickets thorned,
By delicate miniature dainty flowers adorned!

I climb your crown, and lo! a sight surprising
Of sea in front uprising, steep and wide:
    And scattered ships ascending
    To heaven, lost in the blending
Of distant blues, where water and sky divide,
Urging their engines against wind and tide,
    And all so small and slow
They seem to be wearily pointing the way they would go.

The accumulated murmur of soft plashing,
Of waves on rocks dashing and searching the sands,
    Takes my ear, in the veering
    Baffled wind, as rearing
Upright at the cliff, to the gullies and rifts he stands;
And his conquering surges scour out over the lands;
    While again at the foot of the downs
He masses his strength to recover the topmost crowns.

8

SPRING

ODE I

INVITATION TO THE COUNTRY

AGAIN with pleasant green
Has Spring renewed the wood,
And where the bare trunks stood
Are leafy arbours seen ;
And back on budding boughs
Come birds, to court and pair,
Whose rival amorous vows
Amaze the scented air.

The freshets are unbound,
And leaping from the hill,
Their mossy banks refill
With streams of light and sound :
And scattered down the meads,
From hour to hour unfold
A thousand buds and beads
In stars and cups of gold.

Now hear, and see, and note,
The farms are all astir,
And every labourer
Has doffed his winter coat;
And how with specks of white
They dot the brown hillside,
Or jaunt and sing outright
As by their teams they stride.

Book II

They sing to feel the Sun
Regain his wanton strength;
To know the year at length
Rewards their labour done;
To see the rootless stake
They set bare in the ground,
Burst into leaf, and shake
Its grateful scent around.

Ah now an evil lot
Is his, who toils for gain,
Where crowded chimneys stain
The heavens his choice forgot;
'Tis on the blighted trees
That deck his garden dim,
And in the tainted breeze,
That sweet Spring comes to him.

Far sooner I would choose
The life of brutes that bask,
Than set myself a task,
Which inborn powers refuse:
And rather far enjoy
The body, than invent
A duty, to destroy
The ease which nature sent;

And country life I praise,
And lead, because I find
The philosophic mind
Can take no middle ways;
She will not leave her love
To mix with men, her art
Is all to strive above
The crowd, or stand apart.

Thrice happy he, the rare
Prometheus, who can play
With hidden things, and lay
New realms of nature bare;
Whose venturous step has trod
Hell underfoot, and won
A crown from man and God
For all that he has done.—

That highest gift of all,
Since crabbèd fate did flood
My heart with sluggish blood,
I look not mine to call;
But, like a truant freed,
Fly to the woods, and claim
A pleasure for the deed
Of my inglorious name:

And am content, denied
The best, in choosing right;
For Nature can delight
Fancies unoccupied
With ecstasies so sweet
As none can even guess,
Who walk not with the feet
Of joy in idleness.

Then leave your joyless ways,
My friend, my joys to see.
The day you come shall be
The choice of chosen days:
You shall be lost, and learn
New being, and forget
The world, till your return
Shall bring your first regret.

Book II

SPRING

ODE II

REPLY

BEHOLD! the radiant Spring,
In splendour decked anew,
Down from her heaven of blue
Returns on sunlit wing:
The zephyrs of her train
In fleecy clouds disport,
And birds to greet her reign
Summon their silvan court.

And here in street and square
The prisoned trees contest
Her favour with the best,
To robe themselves full fair:
And forth their buds provoke,
Forgetting winter brown,
And all the mire and smoke
That wrapped the dingy town.

Now he that loves indeed
His pleasure must awake,
Lest any pleasure take
Its flight, and he not heed;
For of his few short years
Another now invites
His hungry soul, and cheers
His life with new delights.

(255)

And who loves Nature more
Than he, whose painful art
Has taught and skilled his heart
To read her skill and lore?
Whose spirit leaps more high,
Plucking the pale primrose,
Than his whose feet must fly
The pasture where it grows?

One long in city pent
Forgets, or must complain:
But think not I can stain
My heaven with discontent;
Nor wallow with that sad,
Backsliding herd, who cry
That Truth must make man bad,
And pleasure is a lie.

Rather while Reason lives
To mark me from the beast,
I'll teach her serve at least
To heal the wound she gives:
Nor need she strain her powers
Beyond a common flight,
To make the passing hours
Happy from morn till night.

Since health our toil rewards,
And strength is labour's prize,
I hate not, nor despise
The work my lot accords;
Nor fret with fears unkind
The tender joys, that bless
My hard-won peace of mind,
In hours of idleness.

Then what charm company
Can give, know I,—if wine
Go round, or throats combine
To set dumb music free.
Or deep in wintertide
When winds without make moan,
I love my own fireside
Not least when most alone.

Then oft I turn the page
In which our country's name,
Spoiling the Greek of fame,
Shall sound in every age:
Or some Terentian play
Renew, whose excellent
Adjusted folds betray
How once Menander went.

Or if grave study suit
The yet unwearied brain,
Plato can teach again,
And Socrates dispute;
Till fancy in a dream
Confront their souls with mine,
Crowning the mind supreme,
And her delights divine.

While pleasure yet can be
Pleasant, and fancy sweet,
I bid all care retreat
From my philosophy;
Which, when I come to try
Your simpler life, will find,
I doubt not, joys to vie
With those I leave behind.

S

10

ELEGY

AMONG THE TOMBS

SAD, sombre place, beneath whose antique yews
I come, unquiet sorrows to control;
Amid thy silent mossgrown graves to muse
With my neglected solitary soul;
And to poetic sadness care confide,
Trusting sweet Melancholy for my guide:

They will not ask why in thy shades I stray,
Among the tombs finding my rare delight,
Beneath the sun at indolent noonday,
Or in the windy moon-enchanted night,
Who have once reined in their steeds at any shrine,
And given them water from the well divine.—

The orchards are all ripened, and the sun
Spots the deserted gleanings with decay;
The seeds are perfected: his work is done,
And Autumn lingers but to outsmile the May;
Bidding his tinted leaves glide, bidding clear
Unto clear skies the birds applaud the year.

Lo, here I sit, and to the world I call,
The world my solemn fancy leaves behind,
Come! pass within the inviolable wall,
Come pride, come pleasure, come distracted mind;
Within the fated refuge, hither, turn,
And learn your wisdom ere 'tis late to learn.

Come with me now, and taste the fount of tears;
For many eyes have sanctified this spot,
Where grief's unbroken lineage endears
The charm untimely Folly injures not,
And slays the intruding thoughts, that overleap
The simple fence its holiness doth keep.

Book II

Read the worn names of the forgotten dead,
Their pompous legends will no smile awake;
Even the vainglorious title o'er the head
Wins its pride pardon for its sorrow's sake;
And carven Loves scorn not their dusty prize,
Though fallen so far from tender sympathies.

Here where a mother laid her only son,
Here where a lover left his bride, below
The treasured names their own are added on
To those whom they have followed long ago:
Sealing the record of the tears they shed,
That 'where their treasure there their hearts are fled.'

Grandfather, father, son, and then again
Child, grandchild, and great-grandchild laid beneath
Numbered in turn among the sons of men,
And gathered each one in his turn to death:
While he that occupies their house and name
To-day,—to-morrow too their grave shall claim.

And where are all their spirits? Ah! could we tell
The manner of our being when we die,
And see beyond the scene we know so well
The country that so much obscured doth lie!
With brightest visions our fond hopes repair,
Or crown our melancholy with despair;

From death, still death, still would a comfort come:
Since of this world the essential joy must fall
In all distributed, in each thing some,
In nothing all, and all complete in all;
Till pleasure, ageing to her full increase,
Puts on perfection, and is throned in peace.

Yea, sweetest peace, unsought-for, undesired,
Loathed and misnamed, 'tis thee I worship here :
Though in most black habiliments attired,
Thou art sweet peace, and thee I cannot fear.
Nay, were my last hope quenched, I here would sit
And praise the annihilation of the pit.

Nor quickly disenchanted will my feet
Back to the busy town return, but yet
Linger, ere I my loving friends would greet,
Or touch their hands, or share without regret
The warmth of that kind hearth, whose sacred ties
Only shall dim with tears my dying eyes.

II

DEJECTION

WHEREFORE to-night so full of care,
My soul, revolving hopeless strife,
Pointing at hindrance, and the bare
Painful escapes of fitful life?

Shaping the doom that may befall
By precedent of terror past :
By love dishonoured, and the call
Of friendship slighted at the last?

By treasured names, the little store
That memory out of wreck could save
Of loving hearts, that gone before
Call their old comrade to the grave?

O soul, be patient : thou shalt find
A little matter mend all this ;
Some strain of music to thy mind,
Some praise for skill not spent amiss.

Again shall pleasure overflow
Thy cup with sweetness, thou shalt taste
Nothing but sweetness, and shalt grow
Half sad for sweetness run to waste.

O happy life! I hear thee sing,
O rare delight of mortal stuff!
I praise my days for all they bring,
Yet are they only not enough.

12

MORNING HYMN

O GOLDEN Sun, whose ray
My path illumineth:
Light of the circling day,
Whose night is birth and death:

That dost not stint the prime
Of wise and strong, nor stay
The changeful ordering time,
That brings their sure decay:

Though thou, the central sphere,
Dost seem to turn around
Thy creature world, and near
As father fond art found;

Thereon, as from above
To shine, and make rejoice
With beauty, life, and love,
The garden of thy choice,

To dress the jocund Spring
With bounteous promise gay
Of hotter months, that bring
The full perfected day;

To touch with richest gold
The ripe fruit, ere it fall;
And smile through cloud and cold
On Winter's funeral.

Now with resplendent flood
Gladden my waking eyes,
And stir my slothful blood
To joyous enterprise.

Arise, arise, as when
At first God said LIGHT BE!
That He might make us men
With eyes His light to see.

Scatter the clouds that hide
The face of heaven, and show
Where sweet Peace doth abide,
Where Truth and Beauty grow.

Awaken, cheer, adorn,
Invite, inspire, assure
The joys that praise thy morn,
The toil thy noons mature:

And soothe the eve of day,
That darkens back to death;
O golden Sun, whose ray
Our path illumineth!

13

I HAVE loved flowers that fade,
Within whose magic tents
Rich hues have marriage made
With sweet unmemoried scents:
A honeymoon delight,—
A joy of love at sight,
That ages in an hour:—
My song be like a flower!

I have loved airs, that die
Before their charm is writ
Along a liquid sky
Trembling to welcome it.
Notes, that with pulse of fire
Proclaim the spirit's desire,
Then die, and are nowhere:—
My song be like an air!

Die, song, die like a breath,
And wither as a bloom:
Fear not a flowery death,
Dread not an airy tomb!
Fly with delight, fly hence!
'Twas thine love's tender sense
To feast; now on thy bier
Beauty shall shed a tear.

BOOK III

TO

R. W. D.

I

O MY vague desires!
Ye lambent flames of the soul, her offspring fires:
That are my soul herself in pangs sublime
Rising and flying to heaven before her time:

What doth tempt you forth
To drown in the south or shiver in the frosty north?
What seek ye or find ye in your random flying,
Ever soaring aloft, soaring and dying?

Joy, the joy of flight!
They hide in the sun, they flare and dance in the night;
Gone up, gone out of sight: and ever again
Follow fresh tongues of fire, fresh pangs of pain.

Ah! they burn my soul,
The fires, devour my soul that once was whole:
She is scattered in fiery phantoms day by day,
But whither, whither? ay whither? away, away!

Could I but control
These vague desires, these leaping flames of the soul:
Could I but quench the fire: ah! could I stay
My soul that flieth, alas, and dieth away!

LONDON SNOW

WHEN men were all asleep the snow came flying,
In large white flakes falling on the city brown,
Stealthily and perpetually settling and loosely lying,
   Hushing the latest traffic of the drowsy town;
Deadening, muffling, stifling its murmurs failing;
Lazily and incessantly floating down and down:
   Silently sifting and veiling road, roof and railing;
Hiding difference, making unevenness even,
Into angles and crevices softly drifting and sailing.
   All night it fell, and when full inches seven
It lay in the depth of its uncompacted lightness,
The clouds blew off from a high and frosty heaven;
   And all woke earlier for the unaccustomed brightness
Of the winter dawning, the strange unheavenly glare:
The eye marvelled—marvelled at the dazzling whiteness;
   The ear hearkened to the stillness of the solemn air;
No sound of wheel rumbling nor of foot falling,
And the busy morning cries came thin and spare.
   Then boys I heard, as they went to school, calling,
They gathered up the crystal manna to freeze
Their tongues with tasting, their hands with snowballing;
   Or rioted in a drift, plunging up to the knees;
Or peering up from under the white-mossed wonder,
'O look at the trees!' they cried, 'O look at the trees!'
   With lessened load a few carts creak and blunder,
Following along the white deserted way,
A country company long dispersed asunder:
   When now already the sun, in pale display
Standing by Paul's high dome, spread forth below
His sparkling beams, and awoke the stir of the day.

For now doors open, and war is waged with the snow;
And trains of sombre men, past tale of number,
Tread long brown paths, as toward their toil they go:
    But even for them awhile no cares encumber
Their minds diverted; the daily word is unspoken,
The daily thoughts of labour and sorrow slumber
At the sight of the beauty that greets them, for the charm
    they have broken.

3

THE VOICE OF NATURE

I STAND on the cliff and watch the veiled sun paling
    A silver field afar in the mournful sea,
The scourge of the surf, and plaintive gulls sailing
    At ease on the gale that smites the shuddering lea:
        Whose smile severe and chaste
    June never hath stirred to vanity, nor age defaced.
In lofty thought strive, O spirit, for ever:
In courage and strength pursue thine own endeavour.

Ah! if it were only for thee, thou restless ocean
    Of waves that follow and roar, the sweep of the tides;
Wer't only for thee, impetuous wind, whose motion
    Precipitate all o'errides, and turns, nor abides:
        For you sad birds and fair,
    Or only for thee, bleak cliff, erect in the air;
Then well could I read wisdom in every feature,
O well should I understand the voice of Nature.

But far away, I think, in the Thames valley,
    The silent river glides by flowery banks:
And birds sing sweetly in branches that arch an alley
    Of cloistered trees, moss-grown in their ancient ranks:
        Where if a light air stray,
    'Tis laden with hum of bees and scent of may.

Love and peace be thine, O spirit, for ever :
Serve thy sweet desire : despise endeavour.

And if it were only for thee, entrancèd river,
   That scarce dost rock the lily on her airy stem,
Or stir a wave to murmur, or a rush to quiver;
     Wer't but for the woods, and summer asleep in them :
       For you my bowers green,
   My hedges of rose and woodbine, with walks between,
Then well could I read wisdom in every feature,
O well should I understand the voice of Nature.

4

ON A DEAD CHILD

Perfect little body, without fault or stain on thee,
   With promise of strength and manhood full and fair !
     Though cold and stark and bare,
The bloom and the charm of life doth awhile remain on thee.

Thy mother's treasure wert thou ;—alas ! no longer
   To visit her heart with wondrous joy ; to be
     Thy father's pride ;—ah, he
Must gather his faith together, and his strength make stronger.

To me, as I move thee now in the last duty,
   Dost thou with a turn or gesture anon respond ;
     Startling my fancy fond
With a chance attitude of the head, a freak of beauty.

Thy hand clasps, as 'twas wont, my finger, and holds it :
   But the grasp is the clasp of Death, heartbreaking and stiff ;
     Yet feels to my hand as if
'Twas still thy will, thy pleasure and trust that enfolds it.

(267)

So I lay thee there, thy sunken eyelids closing,—
  Go lie thou there in thy coffin, thy last little bed !—
      Propping thy wise, sad head,
Thy firm, pale hands across thy chest disposing.

So quiet ! doth the change content thee ?—Death, whither
      hath he taken thee ?
  To a world, do I think, that rights the disaster of this ?
      The vision of which I miss,
Who weep for the body, and wish but to warm thee and
      awaken thee ?

Ah ! little at best can all our hopes avail us
  To lift this sorrow, or cheer us, when in the dark,
      Unwilling, alone we embark,
And the things we have seen and have known and have
      heard of, fail us.

5

THE PHILOSOPHER TO HIS MISTRESS

BECAUSE thou canst not see,
Because thou canst not know
The black and hopeless woe
That hath encompassed me :
Because, should I confess
The thought of my despair,
My words would wound thee less
Than swords can hurt the air :

Because with thee I seem
As one invited near
To taste the faery cheer
Of spirits in a dream ;
Of whom he knoweth nought
Save that they vie to make
All motion, voice and thought
A pleasure for his sake :

(268)

Therefore more sweet and strange
Has been the mystery
Of thy long love to me,
That doth not quit, nor change,
Nor tax my solemn heart,
That kisseth in a gloom,
Knowing not who thou art
That givest, nor to whom.

Therefore the tender touch
Is more ; more dear the smile :
And thy light words beguile
My wisdom overmuch :
And O with swiftness fly
The fancies of my song
To happy worlds, where I
Still in thy love belong.

6

HASTE on, my joys ! your treasure lies
    In swift, unceasing flight.
O haste : for while your beauty flies
    I seize your full delight.
Lo ! I have seen the scented flower,
    Whose tender stems I cull,
For her brief date and meted hour
    Appear more beautiful.

O youth, O strength, O most divine
    For that so short ye prove ;
Were but your rare gifts longer mine,
    Ye scarce would win my love.
Nay, life itself the heart would spurn,
    Did once the days restore
The days, that once enjoyed return,
    Return—ah ! nevermore.

7

INDOLENCE

WE left the city when the summer day
Had verged already on its hot decline,
And charmèd Indolence in languor lay
In her gay gardens, 'neath her towers divine:
'Farewell,' we said, 'dear city of youth and dream!'
And in our boat we stepped and took the stream.

All through that idle afternoon we strayed
Upon our proposed travel well begun,
As loitering by the woodland's dreamy shade,
Past shallow islets floating in the sun,
Or searching down the banks for rarer flowers
We lingered out the pleasurable hours.

Till when that loveliest came, which mowers home
Turns from their longest labour, as we steered
Along a straitened channel flecked with foam,
We lost our landscape wide, and slowly neared
An ancient bridge, that like a blind wall lay
Low on its buried vaults to block the way.

Then soon the narrow tunnels broader showed,
Where with its arches three it sucked the mass
Of water, that in swirl thereunder flowed,
Or stood piled at the piers waiting to pass;
And pulling for the middle span, we drew
The tender blades aboard and floated through.

But past the bridge what change we found below!
The stream, that all day long had laughed and played
Betwixt the happy shires, ran dark and slow,
And with its easy flood no murmur made:
And weeds spread on its surface, and about
The stagnant margin reared their stout heads out.

Book III

Upon the left high elms, with giant wood
Skirting the water-meadows, interwove
Their slumbrous crowns, o'ershadowing where they stood
The floor and heavy pillars of the grove:
And in the shade, through reeds and sedges dank,
A footpath led along the moated bank.

Across, all down the right, an old brick wall,
Above and o'er the channel, red did lean;
Here buttressed up, and bulging there to fall,
Tufted with grass and plants and lichen green;
And crumbling to the flood, which at its base
Slid gently nor disturbed its mirrored face.

Sheer on the wall the houses rose, their backs
All windowless, neglected and awry,
With tottering coigns, and crooked chimney stacks;
And here and there an unused door, set high
Above the fragments of its mouldering stair,
With rail and broken step led out on air.

Beyond, deserted wharfs and vacant sheds,
With empty boats and barges moored along,
And rafts half-sunken, fringed with weedy shreds,
And sodden beams, once soaked to season strong.
No sight of man, nor sight of life, no stroke,
No voice the somnolence and silence broke.

Then I who rowed leant on my oar, whose drip
Fell without sparkle, and I rowed no more;
And he that steered moved neither hand nor lip,
But turned his wondering eye from shore to shore;
And our trim boat let her swift motion die,
Between the dim reflections floating by.

8

I PRAISE the tender flower,
That on a mournful day
Bloomed in my garden bower
And made the winter gay.
Its loveliness contented
　My heart tormented.

I praise the gentle maid
Whose happy voice and smile
To confidence betrayed
My doleful heart awhile:
And gave my spirit deploring
　Fresh wings for soaring.

The maid for very fear
Of love I durst not tell:
The rose could never hear,
Though I bespake her well:
So in my song I bind them
　For all to find them.

9

A WINTER'S night with the snow about:
'Twas silent within and cold without:
Both father and mother to bed were gone:
The son sat yet by the fire alone.

He gazed on the fire, and dreamed again
Of one that was now no more among men:
As still he sat and never aware
How close was the spirit beside his chair.

Nay, sad were his thoughts, for he wept and said
Ah, woe for the dead! ah, woe for the dead!
How heavy the earth lies now on her breast,
The lips that I kissed, and the hand I pressed.

The spirit he saw not, he could not hear
The comforting word she spake in his ear:
His heart in the grave with her mouldering clay
No welcome gave—and she fled away.

10

My bed and pillow are cold,
My heart is faint with dread,
The air hath an odour of mould,
I dream I lie with the dead:
    I cannot move,
    O come to me, Love,
    Or else I am dead.

The feet I hear on the floor
Tread heavily overhead:
O Love, come down to the door,
Come, Love, come, ere I be dead:
    Make shine thy light,
    O Love, in the night;
    Or else I am dead.

11

O THOU unfaithful, still as ever dearest
That in thy beauty to my eyes appearest
In fancy rising now to re-awaken
    My love unshaken;

All thou'st forgotten, but no change can free thee,
No hate unmake thee; as thou wert I see thee,
And am contented, eye from fond eye meeting
    Its ample greeting.

O thou my star of stars, among things wholly
Devoted, sacred, dim and melancholy,
The only joy of all the joys I cherished
      That hast not perished,

Why now on others squand'rest thou the treasure,
That to be jealous of is still my pleasure :
As still I dream 'tis me whom thou invitest,
      Me thou delightest ?

But day by day my joy hath feebler being,
The fading picture tires my painful seeing,
And faery fancy leaves her habitation
      To desolation.

Of two things open left for lovers parted
'Twas thine to scorn the past and go lighthearted :
But I would ever dream I still possess it,
      And thus caress it.

12

    Thou didst delight my eyes :
    Yet who am I ? nor first
    Nor last nor best, that durst
    Once dream of thee for prize ;
    Nor this the only time
    Thou shalt set love to rhyme.

    Thou didst delight my ear :
    Ah ! little praise ; thy voice
    Makes other hearts rejoice,
    Makes all ears glad that hear ;
    And short my joy : but yet,
    O song, do not forget !

Book III

For what wert thou to me?
How shall I say?   The moon,
That poured her midnight noon
Upon his wrecking sea;—
A sail, that for a day
Has cheered the castaway.

13

Joy, sweetest lifeborn joy, where dost thou dwell?
Upon the formless moments of our being
Flitting, to mock the ear that heareth well,
To escape the trainèd eye that strains in seeing,
Dost thou fly with us whither we are fleeing;
Or home in our creations, to withstand
Black-wingèd death, that slays the making hand?

The making mind, that must untimely perish
Amidst its work which time may not destroy,
The beauteous forms which man shall love to cherish,
The glorious songs that combat earth's annoy?
Thou dost dwell here, I know, divinest Joy:
But they who build thy towers fair and strong,
Of all that toil, feel most of care and wrong.

Sense is so tender, O and hope so high,
That common pleasures mock their hope and sense;
And swifter than doth lightning from the sky
The ecstasy they pine for flashes hence,
Leaving the darkness and the woe immense,
Wherewith it seems no thread of life was woven,
Nor doth the track remain where once 'twas cloven.

And heaven and all the stable elements
That guard God's purpose mock us, though the mind
Be spent in searching: for his old intents
We see were never for our joy designed:
They shine as doth the bright sun on the blind,

Or like his pensioned stars, that hymn above
His praise, but not toward us, that God is Love.

For who so well hath wooed the maiden hours
As quite to have won the worth of their rich show,
To rob the night of mystery, or the flowers
Of their sweet delicacy ere they go?
Nay, even the dear occasion when we know,
We miss the joy, and on the gliding day
The special glories float and pass away.

Only life's common plod: still to repair
The body and the thing which perisheth:
The soil, the smutch, the toil and ache and wear,
The grinding enginry of blood and breath,
Pain's random darts, the heartless spade of death;
All is but grief, and heavily we call
On the last terror for the end of all.

Then comes the happy moment: not a stir
In any tree, no portent in the sky:
The morn doth neither hasten nor defer,
The morrow hath no name to call it by,
But life and joy are one,—we know not why,—
As though our very blood long breathless lain
Had tasted of the breath of God again.

And having tasted it I speak of it,
And praise him thinking how I trembled then
When his touch strengthened me, as now I sit
In wonder, reaching out beyond my ken,
Reaching to turn the day back, and my pen
Urging to tell a tale which told would seem
The witless phantasy of them that dream.

But O most blessèd truth, for truth thou art,
Abide thou with me till my life shall end.
Divinity hath surely touched my heart;
I have possessed more joy than earth can lend:
I may attain what time shall never spend.
Only let not my duller days destroy
The memory of thy witness and my joy.

14

THE full moon from her cloudless skies
Turneth her face, I think, on me;
And from the hour when she doth rise
Till when she sets, none else will see.

One only other ray she hath,
That makes an angle close with mine,
And glancing down its happy path
Upon another spot doth shine.

But that ray too is sent to me,
For where it lights there dwells my heart:
And if I were where I would be,
Both rays would shine, love, where thou art.

15

AWAKE, my heart, to be loved, awake, awake!
The darkness silvers away, the morn doth break,
It leaps in the sky: unrisen lustres slake
The o'ertaken moon.   Awake, O heart, awake!

She too that loveth awaketh and hopes for thee;
Her eyes already have sped the shades that flee,
Already they watch the path thy feet shall take:
Awake, O heart, to be loved, awake, awake!

And if thou tarry from her,—if this could be,—
She cometh herself, O heart, to be loved, to thee;
For thee would unashamèd herself forsake:
Awake to be loved, my heart, awake, awake!

Awake, the land is scattered with light, and see,
Uncanopied sleep is flying from field and tree :
And blossoming boughs of April in laughter shake ;
Awake, O heart, to be loved, awake, awake !

Lo all things wake and tarry and look for thee :
She looketh and saith, 'O sun, now bring him to me.
Come more adored, O adored, for his coming's sake,
And awake my heart to be loved : awake, awake !'

16

SONG

I LOVE my lady's eyes
Above the beauties rare
She most is wont to prize,
Above her sunny hair,
And all that face to face
Her glass repeats of grace.

For those are still the same
To her and all that see :
But oh ! her eyes will flame
When they do look on me :
And so above the rest
I love her eyes the best.

Now say, [*Say, O say ! saith the music*]
　　who likes my song ?—
I knew you by your eyes,
That rest on nothing long,
And have forgot surprise ;
And stray [*Stray, O stray ! saith the music*]
　　as mine will stray,
The while my love 's away.

Book III

17

Since thou, O fondest and truest,
Hast loved me best and longest,
And now with trust the strongest
The joy of my heart renewest;

Since thou art dearer and dearer
While other hearts grow colder
And ever, as love is older,
More lovingly drawest nearer:

Since now I see in the measure
Of all my giving and taking,
Thou wert my hand in the making,
The sense and soul of my pleasure;

The good I have ne'er repaid thee
In heaven I pray be recorded,
And all thy love rewarded
By God, thy master that made thee.

18

The evening darkens over
After a day so bright
The windcapt waves discover
That wild will be the night.
There's sound of distant thunder.

The latest sea-birds hover
Along the cliff's sheer height;
As in the memory wander
Last flutterings of delight,
White wings lost on the white.

There's not a ship in sight;
And as the sun goes under
Thick clouds conspire to cover
The moon that should rise yonder.
Thou art alone, fond lover.

19

O YOUTH whose hope is high,
Who dost to Truth aspire,
Whether thou live or die,
O look not back nor tire.

Thou that art bold to fly
Through tempest, flood and fire,
Nor dost not shrink to try
Thy heart in torments dire:

If thou canst Death defy,
If thy Faith is entire,
Press onward, for thine eye
Shall see thy heart's desire.

Beauty and love are nigh,
And with their deathless quire
Soon shall thine eager cry
Be numbered and expire.

BOOK IV

TO

L. B. C. L. M.

I

I LOVE all beauteous things,
   I seek and adore them ;
God hath no better praise,
And man in his hasty days
   Is honoured for them.

I too will something make
   And joy in the making ;
Altho' to-morrow it seem
Like the empty words of a dream
   Remembered on waking.

2

My spirit sang all day
   O my joy.
Nothing my tongue could say,
   Only My joy !

My heart an echo caught—
   O my joy—
And spake, Tell me thy thought,
   Hide not thy joy.

My eyes gan peer around,—
  O my joy—
What beauty hast thou found?
  Shew us thy joy.

My jealous ears grew whist;—
  O my joy—
Music from heaven is 't,
  Sent for our joy?

She also came and heard;
  O my joy,
What, said she, is this word?
  What is thy joy?

And I replied, O see,
  O my joy,
'Tis thee, I cried, 'tis thee:
  Thou art my joy.

3

THE upper skies are palest blue
Mottled with pearl and fretted snow:
With tattered fleece of inky hue
Close overhead the storm-clouds go.

Their shadows fly along the hill
And o'er the crest mount one by one:
The whitened planking of the mill
Is now in shade and now in sun.

4

THE clouds have left the sky,
The wind hath left the sea,
The half-moon up on high
Shrinketh her face of dree

She lightens on the comb
Of leaden waves, that roar
And thrust their hurried foam
Up on the dusky shore.

Behind the western bars
The shrouded day retreats,
And unperceived the stars
Steal to their sovran seats.

And whiter grows the foam,
The small moon lightens more;
And as I turn me home,
My shadow walks before.

5

LAST WEEK OF FEBRUARY, 1890

HARK to the merry birds, hark how they sing!
    Although 'tis not yet spring
        And keen the air;
Hale Winter, half resigning ere he go,
    Doth to his heiress shew
        His kingdom fair.

In patient russet is his forest spread,
    All bright with bramble red,
        With beechen moss
And holly sheen: the oak silver and stark
    Sunneth his aged bark
        And wrinkled boss.

But neath the ruin of the withered brake
    Primroses now awake
       From nursing shades :
The crumpled carpet of the dry leaves brown
    Avails not to keep down
       The hyacinth blades.

The hazel hath put forth his tassels ruffed ;
    The willow's flossy tuft
       Hath slipped him free :
The rose amid her ransacked orange hips
    Braggeth the tender tips
       Of bowers to be.

A black rook stirs the branches here and there,
    Foraging to repair
       His broken home :
And hark, on the ash-boughs ! Never thrush did sing
    Louder in praise of spring,
       When spring is come.

6

APRIL, 1885

WANTON with long delay the gay spring leaping cometh ;
The blackthorn starreth now his bough on the eve of May :
All day in the sweet box-tree the bee for pleasure hummeth :
The cuckoo sends afloat his note on the air all day.

Now dewy nights again and rain in gentle shower
At root of tree and flower have quenched the winter's drouth :
On high the hot sun smiles, and banks of cloud uptower
In bulging heads that crowd for miles the dazzling south.

7

Gáy Róbin is seen no more :
   He is gone with the snow,
   For winter is o'er
   And Robin will go.
In need he was fed, and now he is fled
   Away to his secret nest.
   No more will he stand
   Begging for crumbs,
   No longer he comes
   Beseeching our hand
   And showing his breast
   At window and door :—
Gay Robin is seen no more.

Blithe Robin is heard no more :
   He gave us his song
   When summer was o'er
   And winter was long :
He sang for his bread and now he is fled
   Away to his secret nest.
   And there in the green
   Early and late
   Alone to his mate
   He pipeth unseen
   And swelleth his breast ;
   For us it is o'er :—
Blithe Robin is heard no more.

8

Spring goeth all in white,
Crowned with milk-white may :
In fleecy flocks of light
O'er heaven the white clouds stray :

White butterflies in the air ;
White daisies prank the ground :
The cherry and hoary pear
Scatter their snow around.

9

My eyes for beauty pine,
My soul for Goddës grace :
No other care nor hope is mine ;
To heaven I turn my face.

One splendour thence is shed
From all the stars above :
'Tis namèd when God's name is said,
'Tis Love, 'tis heavenly Love.

And every gentle heart,
That burns with true desire,
Is lit from eyes that mirror part
Of that celestial fire.

10

O Love, my muse, how was 't for me
    Among the best to dare,
In thy high courts that bowed the knee
    With sacrifice and prayer ?

Their mighty offerings at thy shrine
  Shamed me, who nothing bore
Their suits were mockeries of mine,
  I sued for so much more.

Full many I met that crowned with bay
  In triumph home returned,
And many a master on the way
  Proud of the prize I scorned.

I wished no garland on my head
  Nor treasure in my hand;
My gift the longing that me led,
  My prayer thy high command,

My love, my muse; and when I spake
  Thou mad'st me thine that day,
And more than hundred hearts could take
  Gav'st me to bear away.

I I

Love on my heart from heaven fell,
Soft as the dew on flowers of spring,
Sweet as the hidden drops that swell
Their honey-throated chalicing.

Now never from him do I part,
Hosanna evermore I cry:
I taste his savour in my heart,
And bid all praise him as do I.

Without him noughtsoever is,
Nor was afore, nor e'er shall be:
Nor any other joy than his
Wish I for mine to comfort me.

12

THE hill pines were sighing,
O'ercast and chill was the day :
A mist in the valley lying
Blotted the pleasant May.

But deep in the glen's bosom
Summer slept in the fire
Of the odorous gorse-blossom
And the hot scent of the brier.

A ribald cuckoo clamoured,
And out of the copse the stroke
Of the iron axe that hammered
The iron heart of the oak.

Anon a sound appalling,
As a hundred years of pride
Crashed, in the silence falling :
And the shadowy pine-trees sighed.

13

THE WINDMILL

THE green corn waving in the dale,
The ripe grass waving on the hill :
I lean across the paddock pale
And gaze upon the giddy mill.

Its hurtling sails a mighty sweep
Cut thro' the air : with rushing sound
Each strikes in fury down the steep,
Rattles, and whirls in chase around.

Beside his sacks the miller stands
On high within the open door:
A book and pencil in his hands,
His grist and meal he reckoneth o'er.

His tireless merry slave the wind
Is busy with his work to-day:
From whencesoe'er, he comes to grind;
He hath a will and knows the way.

He gives the creaking sails a spin,
The circling millstones faster flee,
The shuddering timbers groan within,
And down the shoot the meal runs free.

The miller giveth him no thanks,
And doth not much his work o'erlook:
He stands beside the sacks, and ranks
The figures in his dusty book.

14

WHEN June is come, then all the day
I'll sit with my love in the scented hay:
And watch the sunshot palaces high,
That the white clouds build in the breezy sky.

She singeth, and I do make her a song,
And read sweet poems the whole day long:
Unseen as we lie in our haybuilt home.
O life is delight when June is come.

15

THE pinks along my garden walks
Have all shot forth their summer stalks,
Thronging their buds 'mong tulips hot,
    And blue forget-me-not.

Their dazzling snows forth-bursting soon
Will lade the idle breath of June :
And waken thro' the fragrant night
　　　To steal the pale moonlight.

The nightingale at end of May
Lingers each year for their display ,
Till when he sees their blossoms blown,
　　　　He knows the spring is flown.

June's birth they greet, and when their bloom
Dislustres, withering on his tomb,
Then summer hath a shortening day;
　　　　And steps slow to decay.

16

　　FIRE of heaven, whose starry arrow
　　Pierces the veil of timeless night :
　　Molten spheres, whose tempests narrow
　　Their floods to a beam of gentle light,
To charm with a moon-ray quenched from fire
The land of delight, the land of desire !

　　Smile of love, a flower planted,
　　Sprung in the garden of joy that art :
　　Eyes that shine with a glow enchanted,
　　Whose spreading fires encircle my heart,
And warm with a noon-ray drenched in fire
My land of delight, my land of desire !

17

　　THE idle life I lead
　　Is like a pleasant sleep,
　　Wherein I rest and heed
　　The dreams that by me sweep

And still of all my dreams
In turn so swiftly past,
Each in its fancy seems
A nobler than the last.

And every eve I say,
Noting my step in bliss,
That I have known no day
In all my life like this.

18

ANGEL spirits of sleep,
White-robed, with silver hair;
In your meadows fair,
Where the willows weep,
And the sad moonbeam
On the gliding stream
Writes her scattered dream:

Angel spirits of sleep,
Dancing to the weir
In the hollow roar
Of its waters deep;
Know ye how men say
That ye haunt no more
Isle and grassy shore
With your moonlit play;
That ye dance not here,
White-robed spirits of sleep,
All the summer night
Threading dances light?

19

ANNIVERSARY

WHAT is sweeter than new-mown hay,
Fresher than winds o'er-sea that blow,
Innocent above children's play,
Fairer and purer than winter snow,
Frolic as are the morns of May?
   —If it should be what best I know!

What is richer than thoughts that stray
From reading of poems that smoothly flow?
What is solemn like the delay
Of concords linked in a music slow
Dying thro' vaulted aisles away?
   —If it should be what best I know!

What gives faith to me when I pray,
Setteth my heart with joy aglow,
Filleth my song with fancies gay,
Maketh the heaven to which I go,
The gladness of earth that lasteth for aye?
   —If it should be what best I know!

But tell me thou—'twas on this day
That first we loved five years ago—
If 'tis a thing that I can say,
   Though it must be what best we know.

20

THE summer trees are tempest-torn,
The hills are wrapped in a mantle wide
Of folding rain by the mad wind borne
   Across the country side.

His scourge of fury is lashing down
The delicate-rankèd golden corn,
That never more shall rear its crown
    And curtsey to the morn.

There shews no care in heaven to save
Man's pitiful patience, or provide
A season for the season's slave,
    Whose trust hath toiled and died.

So my proud spirit in me is sad,
A wreck of fairer fields to mourn,
The ruin of golden hopes she had,
    My delicate-rankèd corn.

21

THE birds that sing on autumn eves
Among the golden-tinted leaves,
Are but the few that true remain
Of budding May's rejoicing train.

Like autumn flowers that brave the frost,
And make their show when hope is lost,
These 'mong the fruits and mellow scent
Mourn not the high-sunned summer spent.

Their notes thro' all the jocund spring
Were mixed in merry musicking:
They sang for love the whole day long,
But now their love is all for song.

Now each hath perfected his lay
To praise the year that hastes away:
They sit on boughs apart, and vie
In single songs and rich reply:

And oft as in the copse I hear
These anthems of the dying year,
The passions, once her peace that stole,
With flattering love my heart console.

22

WHEN my love was away,
Full three days were not sped,
I caught my fancy astray
Thinking if she were dead,

And I alone, alone:
It seemed in my misery
In all the world was none
Ever so lone as I.

I wept; but it did not shame
Nor comfort my heart: away
I rode as I might, and came
To my love at close of day.

The sight of her stilled my fears,
My fairest-hearted love:
And yet in her eyes were tears:
Which when I questioned of,

O now thou art come, she cried,
'Tis fled: but I thought to-day
I never could here abide,
If thou wert longer away.

23

THE storm is over, the land hushes to rest:
The tyrannous wind, its strength fordone,
Is fallen back in the west
To couch with the sinking sun.
The last clouds fare
With fainting speed, and their thin streamers fly
In melting drifts of the sky.
Already the birds in the air

Appear again ; the rooks return to their haunt,
And one by one,
Proclaiming aloud their care,
Renew their peaceful chant.

Torn and shattered the trees their branches again reset,
They trim afresh the fair
Few green and golden leaves withheld from the storm,
And awhile will be handsome yet.
To-morrow's sun shall caress
Their remnant of loveliness :
In quiet days for a time
Sad Autumn lingering warm
Shall humour their faded prime.

But ah ! the leaves of summer that lie on the ground !
What havoc !   The laughing timbrels of June,
That curtained the birds' cradles, and screened their song,
That sheltered the cooing doves at noon,
Of airy fans the delicate throng,—
Torn and scattered around :
Far out afield they lie,
In the watery furrows die,
In grassy pools of the flood they sink and drown,
Green-golden, orange, vermilion, golden and brown,
The high year's flaunting crown
Shattered and trampled down.

The day is done : the tired land looks for night :
She prays to the night to keep
In peace her nerves of delight :
While silver mist upstealeth silently,
And the broad cloud-driving moon in the clear sky
Lifts o'er the firs her shining shield,
And in her tranquil light
Sleep falls on forest and field.
Sée ! sléep hath fallen : the trees are asleep :
The night is come.   The land is wrapt in sleep.

24

YE thrilled me once, ye mournful strains,
    Ye anthems of plaintive woe,
My spirit was sad when I was young;
    Ah sorrowful long-ago!
But since I have found the beauty of joy
    I have done with proud dismay:
For howsoe'er man hug his care
    The best of his art is gay.

And yet if voices of fancy's choir
    Again in mine ear awake
Your old lament, 'tis dear to me still,
    Nor all for memory's sake:
'Tis like the dirge of sorrow dead,
    Whose tears are wiped away;
Or drops of the shower when rain is o'er,
    That jewel the brightened day.

25

SAY who is this with silvered hair,
    So pale and worn and thin,
Who passeth here, and passeth there,
    And looketh out and in?

That useth not our garb nor tongue
    And knoweth things untold:
Who teacheth pleasure to the young,
    And wisdom to the old?

No toil he maketh his by day,
    No home his own by night;
But wheresoe'er he take his way,
    He killeth our delight.

Since he is come there's nothing wise
    Nor fair in man or child,
Unless his deep divining eyes
    Have looked on it and smiled.

Whence came he hither all alone
    Among our folk to spy?
There's nought that we can call our own,
    Till he shall hap to die.

And I would dig his grave full deep
    Beneath the churchyard yew,
Lest thence his wizard eyes might peep
    To mark the things we do.

26

CROWN Winter with green,
And give him good drink
To physic his spleen
Or ever he think.

His mouth to the bowl,
His feet to the fire;
And let him, good soul,
No comfort desire.

So merry he be,
I bid him abide:
And merry be we
This good Yuletide.

27

THE snow lies sprinkled on the beach,
And whitens all the marshy lea :
The sad gulls wail adown the gale,
The day is dark and black the sea.
  Shorn of their crests the blighted waves
With driven foam the offing fleck :
The ebb is low and barely laves
The red rust of the giant wreck.

On such a stony, breaking beach
My childhood chanced and chose to be :
'Twas here I played, and musing made
My friend the melancholy sea.
  He from his dim enchanted caves
With shuddering roar and onrush wild
Fell down in sacrificial waves
At feet of his exulting child.

Unto a spirit too light for fear
His wrath was mirth, his wail was glee :—
My heart is now too fixed to bow
Tho' all his tempests howl at me :
  For to the gain life's summer saves,
My solemn joy's increasing store,
The tossing of his mournful waves
Makes sweetest music evermore.

28

MY spirit kisseth thine,
My spirit embraceth thee :
I feel thy being twine
Her graces over me,

In the life-kindling fold
Of God's breath ; where on high,
In furthest space untold
Like a lost world I lie :

And o'er my dreaming plains
Lightens, most pale and fair,
A moon that never wanes ;
Or more, if I compare,

Like what the shepherd sees
On late mid-winter dawns,
When thro' the branchèd trees,
O'er the white-frosted lawns,

The huge unclouded sun,
Surprising the world whist,
Is all uprisen thereon,
Golden with melting mist.

29

ARIEL, O,—my angel, my own,—
Whither away then art thou flown
    Beyond my spirit's dominion ?
That makest my heart run over with rhyme,
Renewing at will my youth for a time,
    My servant, my pretty minion.

Now indeed I have cause to mourn,
Now thou returnest scorn for scorn :
    Leave me not to my folly :
For when thou art with me is none so gay
As I, and none when thou'rt away
    Was ever so melancholy.

30

LAUS DEO

LET praise devote thy work, and skill employ
Thy whole mind, and thy heart be lost in joy.
Well-doing bringeth pride, this constant thought
Humility, that thy best done is nought.
Man doeth nothing well, be it great or small,
Save to praise God; but that hath savèd all:
For God requires no more than thou hast done,
And takes thy work to bless it for his own.

BOOK V

DEDICATED TO M. G. K.

I

THE WINNOWERS

BETWIXT two billows of the downs
    The little hamlet lies,
And nothing sees but the bald crowns
    Of the hills, and the blue skies.

Clustering beneath the long descent
    And grey slopes of the wold,
The red roofs nestle, oversprent
    With lichen yellow as gold.

We found it in the mid-day sun
    Basking, what time of year
The thrush his singing has begun,
    Ere the first leaves appear.

High from his load a woodman pitched
    His faggots on the stack :
Knee-deep in straw the cattle twitched
    Sweet hay from crib and rack :

And from the barn hard by was borne
    A steady muffled din,
By which we knew that threshèd corn
    Was winnowing, and went in.

(301)

The sunbeams on the motey air
 Streamed through the open door,
And on the brown arms moving bare,
 And the grain upon the floor.

One turns the crank, one stoops to feed
 The hopper, lest it lack,
One in the bushel scoops the seed,
 One stands to hold the sack.

We watched the good grain rattle down,
 And the awns fly in the draught;
To see us both so pensive grown
 The honest labourers laughed :

Merry they were, because the wheat
 Was clean and plump and good,
Pleasant to hand and eye, and meet
 For market and for food.

It chanced we from the city were,
 And had not gat us free
In spirit from the store and stir
 Of its immensity :

But here we found ourselves again.
 Where humble harvests bring
After much toil but little grain,
 'Tis merry winnowing.

2

THE AFFLICTION OF RICHARD

Love not too much. But how,
When thou hast made me such,
And dost thy gifts bestow,
How can I love too much ?

Though I must fear to lose,
And drown my joy in care,
With all its thorns I choose
The path of love and prayer.

Though thou, I know not why,
Didst kill my childish trust,
That breach with toil did I
Repair, because I must :
   And spite of frighting schemes,
With which the fiends of Hell
Blaspheme thee in my dreams,
So far I have hoped well.

But what the heavenly key,
What marvel in me wrought
Shall quite exculpate thee,
I have no shadow of thought.
   What am I that complain ?
The love, from which began
My question sad and vain,
Justifies thee to man.

3

SINCE to be loved endures,
   To love is wise :
Earth hath no good but yours,
   Brave, joyful eyes :

Earth hath no sin but thine,
   Dull eye of scorn :
O'er thee the sun doth pine
   And angels mourn.

4

THE GARDEN IN SEPTEMBER

Now thin mists temper the slow-ripening beams
Of the September sun : his golden gleams
On gaudy flowers shine, that prank the rows
Of high-grown hollyhocks, and all tall shows
That Autumn flaunteth in his bushy bowers ;
Where tomtits, hanging from the drooping heads
Of giant sunflowers, peck the nutty seeds ;
And in the feathery aster bees on wing
Seize and set free the honied flowers,
Till thousand stars leap with their visiting :
While ever across the path mazily flit,
Unpiloted in the sun,
The dreamy butterflies
With dazzling colours powdered and soft glooms,
White, black and crimson stripes, and peacock eyes,
Or on chance flowers sit,
With idle effort plundering one by one
The nectaries of deepest-throated blooms.

With gentle flaws the western breeze
Into the garden saileth,
Scarce here and there stirring the single trees,
For his sharpness he vaileth :
So long a comrade of the bearded corn,
Now from the stubbles whence the shocks are borne,
O'er dewy lawns he turns to stray,
As mindful of the kisses and soft play
Wherewith he enamoured the light-hearted May,
Ere he deserted her ;
Lover of fragrance, and too late repents ;
Nor more of heavy hyacinth now may drink,
Nor spicy pink,

Nor summer's rose, nor garnered lavender,
But the few lingering scents
Of streakèd pea, and gillyflower, and stocks
Of courtly purple, and aromatic phlox.

And at all times to hear are drowsy tones
Of dizzy flies, and humming drones,
With sudden flap of pigeon wings in the sky,
Or the wild cry
Of thirsty rooks, that scour ascare
The distant blue, to watering as they fare
With creaking pinions, or—on business bent,
If aught their ancient polity displease,—
Come gathering to their colony, and there
Settling in ragged parliament,
Some stormy council hold in the high trees.

5

So sweet love seemed that April morn,
When first we kissed beside the thorn,
So strangely sweet, it was not strange
We thought that love could never change.

But I can tell—let truth be told—
That love will change in growing old;
Though day by day is nought to see,
So delicate his motions be.

And in the end 'twill come to pass
Quite to forget what once he was,
Nor even in fancy to recall
The pleasure that was all in all.

His little spring, that sweet we found,
So deep in summer floods is drowned,
I wonder, bathed in joy complete,
How love so young could be so sweet.

6

LARKS

WHAT voice of gladness, hark!
In heaven is ringing?
From the sad fields the lark
Is upward winging.

High through the mournful mist that blots our day
Their songs betray them soaring in the grey.
See them! Nay, they
In sunlight swim; above the furthest stain
Of cloud attain; their hearts in music rain
Upon the plain.

Sweet birds, far out of sight
Your songs of pleasure
Dome us with joy as bright
As heaven's best azure.

7

THE PALM WILLOW

SEE, whirling snow sprinkles the starvèd fields,
The birds have stayed to sing;
No covert yet their fairy harbour yields.
When cometh Spring?
Ah! in their tiny throats what songs unborn
Are quenched each morn.

The lenten lilies, through the frost that push,
Their yellow heads withhold:
The woodland willow stands a lonely bush
Of nebulous gold;
There the Spring-goddess cowers in faint attire
Of frightened fire.

8

ASIAN BIRDS

In this May-month, by grace
    of heaven, things shoot apace.
The waiting multitude
    of fair boughs in the wood,
How few days have arrayed
    their beauty in green shade.

What have I seen or heard?
    it was the yellow bird
Sang in the tree: he flew
    a flame against the blue;
Upward he flashed.   Again,
    hark! 'tis his heavenly strain.

Another! Hush! Behold,
    many, like boats of gold,
From waving branch to branch
    their airy bodies launch.
What music is like this,
    where each note is a kiss?

The golden willows lift
    their boughs the sun to sift:
Their sprays they droop to screen
    the sky with veils of green,
A floating cage of song,
    where feathered lovers throng.

How the delicious notes
    come bubbling from their throats!
Full and sweet how they are shed
    like round pearls from a thread!
The motions of their flight
    are wishes of delight.

Hearing their song I trace
　the secret of their grace.
Ah, could I this fair time
　so fashion into rhyme,
The poem that I sing
　would be the voice of spring.

9

JANUARY

COLD is the winter day, misty and dark :
　The sunless sky with faded gleams is rent:
And patches of thin snow outlying, mark
　The landscape with a drear disfigurement.

The trees their mournful branches lift aloft :
　The oak with knotty twigs is full of trust,
With bud-thronged bough the cherry in the croft;
　The chestnut holds her gluey knops upthrust.

No birds sing, but the starling chaps his bill
　And chatters mockingly ; the newborn lambs
Within their strawbuilt fold beneath the hill
　Answer with plaintive cry their bleating dams.

Their voices melt in welcome dreams of spring,
　Green grass and leafy trees and sunny skies:
My fancy decks the woods, the thrushes sing,
　Meadows are gay, bees hum and scents arise.

And God the Maker doth my heart grow bold
　To praise for wintry works not understood,
Who all the worlds and ages doth behold,
　Evil and good as one, and all as good.

10

A ROBIN

FLAME-THROATED robin on the topmost bough
　　Of the leafless oak, what singest thou?
　　　　Hark! he telleth how—
　　'Spring is coming now; Spring is coming now.

Now ruddy are the elm-tops against the blue sky,
　　The pale larch donneth her jewelry;
　　　　Red fir and black fir sigh,
　　And I am lamenting the year gone by.

The bushes where I nested are all cut down,
　　They are felling the tall trees one by one,
　　　　And my mate is dead and gone,
　　In the winter she died and left me lone.

She lay in the thicket where I fear to go;
　　For when the March-winds after the snow
　　　　The leaves away did blow,
　　She was not there, and my heart is woe:

And sad is my song, when I begin to sing,
　　As I sit in the sunshine this merry spring:
　　　　Like a withered leaf I cling
　　To the white oak-bough, while the wood doth ring.

Spring is coming now, the sun again is gay;
　　Each day like a last spring's happy day.'—
　　　　Thus sang he; then from his spray
　　He saw me listening and flew away.

11

I NEVER shall love the snow again
　　　　Since Maurice died:
With corniced drift it blocked the lane
And sheeted in a desolate plain
　　　　The country side.

The trees with silvery rime bedight
  Their branches bare.
By day no sun appeared ; by night
The hidden moon shed thievish light
  In the misty air.

We fed the birds that flew around
  In flocks to be fed :
No shelter in holly or brake they found.
The speckled thrush on the frozen ground
  Lay frozen and dead.

We skated on stream and pond ; we cut
  The crinching snow
To Doric temple or Arctic hut ;
We laughed and sang at nightfall, shut
  By the fireside glow.

Yet grudged we our keen delights before
  Maurice should come.
We said, In-door or out-of-door
We shall love life for a month or more,
  When he is home.

They brought him home ; 'twas two days late
  For Christmas day :
Wrapped in white, in solemn state,
A flower in his hand, all still and straight
  Our Maurice lay.

And two days ere the year outgave
  We laid him low.
The best of us truly were not brave,
When we laid Maurice down in his grave
  Under the snow.

12

NIGHTINGALES

BEAUTIFUL must be the mountains whence ye come,
And bright in the fruitful valleys the streams, wherefrom
Ye learn your song:
Where are those starry woods? O might I wander there,
Among the flowers, which in that heavenly air
Bloom the year long!

Nay, barren are those mountains and spent the streams:
Our song is the voice of desire, that haunts our dreams,
A throe of the heart,
Whose pining visions dim, forbidden hopes profound,
No dying cadence nor long sigh can sound,
For all our art.

Alone, aloud in the raptured ear of men
We pour our dark nocturnal secret; and then,
As night is withdrawn
From these sweet-springing meads and bursting boughs of
May,
Dream, while the innumerable choir of day
Welcome the dawn.

13

A SONG of my heart, as the sun peered o'er the sea,
Was born at morning to me:
And out of my treasure-house it chose
A melody, that arose

Of all fair sounds that I love, remembered together
In one; and I knew not whether
From waves of rustling wheat it was,
Recoveringly that pass:

Or a hum of bees in the queenly robes of the lime:
    Or a descant in pairing time
Of warbling birds: or watery bells
    Of rivulets in the hills:

Or whether on blazing downs a high lark's hymn
    Alone in the azure dim:
Or a sough of pines, when the midnight wold
    Is solitary and cold:

Or a lapping river-ripple all day chiding
    The bow of my wherry gliding
Down Thames, between his flowery shores
    Re-echoing to the oars:

Or anthem notes, wherever in archèd quires
    The unheeded music twires,
And, centuries by, to the stony shade
    Flies following and to fade:

Or a homely prattle of children's voices gay
    'Mong garden joys at play:
Or a sundown chaunting of solemn rooks:
    Or memory of my books,

Which hold the words that poets in many a tongue
    To the irksome world have sung:
Or the voice, my happy lover, of thee
    Now separated from me.

A ruby of fire in the burning sleep of my brain
    Long hid my thought had lain,
Forgotten dreams of a thousand days
    Ingathering to its rays,

The light of life in darkness tempering long;
    Till now a perfect song,
A jewel of jewels it leapt above
    To the coronal of my love.

Book V

FOUNDER'S DAY. A SECULAR ODE ON THE NINTH JUBILEE OF ETON COLLEGE

CHRIST and his Mother, heavenly maid,
Mary, in whose fair name was laid
Eton's corner, bless our youth
With truth, and purity, mother of truth!

O ye, 'neath breezy skies of June,
By silver Thames's lulling tune,
In shade of willow or oak, who try
The golden gates of poesy;

Or on the tabled sward all day
Match your strength in England's play,
Scholars of Henry, giving grace
To toil and force in game or race;

Exceed the prayer and keep the fame
Of him, the sorrowful king, who came
Here in his realm a realm to found,
Where he might stand for ever crowned.

Or whether with naked bodies flashing
Ye plunge in the lashing weir; or dashing
The oars of cedar skiffs, ye strain
Round the rushes and home again;—

Or what pursuit soe'er it be
That makes your mingled presence free,
When by the schoolgate 'neath the limes
Ye muster waiting the lazy chimes;

May Peace, that conquereth sin and death,
Temper for you her sword of faith;
Crown with honour the loving eyes,
And touch with mirth the mouth of the wise.

Here is eternal spring: for you
The very stars of heaven are new;
And aged Fame again is born,
Fresh as a peeping flower of morn.

For you shall Shakespeare's scene unroll,
Mozart shall steal your ravished soul,
Homer his bardic hymn rehearse,
Virgil recite his maiden verse.

Now learn, love, have, do, be the best;
Each in one thing excel the rest:
Strive; and hold fast this truth of heaven—
To him that hath shall more be given.

Slow on your dial the shadows creep,
So many hours for food and sleep,
So many hours till study tire,
So many hours for heart's desire.

These suns and moons shall memory save,
Mirrors bright for her magic cave;
Wherein may steadfast eyes behold
A self that groweth never old.

O in such prime enjoy your lot,
And when ye leave regret it not;
With wishing gifts in festal state
Pass ye the angel-sworded gate.

Then to the world let shine your light,
Children in play be lions in fight,
And match with red immortal deeds
The victory that made ring the meads:

Or by firm wisdom save your land
From giddy head and grasping hand:
IMPROVE THE BEST; so shall your sons
Better what ye have bettered once.

Send them here to the court of grace
Bearing your name to fill your place:
Ye in their time shall live again
The happy dream of Henry's reign:

And on his day your steps be bent
Where, saint and king, crowned with content,
He biddeth a prayer to bless his youth
With truth, and purity, mother of truth.

15

THE north wind came up yesternight
  With the new year's full moon,
And rising as she gained her height,
  Grew to a tempest soon.
Yet found he not on heaven's face
  A task of cloud to clear;
There was no speck that he might chase
  Off the blue hemisphere,
Nor vapour from the land to drive:
  The frost-bound country held
Nought motionable or alive,
  That 'gainst his wrath rebelled.
There scarce was hanging in the wood
  A shrivelled leaf to reave;

No bud had burst its swathing hood
 That he could rend or grieve :
Only the tall tree-skeletons,
 Where they were shadowed all,
Wavered a little on the stones,
 And on the white church-wall.

—Like as an artist in his mood,
 Who reckons all as nought,
So he may quickly paint his nude,
 Unutterable thought :
So Nature in a frenzied hour
 By day or night will show
Dim indications of the power
 That doometh man to woe.
Ah, many have my visions been,
 And some I know full well :
I would that all that I have seen
 Were fit for speech to tell.—

And by the churchyard as I came,
 It seemed my spirit passed
Into a land that hath no name,
 Grey, melancholy and vast ;
Where nothing comes : but Memory,
 The widowed queen of Death,
Reigns, and with fixed, sepulchral eye
 All slumber banisheth.
Each grain of writhen dust, that drapes
 That sickly, staring shore,
Its old chaotic change of shapes
 Remembers evermore.
And ghosts of cities long decayed
 And ruined shrines of Fate
Gather the paths, that Time hath made
 Foolish and desolate.

Nor winter there hath hope of spring,
    Nor the pale night of day,
Since the old king with scorpion sting
    Hath done himself away.

          *   *

The morn was calm ; the wind's last breath
    Had fal'n : in solemn hush
The golden moon went down beneath
    The dawning's crimson flush.

16

NORTH WIND IN OCTOBER

In the golden glade the chestnuts are fallen all ;
From the sered boughs of the oak the acorns fall :
The beech scatters her ruddy fire ;
The lime hath stripped to the cold,
And standeth naked above her yellow attire :
The larch thinneth her spire
To lay the ways of the wood with cloth of gold.

    Out of the golden-green and white
Of the brake the fir-trees stand upright
In the forest of flame, and wave aloft
To the blue of heaven their blue-green tuftings soft.

But swiftly in shuddering gloom the splendours fail,
As the harrying North-wind beareth
A cloud of skirmishing hail
The grievèd woodland to smite :
In a hurricane through the trees he teareth,
Raking the boughs and the leaves rending,
And whistleth to the descending
Blows of his icy flail.
Gold and snow he mixeth in spite,
And whirleth afar ; as away on his winnowing flight
He passeth, and all again for awhile is bright.

17

FIRST SPRING MORNING

A CHILD'S POEM.

Look! Look! the spring is come:
O feel the gentle air,
That wanders thro' the boughs to burst
The thick buds everywhere!
The birds are glad to see
The high unclouded sun:
Winter is fled away, they sing,
The gay time is begun.

Adown the meadows green
Let us go dance and play,
And look for violets in the lane,
And ramble far away
To gather primroses,
That in the woodland grow,
And hunt for oxlips, or if yet
The blades of bluebells show:

There the old woodman gruff
Hath half the coppice cut,
And weaves the hurdles all day long
Beside his willow hut.
We'll steal on him, and then
Startle him, all with glee
Singing our song of winter fled
And summer soon to be.

18

A VILLAGER

There was no lad handsomer than Willie was
The day that he came to father's house :
There was none had an eye as soft an' blue
As Willie's was, when he came to woo.

To a labouring life though bound thee be,
An' I on my father's ground live free,
I'll take thee, I said, for thy manly grace,
Thy gentle voice an' thy loving face.

'Tis forty years now since we were wed :
We are ailing an' grey needs not to be said :
But Willie's eye is as blue an' soft
As the day when he wooed me in father's croft.

Yet changed am I in body an' mind,
For Willie to me has ne'er been kind :
Merrily drinking an' singing with the men
He 'ud come home late six nights o' the se'n.

An' since the children be grown an' gone
He 'as shunned the house an' left me lone :
An' less an' less he brings me in
Of the little he now has strength to win.

The roof lets through the wind an' the wet,
An' master won't mend it with us in 's debt :
An' all looks every day more worn,
An' the best of my gowns be shabby an' torn.

No wonder if words hav' a-grown to blows ;
That matters not while nobody knows :
For love him I shall to the end of life,
An' be, as I swore, his own true wife.

An' when I am gone, he'll turn, an' see
His folly an' wrong, an' be sorry for me :
An' come to me there in the land o' bliss
To give me the love I looked for in this.

19

WEEP not to-day : why should this sadness be?
  Learn in present fears
  To o'ermaster those tears
  That unhindered conquer thee.

Think on thy past valour, thy future praise :
  Up, sad heart, nor faint
  In ungracious complaint,
  Or a prayer for better days.

Daily thy life shortens, the grave's dark peace
  Draweth surely nigh,
  When good-night is good-bye ;
  For the sleeping shall not cease.

Fight, to be found fighting : nor far away
  Deem, nor strange thy doom.
  Like this sorrow 'twill come,
  And the day will be to-day.

NEW POEMS

PREVIOUS EDITION

Collected for the first time in 1899. *Smith, Elder & Co. Vol. II.*
See notes at end of that volume.

NEW POEMS

ECLOGUE I

THE MONTHS

BASIL AND EDWARD

MAN hath with man on earth no holier bond
Than that the Muse weaves with her dreamy thread :
Nor e'er was such transcendent love more fond
Than that which Edward unto Basil led,
Wandering alone across the woody shires
To hear the living voice of that wide heart,
To see the eyes that read the world's desires,
And touch the hand that wrote the roving rhyme.
Diverse their lots as distant were their homes,
And since that early meeting, jealous Time
Knitting their loves had held their lives apart.

But now again were these fine lovers met
And sat together on a rocky hill
Looking upon the vales of Somerset,
Where the far sea gleam'd o'er the bosky combes,
Satisfying their spirits the livelong day
With various mirth and revelation due
And delicate intimacy of delight,
As there in happy indolence they lay
And drank the sun, while round the breezy height
Beneath their feet rabbit and listless ewe
Nibbled the scented herb and grass at will.

Much talked they at their ease; and at the last
Spoke Edward thus, '"Twas on this very hill
This time of the year,—but now twelve years are past,—
That you provoked in verse my younger skill
To praise the months against your rival song;
And ere the sun had westered ten degrees
Our rhyme had brought him thro' the Zodiac.
Have you remembered?'—Basil answer'd back,
'Guest of my solace, how could I forget?
Years fly as months that seem'd in youth so long.
The precious life that, like indifferent gold,
Is disregarded in its worth to hold
Some jewel of love that God therein would set,
It passeth and is gone.'—'And yet not all,'
Edward replied: 'The passion as I please
Of that past day I can to-day recall;
And if but you, as I, remember yet
Your part thereof, and will again rehearse,
For half an hour we may old Time outwit.'
And Basil said, 'Alas for my poor verse!
What happy memory of it still endures
Will thank your love: I have forgotten it.
Speak you my stanzas, I will ransom yours.
Begin you then as I that day began,
And I will follow as your answers ran.'

JANUARY

ED. The moon that mounts the sun's deserted way,
Turns the long winter night to a silver day;
But setteth golden in face of the solemn sight
Of her lord arising upon a world of white.

FEBRUARY

BA. I have in my heart a vision of spring begun
In a sheltering wood, that feels the kiss of the sun:
And a thrush adoreth the melting day that dies
In clouds of purple afloat upon saffron skies.

MARCH

ED. Now carol the birds at dawn, and some new lay
Announceth a homecome voyager every day.
Beneath the tufted sallows the streamlet thrills
With the leaping trout and the gleam of the daffodils.

APRIL

BA. Then laugheth the year; with flowers the meads are
    bright;
The bursting branches are tipped with flames of light:
The landscape is light; the dark clouds flee above,
And the shades of the land are a blue that is deep as love.

MAY

ED. But if you have seen a village all red and old
In cherry-orchards a-sprinkle with white and gold,
By a hawthorn seated, or a witch-elm flowering high,
A gay breeze making riot in the waving rye!

JUNE

BA. Then night retires from heaven; the high winds go
A-sailing in cloud-pavilions of cavern'd snow.
O June, sweet Philomel sang thy cradle-lay;
In rosy revel thy spirit shall pass away.

JULY

ED. Heavy is the green of the fields, heavy the trees
With foliage hang, drowsy the hum of bees
In the thund'rous air: the crowded scents lie low:
Thro' tangle of weeds the river runneth slow.

AUGUST

BA. A reaper with dusty shoon and hat of straw
On the yellow field, his scythe in his armës braw:
Beneath the tall grey trees resting at noon
From sweat and swink with scythe and dusty shoon.

(325)

SEPTEMBER

ED. Earth's flaunting flower of passion fadeth fair
To ripening fruit in sunlit veils of the air,
As the art of man makes wisdom to glorify
The beauty and love of life born else to die.

OCTOBER

BA. On frosty morns with the woods aflame, down, down
The golden spoils fall thick from the chestnut crown.
May Autumn in tranquil glory her riches spend,
With mellow apples her orchard-branches bend.

NOVEMBER

ED. Sad mists have hid the sun, the land is forlorn:
The plough is afield, the hunter windeth his horn.
Dame Prudence looketh well to her winter stores,
And many a wise man finds his pleasure indoors.

DECEMBER

BA. I pray thee don thy jerkin of olden time,
Bring us good ice, and silver the trees with rime;
And I will good cheer, good music and wine bestow,
When the Christmas guest comes galloping over the snow.

Thus they in verse alternate sang the year
For rabbit shy and listless ewe to hear,
Among the grey rocks on the mountain green
Beneath the sky in fair and pastoral scene,
Like those Sicilian swains, whose doric tongue
After two thousand years is ever young,—
Sweet the pine's murmur, and, shepherd, sweet thy pipe,—
Or that which gentle Virgil, yet unripe,
Of Tityrus sang under the spreading beech
And gave to rustic clowns immortal speech,
By rocky fountain or on flowery mead

Bidding their idle flocks at will to feed,
While they, retreated to some bosky glade,
Together told their loves, and as they played
Sang what sweet thing soe'er the poet feigned:
    But these were men when good Victoria reigned,
Poets themselves, who without shepherd gear
Each of his native fancy sang the year.

ECLOGUE II

GIOVANNI DUPRÈ

LAWRENCE AND RICHARD

LAWRENCE

LOOK down the river—against the western sky—
The Ponte Santa Trinità—what throng
Slowly trails o'er with waving banners high,
With foot and horse! Surely they bear along
The spoil of one whom Florence honoureth:
And hark! the drum, the trumpeting dismay,
The wail of the triumphal march of death.

RICHARD

'Twill be the funeral of Giovánn Duprè
Wending to Santa Croce. Let us go
And see what relic of old splendour cheers
The dying ritual.

LAWRENCE

                    They esteem him well
To lay his bones with Michael Angelo.
Who might he be?

RICHARD

                    He too a sculptor, one
Who left a work long to resist the years.

LAWRENCE

You make me question further.

RICHARD
                    I can tell
All as we walk.   A poor woodcarver's son,
Prenticed to cut his father's rude designs
(We have it from himself), maker of shrines,
In his mean workshop in Siena dreamed ;
And saw as gods the artists of the earth,
And long'd to stand on their immortal shore,
And be as they, who in his vision gleam'd,
Dowering the world with grace for evermore.
So, taxing rest and leisure to one aim,
The boy of single will and inbred skill
Rose step by step to academic fame.

LAWRENCE
Do I not know him then ?   His figures fill
The tympana o'er Santa Croce's gate ;
In the museum too, his Cain, that stands
A left-handed discobolos . . . . .

RICHARD
                    So great
His vogue, that elder art of classic worth
Went to the wall to give his statues room ;
And last—his country's praise could do no more—
He cut the stone that honoured good Cavour.

LAWRENCE
I have seen the things.

RICHARD
                    He, finding in his hands
His life-desire possest, fell not in gloom,
Nor froth'd in vanity : his Sabbath earn'd
He look'd to spend in meditative rest :
So laying chisel by, he took a pen
To tell his story to his countrymen,
And prove (he did it) that the flower of all,
Rarest to attain, is in the power of all.

LAWRENCE

Yet nought he ever made, that I have learn'd,
In wood or stone deserved, nay not his best,
The Greek or Tuscan name for beautiful.
'Twas level with its praise, had force to pull
Favour from fashion.

RICHARD

           Yet he made one thing
Worthy of the lily city in her spring;
For while in vain the forms of beauty he aped,
A perfect spirit in himself he shaped;
And all his lifetime doing less than well
Where he profess'd nor doubted to excel,
Now, where he had no scholarship, but drew
His art from love, 'twas better than he knew:
And when he sat to write, lo! by him stood
The heavenly Muse, who smiles on all things good;
And for his truth's sake, for his stainless mind,
His homely love and faith, she now grew kind,
And changed the crown, that from the folk he got,
For her green laurel, and he knew it not.

LAWRENCE

Ah! Love of Beauty! This man then mistook
Ambition for her?

RICHARD

        In simplicity
Erring he kept his truth; and in his book
The statue of his grace is fair to see.

LAWRENCE

Then buried with their great he well may be.

RICHARD

And number'd with the saints, not among them
Who painted saints. Join we his requiem.

ECLOGUE III

FOURTH OF JUNE AT ETON

RICHARD AND GODFREY

RICHARD

BENEATH the wattled bank the eddies swarm
In wandering dimples o'er the shady pool:
The same their chase as when I was at school;
The same the music, where in shallows warm
The current, sunder'd by the bushy isles,
Returns to join the main, and struggles free
Above the willows, gurgling thro' the piles:
Nothing is changed, and yet how changed are we!
—What can bring Godfrey to the Muses' bower?

GODFREY

What but brings you?   The festal day of the year;
To live in boyish memories for an hour;
See and be seen: tho' you come seldom here.

RICHARD

Dread of the pang it was, fear to behold
What once was all myself, that kept me away.

GODFREY

You miss new pleasures coveting the old.

RICHARD

They need have prudence, who in courage lack;
'Twas that I might go on I looked not back.

GODFREY

Of all our company he, who, we say,
Fruited the laughing flower of liberty!

(330)

RICHARD

Ah ! had I my desire, so should it be.

GODFREY

Nay, but I know this melancholy mood ;
'Twas your poetic fancy when a boy.

RICHARD

For Fancy cannot live on real food :
In youth she will despise familiar joy
To dwell in mournful shades ; as they grow real,
Then buildeth she of joy her far ideal.

GODFREY

And so perverteth all.   This stream to me
Sings, and in sunny ripples lingeringly
The water saith 'Ah me ! where have I lept ?
Into what garden of life ? what banks are these,
What secret lawns, what ancient towers and trees ?
Where the young sons of heav'n, with shouts of play
Or low delighted speech, welcome the day,
As if the poetry of the earth had slept
To wake in ecstasy.   O stay me ! alas !
Stay me, ye happy isles, ere that I pass
Without a memory on my sullen course
By the black city to the tossing seas !'

RICHARD

So might this old oak say 'My heart is sere ;
With greater effort every year I force
My stubborn leafage : soon my branch will crack,
And I shall fall or perish in the wrack :
And here another tree its crown will rear,
And see for centuries the boys at play :
And 'neath its boughs, on some fine holiday,
Old men shall prate as these.'   Come see the game.

GODFREY

Yes, if you will.   'Tis all one picture fair.

RICHARD

Made in a mirror, and who looketh there
Must see himself.   Is not a dream the same?

GODFREY

Life is a dream.

RICHARD

And you, who say it, seem
Dreaming to speak to a phantom in a dream.

4

ELEGY

THE SUMMER-HOUSE ON THE MOUND

How well my eyes remember the dim path!
My homing heart no happier playground hath.
I need not close my lids but it appears
Through the bewilderment of forty years
To tempt my feet, my childish feet, between
Its leafy walls, beneath its arching green;
Fairer than dream of sleep, than Hope more fair
Leading to dreamless sleep her sister Care.

There grew two fellow limes, two rising trees,
Shadowing the lawn, the summer haunt of bees,
Whose stems, engraved with many a russet scar
From the spear-hurlings of our mimic war,
Pillar'd the portico to that wide walk,
A mossy terrace of the native chalk
Fashion'd, that led thro' the dark shades around
Straight to the wooden temple on the mound.
There live the memories of my early days,
There still with childish heart my spirit plays;

Yea, terror-stricken by the fiend despair
When she hath fled me, I have found her there;
And there 'tis ever noon, and glad suns bring
Alternate days of summer and of spring,
With childish thought, and childish faces bright,
And all unknown save but the hour's delight.

High on the mound the ivied arbour stood,
A dome of straw upheld on rustic wood:
Hidden in fern the steps of the ascent,
Whereby unto the southern front we went,
And from the dark plantation climbing free,
Over a valley look'd out on the sea.
That sea is ever bright and blue, the sky
Serene and blue, and ever white ships lie
High on the horizon steadfast in full sail,
Or nearer in the roads pass within hail,
Of naked brigs and barques that windbound ride
At their taut cables heading to the tide.

There many an hour I have sat to watch; nay, now
The brazen disk is cold against my brow,
And in my sight a circle of the sea
Enlarged to swiftness, where the salt waves flee,
And ships in stately motion pass so near
That what I see is speaking to my ear:
I hear the waves dash and the tackle strain,
The canvas flap, the rattle of the chain
That runs out thro' the hawse, the clank of the winch
Winding the rusty cable inch by inch,
Till half I wonder if they have no care,
Those sailors, that my glass is brought to bear
On all their doings, if I vex them not
On every petty task of their rough lot
Prying and spying, searching every craft
From painted truck to gunnel, fore and aft,—

Thro' idle Sundays as I have watch'd them lean
Long hours upon the rail, or neath its screen
Prone on the deck to lie outstretch'd at length,
Sunk in renewal of their wearied strength.

But what a feast of joy to me, if some
Fast-sailing frigate to the Channel come
Back'd here her topsail, or brought gently up
Let from her bow the splashing anchor drop,
By faint contrary wind stay'd in her cruise,
The *Phaethon* or dancing *Arethuse*,
Or some immense three-decker of the line,
Romantic as the tale of Troy divine;
Ere yet our iron age had doom'd to fall
The towering freeboard of the wooden wall,
And for the engines of a mightier Mars
Clipp'd their wide wings, and dock'd their soaring spars.
The gale that in their tackle sang, the wave
That neath their gilded galleries dasht so brave
Lost then their merriment, nor look to play
With the heavy-hearted monsters of to-day.

One noon in March upon that anchoring ground
Came Napier's fleet unto the Baltic bound:
Cloudless the sky and calm and blue the sea,
As round Saint Margaret's cliff mysteriously,
Those murderous queens walking in Sabbath sleep
Glided in line upon the windless deep:
For in those days was first seen low and black
Beside the full-rigg'd mast the strange smoke-stack,
And neath their stern revolv'd the twisted fan.
Many I knew as soon as I might scan,
The heavy *Royal George*, the *Acre* bright,
The *Hogue* and *Ajax*, and could name aright
Others that I remember now no more;
But chief, her blue flag flying at the fore,

With fighting guns a hundred thirty and one,
The Admiral ship *The Duke of Wellington*,
Whereon sail'd George, who in her gig had flown
The silken ensign by our sisters sewn.
The iron Duke himself,—whose soldier fame
To England's proudest ship had given her name,
And whose white hairs in this my earliest scene
Had scarce more honour'd than accustom'd been,—
Was two years since to his last haven past:
I had seen his castle-flag to fall half-mast
One morn as I sat looking on the sea,
When thus all England's grief came first to me,
Who hold my childhood favour'd that I knew
So well the face that won at Waterloo.

But now 'tis other wars, and other men ;—
The year that Napier sail'd, my years were ten—
Yea, and new homes and loves my heart hath found :
A priest has there usurped the ivied mound,
The bell that call'd to horse calls now to prayers,
And silent nuns tread the familiar stairs.
Within the peach-clad walls that old outlaw,
The Roman wolf, scratches with privy paw.

5

O LOVE, I complain,
Complain of thee often,
Because thou dost soften
    My being to pain :

    Thou makest me fear
The mind that createth,
That loves not nor hateth
    In justice austere ;

Who, ere he make one,
With millions toyeth,
And lightly destroyeth
    Whate'er is begun.

An' wer't not for thee,
My glorious passion,
My heart I could fashion
    To sternness, as he.

But thee, Love, he made
Lest man should defy him,
Connive and outvie him,
    And not be afraid:

Nay, thee, Love, he gave
His terrors to cover,
And turn to a lover
    His insolent slave.

6

THE SOUTH WIND

THE south wind rose at dusk of the winter day,
The warm breath of the western sea
Circling wrapp'd the isle with his cloke of cloud,
And it now reach'd even to me, at dusk of the day,
And moan'd in the branches aloud:
While here and there, in patches of dark space,
A star shone forth from its heavenly place,
As a spark that is borne in the smoky chase;
And, looking up, there fell on my face—
Could it be drops of rain
Soft as the wind, that fell on my face?
Gossamers light as threads of the summer dawn,

(336)

Suck'd by the sun from midmost calms of the main,
From groves of coral islands secretly drawn,
O'er half the round of earth to be driven,
Now to fall on my face
In silky skeins spun from the mists of heaven.

Who art thou, in wind and darkness and soft rain
Thyself that robest, that bendest in sighing pines
To whisper thy truth? that usest for signs
A hurried glimpse of the moon, the glance of a star
In the rifted sky?
Who art thou, that with thee I
Woo and am wooed?
That robing thyself in darkness and soft rain
Choosest my chosen solitude,
Coming so far
To tell thy secret again,
As a mother her child, in her folding arm
Of a winter night by a flickering fire,
Telleth the same tale o'er and o'er
With gentle voice, and I never tire,
So imperceptibly changeth the charm,
As Love on buried ecstasy buildeth his tower,
—Like as the stem that beareth the flower
By trembling is knit to power;—
Ah! long ago
In thy first rapture I renounced my lot,
The vanity, the despondency and the woe,
And seeking thee to know
Well was 't for me, and evermore
I am thine, I know not what.

For me thou seekest ever, me wondering a day
In the eternal alternations, me
Free for a stolen moment of chance
To dream a beautiful dream

In the everlasting dance
Of speechless worlds, the unsearchable scheme,
To me thou findest the way,
Me and whomsoe'er
I have found my dream to share
Still with thy charm encircling; even to-night
To me and my love in darkness and soft rain
Under the sighing pines thou comest again,
And staying our speech with mystery of delight,
Of the kiss that I give a wonder thou makest,
And the kiss that I take thou takest.

7

I CLIMB the mossy bank of the glade:
My love awaiteth me in the shade.

She holdeth a book that she never heedeth:
In Goddës work her spirit readeth.

She is all to me, and I to her:
When we embrace, the stars confer.

O my love, from beyond the sky
I am calling thy heart, and who but I?

Fresh as love is the breeze of June,
In the dappled shade of the summer noon.

Catullus, throwing his heart away,
Gave fewer kisses every day.

Heracleitus, spending his youth
In search of wisdom, had less of truth.

Flame of fire was the poet's desire:
The thinker found that life was fire.

O my love! my song is done:
My kiss hath both their fires in one.

(338)

8

To my love I whisper, and say
Knowest thou why I love thee?—Nay:
Nay, she saith; O tell me again.—

When in her ear the secret I tell,
She smileth with joy incredible—

Ha! she is vain—O nay—
Then tell us!—Nay, O nay.

But this is in my heart,
That Love is Nature's perfect art,
And man hath got his fancy hence,
To clothe his thought in forms of sense.

Fair are thy works, O man, and fair
Thy dreams of soul in garments rare,
Beautiful past compare,
Yea, godlike when thou hast the skill
To steal a stir of the heavenly thrill:

But O, have care, have care!
'Tis envious even to dare:
And many a fiend is watching well
To flush thy reed with the fire of hell.

9

My delight and thy delight
Walking, like two angels white,
In the gardens of the night:

My desire and thy desire
Twining to a tongue of fire,
Leaping live, and laughing higher;

Thro' the everlasting strife
In the mystery of life.

Love, from whom the world begun,
Hath the secret of the sun.

Love can tell, and love alone,
Whence the million stars were strewn,
Why each atom knows its own,
How, in spite of woe and death,
Gay is life, and sweet is breath:

This he taught us, this we knew,
Happy in his science true,
Hand in hand as we stood
Neath the shadows of the wood.
Heart to heart as we lay
In the dawning of the day.

10

SEPTUAGESIMA

Now all the windows with frost are blinded,
    As punctual day with greedy smile
Lifts like a Cyclops evil-minded
    His ruddy eyeball over the isle.

In an hour 'tis paled, in an hour ascended
    A dazzling light in the cloudless grey.
Steel is the ice; the snow unblended
    Is trod to dust on the white highway.

The lambkins frisk; the shepherd is melting
    Drink for the ewes with a fire of straw:
The red flames leap at the wild air pelting
    Bitterly thro' the leafless shaw.

Around, from many a village steeple
   The sabbath-bells hum over the snow:
I give a blessing to parson and people
   Across the fields as away I go.

Over the hills and over the meadows
   Gay is my way till day be done:
Blue as the heaven are all the shadows,
   And every light is gold in the sun.

I I

THE sea keeps not the Sabbath day,
His waves come rolling evermore;
His noisy toil grindeth the shore,
And all the cliff is drencht with spray.

   Here as we sit, my love and I,
Under the pine upon the hill,
The sadness of the clouded sky,
The bitter wind, the gloomy roar,
The seamew's melancholy cry
With loving fancy suit but ill.

   We talk of moons and cooling suns,
Of geologic time and tide,
The eternal sluggards that abide
While our fair love so swiftly runs,

   Of nature that doth half consent
That man should guess her dreary scheme
Lest he should live too well content
In his fair house of mirth and dream:

   Whose labour irks his ageing heart,
His heart that wearies of desire,
Being so fugitive a part
Of what so slowly must expire.

She in her agelong toil and care
Persistent, wearies not nor stays,
Mocking alike hope and despair.

—Ah, but she too can mock our praise,
Enchanted on her brighter days,

Days, that the thought of grief refuse,
Days that are one with human art,
Worthy of the Virgilian muse,
Fit for the gaiety of Mozart.

12

RIDING adown the country lanes
    One day in spring,
Heavy at heart with all the pains
    Of man's imagining :—

The mist was not yet melted quite
    Into the sky :
The small round sun was dazzling white,
    The merry larks sang high :

The grassy northern slopes were laid
    In sparkling dew,
Out of the slow-retreating shade
    Turning from sleep anew :

Deep in the sunny vale a burn
    Ran with the lane,
O'erhung with ivy, moss and fern
    It laughed in joyful strain :

And primroses shot long and lush
    Their cluster'd cream ;
Robin and wren and amorous thrush
    Carol'd above the stream :

The stillness of the lenten air
    Call'd into sound
The motions of all life that were
    In field and farm around:

So fair it was, so sweet and bright,
    The jocund Spring
Awoke in me the old delight
    Of man's imagining,

Riding adown the country lanes:
    The larks sang high.—
O heart! for all thy griefs and pains
    Thou shalt be loth to die.

13

PATER FILIO

SENSE with keenest edge unusèd,
    Yet unsteel'd by scathing fire;
Lovely feet as yet unbruisèd
    On the ways of dark desire;
Sweetest hope that lookest smiling
O'er the wilderness defiling!

Why such beauty, to be blighted
    By the swarm of foul destruction?
Why such innocence delighted,
    When sin stalks to thy seduction?
All the litanies e'er chaunted
Shall not keep thy faith undaunted.

I have pray'd the sainted Morning
    To unclasp her hands to hold thee;
From resignful Eve's adorning
    Stol'n a robe of peace to enfold thee;
With all charms of man's contriving
Arm'd thee for thy lonely striving.

Me too once unthinking Nature,
   —Whence Love's timeless mockery took me,—
Fashion'd so divine a creature,
   Yea, and like a beast forsook me.
I forgave, but tell the measure
Of her crime in thee, my treasure.

14

NOVEMBER

THE lonely season in lonely lands, when fled
Are half the birds, and mists lie low, and the sun
Is rarely seen, nor strayeth far from his bed ;
The short days pass unwelcomed one by one.

   Out by the ricks the mantled engine stands
Crestfallen, deserted,—for now all hands
Are told to the plough,—and ere it is dawn appear
The teams following and crossing far and near,
As hour by hour they broaden the brown bands
Of the striped fields ; and behind them firk and prance
The heavy rooks, and daws grey-pated dance :
As awhile, surmounting a crest, in sharp outline
(A miniature of toil, a gem's design,)
They are pictured, horses and men, or now near by
Above the lane they shout lifting the share,
By the trim hedgerow bloom'd with purple air ;
Where, under the thorns, dead leaves in huddle lie
Packed by the gales of Autumn, and in and out
The small wrens glide
With a happy note of cheer,
And yellow amorets flutter above and about,
Gay, familiar in fear.

And now, if the night shall be cold, across the sky
Linnets and twites, in small flocks helter-skelter,
All the afternoon to the gardens fly,
From thistle-pastures hurrying to gain the shelter
Of American rhododendron or cherry-laurel:
And here and there, near chilly setting of sun,
In an isolated tree a congregation
Of starlings chatter and chide,
Thickset as summer leaves, in garrulous quarrel:
Suddenly they hush as one,—
The tree top springs,—
And off, with a whirr of wings,
They fly by the score
To the holly-thicket, and there with myriads more
Dispute for the roosts; and from the unseen nation
A babel of tongues, like running water unceasing,
Makes live the wood, the flocking cries increasing,
Wrangling discordantly, incessantly,
While falls the night on them self-occupied;
The long dark night, that lengthens slow,
Deepening with Winter to starve grass and tree,
And soon to bury in snow
The Earth, that, sleeping 'neath her frozen stole,
Shall dream a dream crept from the sunless pole
Of how her end shall be.

15

WINTER NIGHTFALL

THE day begins to droop,—
    Its course is done:
But nothing tells the place
    Of the setting sun.

The hazy darkness deepens,
    And up the lane
You may hear, but cannot see,
    The homing wain.

An engine pants and hums
    In the farm hard by:
Its lowering smoke is lost
    In the lowering sky.

The soaking branches drip,
    And all night through
The dropping will not cease
    In the avenue.

A tall man there in the house
    Must keep his chair:
He knows he will never again
    Breathe the spring air:

His heart is worn with work;
    He is giddy and sick
If he rise to go as far
    As the nearest rick:

He thinks of his morn of life,
    His hale, strong years;
And braves as he may the night
    Of darkness and tears.

16

SINCE we loved,—(the earth that shook
As we kissed, fresh beauty took)—
Love hath been as poets paint,
Life as heaven is to a saint;

All my joys my hope excel,
All my work hath prosper'd well,
All my songs have happy been,
O my love, my life, my queen.

17

WHEN Death to either shall come,—
   I pray it be first to me,—
Be happy as ever at home,
   If so, as I wish, it be.

Possess thy heart, my own;
   And sing to the child on thy knee,
Or read to thyself alone
   The songs that I made for thee.

18

WISHES

I WISH'D to sing thy grace, but nought
Found upon earth that could compare:
Some day, maybe, in heaven, I thought,—
If I should win the welcome there,—

There might I make thee many a song:
But now it is enough to say
I ne'er have done our life the wrong
Of wishing for a happier day.

19

A LOVE LYRIC

WHY art thou sad, my dearest?
What terror is it thou fearest,
Braver who art than I
   The fiend to defy?

Why art thou sad, my dearest?
And why in tears appearest,
Closer than I that wert
   At hiding thy hurt?

(347)

Why art thou sad, my dearest,
Since now my voice thou hearest?
Who with a kiss restore
Thy valour of yore.

20

ΕΡΩΣ

Why hast thou nothing in thy face?
Thou idol of the human race,
Thou tyrant of the human heart,
The flower of lovely youth that art;
Yea, and that standest in thy youth
An image of eternal Truth,
With thy exuberant flesh so fair,
That only Pheidias might compare,
Ere from his chaste marmoreal form
Time had decayed the colours warm;
Like to his gods in thy proud dress,
Thy starry sheen of nakedness.

Surely thy body is thy mind,
For in thy face is nought to find,
Only thy soft unchristen'd smile,
That shadows neither love nor guile,
But shameless will and power immense,
In secret sensuous innocence.

O king of joy, what is thy thought?
I dream thou knowest it is nought,
And wouldst in darkness come, but thou
Makest the light where'er thou go.
Ah yet no victim of thy grace,
None who e'er long'd for thy embrace,
Hath cared to look upon thy face.

THE FAIR BRASS

AN effigy of brass
Trodden by careless feet
Of worshippers that pass,
Beautiful and complete,

Lieth in the sombre aisle
Of this old church unwreckt,
And still from modern style
Shielded by kind neglect.

It shows a warrior arm'd :
Across his iron breast
His hands by death are charm'd
To leave his sword at rest,

Wherewith he led his men
O'ersea, and smote to hell
The astonisht Saracen,
Nor doubted he did well.

Would wé could teach our sons
His trust in face of doom,
Or give our bravest ones
A comparable tomb :

Such as to look on shrives
The heart of half its care ;
So in each line survives
The spirit that made it fair ;

So fair the characters,
With which the dusty scroll,
That tells his title, stirs
A requiem for his soul.

Yet dearer far to me,
And brave as he are they,
Who fight by land and sea
For England at this day;

Whose vile memorials,
In mournful marbles gilt,
Deface the beauteous walls
By growing glory built:

Heirs of our antique shrines,
Sires of our future fame,
Whose starry honour shines
In many a noble name

Across the deathful days,
Link'd in the brotherhood
That loves our country's praise,
And lives for heavenly good.

22

THE DUTEOUS HEART

Spirit of grace and beauty,
Whom men so much miscall:
Maidenly, modest duty,
I cry thee fair befall!

Pity for them that shun thee,
Sorrow for them that hate,
Glory, hath any won thee
To dwell in high estate!

But rather thou delightest
To walk in humble ways,
Keeping thy favour brightest
Uncrown'd by foolish praise;

In such retirement dwelling,
Where, hath the worldling been,
He straight returneth telling
Of sights that he hath seen,

Of simple men and truest
Faces of girl and boy;
The souls whom thou enduest
With gentle peace and joy.

Fair from my song befall thee,
Spirit of beauty and grace!
Men that so much miscall thee
Have never seen thy face.

23

THE IDLE FLOWERS

I HAVE sown upon the fields
Eyebright and Pimpernel,
And Pansy and Poppy-seed
Ripen'd and scatter'd well,

And silver Lady-smock
The meads with light to fill,
Cowslip and Buttercup,
Daisy and Daffodil;

King-cup and Fleur-de-lys
Upon the marsh to meet
With Comfrey, Watermint,
Loose-strife and Meadowsweet;

And all along the stream
My care hath not forgot
Crowfoot's white galaxy
And love's Forget-me-not:

(351)

And where high grasses wave
Shall great Moon-daisies blink,
With Rattle and Sorrel sharp
And Robin's ragged pink.

 Thick on the woodland floor
Gay company shall be,
Primrose and Hyacinth
And frail Anemone,

Perennial Strawberry-bloom,
Woodsorrel's pencilled veil,
Dishevel'd Willow-weed
And Orchis purple and pale,

Bugle, that blushes blue,
And Woodruff's snowy gem,
Proud Foxglove's finger-bells
And Spurge with milky stem.

 High on the downs so bare,
Where thou dost love to climb,
Pink Thrift and Milkwort are,
Lotus and scented Thyme;

 And in the shady lanes
Bold Arum's hood of green,
Herb Robert, Violet,
Starwort and Celandine;

 And by the dusty road
Bedstraw and Mullein tall,
With red Valerian
And Toadflax on the wall,

Yarrow and Chicory,
That hath for hue no like,
Silene and Mallow mild
And Agrimony's spike,

Blue-eyed Veronicas
And grey-faced Scabious
And downy Silverweed
And striped Convolvulus:

Harebell shall haunt the banks,
And thro' the hedgerow peer
Withwind and Snapdragon
And Nightshade's flower of fear.

And where men never sow,
Have I my Thistles set,
Ragwort and stiff Wormwood
And straggling Mignonette,

Bugloss and Burdock rank
And prickly Teasel high,
With Umbels yellow and white,
That come to kexes dry.

Pale Chlora shalt thou find,
Sun-loving Centaury,
Cranesbill and Sinjunwort,
Cinquefoil and Betony:

Shock-headed Dandelion,
That drank the fire of the sun:
Hawkweed and Marigold,
Cornflower and Campion.

Let Oak and Ash grow strong,
Let Beech her branches spread;
Let Grass and Barley throng
And waving Wheat for bread;

Be share and sickle bright
To labour at all hours;
For thee and thy delight
I have made the idle flowers.

But now 'tis Winter, child,
And bitter northwinds blow,
The ways are wet and wild,
The land is laid in snow.

24

DUNSTONE HILL

A COTTAGE built of native stone
Stands on the mountain-moor alone,
High from man's dwelling on the wide
And solitary mountain-side,

The purple mountain-side, where all
The dewy night the meteors fall,
And the pale stars musically set
To the watery bells of the rivulet,

And all day long, purple and dun,
The vast moors stretch beneath the sun,
The wide wind passeth fresh and hale,
And whirring grouse and blackcock sail.

Ah, heavenly Peace, where dost thou dwell?
Surely 'twas here thou hadst a cell,
Till flaming Love, wandering astray
With fury and blood, drove thee away.—

Far down across the valley deep
The town is hid in smoky sleep,
At moonless nightfall wakening slow
Upon the dark with lurid glow:

Beyond, afar the widening view
Merges into the soften'd blue,
Cornfield and forest, hill and stream,
Fair England in her pastoral dream.

To one who looketh from this hill
Life seems asleep, all is so still :
Nought passeth save the travelling shade
Of clouds on high that float and fade :

Nor since this landscape saw the sun
Might other motion o'er it run,
Till to man's scheming heart it came
To make a steed of steel and flame.

Him may you mark in every vale
Moving beneath his fleecy trail,
And tell whene'er the motions die
Where every town and hamlet lie.

He gives the distance life to-day,
Rushing upon his level'd way
From man's abode to man's abode,
And mocks the Roman's vaunted road,

Which o'er the moor purple and dun
Still wanders white beneath the sun,
Deserted now of men and lone
Save for this cot of native stone.

There ever by the whiten'd wall
Standeth a maiden fair and tall,
And all day long in vacant dream
Watcheth afar the flying steam.

25

SCREAMING TARN

THE saddest place that e'er I saw
    Is the deep tarn above the inn
That crowns the mountain-road, whereby
    One southward bound his way must win.

Sunk on the table of the ridge
　　From its deep shores is nought to see:
The unresting wind lashes and chills
　　Its shivering ripples ceaselessly.

Three sides 'tis banked with stones aslant,
　　And down the fourth the rushes grow,
And yellow sedge fringing the edge
　　With lengthen'd image all arow.

'Tis square and black, and on its face
　　When noon is still, the mirror'd sky
Looks dark and further from the earth
　　Than when you gaze at it on high.

At mid of night, if one be there,
　　—So say the people of the hill—
A fearful shriek of death is heard,
　　One sudden scream both loud and shrill.

And some have seen on stilly nights,
　　And when the moon was clear and round,
Bubbles which to the surface swam
　　And burst as if they held the sound.—

'Twas in the days ere hapless Charles
　　Losing his crown had lost his head,
This tale is told of him who kept
　　The inn upon the watershed:

He was a lowbred ruin'd man
　　Whom lawless times set free from fear:
One evening to his house there rode
　　A young and gentle cavalier.

With curling hair and linen fair
　　And jewel-hilted sword he went;
The horse he rode he had ridden far,
　　And he was with his journey spent.

He asked a lodging for the night,
   His valise from his steed unbound,
He let none bear it but himself
   And set it by him on the ground.

'Here's gold or jewels,' thought the host,
   'That's carrying south to find the king.'
He chattered many a loyal word,
   And scraps of royal airs gan sing.

His guest thereat grew more at ease
   And o'er his wine he gave a toast,
But little ate, and to his room
   Carried his sack behind the host.

'Now rest you well,' the host he said,
   But of his wish the word fell wide;
Nor did he now forget his son
   Who fell in fight by Cromwell's side.

Revenge and poverty have brought
   Full gentler heart than his to crime;
And he was one by nature rude,
   Born to foul deeds at any time.

With unshod feet at dead of night
   In stealth he to the guest-room crept,
Lantern and dagger in his hand,
   And stabbed his victim while he slept.

But as he struck a scream there came,
   A fearful scream so loud and shrill:
He whelm'd the face with pillows o'er,
   And lean'd till all had long been still.

Then to the face the flame he held
   To see there should no life remain :—
When lo! his brutal heart was quell'd:
   'Twas a fair woman he had slain.

The tan upon her face was paint,
　　The manly hair was torn away,
Soft was the breast that he had pierced ;
　　Beautiful in her death she lay.

His was no heart to faint at crime,
　　Tho' half he wished the deed undone.
He pulled the valise from the bed
　　To find what booty he had won.

He cut the straps, and pushed within
　　His murderous fingers to their theft.
A deathly sweat came o'er his brow,
　　He had no sense nor meaning left.

He touched not gold, it was not cold,
　　It was not hard, it felt like flesh.
He drew out by the curling hair
　　A young man's head, and murder'd fresh ;

A young man's head, cut by the neck.
　　But what was dreader still to see,
Her whom he had slain he saw again,
　　The twain were like as like can be.

Brother and sister if they were,
　　Both in one shroud they now were wound,—
Across his back and down the stair,
　　Out of the house without a sound.

He made his way unto the tarn,
　　The night was dark and still and dank ;
The ripple chuckling neath the boat
　　Laughed as he drew it to the bank.

Upon the bottom of the boat
　　He laid his burden flat and low,
And on them laid the square sandstones
　　That round about the margin go.

Stone upon stone he weighed them down,
    Until the boat would hold no more ;
The freeboard now was scarce an inch :
    He stripp'd his clothes and push'd from shore.

All naked to the middle pool
    He swam behind in the dark night ;
And there he let the water in
    And sank his terror out of sight.

He swam ashore, and donn'd his dress,
    And scraped his bloody fingers clean ;
Ran home and on his victim's steed
    Mounted, and never more was seen.

But to a comrade ere he died
    He told his story guess'd of none :
So from his lips the crime returned
    To haunt the spot where it was done.

26

THE ISLE OF ACHILLES

(FROM THE GREEK)

Τὸν φίλτατόν σοι παῖδ' ἐμοί τ', Ἀχιλλέα
ὄψει δόμους ναίοντα νησιωτικοὺς
Λευκὴν κατ' ἀκτὴν ἐντὸς Εὐξείνου πόρου.
Eur. And. 1250.

Voyaging northwards by the western strand
Of the Euxine sea we came to where the land
Sinks low in salt morass and wooded plain :
Here mighty Ister pushes to the main,
Forking his turbid flood in channels three
To plough the sands wherewith he chokes the sea.

Against his middle arm, not many a mile
In the offing of black water is the isle
Named of Achilles, or as Leukê known,
Which tender Thetis, counselling alone
With her wise sire beneath the ocean-wave
Unto her child's departed spirit gave,
Where he might still his love and fame enjoy,
Through the vain Danaan cause fordone at Troy.
Thither Achilles passed, and long fulfill'd
His earthly lot, as the high gods had will'd,
Far from the rivalries of men, from strife,
From arms, from woman's love and toil of life.
Now of his lone abode I will unfold
What there I saw, or was by others told.

There is in truth a temple on the isle;
Therein a wooden statue of rude style
And workmanship antique with helm of lead:
Else all is desert, uninhabited;
Only a few goats browse the wind-swept rocks,
And oft the stragglers of their starving flocks
Are caught and sacrificed by whomsoe'er,
Whoever of chance or purpose hither fare:
About the fence lie strewn their bleaching bones.

But in the temple jewels and precious stones,
Upheapt with golden rings and vials lie,
Thankofferings to Achilles, and thereby,
Written or scratch'd upon the walls in view,
Inscriptions, with the givers' names thereto,
Some in Romaic character, some Greek,
As each man in the tongue that he might speak
Wrote verse of praise, or prayer for good to come,
To Achilles most, but to Patroclus some;
For those who strongly would Achilles move
Approach him by the pathway of his love.

Thousands of birds frequent the sheltering shrine,
The dippers and the swimmers of the brine,
Sea-mew and gull and diving cormorant,
Fishers that on the high cliff make their haunt
Sheer inaccessible, and sun themselves
Huddled arow upon the narrow shelves :—
And surely no like wonder e'er hath been
As that such birds should keep the temple clean;
But thus they do : at earliest dawn of day
They flock to sea and in the waters play,
And when they well have wet their plumage light,
Back to the sanctuary they take flight
Splashing the walls and columns with fresh brine,
Till all the stone doth fairly drip and shine,
When off again they skim asea for more
And soon returning sprinkle steps and floor,
And sweep all cleanly with their wide-spread wings.

From other men I have learnt further things.
If any of free purpose, thus they tell,
Sail'd hither to consult the oracle,—
For oracle there was,—they sacrificed
Such victims as they brought, if such sufficed,
And some they slew, some to the god set free :
But they who driven from their course at sea
Chanced on the isle, took of the goats thereon
And pray'd Achilles to accept his own.
Then made they a gift, and when they had offer'd once,
If to their question there was no response,
They added to the gift and asked again ;
Yea twice and more, until the god should deign
Answer to give, their offering they renew'd ;
Whereby great riches to the shrine ensued.
And when both sacrifice and gifts were made
They worship'd at the shrine, and as they pray'd

Sailors aver that often hath been seen
A man like to a god, of warrior mien,
A beauteous form of figure swift and strong;
Down on his shoulders his light hair hung long
And his full armour was enchast with gold:
While some, who with their eyes might nought behold,
Say that with music strange the air was stir'd;
And some there are, who have both seen and heard:
And if a man wish to be favour'd more,
He need but spend one night upon the shore;
To him in sleep Achilles will appear
And lead him to his tent, and with good cheer
Show him all friendliness that men desire;
Patroclus pours the wine, and he his lyre
Takes from the pole and plays the strains thereon
Which Cheiron taught him first on Pelion.

These things I tell as they were told to me,
Nor do I question but it well may be:
For sure I am that, if man ever was,
Achilles was a hero, both because
Of his high birth and beauty, his country's call
His valour of soul, his early death withal,
For Homer's praise, the crown of human art;
And that above all praise he had at heart
A gentler passion in her sovran sway,
And when his love died threw his life away.

27

AN ANNIVERSARY

HE

BRIGHT, my belovèd, be thy day,
   This eve of Summer's fall:
And Autumn mass his flowers gay
   To crown thy festival!

SHE

I care not if the morn be bright,
   Living in thy love-rays:
No flower I need for my delight,
   Being crownèd with thy praise.

HE

O many years and joyfully
   This sun to thee return;
Ever all men speak well of thee,
   Nor any angel mourn!

SHE

For length of life I would not pray,
   If thy life were to seek;
Nor ask what men and angels say
   But when of thee they speak.

HE

Arise! The sky hath heard my song,
   The flowers o'erhear thy praise;
And little loves are waking long
   To wish thee happy days.

28

REGINA CARA

JUBILEE-SONG, FOR MUSIC, 1897

HARK! The world is full of thy praise,
England's Queen of many days;
Who, knowing how to rule the free,
Hast given a crown to monarchy.

Honour, Truth and growing Peace
Follow Britannia's wide increase,
And Nature yield her strength unknown
To the wisdom born beneath thy throne!

In wisdom and love firm is thy fame:
Enemies bow to revere thy name:
The world shall never tire to tell
Praise of the queen that reignèd well.

O FELIX ANIMA, DOMINA PRAECLARA,
AMORE SEMPER CORONABERE
REGINA CARA.

LATER POEMS

OCCASIONAL ODES &C.

PREVIOUS PUBLICATIONS

1. *Monthly Review.   February,* 1903.
2. *Daniel Press.   Poems by A. Buckton.*
   1901.
3, 4. *Saturday Review.*
5. *' The Sheaf.'   June,* 1902.
6. *English Review.   March,* 1911.
7. *Academy.   April* 1, 1905.
8, 9. *Monthly Review.   June,* 1904.
11. *Speaker.*
12. *Monthly Review.   March,* 1902.
13. *' Wayfarer's Love.'* 1904.
14. *Saturday Review.   April* 13, 1907.
   Book of the Oxford Pageant.   July,
   1907.
15, 16. *Published with the Music by*
   Novello, Ewer & Co.

LATER POEMS

RECOLLECTIONS OF SOLITUDE
An Elegy

ENDED are many days, and now but few
Remain; since therefore it is happy and true
That memoried joys keep ever their delight,
Like steadfast stars in the blue vault of night,
While hours of pain (among those heavenly spheres
Like falling meteors, the martyr's tears)
Dart their long trails at random, and anon,
Ere we exclaim, pass, and for aye are gone;
Therefore my heedy thought will oft restore
The long light-hearted days that are no more,
Save where in her memorial crypt they shine
Spangling the silent past with joy divine.

But why in dream of this enchanted mood
Should all my boyhood seem a solitude?
Good reason know I, when I wander there,
In that transmuted scene, why all is fair;
The woods as when in holiday of spring
Million buds burst, and flowers are blossoming;
The meadows deep in grass, the fields unshorn
In beauty of the multitudinous corn,
Where the strait alleys hide me, wall'd between
High bloomy stalks and rustling banners green;
The gardens, too, in dazzling hues full-blown,
With wafted scent and blazing petals strewn;
The orchards reddening thro' the patient hours,
While idle autumn in his mossy bowers

Inviteth meditation to endear
The sanctuaries of the mellowing year;
And every spot wherein I loved to stray
Hath borrowed radiance of eternal day;
But why am I ever alone, alone?
Here in the corner of a field my throne,
Now in the branching chair of some tall tree
Drinking the gale in bird-like liberty;
Or to the seashore wandered in the sun
To watch the fateful waves break one by one ;
Or if on basking downs supine I lie
Bathing my spirit in blue calms of the sky ;
Or to the river bank am stolen by night
Hearkening unto the moonlit ripple bright
That warbles o'er the shallows of smooth stone ;
Why should my memory find me all alone,
When I had such companions every day
Jocund and dear?   'Twixt glimpses of their play
'Tis a vast solitude, wherein I see
Only myself and what I came to be.

    Yet never think, dear spirits, if now ye may
Remember aught of that brief earthly day,
Ere ye the mournful Stygian river crost,
From our familiar home too early lost,—
O never think that I your tears forget,
Or that I loved not well, or love not yet.
    Nor ye who held my heart in passion's chain,—
As kings and queens succeed in glorious reign—
When, as a man, I made you to outvie
God's work, and, as a god, then set you by
Among the sainted throng in holiest shrine
Of mythic creed and poetry divine;
True was my faith, and still your loves endure,
The jewels of my fancy, bright and pure.

Nor only in fair places do I see
The picture fair now it has ceased to be :
For fate once led me, and myself some days
Did I devote, to dull laborious ways,
By soaring thought detained to tread full low,—
Yea might I say unbeauteous paths of woe
And dreary abodes, had not my youthful sprite
Hallow'd each nook with legends of delight.

Ah ! o'er that smoky town who looketh now
By winter sunset from the dark hill-brow,
Under the dying trees exultantly
Nursing the sting of human tragedy ?
Or in that little room upstair'd so high,
Where London's roofs in thickest huddle lie,
Who now returns at evening to entice
To his fireside the joys of Paradise ?
Once sacred was that hearth, and bright the air ;
The flame of man's redemption flickered there,
In worship of those spirits, whose deathless fames
Have thrilled the stars of heaven to hear their names ;
They that excell'd in wisdom to create
Beauty, with mortal passion conquering fate ;
And, mid the sovran powers of elder time,
The loveliness of music and new rhyme,
The masters young that first enthrallèd me ;
Of whom if I should name, whom then but thee,
Sweet Shelley, or the boy whose book was found
Thrust in thy bosom on thy body drowned ?

O mighty Muse, wooer of virgin thought,
Beside thy charm all else counteth as nought ;
The revelation of thy smile doth make
Him whom thou lovest reckless for thy sake ;
Earthborn of suffering, that knowest well
To call thine own, and with enamouring spell

Feedest the stolen powers of godlike youth
On dear imagination's only truth,
Building with song a temple of desire;
And with the yearning music of thy quire,
In nuptial sacrament of thought and sense
Hallowest for toil the hours of indolence:
Thou in thy melancholic beauty drest,
Subduest ill to serve thy fair behest,
With tragic tears, and sevenfold purified
Silver of mirth; and with extremest pride,
With secret doctrine and unfathomed lore
Remainest yet a child for evermore,
The only enchantress of the earth that art
To cheer his day and staunch man's bleeding heart.

    O heavenly Muse, for heavenly thee we call
Who in the fire of love refinest all,
Accurst is he who heark'neth not thy voice;
But happy he who, numbered of thy choice,
Walketh aloof from nature's clouded plan:
For all God's world is but the thought of man;
Wherein hast thou re-formed a world apart,
The mutual mirror of his better heart.
There is no foulness, misery, nor sin,
But he who loves finds his desire therein,
And there with thee in lonely commerce lives:
Nay, all that nature gave or fortune gives,
Joys that his spirit is most jealous of,
His only-embraced and best-deserving love,
Who walketh in the noon of heavenly praise,
The troubled godhead of his children's gaze,
Wear thine eternity, and are loved best
By thee transfigured and in thee possest;
Who madest beauty, and from thy boundless store
Of beauty shalt create for evermore.

1900.

2

A VIGNETTE

Among the meadows
   lightly going,
With worship and joy
   my heart o'erflowing,

Far from town
   and toil of living,
To a holy day
   my spirit giving, . . .

    *   *   *

Thou tender flower,
   I kneel beside thee
Wondering why God
   so beautified thee.—

An answering thought
   within me springeth,
A bloom of the mind
   her vision bringeth.

Between the dim hills'
   distant azure
And flowery foreground
   of sparkling pleasure

I see the company
   of figures sainted,
For whom the picture
   of earth was painted,

Those robèd seërs
   who made man's story
The crown of Nature,
   Her cause his glory.

They walk in the city
   which they have builded,
The city of God
   from evil shielded :

To them for canopy
   the vault of heaven,
The flowery earth
   for carpet is given ;

Whereon I wander
   not unknowing,
With worship and joy
   my heart o'erflowing.

1901.

3

MILLICENT

THOU dimpled Millicent, of merry guesses,
Strong-limb'd and tall, tossing thy wayward tresses,
What mystery of the heart can so surprise
The mirth and music of thy brimming eyes?

Pale-brow, thou knowest not and diest to learn
The mortal secret that doth in thee burn ;
With look imploring ' If you love me, tell,
What is it in me that you love so well ? '

And suddenly thou stakest all thy charms,
And leapest on me ; and in thy circling arms
When almost stifled with their wild embrace,
I feel thy hot tears sheltering on my face.

(372)

1901.

4

VIVAMUS

WHEN thou didst give thy love to me,
    Asking no more of gods or men
I vow'd I would contented be,
    If Fate should grant us summers ten.

But now that twice the term is sped,
    And ever young my heart and gay,
I fear the words that then I said,
    And turn my face from Fate away.

To bid thee happily good-bye
    I have no hope that I can see,
No way that I shall bravely die,
    Unless I give my life for thee.

1901.

5

ONE grief of thine
    if truth be confest
Was joy to me ;
    for it drave to my breast
Thee, to my heart
    to find thy rest.

How long it was
    I never shall know :
I watcht the earth
    so stately and slow,
And the ancient things
    that waste and grow.

But now for me
    what speed devours
Our heavenly life,
    our brilliant hours!
How fast they fly,
    the stars and flowers!

6

In still midsummer night
    When the moon is late
And the stars all watery and white
    For her coming wait,

A spirit, whose eyes are possest
    By wonder new,
Passeth—her arms upon her breast
    Enwrapt from the dew

In a raiment of azure fold
    With diaper
Of flower'd embroidery of gold
    Bestarr'd with silver.

The daisy folk are awake
    Their carpet to spread,
And the thron'd stars gazing on her make
    Fresh crowns for her head,

Netted in her floating hair
    As she drifteth free
Between the star-blossoming air
    And starry lea,

From the silent-shadow'd vale
    By the west wind drawn
Aloft to melt into the pale
    Moonrise of dawn.

1910.

7
MELANCHOLIA

THE sickness of desire, that in dark days
Looks on the imagination of despair,
Forgetteth man, and stinteth God his praise;
Nor but in sleep findeth a cure for care.

Incertainty that once gave scope to dream
Of laughing enterprise and glory untold,
Is now a blackness that no stars redeem,
A wall of terror in a night of cold.

Fool! thou that hast impossibly desired
And now impatiently despairest, see
How nought is changed: Joy's wisdom is attired
Splendid for others' eyes if not for thee:
Not love or beauty or youth from earth is fled:
If they delite thee not, 'tis thou art dead.   1904.

8
TO THE PRESIDENT OF MAGDALEN COLLEGE, OXFORD

SINCE now from woodland mist and flooded clay
I am fled beside the steep Devonian shore,
Nor stand for welcome at your gothic door,
'Neath the fair tower of Magdalen and May,
Such tribute, Warren, as fond poets pay
For generous esteem, I write, not more
Enhearten'd than my need is, reckoning o'er
My life-long wanderings on the heavenly way:

But well-befriended we become good friends,
Well-honour'd honourable; and all attain
Somewhat by fathering what fortune sends.
I bid your presidency a long reign,
True friend; and may your praise to greater ends
Aid better men than I, nor me in vain.

(375)

9

TO JOSEPH JOACHIM

Belov'd of all to whom that Muse is dear
Who hid her spirit of rapture from the Greek,
Whereby our art excelleth the antique,
Perfecting formal beauty to the ear;
Thou that hast been in England many a year
The interpreter who left us nought to seek,
Making Beethoven's inmost passion speak,
Bringing the soul of great Sebastian near·

　　Their music liveth ever, and 'tis just
That thou, good Joachim, so high thy skill,
Rank (as thou shalt upon the heavenly hill)
Laurel'd with them, for thy ennobling trust
Remember'd when thy loving hand is still
And every ear that heard thee stopt with dust.

10

TO THOS. FLOYD

How fares it, friend, since I by Fate annoy'd
Left the old home in need of livelier play
For body and mind? How fare, this many a day,
The stubborn thews and ageless heart of Floyd?
If not too well with country sport employ'd,
Visit my flock, the breezy hill that they
Choose for their fold ; and see, for thence you may,
From rising walls all roofless yet and void,

 The lovely city, thronging tower and spire,
The mind of the wide landscape, dreaming deep,
Grey-silvery in the vale ; a shrine where keep
Memorial hopes their pale celestial fire :
Like man's immortal conscience of desire,
The spirit that watcheth in me ev'n in my sleep.

1906.

II

LA GLOIRE DE VOLTAIRE

A.

Je donnerais pour revivre à vingt ans
L'or de Rothschild, la gloire de Voltaire.
I like that : Béranger in his printems,
Voltaire and Rothschild : what three graces there
Foot it together !   But of old Voltaire,
I'd ask what Béranger found so sublime
In that man's glory to adorn his rhyme.
Was it mere fame ?

B.

          Nay : for as wide a fame
Was won by the gold-garnering millionaire,
Who in the poet's verse might read his name :
And what is that ? when so much froth and scum
Float down the stream of Time (as Bacon saith),
What is that for deliverance from the death ?
Could any sober man be proud to hold
A lease of common talk, or die consoled
For thinking that on lips of fools to come
He'll live with Pontius Pilate and Tom Thumb ?
That were more like eternal punishment,
The true fool's Paradise by all consent.
Béranger thought to set a crown on merit.

A.

Man's merit ! and to crown it in Voltaire ?
The modest eye, the gentle, fearless heart,
The mouth of peace and truth, the angelic spirit !
Why Arouet was *soufflé* with the leaven,

Of which the little flock was bid beware:
His very ambition was to play a part;
Indifferent whether he did wrong or right,
So he won credit; eager to deny
A lie that failed, by adding lie to lie;
Repaying evil unto seven-times-seven;
A fount of slander, flattery and spite;
Vain, irritable; true but to his face
Of mockery and mischievous grimace,
A monkey of the schools, the saints' despair!

B.

Yet for his voice half Europe stood at pause
To hear, and when he spoke rang with applause.

A.

Granted he was a wonder of his kind.
There is a devilish mockery in things
Which only a born devil can enjoy.
True banter is of melancholy mind,
Akin to madness; thus must Shakespeare toy
With Hamlet's reason, ere his fine art dare
Push his relentless humour to the quick;
And so his mortal thrusts pierce not the skin.
But for the superficial bickerings
That poison life and never seem to prick,
The reasonable educated grin,
Truly no wag is equal to Voltaire,
His never-dying ripple, wide and light,
Has nigh the force of Nature: to compare,
'Tis like the ocean when the sky is bright,
And the cold north-wind tickles with surprise
The briny levels of the infinite sea.
—Shall we conclude his merit was his wit,
His magic art and versatility?

B.

And think of those foredoom'd in Dante's pit,
Who, sunk at bottom of the loathly slough,
Made the black mud up-bubble with their sighs;
And all because they were unkind to Mirth,
And went with smoky heart and gloomy brow
The while they lived upon the pleasant earth
In the sweet air that rallies to the sun,
And ne'er so much as smiled or gave God thanks:
Surely a sparkle of the Frenchman's fun
Had rescued all their souls.

A.

                    I think I see
The Deity who in this Heaven abides,
Le bon Dieu, holding both his aching sides,
With radiant face of Pan, ruddy and hairy:
Give him his famous whistles and goat-shanks,
And then present him to Alighieri.

B.

Nay, 'twixt the Frenchman and the Florentine
I ask no truce, grave Dante weaving well
His dark-eyed thought into a song divine,
Drawing high poetry from heaven and hell—
And him who lightly mockt at all in turn.

A

It follow'd from his mundane thought of art
That he contemn'd religion : his concern
Was comfort, taste, and wit : he had no heart
For man's attempt to build and beautify
His home in Nature ; so he set all by
That wisdom had evolved with purpose kind ;

Stamped it as folly, or as fraud attacked;
Never discerning how his callow zest
Was impiously defiling his own nest;
Whereas the least philosophy may find
The truths are the ideas; the sole fact
Is the long story of man's growing mind.

B.

Upon your thistle now I see my fig—
Béranger thought of Voltaire as a seer,
A latter-day John Baptist in a wig;
A herald of that furious gospel-storm
Of words and blood, that made the nations fear;
When sickening France adulterously sinn'd
With Virtue, and went mad conceiving wind.
He ranks him with those captains of reform,
Luther and Calvin; who, whate'er they taught,
Led folk from superstition to free thought.

A.

They did.   But whence or whither led Voltaire?
The steward with fifty talents given in charge,
Who spent them on himself, and liv'd at large;
His only virtue that he did not hide
The pounds, but squander'd them to serve his pride;
His praise that, cunning in his generation,
He of the heavenly treasure did not spare
To win himself an earthly habitation.

B.

Deny him not this laurel, nor to France
The apostolate of modern tolerance:
Their Theseus he, who slew the Minotaur,
The Dragon Persecution, in which war
He tipp'd the shafts that made the devil bleed;

And won a victory that hath overcome
Many misdoings in a well-done deed;
And more, I think, the mind of Christ revealing,
Yea, more of common-sense and human feeling
Than all the Creeds and Bulls of Christendom.

A.

Yet was he only one of them that slew:
The fiend had taken a deadly wound from Bayle;
And did he 'roar to see his kingdom fail'
'Neath Robespierre, or raise his head anew?
Nay, Voltaire's teaching never cured the heart:
The lack of human feeling blots his art.
When most his phrase with indignation burns,
Still to the gallery his face he turns.

B.

You bear him hard.   Men are of common stuff,
Each hath some fault, and he had faults enough:
But of all slanderers that ever were
A virtuous critic is the most unfair.
In greatness ever is some good to see;
And what is character, unless it be
The colour of persistent qualities,
That, like a ground in painting, balances
All hues and forms, combining with one tone
Whatever lights or shades are on it thrown?
Now Voltaire had of Nature a rich ground,
Two virtues rarely in conjunction found:
Industry, which no pedant could excel,
He matched with gaiety inexhaustible;
And with heroic courage held these fast,
As sailors nail their colours to the mast,
With ruling excellence atoning all.
Though, for the rest, he still for praise may call;

Prudent to gain, as generous to share
Le superflu, chose si nécessaire ;
To most a rare companion above scorn,
To not a few a kind, devoted friend
Through his long battling life, which in the end
He strove with good works richly to adorn.
I have admired, and why should I abuse
A man who can so long and well amuse?

A.

To some Parisian art there's this objection,
'Tis mediocrity pushed to perfection.

B.

'Judge not,' say I, 'and ye shall not be judged!'

A.

Let me say, 'praise men, if ye would be praised:'
Let your unwholesome flattery flow ungrudged,
And with ungrudging measure shall men pour
Their stifling homage back till ye be crazed,
And sane men humour you as fools past cure.
But these wise maxims deal not with the dead,
'Tis by example that the young are led,
And judgement owes its kindness but to them;
Nor will I praise, call you me hard or nice,
One that degraded art, and varnished vice.
They that praise ill thereby themselves condemn.

B.

Béranger could not praise.

A.

            Few are who can;
Not he: if ever he assay'd to impart
A title loftier than his own renown,

Native irreverence defied his art,
His fingers soil'd the lustre of his crown.
Here he adored what he was envious of,
The vogue and dazzling fashion of the man.
But man's true praise, the poet's praise, is love.

B.

And that, perhaps, was hardly his affair . . .
Pray, now, what set you talking of Voltaire?

A.

This only, that in weeding out my shelves,
In fatherly regard for babes upgrown,
Until they learn to garden for themselves,
Much as I like to keep my sets entire,
When I came out to you I had just thrown
Three of his precious works behind the fire.

12

TO ROBERT BURNS

AN EPISTLE ON INSTINCT

I

THOU art a poet, Robbie Burns,
Master of words and witty turns,
Of lilting songs and merry yarns,
    Drinking and kissing:
There's much in all thy small concerns,
    But more that's missing.

2

The wisdom of thy common sense,
Thy honest hate of vain pretence,
Thy love and wide benevolence
    Full often lead thee
Where feeling is its own defence;
    Yet while I read thee,

(384)

3

It seems but chance that all our race
Trod not the path of thy disgrace,
And, living freely to embrace
    The moment's pleasure,
Snatch'd not a kiss of Nature's face
    For all her treasure.

4

The feelings soft, the spirits gay
Entice on such a flowery way,
And sovran youth in high heyday
    Hath such a fashion
To glorify the bragging sway
    Of sensual passion.

5

But rakel Chance and Fortune blind
Had not the power:—Eternal Mind
Led man upon a way design'd,
    By strait selection
Of pleasurable ways, to find
    Severe perfection.

6

For Nature did not idly spend
Pleasure: she ruled it should attend
On every act that doth amend
    Our life's condition:
'Tis therefore not well-being's end,
    But its fruition.

7

Beasts that inherited delight
In what promoted health or might,
Survived their cousins in the fight:
    If some—like Adam—
Prefer'd the wrong tree to the right,
    The devil had 'em.

8

So when man's Reason took the reins,
She found that she was saved her pains;
She had but to approve the gains
   Of agelong inscience,
And spin it fresh into her brains
    As moral conscience.

9

But Instinct in the beasts that live
Is of three kinds; (Nature did give
To man three shakings in her sieve)—
   The first is Racial,
The second Self-preservative,
    The third is Social.

10

Without the first no race could be,
So 'tis the strongest of the three;
Nay, of such forceful tyranny
   'Tis hard to attune it,
Because 'twas never made to agree
    To serve the unit:

11

Art will not picture it, its name
In common talk is utter shame:
And yet hath Reason learn'd to tame
   Its conflagration
Into a sacramental flame
    Of consecration.

12

Those hundred thousand years, ah me!
Of budding soul! What slow degree,
With aim so dim, so true! We see,
   Now that we know them,
Our humble cave-folk ancestry,
    How much we owe them:

13

While with the savage beasts around
They fought at odds, yet underground
Their miserable life was sound;
   Their loves and quarrels
Did well th' ideal bases found
   Of art and morals:

14

One prime distinction, Good and Ill,
Was all their notion, all their skill;—
But Unity stands next to Nil;—
   Want of analysis
Saved them from doubts that wreck the Will
   With pale paralysis.

15

In vain philosophers dispute
'Is Good or Pleasure our pursuit?'—
The fruit likes man, not man the fruit;
   The good that likes him,
The good man's pleasure 'tis to do 't;
   That's how it strikes him.

16

Tho' Science hide beneath her feet
The point where moral reasonings meet,
The vicious circle is complete;
   There is no lodgement
Save Aristotle's own retreat,
   The just man's judgement.

17

And if thou wert not that just man,
Wild Robin, born to crown his plan,
We shall not for that matter ban
   Thy petty treason,
Nor closely thy defection scan
   From highest Reason.

18

Thou might'st have lived like Robin Hood
Waylaying Abbots in the wood,
Doing whate'er thee-seemèd good,
   The law defying,
And 'mong the people's heroes stood
   Living and dying :

19

Yet better bow than his thou bendest,
And well the poor man thou befriendest,
And oftentime an ill amendest ;
   When, if truth touch thee,
Sharply the arrow home thou sendest ;
   There 's none can match thee.

20

So pity it is thou knew'st the teen
Of sad remorse : the Might-have-been
Shall not o'ercloud thy merry scene
   With vain repentance,
Nor forfeit from thy spirit keen
   My friendly sentence.

13

THE PORTRAIT OF A GRANDFATHER

With mild eyes agaze, and lips ready to speak,
Whereon the yearning of love, the warning of wisdom plays,
One portrait ever charms me and teaches me when I seek :
   It is of him whom I, remembering my young days,
Imagine fathering my father ; when he, in sonship afore,
Liv'd honouring and obeying the eyes now pictur'd agaze,
   The lips ready to speak, that promise but speak no more.

O high parental claim, that were not but for the knowing,
O fateful bond of duty, O more than body that bore,
   The smile that guides me to right, the gaze that follows
       my going,
How had I stray'd without thee! and yet how few will seek
The spirit-hands, that heaven, in tender-free bestowing,
   Holds to her children, to guide the wandering and aid
       the weak.

And Thee! ah what of thee, thou lover of men? if truly
A painter had stell'd thee there, with thy lips ready to speak,
   In all-fathering passion to souls enchanted newly,
—Tenderer call than of sire to son, or of lover to maiden,—
Ever ready to speak to us, if we will hearken duly,
   'Come, O come unto me, ye weary and heavy-laden!'

                        [1880.]

14

AN INVITATION TO THE OXFORD PAGEANT, JULY 1907

FAIR lady of learning, playfellow of spring,
   Who to thy towery hospice in the vale
Invitest all, with queenly claim to bring
   Scholars from every land within thy pale;
   If aught our pageantry may now avail
To paint thine antique story to the eye,
Inspire the scene, and bid thy herald cry
   Welcome to all, and to all comers hail!

Come hither, then he crieth, and hail to all.
   Bow each his heart a pilgrim at her shrine,
Whatever chance hath led you to my call,
   Ye that love pomp, and ye that seek a sign,

Or on the low earth look for things divine;
Nor ye, whom reverend Camus near-allied,
Writes in the roll of his ennobled pride,
    Refrain your praise and love to mix with mine.

Praise her, the mother of celestial moods,
    Who o'er the saints' inviolate array
Hath starr'd her robe of fair beatitudes
    With jewels worn by Hellas, on the day
    She grew from girlhood into wisdom gay;
And hath laid by her crozier, evermore
With both hands gathering to enrich her store,
    And make her courts with music ring alway.

Love her, for that the world is in her heart,
    Man's rude antiquity and doubtful goal,
The heaven-enthralling luxury of art,
    The burden'd pleading of his clay-bound soul,
    The mutual office of delight and dole,
The merry laugh of youth, the joy of life
Older than thought, and the unamending strife
    'Twixt liberty and politic control.

There is none holier, not the lilied town
    By Arno, whither the spirit of Athens fled,
Escap't from Hades to a less renown,
    Yet joyful to be risen from the dead;
    Nor she whose wide imperious arms were spread
To spoil mankind, until the avenger came
In darkening storm, and left a ruin'd name,
    A triple crown upon a vanquish't head.

What love in myriad hearts in every clime
    The vision of her beauty calls to pray'r:
Where at his feet Himâlaya sublime
    Holds up aslope the Arabian floods, or where

Patriarchal Nile rears at his watery stair;
In the broad islands of the Antipodes,
By Esperanza, or in the coral seas
    Where Buddha's vain pagodas throng the air;

Or where the chivalry of Nipon smote
    The wily Muscovite, intent to creep
Around the world with half his pride afloat,
    And sent his battle to the soundless deep;
    Or with our pilgrim-kin, and them that reap
The prairie-corn beyond cold Labrador
To California and the Alaskan shore,
    Her exiled sons their pious memory keep:

Bright memories of young poetic pleasure
    In free companionship, the loving stress
Of all life-beauty lull'd in studious leisure,
    When every Muse was jocund with excess
    Of fine delight and tremulous happiness;
The breath of an indolent unbridled June,
When delicate thought fell from the dreamy moon:
    But now strange care, sorrow, and grief oppress.

' *Ah! fewer tears shall be,*—'tis thus they dream,—
    Ah, fewer, softer tears, when we lie low:
On younger brows shall brighter laurel gleam:
    Lovelier and earlier shall the rosebuds blow.'
    For in this hope she nurs'd them, and to know
That Truth, while men regard a tetter'd page,
Leaps on the mountains, and from age to age
    Reveals the dayspring's inexhausted glow.

Yet all their joy is mingled with regret:
    As the lone scholar on a neighbouring height,
Brooding disconsolate with eyelids wet
    Ere o'er the unkind world he took his flight,

Look'd down upon her festal lamps at night,
And while the far call of her warning bell
Reach't to his heart, sang us his fond farewell,
    Beneath the stars thinking of lost delight;

'Farewell! for whether we be young or old,
    Thou dost remain, but we shall pass away:
Time shall against himself thy house uphold,
    And build thy sanctuary from decay;
    Children unborn shall be thy pride and stay.
May Earth protect thee, and thy sons be true;
And God with heavenly food thy life renew,
    Thy pleasure and thy grace from day to day.'

15

ODE TO MUSIC

WRITTEN FOR THE BICENTENARY COMMEMORATION OF

HENRY PURCELL

*Music composed by Sir Hubert Parry, and performed at the
Leeds Festival and Commemoration Festival in
London, 1895*

I

MYRIAD-VOICED Queen, Enchantress of the air,
Bride of the life of man! With tuneful reed,
With string and horn and high-adoring quire
Thy welcome we prepare.
In silver-speaking mirrors of desire,

(392)

In joyous ravishment of mystery draw thou near,
With heavenly echo of thoughts, that dreaming lie
Chain'd in unborn oblivion drear,
Thy many-hearted grace restore
Unto our isle our own to be,
And make again our Graces three.

II

Turn, O return!   In merry England
Foster'd thou wert with infant Liberty.
Her gloried oaks, that stand
With trembling leaves and giant heart
Drinking in beauty from the summer moon,
Her wild-wood once was dear to thee.

There the birds with tiny art
Earth's immemorial cradle-tune
Warble at dawn to fern and fawn,
In the budding thickets making merry;
And for their love the primrose faint
Floods the green shade with youthful scent.

Come, thy jocund spring renew
By hyacinthine lakes of blue:
Thy beauty shall enchant the buxom May;
And all the summer months shall strew thy way,
And rose and honeysuckle rear
Their flowery screens, till under fruit and berry
The tall brake groweth golden with the year.

III

Thee fair Poetry oft hath sought,
Wandering lone in wayward thought,
On level meads by gliding streams,
When summer noon is full of dreams:
And thy loved airs her soul invade,
Haunting retired the willow shade.

Or in some wallèd orchard nook
She communes with her ancient book,
Beneath the branches laden low;
While the high sun o'er bosom'd snow
Smiteth all day the long hill-side
With ripening cornfields waving wide.

There if thou linger all the year,
No jar of man can reach thine ear,
Or sweetly comes, as when the sound
From hidden villages around,
Threading the woody knolls, is borne
Of bells that dong the Sabbath morn.

IV

1

The sea with melancholy war
Moateth about our castled shore;
His world-wide elemental moan
Girdeth our lives with tragic zone.

He, ere men dared his watery path,
Fenced them aloof in wrath;
Their jealous brotherhoods
Sund'ring with bitter floods:
Till science grew and skill,
And their adventurous will
Challenged his boundaries, and went free
To know the round world, and the sea
From midday night to midnight sun
Binding all nations into one.

2

Yet shall his storm and mastering wave
Assure the empire to the brave;

And to his billowy bass belongs
The music of our patriot songs,
When to the wind his ridges go
In furious following, careering a-row,
Lasht with hail and withering snow :
And ever undaunted hearts outride
   His rushing waters wide.

3

   But when the winds fatigued or fled
Have left the drooping barks unsped,
And nothing stirs his idle plain
Save fire-breathed ships with silvery train,
While lovingly his waves he layeth,
And his slow heart in passion swells
To the pale moon in heav'n that strayeth,
And all his mighty music deep
Whispers among the heapèd shells,
Or in dark caverns lies asleep ;—
   Then dreams of Peace invite,
Haunting our shore with kisses light :
Nay—even Love's Paphian Queen hath come
Out of her long retirèd home
To show again her beauty bright ;
And twice or thrice in sight hath play'd
Of a young lover unaffray'd,
And all his verse immortal made.

V

1

   Love to Love calleth,
   Love unto Love replieth :
From the ends of the earth, drawn by invisible bands,
Over the dawning and darkening lands
   Love cometh to Love.

To the pangs of desire;
To the heart by courage and might
Escaped from hell,
From the torment of raging fire,
From the sighs of the drowning main,
From shipwreck of fear and pain,
From the terror of night.

2

All mankind by Love shall be banded
To combat Evil, the many-handed:
For the spirit of man on beauty feedeth,
The airy fancy he heedeth,
He regardeth Truth in the heavenly height,
In changeful pavilions of loveliness dight,
The sovran sun that knows not the night;
He loveth the beauty of earth,
And the sweet birds' mirth;
And out of his heart there falleth
A melody-making river
Of passion, that runneth ever
To the ends of the earth and crieth,
That yearneth and calleth;
And Love from the heart of man
To the heart of man replieth:
On the wings of desire
Love cometh to Love.

VI

1

To me, to me, fair hearted Goddess, come,
To Sorrow come,
Where by the grave I linger dumb;
With sorrow bow thine head,
For all my beauty is dead,

Leave Freedom's vaunt and playful thought awhile,
Come with thine unimpassioned smile
Of heavenly peace. and with thy fourfold choir
    Of fair uncloying harmony
Unveil the palaces where man's desire
Keepeth celestial solemnity.

2

Lament, fair hearted queen, lament with me :
For when thy seer died no song was sung,
Nor for our heroes fal'n by land or sea
    Hath honour found a tongue :
Nor aught of beauty for their tomb can frame
    Worthy their noble name.
Let Mirth go bare : make mute thy dancing string :
With thy majestic consolation
Sweeten our suffering.
Speak thou my woe ; that from her pain
My spirit arise to see again
The Truth unknown that keeps our faith,
The Beauty unseen that bates our breath,
The heaven that doth our joy renew,
And drinketh up our tears as dew.

VII

DIRGE

Man born of desire
Cometh out of the night,
A wandering spark of fire,
A lonely word of eternal thought
Echoing in chance and forgot.

I

He seeth the sun,
He calleth the stars by name,

(397)

He saluteth the flowers.—
Wonders of land and sea,
The mountain towers
Of ice and air
He seeth, and calleth them fair :
　Then he hideth his face ;—
Whence he came to pass away
Where all is forgot,
Unmade—lost for aye
With the things that are not.

2

　He striveth to know,
To unravel the Mind
That veileth in horror :
He wills to adore.
In wisdom he walketh
And loveth his kind ;
His labouring breath
Would keep evermore :
　Then he hideth his face ;—
Whence he came to pass away
Where all is forgot,
Unmade—lost for aye
With the things that are not.

3

　He dreameth of beauty,
He seeks to create
Fairer and fairer
To vanquish his Fate ;
No hindrance he—
No curse will brook,
He maketh a law
No ill shall be :

Then he hideth his face;—
Whence he came to pass away
Where all is forgot,
Unmade—lost for aye
With the things that are not.

VIII

Rejoice, ye dead, where'er your spirits dwell,
Rejoice that yet on earth your fame is bright,
And that your names, remember'd day and night,
Live on the lips of those who love you well.
　'Tis ye that conquer'd have the powers of Hell
Each with the special grace of your delight;
Ye are the world's creators, and by might
Alone of Heavenly love ye did excel.

　　Now ye are starry names
　　Behind the sun ye climb
　　To light the glooms of Time
　　With deathless flames.

IX

Open for me the gates of delight,
The gates of the garden of man's desire;
Where spirits touch'd by heavenly fire
　Have planted the trees of life.—
Their branches in beauty are spread,
　　Their fruit divine
To the nations is given for bread,
　And crush'd into wine.

To thee, O man, the sun his truth hath given,
The moon hath whisper'd in love her silvery dreams;
Night hath unlockt the starry heaven,
The sea the trust of his streams:

And the rapture of woodland spring
    Is stay'd in its flying;
    And Death cannot sting
    Its beauty undying.

Fear and Pity disentwine
Their aching beams in colours fine;
Pain and woe forgo their might.
After darkness thy leaping sight,
After dumbness thy dancing sound,
After fainting thy heavenly flight,
After sorrow thy pleasure crown'd:
O enter the garden of thy delight,
    Thy solace is found.

X

    To us, O Queen of sinless grace,
    Now at our prayer unveil thy face:
    Awake again thy beauty free;
    Return and make our Graces three.
And with our thronging strength to the ends of the earth
Thy myriad-voicèd loveliness go forth,
    To lead o'er all the world's wide ways
      God's everlasting praise,
      And every heart inspire
With the joy of man in the beauty of Love's desire.

16

A HYMN OF NATURE

AN ODE WRITTEN FOR MUSIC

*The music composed by Sir Hubert Parry, performed at
the Gloucester Festival, 1898*

I

POWER eternal, power unknown, uncreate:
Force of force, fate of fate.

Beauty and light are thy seeing,
Wisdom and right thy decreeing,
Life of life is thy being.
In the smile of thine infinite starry gleam,
Without beginning or end,
Measure or number,
Beyond time and space,
Without foe or friend,
In the void of thy formless embrace,
All things pass as a dream
Of thine ùnbroken slumber.

II

Gloom and the night are thine:
On the face of thy mirror darkness and terror,
The smoke of thy blood, the frost of thy breath.

In silence and woful awe
Thy harrying angels of death
Destroy whate'er thou makest—
Makest, destroyest, destroyest and makest.
Thy gems of life thou dost squander,

(401)

Their virginal beauty givest to plunder,
Doomest to uttermost regions of age-long ice
    To starve and expire:
    Consumest with glance of fire,
    Or back to confusion shakest
With earthquake, elemental storm and thunder.

III

    In ways of beauty and peace
    Fair desire, companion of man,
    Leadeth the children of earth.

    As when the storm doth cease,
The loving sun the clouds dispelleth,
And woodland walks are sweet in spring;
    The birds they merrily sing
    And every flower-bud swelleth.
    Or where the heav'ns o'erspan
        The lonely downs
        When summer is high:
    Below their breezy crowns
        And grassy steep
Spreadeth the infinite smile of the sunlit sea;
    Whereon the white ships swim,
    And steal to havens far
    Across the horizon dim,
Or lie becalm'd upon the windless deep,
    Like thoughts of beauty and peace,
    When the storm doth cease,
And fair desire, companion of man,
    Leadeth the children of earth.

IV

Man, born to toil, in his labour rejoiceth;
His voice is heard in the morn:

He armeth his hand and sallieth forth
To engage with the generous teeming earth,
    And drinks from the rocky rills
        The laughter of life.

Or else, in crowded cities gathering close,
    He traffics morn and eve
    In thronging market-halls;
    Or within echoing walls
    Of busy arsenals
Weldeth the stubborn iron to engines vast;
    Or tends the thousand looms
    Where, with black smoke o'ercast,
    The land mourns in deep glooms.

    Life is toil, and life is good:
    There in loving brotherhood
    Beateth the nation's heart of fire.
    Strife! Strife! The strife is strong!
There battle thought and voice, and spirits conspire
In joyous dance around the tree of life,
    And from the ringing choir
Riseth the praise of God from hearts in tuneful song.

           V

    Hark! What spirit doth entreat
    The love-obedient air?
    All the pomp of his delight
    Revels on the ravisht night,
    Wandering wilful, soaring fair:
    There! 'Tis there, 'tis there.
    Like a flower of primal fire
    Late redeem'd by man's desire.

    Away, on wings away
    My spirit far hath flown,

To a land of love and peace,
        Of beauty unknown.
The world that earth-born man,
By evil undismay'd,
Out of the breath of God
Hath for his heaven made.

Where all his dreams soe'er
Of holy things and fair
In splendour are upgrown,
Which thro' the toilsome years
Martyrs and faithful seers
And poets with holy tears
        Of hope have sown.

There, beyond power of ill,
In joy and blessing crown'd,
Christ with His lamp of truth
Sitteth upon the hill
Of everlasting youth,
And calls His saints around.

VI

Sweet compassionate tears
Have dimm'd my earthly sight,
Tears of love, the showers wherewith
The eternal morn is bright:
Dews of the heav'nly spheres.
With tears my eyes are wet,
Tears not of vain regret,
Tears of no lost delight,
Dews of the heav'nly spheres
Have dimm'd my earthly sight,
Sweet compassionate tears

Odes

VII

Gird on thy sword, O man, thy strength endue,
In fair desire thine earth-born joy renew.
Live thou thy life beneath the making sun
Till Beauty, Truth, and Love in thee are one.

Thro' thousand ages hath thy childhood run:
On timeless ruin hath thy glory been:
From the forgotten night of loves fordone
Thou risest in the dawn of hopes unseen.

Higher and higher shall thy thoughts aspire,
Unto the stars of heaven, and pass away,
And earth renew the buds of thy desire
In fleeting blooms of everlasting day.

Thy work with beauty crown, thy life with love;
Thy mind with truth uplift to God above:
For whom all is, from whom was all begun,
In whom all Beauty, Truth, and Love are one.

Poems
in
Classical Prosody

PREVIOUS PUBLICATIONS

Ep. I. Daniel Press. 1903.

,, *II.* Monthly Review. July, 1903, with an abstract of Stone's Prosody, as there used.

No. 7. In ' Pelican,' C.C.C., Oxford.

,, 8. English Review. March, 1912.

,, 20. New Quarterly. Jan. 1909, with an essay on the Virgilian Hexameter, &c.

,, 20 & 21. Ibant Obscuri. Clarendon Press. 1916: with reprint of summary of Stone's Prosody accompanied by ' later observations & modifications'.

THESE experiments in quantitive verse were made in fulfilment of a promise to William Johnson Stone that I would some day test his theory. His premature death converted my consent into a serious obligation. This personal explanation is due to myself for two reasons : because I might otherwise appear firstly as an advocate of the system, secondly as responsible for Stone's determination of the lengths of English syllables. Before writing quantitive verse it is necessary to learn to *think* in quantities. This is no light task, and a beginner requires fixed rules. Except for a few minor details, which I had disputed with Mr. Stone, I was bound to take his rules as he had elaborated them ; and it was not until I had made some progress and could think fairly well in his prosody that I seriously criticized it. The two chief errors that I find in it are that he relied too much on the quality of a vowel in determining its syllabic length, and that he regarded the *h* as *always* consonantal in quality. His valuation of the *er* sound is doubtful, but defensible and convenient, and I have never discarded it. My earlier experiments contain therefore a good many 'false quantities', and these, where they could not be very easily (though *inconsistently*) amended, I have left, and marked most of them in the text : a few false quantities do not make a poem less readable. Thus a long mark over a syllable means that Stone reckoned it as long, and that the verse requires it to be so pronounced, but that I regard it as short, or at least as *doubtful*. For example on p. 414 *Rūin* is thus written. Of all accented long vowels in 'open' position the long *u* seems perhaps to retain its quantity best, but there is evidence that Tennyson held it to be shortened, and I do not know whether it might be an exception or go with thĕory, pīety, pŏetry, &c. Again, where a final syllable should be lengthened or not shortened by position, but lacks its consonantal support, I have put a ˇ in the gap: these weak places are chiefly due to my accepting Stone's unchanging valuation of *h*. My emancipation from Stone's rules was gradual, so that I have not been able to distinguish definitely my earlier experiments from the later, in which the quantities are such as I have now come to approve of: but my line-for-line paraphrase of Virgil is such a later experiment. It was accompanied in the *New Quarterly* by a long examination of the Virgilian hexameter, to which I would refer any one who is interested in the subject. In these English hexameters I have used and advocate the use of Miltonic elision. The mark ˡ in the text shows where I have purposely allowed a short syllable to sustain a long place. Though the difficulty of adapting our English syllables to the Greek rules is very great, and even deterrent—for I cannot pretend to have attained to an absolutely consistent scheme—yet the experiments that I have made reveal a vast unexplored field of delicate and expressive rhythms hitherto unknown in our poetry : and this amply rewarded me for my friendly undertaking.

EPISTLE I

to L. M.

WINTRY DELIGHTS

Now in wintry delights, and long fireside meditation,
'Twixt studies and routine paying due court to the Muses,
My solace in solitude, when broken roads barricade me
Mudbound, unvisited for months with my merry children,
Grateful t'ward Providence, and heeding a slander against me
Less than a rheum, think of me to-day, dear Līonel, and take
This letter as some account of Will Stone's versification.

  We, whose first memories reach half of a century backward,
May praise our fortune to have outliv'd so many dangers,—
Faultiness of Nature's unruly machinery or man's—;   10
For, once born, whatever 'tis worth, LIFE is to be held to,
Its mere persistence esteem'd as rēal attainment,
Its crown of silver reverenc'd as one promise of youth
Fruiting, of existence one needful purpose accomplish'd:
And 'twere worth the living, howe'er unkindly bereft of
Those joys and comforts, throu' which we chiefly regard it:
Nay,—set aside the pleasant unhinder'd order of our life,
Our happy enchantments of Fortune, easy surroundings,
Courteous acquaintance, dwelling in fair homes, the delight of
Long-plann'd excursions, the romance of journeying in lands
Historic, of sēeing their glory, the famous adornments   21
Giv'n to memorial Earth by man, decorator of all-time,
(—As wē saw with virginal eyes travelling to behold them,—)
Her gorgeous palaces,ᵛher tow'rs and stately cathedrals;
Where the turrets and domes of pictured Tuscany slumber,

Or the havoc'd splendours of Rome imperial, or where
Glare the fretted minarets and mosks of trespassing Islam,
And old Nilus, amid the mummied suzerainty of Egypt,
Glideth, a godly presence, consciously regardless of all things,
Save his unending toil and ēternal recollections :— 30

    Set these out of account, and with them too put away ART,
Those ravishings of mind, those sensuous intelligences,
By whose grace the elect enjoy their sacred aloofness
From Life's meagre affairs, in beauty's rēgenerate youth
Reading immortality's sublime revelation, adoring
Their own heav'nly desire ; nor alone in worship assist they,
But take, call'd of God, part and pleasure in crēation
Of that beauty, the first of His first purposes extoll'd :—

    Yea, set aside with these all NATURE's beauty, the wildwood's
Flow'ry domain, the flushing, softcrowding loveliness of
      Spring, 40
Lazy Summer's burning dīal, the serenely solemn spells
Of Sibylline Autumn, with gay-wing'd Plenty departing;
All fair change, whether of seasons or bright recurrent day,
Morning or eve ; the divine night's wonderous empyrean;
High noon's melting azure, his thin cloud-country, the
      landscape
Mountainous or maritime, blue calms of midsummer Ocean,
Broad corn-grown champaign goldwaving in invisible wind,
Wide-water'd pasture, with shade of whispering aspen ;
All whereby Nature winneth our love, fondly appearing
As to caress her children, or all that in exaltation 50
Lifteth aloft our hearts to an unseen glory beyond her :—

    Put these out of account ; yea, more I say, banish also
From the credit sŭm of enjoyment those simple AFFECTIONS,
Whose common exercise informs our natural instinct ;
That, set in our animal flesh-fabric, of our very lifeblood
Draw their subsistence, and even in ungenerous hearts

Root, like plants in stony deserts and 'neath pitiless snows.
Yea, put away all LOVE, the blessings and pīeties of home,
All delicate heart-bonds, vital tendernesses untold,
Joys that fear to be named, feelings too holy to gaze on ;   60
And with his inviolate peace-trīumph his passionate war
Be forgone, his mighty desire, thrilling ecstasies, ardours
Of mystic reverence, his fierce flame-eager emotions,
Idolatrous service, blind faith and ritual of fire.

If from us all these things were taken away, (that is all art
And all beauty whate'er, and all love's varied affection,)
Yet would enough subsist in other concerns to suffice us,
And feed intelligence, and make life's justification.
What this is, if you should ask me, beyond or above the
    rejoicing
In vegetant or brute existence, answer is easy;   70
'Tis the reflective effort of mind that, conscious of itself,
Fares forth exploring nature for principle and cause,
Keenly with all the cunning pleasure and instinct of a hunter,
Who, in craft fashioning weapon and sly snare, tracketh after
His prey flying afield, and that which his arm killeth eateth.

History and SCĪENCE our playthings are : what an untold
Wealth of inexhaustive treasure is stored up for amusement!
Shall the amass'd Earth-structure appeal to me less than in
    early
Childhood an old fives-ball, whose wraps I wondering
    unwound,
Untwining the ravel'd worsted, that mere rubbish and waste
Of leather and shavings had bound and moulded elastic   81
Into a perfect sphere ? Shall not the celestial earth-ball
Equally entertain a mature enquiry, reward our
Examination of its contexture, conglomerated
Of layer'd débris, the erosion of infinite ages ?
Tho' I lack the wizard Darwin's scīentific insight
On the barren sea-beaches of East Patagonia gazing,

I must wond'ring attend, nay learn myself to decipher
Time's rich hīeroglyph, with vast elemental pencil
Scor'd upon Earth's rocky crust,—minute shells slowly
    collecting
        90
Press'd to a stone, uprais'd to a mountain, again to a fine sand
Worn, burying the remains of an alien organic epoch,
In the flat accretions of new sedimentary strata;
All to be crush'd, crumpled, confused, contorted, abandon'd,
Broke, as a child's puzzle is, to be recompos'd with attention;
Nature's history-book, which shē hath torn as asham'd of;
And lest those pictures onᵛher fragmentary pages
Should too lightly reveal frustrate Antiquity, hath laid
Rūin upon rūin, revolution upon revolution:
Yet no single atom, no least insignificant grain   100
But, having order alike of fate, and faulty disorder,
Holds a record of Time, very vestiges of the Creation;
Which who will not attend scorns blindly the only com-
    mandments
By God's finger of old inscribed on table of earth-stone.

This for me wer' enough: yet confin'd Gēology's field
Counts not in all Scīence more than the planet to the Cosmos;
Where our central Sun, almighty material author,
And sustainer, appears as a half-consumed vanishing spark,
Bearing along with it, entangled in immensity's onward
Spiral eddies, the blacken'd dust-motes whirl'd off from
    around it.
        110
But tho' man's microscopical functions measure all things
By his small footprints, finger-spans and ticking of clocks,
And thereby conceive the immense—such multiple extent
As to defy Idēas of imperative cerebration,—
None the less observing, measuring, patiently recording,
Hē mappeth out the utter wilderness of unlimited space;
Carefully weigheth a weight to the sun, reckoneth for it its
    path
Of trackless travelling, the precise momentary places

Of the planets and their satellites, their annual orbits,
Times, perturbations of times, and orbit of orbit.　　120
　　What was Alexander's subduing of Asia, or that
Sheep-worry of Europe, when pigmy Napoleon enter'd
Her sovereign chambers, and her kings with terror eclips'd?
His footsore soldiers inciting across the ravag'd plains,
Thro' bloody fields of death tramping to an ugly disaster?
Shows any crown, set above the promise (so rudely accom-
　　plisht)
Of their fair godlike young faces, a glory to compare
With the immortal olive that circles bold Galileo's
Brows, the laurel'd haloᵛof Newton's unwithering fame?　129
Or what a child's surmise, how trifling a journey Columbus
Adventur'd, to a land like that which he sail'd from arriving,
If compar'd to Bessel's magic divination, awarding
Magnificent Siriusᵛhis dark and invisible bride;
Or when Adams by Cam, (more nearly Leverrier in France,)
From the minutely measur'd vacillation of Uranus, augur'd
Where his mighty brother Neptune went wandering unnamed,
And thro' those thousand-million league-darknesses of space
Drew him slowly whene'er he pass'd, and slowly released
　　him!
Nil admirari!　'Tis surely a most shabby thinker　　139
Who, looking on Nature, finds not the reflection appalling.

　　And if these wonders we must with wonder abandon,
Astronomy's Cosmos, the Immense, and those physical laws
That link mind to matter, laws mutual in revelation,
Which measure and analyse Nature's primordial orgasm,
Lifegiving omnipotential LIGHT, its speed to determine,
Untwist its rainbow of various earthcoloring rays,
Counting strictly to each its own millionth-millimetred
Wave-length, and mapping out on fray'd diffraction of ether
All the adust elements and furnaced alchemy ofᵛheav'n;
Laws which atone the disorder of infinit observation　　150
With tyrannous numbers and abstract théory, closing

Protean Nature with nets of principle exact;
Her metamorphoses transmuting by correlation,
All heat, all chemical concourse or electrical action,
All force and all motion of all matter, or subtle or gross :—
  If we these wonders, I say, with wonder abandon,
Nor can for mental heaviness their high study pursue,
Yet no story of adventures or fabulous exploit
Of famous'd heroes hath so rōmantic a discourse,
As these growing annals of long heav'n-scaling achievement
And far discoveries, which he whoᵛidly neglecteth   161
Is but a boor as truly ridiculous as the village clown,
In whose thought the pleasant sun-ball performeth a circuit
Daily above mother earth, and resteth nightly beneath her.

  Nor will a man, whose mind respects its own operations,
Lightly resign himself to remain in darkness uninform'd,
While any true scīence of fact lies easy within reach
Concerning Nature's ēternal essential object,
Self-matter, embodying substratum of ev'ry relation
Both of Time and Space, at once the machinery and stuff
Of those Idēas ; carrier, giver, only receiver   171
Of such perceptions as arise in sensible organs.
  Now whether each element is a cōherency of equal
Strictly symmetric atoms, or among themselves the atoms are
Like animals in a herd, having each an identity distinct,
—So that atoms of gold compar'd with sulphur or iron
Are but as ancient Greeks compar'd with Chinamen and
      Turks ; —
Nor whether all elements are untransmutable offspring
From one kind or more thro' endless eternity changing,
Or whether invisibles claim rightly the name of immortals,
I make noᵛenquiry ; matter minutely divided   181
Showing a like paradox, with ever-continuous extent,
And, as Adam, the atom will pose as a naked assumption :—
But since all the knowledge which man was born to attain to
Hath these only channels, (which must limit and qualifyᵛit,)

We shall con the grammar, the material alphabet of life,
Yea, ev'n more from error to preserve our inquisitive mind,
Than to secure well-bēing against adversity and ill.
Surely if all is a flux, 'tis well to look into the flūid,
Inspect and question the apparent, shifty behaviour,   190
Wherein lurketh alone our witness of all physical law,
As we read the habits unchanging of invisible things,
Their timeless chronicles, the unintelligent ethic of dust:
In which dense labyrinth he who was guiding avised me,
With caution saying 'Were this globe's area of land
'Wholly cover'd from sight, pack'd close to the watery
        margins
'With mere empty vessels, I could myself put in each one
'Some different substance, and write its formula thereon.'

    Thus would speak the chemist; and Nature's superabun-
        dance,
Her vast infinitude of waste vārīety untold,   200
As⌣her immense extent and inconceivable object,
Squandering activities throughout ēternity, dwarfeth
Man's little aim and hour, his doubtful fancy: what are we?
Our petty selfseekings, our speedily passing affections?
Life having existed so extravagantly before us;
Earth bearing so slight a regard or care for us; and all
After us unconcern'd to remain, strange, beautiful as now.
May not an idle echo⌣of an antique pōetry haunt me,
'Friendship is all feigning, yea⌣all loving is folly only'?
—Yet doth not very mention of antique pōetry and love   210
Quickly recall to better motions my dispirited faith?
And I see man's discontent as witness asserting
His moral idēal, that, born of Nature, is heir to
Her children's titles, which nought may cancel or impugn;
Not wer' of all her works man least, but ranking among them
Highly or ev'n as best, he wrongs himself to imagine
His soul foe to her aim, or from⌣her sanction an outlaw.

(415)

Nay, but just as man should appear more fully accordant
With things not himself, would they rank with˅him as equals:
Judging other creatures he sets them wholly beneath him;
His disquiet among manifold and alien objects   221
Bēing sure evidence, the effect of an understanding,
And perception allow'd by Nature solely to himself.

    Highly then is to be prais'd the resourceful wisdom of
       our time,
That spunged out the written scīence and thēories of life,
And, laying foundation of its knowledge in physical law,
Gave it prēeminence o'er all enquiry, erecting
Superstructive of all, bringing ev'ry research to the object,
Boldly a new scīence of MAN, from dreamy scholastic
Imprisoning set free, and inveterate divination,   230
Into the light of truth, to the touch of history and fact.
    Since 'the proper study of mankind is man',—nor afore-
       time
Was the proverb esteem'd as a truism less than it is now,—
'Tis strange that the method lay out of sight unaccomplisht,
And that we, so late to arrive, should first set a value
On the delusive efforts of human babyhood; and so
Witnessing impatiently the rear of their disappearance,
Upgathering the relics and vestiges of primitive man,
Should ratify˅instinct for scīence, look to the darkness
For light, find a knowledge where 'twas most groping or un-
       known: 240
While civilization's advances mutely regarding
Talk we of old scapegoats, discuss bloodrites, immolations,
Worship of ancestors; explain complexities involved
Of tribal marriages, derivation of early religions,
Priestly taboos, totems, archaic mysteries of trees,
All the devils and dreams abhorr'd of barbarous ages.

    And 'tis a far escape from wires, wheels and penny papers
And the worried congestion of our Victorian era,

Whose many inventions of world-wide luxury have changed
Life's very face :—but enough wē hear of progress, enough
    have   250
Our conscious scïence and comforts trumpeted ; altho'
Hardly can I, who so many years eagerly frequented
Bartholomew's fountain, not speak of things to awaken
Kind old HIPPOCRATES, howe'er hē slumbereth, entomb'd
'Neath the shatter'd winejars and rūined factories of Cos,
Or where hē wander'd in Thessalian Larissa:
For when his doctrine, which Rome had wisely adopted,
Sank lost with the treasures of ᵛher deep-foundering empire,
No ᵛart or scïence grew so contemptible, order'd   259
So by mere folly, windy caprice, superstition and chance,
As boastful MEDICINE, with humours fit for a madhouse,
Save when some Sydenham, like Samson among the Philis-
    tines,
Strode bond-bursting along with a smile of genial instinct.
Nor when here and there some ray, in darkness arising,
Hopefully seem'd to herald the coming dawn, (as when a
    Laennec
Or Jenner invented his meed of worthy remembrance,)
Did one mind foresee, one seer foretell the appearance
Of that unexpected daylight that arose upon our time.
    Who dream'd that living air poison'd our SURGERY, coating
All our sheeny weapons with germs of an invisible death, 270
Till he saw the sterile steel work with immunity, and save
Quickly as its warring scimitars of victory had slain ?
Saw what school-tradition for nature's kind method admir'd,
—In those lifedraining slow cures and bedridden agues,—
Forgotten, or condemn'd as want of care in a surgeon ?
    Tho' MEDICINE makes not so plain an appeal to the vulgar,
Yet she lags not a whit : her pregnant thēory touches
Deeper discoveries, ᵛher more complete revolution
Gives promise of wider benefits in larger abundance.
    Where she nam'd the disease she now separates the
    bacillus;   280

Sets the atoms of offence, those blind and sickly bloodeaters,
'Neath lens and daylight, forcing their foul propagations,
Which had ever prosper'd in dark impunity unguest,
Now to behave in sight, deliver their poisonous extract
And their strange self-brew'd, self-slaying juice to be handled,
Experimented upon, set aside and stor'd to oppose them.

So novel and obscure a research, such hard revelations
Of Nature's cabinet,—tho' with fact amply accordant,
And by hypothesis much dark difficulty resolving,
Are not quickly receiv'd nor approv'd, and sensitive idlers,
Venturing in the profound terrible penetralia of life,   291
Are shock'd byᵛa method that shuns not contamination
With crūel Nature's most secret processes unmaskt.
And yet in all mankind's disappointed history, now first
Haveᵛhis scouts push'd surely withinᵛhis foul enemies' lines,
And his sharpshooters descried their insidious foe,
Those swarming parasites, that barely within the detection
Of manifold search-light, have bred, swimming unsuspected
Thro' man's brain and limbs, slaying with loathly pollution
His beauty's children,ᵛhis sweet scīons of affection,   300
In fev'rous torment and tears, his home desolating
Of their fair innocence, breakingᵛhis proud passionate heart,
And his kindly belief in GOD's good justice arraigning.

With what wildly directed attack, what an armory illjudged,
Has he, (alas, poor man,) with what cumbrous machination
Sought to defend himself from their Lilliputian onslaught;
Aye discharging around him, in obscure night, at a venture,
Ev'ry missile whichᵛhis despair confus'dly imagin'd ;
His simples, compounds, specifics, chemical therapeutics,
Juice of plants, whatever was nam'd in lordly Salerno's   310
Herbaries and gardens, vipers, snails, all animal filth,
Incredible quackeries, the pretentious jugglery of knaves,
Green electricities, saints' bones and priestly anointings.
Fools ! that oppose his one scīentific intelligent hope !
Grant us an hundred years, and man shall hold in abeyance
These foul distempers, and with this world's benefactors

Shall PASTEUR obtain the reward of saintly devotion,
His crown hēroic, who fought not destiny in vain.

'Tis success that attracts : 'twas therefore so many workers
Ran pellmell to the schools of Nature in our generation, 320
While other employments have lack'd their genius and pined.
Our fathers' likings wē thought semibarbarous, our art
Self-consciously sickens in qualms of an æsthetic aura,
Noisily in the shallows splashing and disporting uninspir'd.
Our famed vulgarities whether in speech, taste or amusement,
Are not amended: Is it foolish, hoping for a rescue,
First to appeal to the strong, for health to the healthy
        amongst us?
—For the Sophists' doctrine that GRACE is dȳing of old age
I hold in derision, their inkpot thēories of man,
Of his cradle of art, his deathbed of algebra ;—and see   330
How Scīence has wrought, since we went idling at Eton,
One thing above surmise :—An' if I may dare to remind you
How Vergil praises your lov'd Lucretius, (of whom
My matter and metreᵛhave set you thinking, as I fear,)
In that glory which ends ' et inexorabile fatum
Subjecit pedibus strepitumque Acherontis avari':
Sounded not most empty to us such boast of a pagan,
Strangely to us tutor'd to believe, with faith mediæval,
Torture everlasting to be justly the portion of all souls,
Nor but by the elects' secret prēdestiny escaped?   340
If you think to reply,—making this question in answer,—
' Did the belief disturb for a moment our pleasure in life?'
No.—And men gather in harvest on slopes of an active
Volcano: natheless the terror's ēnormity was there ;
Now 'tis away : Scīence has pierced man's cloudy common-
        sense,
Dow'rd his homely vision with more expansive an embrace,
And the rotten foundation of old superstition exposed.
That trouble of Pascal, those vain paradoxes of Austin,
Those Semitic parables of Paul, those tomes of Aquinas,

All are thrown to the limbo of antediluvian idols,　　350
Only because we learn mankind's true history, and know
That not at all from a high perfection sinfully man fell,
But from baseness arose: We have with sympathy enter'd
Those dark caves, his joyless abodes, where with ravening
　　brutes,
Bear or filthy hyena, he once disputed a shelter:—
That was his Paradise, his garden of Eden,—abandon'd
Ages since to the drift and drip, the cementing accretions
Whence we now separate his bones buried in the stalagma,
His household makeshifts, his hunting tools, his adornments,
From the scatter'd skeletons of a lost prehistoric order,　360
Its mammoth and woolly rhinoceros, the machairodos, and
　　beasts
Whose unnamed pastures the immense Atlantic inundates.
　In what corner of earth lie not dispersed the familiar
Flinty relics of his old primitive stone-cutlery? what child
Kens not now the design, the adapted structure of each one
Of those hand-labor'd chert-flakes, whether axe, chisel, or
　　knife,
Spearhead, barb of arrow, rough plane or rudely serrate saw?
Stones that in our grandsires' time told no sermon, (awaiting
Indestructible, unnumber'd, on chary attention,)
From their prēadamite pulpits now cry Revelation.　　370
　Not to a Greek his chanted epic had mortal allurement,
Conjuring old-world fancies of Ilium and of Olympus,
As this story to me, this tale primæval of unsung,
Unwritten, ancestral fate and adversity, this siege
Of courage and happiness protracted so many thousand
Thousand years in a slow persistent victory of brain
And right hand o'er all the venom'd stings, sharpnesses of
　　fang
And dread fury whate'er Nature, tirelessly devising,
Could develop with tooth, claw, tusk, or horn to oppose them.
See now Herakles, who strangled snakes when an infant　380
In ᵛhis cradle alone; and nought but those petty stonechips

For the battle : 'twas wonder above wonders his achievement :
Yea, and since he thought as a child 'twas natural in him,
Meeting in existence with purposes antagonistic,
Circumstances oppos'd to desire, vast activities, which
Thwarted effort, to assume All-might as spiteful against him.
Nay, as an artist born, impell'd to devise a religion,—
So to relate himself idēally with the immortal,—
This quarrel of reason with what displeas'd his affections
Was not amiss.   The desire and love of beauty possess man :
Art is of all that beauty the best outwardly presented ;   391
Truth to the soul is merely the best that mind can imagine.
No lover ēternal will hold to an older opinion
If but lovelier ideas, with Nature agrēeing,
Are to his understanding offer'd...But enough : 'tis an unsolv'd
Mystery.—Yet man dreams to flatter his dēity saying
'Beautiful is Nature !' rather 'tis various, endless,
And her efforts fertile in error tho' grand in attainment.
If wé, while praising her scheme and infinite order,
Are compell'd to select, our choice condemns the remainder ;
Nor can wisdom honour those loathly polluting offences,   401
Whose very names to the Muse are either accursèd or
    unknown.
Nay, if such foul things thou deemest worthy, the fault was
Making us, O Nature, thy judge and tearful accuser.
    Turn our thought for awhile to the symphonies of
        Beethoven,
Or the rever'd preludes of mighty Sebastian ; Is there
One work of Nature's contrivance beautiful as these ?
Judg'd by beauty alone man wins, as sensuous artist ;
And for other qualities, the spirit's differentia, Nature
Scarce observes them at all : that keen unfaltering insight,   410
Whereby earthly desire's roaming wildernesses are changed
Into a garden a-bloom ; its wandering impossible ways
Into pillar'd avenues, alleys and fair-flow'ry terrac'd walks,
(Where GOD talks with man, as once 'twas fancied of Eden ;)
That transcendental supreme interpreting of sense,

Rendering intelligence passionate with mystery, linking
Sympathy with grandeur, the reserve of dignity with play;
Those soul-formalities, the balance held 'twixt the denīal
And the betrayal of intention, whose masteries invite,
Entice, welcome ever, meet, and with kindliness embrace; 420
Those guarded floodgates of boundless, lovely resources,
Whence nothing ill issues, no distraction nor abortion
Hindering enjoyment, but in easy security flow forth
Ecstasies of fitness, raptures and harmonies of heav'n.
Surely before such work of man, so kindly attemper'd,
Nature must be asham'd, had shē not this ready answer,
' Fool, and who made thee? '—

                    I shall not seem a deserter,
Where in an idle essay my verse to a fancy abandon'd
Praiseth others : rather while art and beauty delight us,
While hope, faith and love are warm and lively in our hearts,
Sweet our earthly desire and dear our human affection,   431
We may, joyfully despising the pedantries of old age,
Hold to the time, nor lose the delight of mortal attainment;
Keenly rejoicing in all that wisdom approves, nor allowing
Ourselves at the challenge of younger craft to be outsailed ;
But trimming our old canvas in all change of weather and
    wind,
Freely without fear urge o'erseas our good vessel onward,
Piloting into the far, unmapp'd futurity.—Farewell.

2

EPISTLE II

TO A SOCIALIST IN LONDON

No˅ethical system, no contemplation or action,
No reason'd attitude of mind nor principle of faith,
Neither Sōcratical wisdom nor saintly devotion,
Buildeth a fortress against heart-ache & compassionate grief,
Nor responds to desire, nor with true mastery yieldeth
Easy repose to the mind; And since all our study endeth
Emptily in full doubt,—fathoming the divine intention
In this one thing alone, that, howsōe'er it affect us,
'Twas never intended for mortal fancy to compass,—
I˅have concluded that from first purposes unknown   10
None should seek to deduce idēal laws to be liv'd by;
And, loving art, am true to the Muse, & pōetry extol:
Therefore 'twas that afore I prais'd & heartily enjoy'd
Your human verses, FRASER, when nobody bought them,
More than again I praise those serious exhortations,
Wherewith you wu'd amend the degraded people about you.
Nay tho' like a prophet with heav'n-sent dignity inspir'd,
With ready convincement and stern example assuring,
Mightily you proclaim your love-messag' in the assembly,
Exhibiting panacēas of ancient ill, propagating   20
Out of a Scotch cerebrum the reforming zeal of a TOLSTOI,
I listen all unmov'd, as a sceptic among the believers.
Yet what a charm has an earnest soul, whom sympathy
     uncheckt
For human suffering has strengthen'd and dedicated
Bravely to serve his kind, to renounce his natural instinct,
And liv' apart, indulging in acts of mercy, delighted
In wisdom's rock-hewn citadel˅her law to illustrate,
Embodying the pattern of self-integrity complete.

(423)

Yea, what a charm pervades discourse, that loftily reason'd
Points the narrow pathway throu' this world's ugly disorder;
How very fair wil appear any gate of cleanliness, open   30
From the city's tumult, its rank impurity, its dread
Vulgarity's triumph : Nay sure *&* bounteous as Truth,
Beautiful in confusion appeareth Simplicity's way.
—'Simple it is, (yóu say) God is good,—Nature is ample,—
'Earth yields plenty for all,—and all might share in abun-
    dance,
'Were profit and labour but fairly divided among them.
'Scarce any laws are needed in our Utopia but these,—
'No fruitless labour to provide mere useless adornment,
'No money encouraging man's sloth *&* slavery, no rents   40
'Of titeld landlords, no pamper'd luxury breeding
'Fleshly disease, worst fiend *&* foe of mind body and soul ;
'All should work, and only produce life's only requirements :
'So with days all halfholidays, toil healthfully enjoy'd,
'Each might, throu' leisure hours of amusement pīety and
    peace,
'In the domestic joys *&* holy community partake.—'
—This wer' a downleveling, my friend ; yoū need, to assure
    me,
Fix a limit to the folk ; else, as their number is increas't,
Their happiness may dwindle away, *&* what was at outset
Goal *&* prize, the provoker of all your wise revolution,   50
Will by subdivision disappear in course of atainment.
When goods areᵛincreas'd, mouths areᵛincreas'd to devour
    them :
If the famine be reliev'd this season in India, next dearth
Will be a worse. Yoū know how one day Herschel acosted
Súch a philanthropical Save-all, who claimed to acomplish
Some greatest happiness for a greatest number ; 'Attend,
    man ;
(Saíd-he) Resólve me anon one query : Suppose Adam and
    Eve
First crēated on Earth but twice ten centuries ere Christ,

That they gat four children in all, who liv'd, getting also
Four to the pair : Had thus mankind ever equaly increast   60
By moderate families but doubling in each generation,
How many souls would now be alive to revise the conun-
    drum
Of greatest happiness ?   No ᵛanswer ?   Well, 'tis a long sum.
Say if on earth such a crowd could stand.   No ?   Pray then
    imágine
All earth's land as a plain, & all this company thereon,
Piled together like peas in a pintpot : How many layers ?
No guess ?   Then how high the column ?   How far wu'd it
    extend
Into the sky ?—To the moon ?—Further—To the sun ?—To
    the sun !   Pshaw !
That column of happy men would reach up, as I fathom its
    height,
Million dīameters of Neptune's infinit' orbit.'   70
    My ᵛ objection   annoys   your   kindly   philanthropy ?—' It
    proves
' Too much.'—Yes nature shows in that scrutiny bankrupt;
Mere matter in deposit gives out.   Yóu wish to determine
No limit of future polities : your actual object
Is to relieve suffering, to repeal injustice acruing
From monied inheritance, which makes a nonentity potent
For public mischief, who might, if usefully harness'd
In common employment, have assisted social order.
Why should Law give fifty talents where Nature alloys one ?
For money is the talent of supreme empery : Gold, Gold   80
Envieth all, getteth all, absorbeth, mastereth all things:
It pusheth out & thrusteth away pitilessly the weak ones,
Those ill-fated, opprest, unfortun'd needy : Beneath them
Yawns the abyss.   Down down they fall, as a stream on a
    mountain,
With ceaseless cataract.   None hearkeneth ; only the silent
Grave, that darkly devours their cry of desperate anguish.
Spáre me the story ; believe more feel this grief than avow it :

'Tis put aside from thought with death's incurable evil;
Left for them, that assume mankind as cause, to lament it.
And what if all Nature ratify this merciless outrage?   90
If her wonder of arch-wonders, her fair animal life,
Her generate creatures, her motion'd warmblooded offspring,
Haunters of the forest & royal country, her antler'd
Mild-gazers, that keep silvan sabbath idly without end;
Her herded galopers, sleeksided stately careerers
Of trembling nostril; her coy unapproachable estrays,
Stealthy treaders, climbers; her leapers furry, lissom-limb'd;
Her timorous burrowers, and grangers thrifty, the sandy
Playmates of the warren; her clumsy-footed, shaggy roamers;
Her soarers, the feather'd fast-fliers, loftily floating   100
Sky-sailers, exiles of high solitudinous eyries;
Her perching carolers, twitterers, & sweetly singing birds:
All ocean's finny clans, mute-mouthers, watery breathers,
Furtive arrow-darters, and fan-tail'd easy balancers,
Silvery-scale, gilt-head, thorn-back, frill'd harlequinading
Globe and slimy ribbon: Shell-builders of many-chamber'd
Pearly dwellings, soft shapes mosslike or starry, adorning
With rich floral fancy the gay rock-garden of ebb-tide:
All life, from the massive-bulkt, ivory-tusht, elephantine
Centēnarian, acknowledging with crouching obeisance   110
Man's will, ev'n to the least petty whiffling ephemeral insect,
Which in a hot sunbeam engend'ring, when summer is high,
Vaunteth an hour his speck of tinsely gaudiness and dies:
Ah! what if all & each of Nature's favorite offspring,
'Mong many distinctions, have this portentous agreement,
MOUTH, STOMACH, INTESTINE? Question that brute appa-
    ratus,
So manifoldly devis'd, set alert with furious instinct:
What doth it interpret but this, that LIFE LIVETH ON LIFE?
That the select creatures, who inherit earth's domination,
Whose happy existence is Nature's intelligent smile,   120
Are bloody survivors of a mortal combat, a-tweenwhiles
Chanting a brief pæan for victory on the battlefield?

Since that of all their kinds most owe their prosperous estate
Unto the art, whereby they more successfully destroy'd
Their weaker brethren, more insatiably devour'd them;
And all fine qualities, their forms pictorial, admired,
Their symmetries, their grace, & beauty, the loveliness of
them,
Were by Murder evolv'd, to 'scape from it or to effect it.

'Surely again (you say) too much is proven, it argues
'Mere horror & despair; unless persuasion avail us   130
'That the moral virtues are man's idĕa, awaken'd
'By the spirit's motions; & therefore not to be conceiv'd
'In Nature's outward & mainly material aspect,
'As that is understood.   You, since you hold that opinion,
'Run your own ship aground invoking Nature against me.'—

Then withdraw the appeal, my friend, to her active alīance;
Bē pessimist Nature with a pitchfork manfully expell'd,
Not to return.   Yet *soul in hand*, with brutal alegiance,
Hunters & warriors *do not forget the comandment*.
See how lively the old animal continueth in them: 140
Of what trifling account they hold life, yet what a practis'd
Art pursue to preserve it: if I should rightly define sport
SLAUGHTER WITH DANGER, what were more serious and brave?
Their love of air, of strength, of wildness, afford us an inkling
Of the delight of beasts, with whom they might innocently
Boast a fellow-feeling, summoning them forth to the combat.
Nay dream not so quickly to see her ladyship expell'd.
Those prowling Līons of stony Kabylia, whose roar
Frights from sleep the huddled herdsmen, soon as the sudden
night
Falls on Mount Atlas, those grave uxorious outlaws   150
Wandering in the Somali desert or waste Kalahari,
Sound a challenge that amid summer-idling London is
answer'd
Haply in Old Bond Street, where some fashionably attired
youth
Daintily stands poising the weapon foredoom'd to appay them:

Or⌄he mentally sighteth a tiger of India, that low
Crouches among the river jungles, or hunts desolating
Grassy Tarâi, 'neath lofty Himálya, or far southward
Outacamund, Mysore's residency, the Nilgherry mountains
By Malabar; yea, and ere-long shall sight him in earnest,
Stalked as a deer, surprised where hē lay slumbering at noon
Under a rock full-gorged, or deep in reedy covert hid   160
By the trackers disturbed : Two grand eyes shall for a moment
Glare upon either side the muzzle.   Woe then to the hunter,
If hē blench !   That fury beclouded in invisible speed
What marksman could arrest ? what mortal abide his arrache-
    ment ?
Standing above the immense carcase hē gratefully praiseth
God for a man-eater so fine, so worthy the slaying.

  See him again ; 'tis war : one hill-rock strongly defended
Checks advance, to be stormed at cost of half the assailants.
Gaily away they go, Highlanders, English, or Irish,   170
Or swart Ghoorkas against the leaden hail, climbing, ascend-
    ing,
Lost in a smoke, scattering, creeping, here there, ever
    upwards :
Till some change cometh o'er confusion.   Who winneth ?
    ah ! see !
Ours have arrived, and he who led their bravery is there.
None that heard will ever forget that far-echoing cheer :
Such heard Nelson, above the crashings & thundering of
    guns :
At Marathon 'twas heard and all time's story remembers.

  See him again, when at home visiting⌄his episcopal uncle :
That good priest contrast with this good captain, assay them :
Find a common-measure equating their rival emotions ;   180
Ēvaporate the rubbish, the degrading pestiferous fuss
Of stuck-up importance, the palatial coterie, weigh out
Then the solids : whose life would claim the award of an
    umpire
For greatest happiness ?   High-priest or soldier ?   Adjudge it

By their books : Let a child give sentence. Ev'n as a magnet
Turns and points to the north, so children's obstinate insight
Flies to the tale of war, hairbreadth scapes, daring achieve-
　　ments,
Discoveries, conquests, the romance of history : these things
Win them away from play to devour with greedy attention
Till they long to be men ; while all that clerkly palaver　190
Tastes like wormwood.—' Avast ! (I hear yoū calling) Avast
　　there !
' I forbid the appeal.'—Well, style my humour atrocious ;
Granted a child cannot understand ; yet see what a huge
　　growth
Stands to be extermin'd, ere you can set dibble in ground.
Nay, more yet ; that mighty forest, whose wildness offends
　　you,
And silences appal, where earth-life self-suffocating
Seethes, lavish as sun-life in a red star's fi'ry corona ;
That waste magnificence, and vain fecundity, breeding
Gīants & parasites embrac'd in flowery tangle,
Interwoven alive and dead, where one tyrannous tree　200
Blights desolating around it a swamp of rank vegetation ;
Where Reason yet dreams unawakt, & throu' the solemn day
Only the monkey chatters, & discordant the parrot screams :
All this is in man's heart with dateless sympathy worshipt,
With filial reverence, & awful pīeties involv'd ;
While that other picture, your formal fancy, the garden
Of your stingy promise, must that not quench his imágin'd
Idēals of beauty, his angel hope of attainment ?
What to him are the level'd borders, the symmetric allot-
　　ments,
Where nothing exceedeth, nothing encroacheth, nor assaileth ;
Where Reason now drudgeth a sad monomaniac, all day　211
Watering & weeding, digging & diligently manuring
Her label'd families, starch-makers, nitrogen-extract-
Purveyors, classified potherbs & empty pretenders
Of medical virtues ; nay ev'n and *their* little impulse

T'ward liberal fruiting disallow'd by stern regulation;
So many beans to a pod, with so many pods to a beanstalk;
Prun'd, pincht, economiz'd miserly til' all is abortion,
Save in such specimens as, but for an extravagant care,
Had miserably perish'd. What madness works to delude
  you,   220
Bēing a man, that yoū see not mankind's predilection
Is for Magnificence, Force, Freedom, Bounty; his inborn
Love for Beauty, his aim to possess, his pride to devise it:
And from everlasting his heart is fixt with affections
Prēengag'd to a few sovranly determinate objects,
Toys of an ēternal distraction. Beautiful is GOLD,
Clear as a trumpet-call, stirring where'er it appeareth
All high pow'rs to battle; with mágisterial ardour
Glowing among the metals, elemental drops of a fire-god's
Life-blood of old outpour'd in Chāos : Mágical also 230
Ev'RY recondite jēwel of Earth, with their seraphim-names,
RUBY, JACYNTH, EMERALD, AMETHYST, SAPPHIRE; amaran-
  thine
Starry essences, elect emblems of purity, heirlooms
Of deathless glories, most like to divine imanences.
Then that heart-gladdening highpriz'd ambrosia, blending
Their dissolute purples *&* golds with sparkling aroma,
That ruddy juice exprest from favour'd vintages, infus'd
With cosmic laughter, when upon some sécular epact
Blandly the sun's old heart is stirr'd to a septennial smile,
Causing strangefortun'd comfort to melancholy mortals : 240
Friend to the flésh, if mind be fatigued ; rallying to the sound
  mind,
When succour is needed 'gainst fainting weariness of flesh;
Shall Wine not be belov'd ? Or now let Aristotle answer
What goods are,—Time leaves the scholar's inventory un-
  chang'd;—
All Virtues *&* Pow'rs, Honour *&* Pleasure, all that in our life
Makes us self-sufficient, Friends, Riches, Comeliness, and
  Strength;

They thatᵛhave these things in plenty desire to retain them,
And win more; while they that lack are pleas'd to desire
    them.
Nay and since possession will leave the desire unappeasèd,
Save in mere appetites that vary with our physical state, 250
Surely delight in goods is an ecstasy rather attendant
On their mental image, than on experienc'd operation.
So the shepherd envies the monarch, the monarch the
    shepherd's lot,—
'O what a life were this, How sweet, how lovely!' the
    king cries.
Whence, I say, as a man feels brave who reads of ACHILLES,
One looking on riches may learn some kindred elation,
And whatever notions of fortune, luxury, comfort,
Genius or virtue, are shown to him, only as aspects
Of possible bēing, 'tis so much gain to desire them;
Learning Magnificence in mean obscurity, tasting   260
Something of all those goods which Fate outwardly denies
    him.
But say none shall again be kíng or prosperous or great,—
Arguing 'all eminence is unequal, unequal is unjust',—
Should that once come about, then alas for this merry England,
Sunk in a grey monotone of drudgery, dreamily poring
O'er her illumin'd page of history, faln to regretful
Worship of ancestors, with nought now left to delight her,
Nought to attain, save one nurst hope, one ambition only
Red Revolution, a wild Reawakening, & a Renaissance.

    Impatiently enough yoū hear me, longing to refute me, 270
While Iᵛin privileg'd pulpit my period expand.
Who could allow such a list of strange miscellaneous items,
So-call'd goods, Strength, Ríches, Honour, Gold, Genius,
    and Wine?
Is not Wisdom above Rubies? more than Coral or Pearl?
Yours is a scheme deep-laid on true distinctive asortment,
Parting use or good from useless or evil asunder;
Dismissing accessories, while half my heathenish invoice

Are Vanity's vanities. Well; truly, as old SOLOMON said,
So they *be*: What is excepted? What scapes his araignment?
Is 't Pleasure or Wisdom? Nay ask THEOLOGIA: Good-
works,   280
Saith-she, offend her nostril. If I distinguish, asserting,
Say, that if I ͮ enjoyed my neighbour's excessive income
I would hire me a string-quartett not an automaton car,
You blame equally both our tastes for luxury, indeed
His shows more of a use. If man's propensity is vain,
Vulgar, inane, unworthy; 'tis also vain to bewail it:
Think you to change his skin? 'Twere scale by scale to
regraft it
With purer traditions; and who shall amend the amenders?
Nay let bé the bubbles, till man grow more solid in mind,
Condemn not the follies: My neighbour's foolery were worse,
Sat he agape listening to Mozart, intently desiring   291
All that time to be rattling alóng on a furious engine
In caoutchouc carapace, with a trail of damnable oilstench.
Yea, blame not the pleasures; they are not enough;
pleasure only
Makes this life liveable: nor scout that doctrine as unsound:
Consider if mankind from puling birth to bitter death
Knew nought but the sorrows, endured unrespited always
Those agonizing assaults which no flesh wholly can escape;
Were his hunger a pang like his starvation, alievement
Thereof a worse torture, like that which full many die with;
Did love burn his soul as fire his skin; did affections   300
Rend his will, as Turks rend men with horses asunder;
Were his labour a breathless effort; his slumber occasion
For visiting Furies to repair his temple of anguish;
Were thoughts all mockeries; slow intelligence a deception;
His mind's far ventures, her voyages into the unseen
But horror & terrified nightmare; None then had ever heard
Praise of a Crēator, nor seen any Dēity worshipped.
'Twas for heav'nly Pleasure that God did first fashion all
thing,

Nor with other benefit would holy Religion attract us
Picturing of Paradise. Consult our Lady's Evangel, 310
Where Saint Luke,—colouring (was it unconsciously, suppose
    you ?)
Fact and fable alike,—contrasts a beggar with a rich man,
And from holding a fool's happiness too greatly in esteem
Makes pleasure ēternal the balance of temporal evil,
And the reverse ; nor shrinks, ascribing thus to the next world
Vaster inequalities, harsher perversity than this.
You have a soul's paradise, its entry the loop of a needle,
Come hither & prithy tell me what I must do to be savèd,
I, that feeding on Idĕals in temperat' estate
Seem so wealthy to poor Lazarus, so needy to Dives : 320
What from my heav'n-bound schooner's dispensable outfit
Has to be cast o'erboard? What see yoū here that offends
    you ?
These myriad volumes, these tons of music :—allow them
Or disallow? Fiddle and trichord?—Must all be relin-
    quished ?
Such toys have not a place in your socīety ; you say
Nobody shall make them, nor made may justly acquire them.
Yet, should a plea be alleged for life's most gracious adorn-
    ment,
For contemplative art's last transcendental achievement,
Grief's almighty solace, frolicking Mirth's Purification,
For Man's unparagon'd High-pōetess, inseparate Muse 330
Companion, the belov'd most dearly among her sisters,
Revivifier of age, fairest instructor of all grace,
His peacemaker alert with varied sympathy, whose speech
Not to arede and love is wholly to miss the celestial
Consolatries, the divine interpreting of physical life,—
Yoū wince? make exception? allow things musical? admit
So many faked viols, penny trumpets, and amateurish
Performers?   Nay, nay ! stand firm, for concession is vain.
Music is outmeasurably a barefaced luxury, her plea 339
Will cover art, (—almost to atone art's vile imitations—);

My Japanese paintings, my fair blue Cheney, Hellenic
Statues and Caroline silver, my beautiful Aldines,
Prized more highly because so few, so fondly familiar,
Need no tongue to defend them against rude hands, that
    assail them
Only because their name is RARITY; hands insensate,
Rending away pitilessly the fair embroideries of life,
That close-clust'ring man, his comfort pared to the outskirts
Of his discomfort, may share in meanness unenvied.
But what if I unveil the figure that closely beside you   350
Half hides his Hell-charred skeleton with mysteries obscene,
That foul one, that Moloch of all Utopias, ancient
Poisoner & destroyer-elect of innumerous unborn?

    Know you the story of our hive-bees, the yellow honey-
      makers,
Whose images from of old have haunted Pŏetry, settling
On the blossoms of man's dream-garden, as on the summer-
    flow'rs,
Pictures of happy toil, sunny glances, gendering always
Such sweet thoughts, as be by slumbrous music awaken'd?
How all their outward happiness,—that fairy demeanour
Of busy contentment, singing at their work,—is an inborn   360
Empty habit, the relics of a time when considerate joy
Truly possest their tiny bodies; when golden abundance
Was not a State-kept hoard; when feasts were plentiful
    indulg'd
With wine well-fermented, or old-stored spicy metheglin:
For they died not then miserably within the second moon
Forgotten, unrespected of all; but slept many winters,
Saw many springs, liv'd, lov'd like men, consciously rejoicing
In Nature's promises, with like hopes and recollections.
Intelligence had brought them Scīence, Genius enter'd;
Seers and sages arose, great Bees, perfecting among them   370
Copious inventions, with man's art worthily compared.
Then was a time when that, which haps not in ages of ages,
Strangely befel: they stole from Nature's secresy one key,

Found the hidden motive which works to variety of kind ;
And thus came wondrously possest of pow'r to determine
Their children's qualities, habitudes, yea their specialized
   form
Masculine or feminine to produce, or asexual offspring
Redow'rd and differenced with such alternative organs
As they chose, to whate'er preferential function adapted,
Wax-pocket or honey-bag, with an instinct rightly acordant.
   We know well the result, but not what causes effected 381
Their decision to prefer so blindly the race to the unit,
As to renounce happiness for a problem, a vain abstraction;
Making home and kingdom a vast egg-factory, wherein
Food and life are stor'd up alike, and strictly proportion'd
In loveless labour with mean anxīety.   Wondrous
Their reason'd motive, their altrūistic obedience
Unto a self-impos'd life-sentence of prison or toil.
Wonder wisely ! then ask if these ingenious insects,
(Who made Natur' against her will their activ' acomplice,
And, methodizing anew her heartless system, averted   391
From their house the torrent of whelming natural increase,)
Are blood-guiltless among their own-born prógeny : What
   skill
Keeps their peace, or what price buys it ?   Alack ! 'tis
   murder,
Murder again.   No worst Oriental despot, assuring
'Gainst birthright or faction or envy his ill-gotten empire,
So decimates his kin, as do these rown-bodied egg-queens
Surprise competitors, and stab their slumbering infants,
Into the wax-cradles replunging their double-edged stings.
Or what a deed of blood some high-day, when the summerᵛ
   hath   400
Their clammy cells o'erbrim'd, and already ripening orchards
And late flow'rs proclaim that starving winter approacheth,
Nor will again any queen lead forth her swarm, dispeopling
Their strawbuilt citadel ; then watch how these busy workers
Cease for awhile from toil ; how crowding upon the devoted

Drones they fall ; those easy fellows gave some provocation ;
Yet 'tis a foul massacre, cold murder of unsuspecting
Life-long companions ; and done bloodthirstily :—is not
Exercise of pow'r a delight ? have yóu not a doctrine
That calls duty pleasure ? What an if they make merry, saying
' Lazy-livers, runagates, evil beasts, greedy devourers,   411
' Too happy and too long ye've liv'd, unashamed to have
    outliv'd
' Your breeders, feeders, warmers and toiling attendants ;
' Had-ye ever been worthy a public good to accomplish,
' Each had nobly perish'd long-ago.   Unneeded, obese ones,
' Impious encumbrance, whose hope of service is over,
' Who did not, now can not, assist the community, YE DIE ! '
   My parable may serve.   What wisdom man hath attain'd to
Came to him of Nature's goodwill throu' tardy selection :
Should her teaching accuse herself and her method impugn,
I may share with her the reproach of approving as artist 421
Far other idēals than what seem needful in action.
This difficulty besets our time.   If you have an answer,
Write me it, as you keep your salt in savour ; or if toil
Grant you an indulgence, here lies fair country, direct then
Your Sabbath excursion westward, and spend a summer-day
Preaching among the lilies what youˇhave preached to the
    chimneys.

3

EVENING

From Wm. Blake [1]

Come, rosy angel, thy coronet donning
Of starry jewels, smile upon ev'ry bed,
    And grant what each day-weary mortal,
      Labourer or lover, asketh of thee.

Smile thou on our loves, enveloping the land
With dusky curtain: consider each blossom
    That timely upcloseth, that opens
      Her treasure of heavy-laden odours.

Now, while the west-wind slumbereth on the lake,
Silently dost thou with delicate shimmer
    O'erbloom the frowning front of awful
      Night to a glance of unearthly silver.

No hungry wild beast rangeth in our forest,
No tiger or wolf prowleth around the fold:
    Keep thou from our sheepcotes the tainting
      Invisible peril of the darkness.

4

POVRE AME AMOUREUSE

From Louise Labé, 1555

(Sapphics)

When to my lone soft bed at eve returning
Sweet desir'd sleep already stealeth o'er me,
My spirit flïeth to the fairy-land of
    her tyrannous love.

[1] There is another alcaic translation from Blake on p. 71 in 'Demeter'. The Ode on p. 72 is iambic, and the Chorus on pp. 53, 54 is in choriambics.

Him then I think fondly to kiss, to hold him
Frankly then to my bosom; I that all day
Have lookèd for˅him suffering, repining,
      yea many long days.

O blessèd sleep, with flatteries beguile me;
So,˅if I ne'er may˅of a surety have˅him,
Grant to my poor soul amorous the dark gift
      of this illusion.

5

THE FOURTH DIMENSION

(*Hendecasyllables*)

TRUEST-HEARTED of early friends, that Eton
Long since gáve to me,—Ah! 'tis all a life-time,—
With my faithfully festive auspication
Of Christmas merriment, this idle item.

  Plato truly believ'd his archetypal
Idĕas to possess the fourth dimension:
For since our solid is triple, but always
Its shade only double, solids as *umbrae*
Must lack equally one dimension also.
Could Plato˅have avoided or denied it?

  So Saint Paul, when in argument opposing
To our earthly bodies bodies celestial,
Meant just those pretty Greek aforesaid abstracts
Of four Plātonical divine dimensions.

  If this be not a holy consolation
More than plumpudding and a turkey roasted,
Whereto you but address a third dimension,
Try it, pray, as a pill to aid digestion:
I can't find anything better to send you.

6

JOHANNES MILTON, Senex

Scazons

SINCE I believe in God the Father Almighty,
Man's Maker and Judge, Overruler of Fortune,
'Twere strange should I praise anything and refuse Him
    praise,
Should love the creature forgetting the Crēator,
Nor unto Himᵛin suff'ring and sorrow turn me :
Nay how coud I withdraw me fromᵛHis embracing ?

But since that I have seen not, andᵗcannot know Him,
Nor in my earthly temple apprehend rightly
His wisdom and the heav'nly purpose ēternal ;
Therefore will I be bound to no studied system
Nor argument, nor with delusion enslave me,
Nor seek to pleáse Him in any foolish invention,
Which my spirit within me, that loveth beauty
And hateth evil, hath reprov'd as unworthy :

But I cherish my freedom in loving service,
Gratefully adoring for delight beyond asking
Or thinking, and in hours of anguish and darkness
Confiding always onᵛHis excellent greatness.

7

PYTHAGORAS

Scazons

THOU vainly, O Man, self-deceiver, exaltest
Thyself the kíng and only thinker of this world,
Where life aboundeth infinite to destroy thee.

Well-guided are thy forces and govern'd bravely,
But like a tyrant crūel or savage monster
Thou disregardest ignorantly all bēing
Save only thine own insubordinate ruling:

As if the flowër held not a happy pact with Spring;
As if the brutes lack'd reason and sorrow's torment;
Or ev'n divine love from the small atoms grew not,
Their grave affection unto thy passion mingling.

An truly were it nobler and better wisdom
To fear the blind thing blindly, lest it espy thee;
And scrupulously do honour to dumb creatures,

No one offending impiously, nor forcing
To service of vile uses ; ordering rather
Thy slave to beauty, compelling lovingkindness.

So should desire, the only priestess of Nature
Divinely inspir'd, like a good monarch rule thee,
And lead thee onward in the consummate motion
Of life eternal unto heav'nly perfection.

Elegiacs

8

AMIEL

WHY, O Maker of all, madest thou man with affections
  Tender above thyself, scrupulous and passionate?
Nay, if compassionate thou art, why, thou lover of men,
  Hidest thou thy face so pitilessly from us?
If thou in priesthoods and altar-glory delitest,
  In torment and tears of trouble and suffering,
Then wert thou displeas'd looking on soft human emotion,
  Thou must scorn the devout love of a sire to a son.
'Twas but vainly of old, Man, making Faith to approach thee,
  Held an imagin'd scheme of providence in honour;
And, to redeem thy praise, judg'd himself cause, took upon
      him
  Humbly the impossible burden of all misery.
Now casteth he away his books and logical idols
  Leaveth again his cell of terrified penitence;
And that stony goddess, his first-born fancy, dethroning,
  Hath made after his own homelier art another;
Made sweet Hope, the modest unportion'd daughter of
      anguish,
  Whose brimming eye sees but dimly what it looketh on;
Dreaming a day when fully, without curse or horrible cross,
  Thou wilt deign to reveal her vision of happiness.

9

AH, what a change! Thou, who didst emptily thy happiness
      seek
  In pleasure, art finding thy pleasure in happiness.
Slave to the soul, whom thou heldest in slavery, art thou?
  Thou, that wert but a vain idol, adored a goddess?

10

WALKING HOME

FROM THE CHINESE

THOUSAND threads of rain and fine white wreathing of air-
mist
Hide from us earth's greenness, hide the enarching azure.
Yet will a breath of Spring homeward convoying attend us,
And the mellow flutings of passionate Philomel.

11

THE RUIN

FROM THE CHINESE

THESE grey stones have rung with mirth and lordly carousel;
Here proud kings mingled pōetry and ruddy wine.
All hath pass'd long ago; nought but this rūin abideth,
Sadly in eyeless trance gazing upon the river.
Wouldst thou know who here visiteth, dwelleth and singeth
also,
Ask the swallows flȳing from sunny-wall'd Italy.

12

REVENANTS

FROM THE FRENCH

AT dead of unseen night ghosts of the departed assembling
Flit to the graves, where each in body had burial.
Ah, then rēvisiting my sad heart their desolate tomb
Troop the desires and loves vainly buried long ago.

13

FROM THE GREEK

MORTAL though I bé, yea ephemeral, if but a moment
  I gaze up to the night's starry domain of heaven,
Then no longer on earth I stand; I touch the Creator,
  And my lively spirit drinketh immortality.

14

ANNIVERSARY

SEE, Love, a year is pass'd : in harvest our summer endeth:
  Praising thee the solemn festival I celebrate.
Unto us all our days are love's anniversaries, each one
  In turn hath ripen'd something of our happiness.
So, lest heart-contented adown life easily floating,
  We note not the passage while living in the delight,
I have honour'd always the attentive vigil of Autumn,
  And thy day set apart holy to fair Memory.

15

COMMUNION OF SAINTS

FROM ANDRÉ CHENIER

WHAT happy bonds together unite you, ye living and dead,
  Your fadeless love-bloom, your manifold memories.

EPITAPHS

16

FIGHT well, my comrades, and prove your bravery.   Me too
  God call'd out, but crown'd early before the battle.

17

I DIED in very flow'r: yet call me not unhappy therefore,
 Ye that against sweet life once a lament have utter'd.

18

WHEN thou, my belovèd, diedst, I saw heaven open,
 And all earthly delight inhabiting Paradise.

19

WHERE thou art better I too were, dearest, anywhere, than
 Wanting thy well-lov'd lovely presence anywhere.

20

IBANT OBSCURI

A line for line paraphrase of a part of
Virgil's Æneid, Bk. VI.

THEY wer' amid the shadows by night in loneliness obscure
Walking forth i' the void and vasty dominyon of Ades;
As by an uncertain moonray secretly illumin'd   270
One goeth in the forest, when heav'n is gloomily clouded,
And black night hath robb'd the colours and beauty from all
  things.
 Here in Hell's very jaws, the threshold of darkening Orcus,
Have the avenging Cares laid their sleepless habitation,
Wailing Grief, pallid Infections, & heart-stricken Old-age,
Dismal Fear, unholy Famine, with low-groveling Want,
Forms of spectral horror, gaunt Toil and Death the devourer,
And Death's drowsy brother, Torpor; with whom, an inane
  rout,   278
All the Pleasures of Sin; there also the Furies in ambusht

(444)

Chamber of iron, afore whose bars wild War bloodyhanded
Raged, and mad Discord high brandisht her venomous locks.

  Midway of all this tract, with secular arms an immense elm
Reareth a crowd of branches, aneath whose leafy protection
Vain dreams thickly nestle, clinging unto the foliage on high :
And many strange creatures of monstrous form and features
Stable about th' entrance, Centaur and Scylla's abortion,
And hundred-handed Briareus, and Lerna's wildbeast
Roaring amain, and clothed in frightful flame the Chimæra,
Gorgons and Harpies, ¹ and Pluto's three-bodied ogre.

  In terror Æneas upheld his sword to defend him,   290
With ready naked point confronting their dreaded onset :
And had not the Sibyl warn'd how these lively spirits were
All incorporeal, flitting in thin maskery of form,
He had assail'd their host, and wounded vainly the void air.

  Hence is a road that led them a-down to the Tartarean
      streams,
Where Acheron's whirlpool impetuous, into the reeky
Deep of Cokytos disgorgeth, with muddy burden.
These floods one ferryman serveth, most awful of aspect,
Of squalor infernal, Chāron : all filthily unkempt
That woolly white cheek-fleece, and fiery the blood-shotten
      eyeballs :   300
On one shoulder a cloak knotted-up his nudity vaunteth.
He himself plieth oar or pole, manageth tiller and sheet,
And the relics of mén in his ash-grey barge ferries over ;
Already old, but green to a god and hearty will age be.

  Now hitherward to the bank much folk were crowding,
      a medley
Of men and matrons ; nor did death's injury conceal
Bravespirited heroes, young maidens beauteous unwed,
And boys borne to the grave in sight of their sorrowing sires.

  Countless as in the forest, at a first white frosting of autumn
Sere leaves fall to the ground ; or like whenas over the ocean
Myriâd birds come thickly flocking, when wintry December 311
Drives them afar southward for shelter upon sunnier shores,

So throng'd they; and each his watery journey demanded,
All to the further bank stretching-oút their arms impatient:
But the sullen boatman took now one now other at will,
While some from the river forbade he', an' drave to a distance.

    Æneas in wonder alike and deep pity then spake.
'Tell-me,' said he, 'my guide, why flock these crowds to the
    water?
Or what seek the spirits? or by what prejudice are these
Rudely denied, while those may upon the solemn river em-
    bark?'   320
T'whom * then briefly again the Avernîan priestess in answer.
'O Son of Anchises, heavn's true-born glorious offspring,
Deep Cokytos it is thou seést & Hell's Stygîan flood,
Whose dread sanctîon alone Jove's oath from falsehood
    assureth.
These whom thou pitiedst, th' outcast and unburied are they;
That ferryman Chāron; those whom his bark carries over
Are the buried; nor ever may mortal across the livid lake
Journey, or e'er upon Earth his bones lie peacefully entomb'd:
Haunting a hundred years this mournful plain they wander
Doom'd for a term, which term expired they win to
    deliv'rance.'   330

    Then he that harken'd stood agaze, his journey arrested,
Grieving at heart and much pitying their unmerited lot.
There miserably fellow'd in death's indignity saw he
Leucaspis with his old Lycian seachieften Orontes,
Whom together from Troy in home-coming over the waters
Wild weather o'ermaster'd, engulphing both shipping and
    men.
And lo! his helmsman, Palinurus, in eager emotion,
Who on th' Afric course, in bright star-light, with a fair wind,
Fell by slumber opprest unheedfully into the wide sea:
Whom i' the gloom when hardly he knew, now changed in
    affliction,   340

   * Line 321. ' T'whom ' is from Milton, in imitation of Virgil's admired
Olli. It is not admitted in the ordinary prosody.

First he addrest. 'What God, tell-me O Palinurus, of all
    gods
Plúckt you away and drown'd i' the swift wake-water aban-
    don'd?
For never erst nor in else hath kind responsive Apollo
Led-me astray, but alone in this thing wholly deluded,
When he aver'd that you, to remote Ausōnia steering,
Safe would arrive. Where now his truth? Is this the
    promis'd faith?'
But he, 'Neither again did Phœbus wrongly bespeak thee,
My general, nor yet did a god in his enmity drown me:
For the tiller, wherewíth I led thy fleet's navigation,
And still clung to, was in my struggling hold of it unshipt, 350
And came with-me' o'erboard. Ah! then, by ev'ry accurst
    sea,
Tho' in utter despair, far less mine own peril awed me
Than my thought o' the ship, what harm might háp to her,
    yawing
In the billows helmless, with a high wind and threatening
    gale.
Two nights and one day buffeted held I to the good spar
Windborne, with the current far-drifting, an' on the second
    morn
Saw, when a great wave raised me aloft, the Italyan highlands;
And swimming-on with effort got ashore, nay already was
    saved,
Had not there the wrecking savages, who spied-me defence-
    less,
Scarce clinging outwearied to a rock, half-drowned & speech-
    less,   360
Beát me to death for hope of an unfound booty upon me.
Now to the wind and tidewash a sport my poor body rolleth.
Wherefore thee, by heav'n's sweet light & airness, I pray,
By thy Sire's memories, thy hope of youthful Iulus,
Rescue-me from these ills, brave master; Go to Velija,
O'er my mortality's spoil cast thou th' all-hallowing dust:

Or better, if so be the goddess, heav'n's lady-Creatress,
Show-thee the way,—nor surely without high favoring impulse
Mak'st thou ventur' across these floods & black Ereban lake,—
Give thy hand-to-me', an' o'er their watery boundary bring
      me   370
Unto the haven of all, death's home of quiet abiding.'
Thus-he lamented, anon spake sternly the maid of Avernus.
'Whence can such unruly desire, Palinurus, assail thee?
Wilt thou th' Eumenidan waters visit unburied? o'erpass
Hell's Stygian barrier? Chāron's boat unbidden enter?
Cease to believe that fate can bé by prayër averted.
Let my sooth a litel thy cruel destiny comfort
Surely the people of all thy new-found country, determin'd
By heav'n-sent omens will achieve thy purification,   379
Build thee a tomb of honour with yearly solemnity ordain'd,
And dedicate for ever thy storied name to the headland.'

    These words lighten awhile his fear, his sadness allaying,
Nor vain was the promise his name should eternally survive.

    They forthwith their journey renew, tending to the water:
Whom when th' old boatman descried silently emerging
Out o' the leafy shadows, advancing t'ward the river-shore,
Angrily gave-he challenge, imperious in salutation.
'Whosoever thou be, that approachest my river all-arm'd,
Stand to announce thyself, nor further make footing onward.
Here 'tis a place of ghosts, of night & drowsy delusion: 390
Forbidden unto living mortals is my Stygian keel:
Truly not Alkides embarkt I cheerfully, nor took
Of Theseus or Pirithous glad custody, nay though
God-sprung were they both, warriors invincible in might:
Hé 'twas would sportively the guard of Tartarus enchain,
Yea and from the palace with gay contumely dragged him:
Théy to ravish Hell's Queen from Pluto's chamber attempted.'

    Then thus th' Amphrysian prophetess spake briefly in
      answer.
'No such doughty designs are ours, Cease thou to be movèd!
Nor these sheeny weapons intend force. Cerberus unvext

Surely for us may affray the spirits with 'howling eternal,   401
And chaste Persephone enjoy her queenly seclusion.
Troian Æneas, bravest and gentlest-hearted,
Hath left earth to behold his father in out-lying Ades.
If the image¹ of a so great virtue doth not affect thee,
Yet this bough'—glittering she reveal'd its golden
    avouchment—
'Thou mayst know.'   Forthwith his bluster of heart was
    appeasèd:
Nor word gave¯he, but admiring the celestial omen,
That bright sprigg of weird for so long period unseen,
Quickly he¯túrneth about his boat, to the margin ap-
    proaching,   410
And the spirits, that along the gun'al benchways sat in order,
Drave he ashore, offering ready room: but when the vessel took
Ponderous Æneas, her timbers crankily straining
Creak'd, an' a brown water came trickling through the upper
    seams.
Natheless both Sibyl ánd Hero, slow wafted across stream,
Safe on th' ooze & slime's hideous desolation alighted.
   Hence the triple-throated bellowings of Cerberus invade
All Hell, where opposite the arrival he lies in a vast den.
But the Sibyl, who mark'd his necklaces of stiffening snakes,
Cast him a cake, poppy-drench'd with drowsiness and honey-
    sweeten'd.   420
He, rabid and distending a-hungry' his triply-cavern'd jaws,
Gulp'd the proffer'd morsel; when slow he¯relaxt his immense
    bulk,
And helplessly diffused fell out-sprawl'd over the whole cave.
Æneas fled by, and left full boldly the streamway,
That biddeth all men across but alloweth ne'er a returning.
   Already now i' the air were voices heard, lamentation,
And shrilly crying of infant souls by th' entry of Ades.
Babes, whom unportion'd of sweet life, unblossoming buds,
One black day carried off and chokt in dusty corruption.—
Next are they who falsely accused were wrongfully condemn'd

Unto the death : but here their lot by justice is order'd. 431
Inquisitor Minos, with his urn, summoning to assembly
His silent council, their deed or slander arraigneth. —
Next the sullen-hearted, who rashly with else-innocent hand
Their own life did-away, for hate or weariness of light,
Imperiling their souls.   How gladly, if only in Earth's air,
Would-they again their toil, discomfort, and pities endure !
Fate obstructs : deep sadness now, unloveliness awful
Rings them about, & Styx with ninefold circle enarmeth.—

    Not far hence they come to a land extensive on all sides; 440
Weeping   Plain   'tis   call'd:—such   name   such   country
    deserveth.

Here the lovers, whom fiery passion hath cruelly consumed,
Hide in leafy alleys ' and pathways bow'ry, sequester'd
By woodland myrtle, nor hath Death their sorrow ended.
Here was Phædra to see, Procris ' and sád Eriphyle,
She of her unfilial deathdoing wound not ashamèd,
Evadne, ' and Pasiphae ' and Laodamia,
And epicene Keneus, a woman to a man metamorphos'd,
Now by Fate converted again to her old feminine form.

    'Mong these shades, her wound yet smarting ruefully, Dido
Wander'd throu' the forest-obscurity ; and Æneas   451
Standing anigh knew surely the dim form, though i' the
    darkness
Veil'd,—as when one seëth a young moon on the horizon,
Or thinketh to ' have seen i' the gloaming her delicate horn;
Tearfully in oncelov'd accents he-lovingly addrest her.
'Unhappy ! ah ! too true 'twas told me ' O unhappy Dido,
Dead thou wert ; to the fell extreme didst thy passion ensue.
And was it I that slew-thee ?   Alas !   Smite falsity, ye
    heav'ns !
And Hell-fury attest-me', if here any sanctity reigneth,
Unwilling, O my Queen, my step thy kingdom abandon'd. 460
Me the command of a god, who here my journey determines
Through   Ereban   darkness,   through   fields   sown   with
    desolation,

Drave⁻me to wrong my heart. Nay tho' deep-pain'd to
    desert thee
I ne'er thought to provoke thy pain of mourning eternal.
Stay yet awhile, ev'n here unlook'd-for again look upon me :
Fly⁻me not ere the supreme words that Fate granteth us are
    said.'
    Thus he : but the spirit was raging, fiercely defiant,
Whom he approach'd with words to appease, with tears for
    atonement.
She to the ground downcast her ¹ eyes in fixity averted;
Nor were her features more by his pleading affected,   470
Than wer' a face of flint, or of ensculptur'd alabaster.
At length she started disdainful, an' angrily withdrew
Into a shady thicket : where her grief kindly Sychæus
Sooth'd with other memories, first love and virginal embrace.
And ever Æneas, to remorse by deep pity soften'd,
With brimming eyes pursued her queenly figure disappearing.
    Thence the Sibyl to the plain's extremest boundary led him,
Where world-fam'd warriors, a lionlike company, haunted.
Here great Tydeus saw he eclips'd, & here the benighted
Phantom of Adrastus, ¹ of stalwart Parthenopæus.   480
Here long mourn'd upon earth went all that prowess of Ilium
Fallen in arms ; whom, when he⁻beheld them, so many and
    great,
Much he⁻bewail'd.   By Thersilochus his mighty brothers
    stood,
Children of Antenor ; here Demetriân Polyphates,
And Idæus, in old chariot-pose dreamily stalking.
Right and left the spirits flocking on stood crowding around
    him ;
Nor their eyes have enough ; they touch, find joy unwonted
Marching in equal stép, and eager of his coming enquire.
But th' Argive leaders, and they that obey'd Agamemnon
When they saw that Trojan in arms come striding among
    them,   490
Old terror invaded their ranks : some fled stricken, as once

They to the ships had fled for shelter ; others the alarm raise,
But their thín utterance mock'd vainly the lips wide parted.
Here too Deiphobus he espied, his fair body mangled,
Cruelly dismember'd, disfeatur'd cruelly his face,
Face and hands ; and lo ! shorn closely from either temple,
Gone wer' his ears, and maim'd each nostril in impious
    outrage.

Barely he⁻knew him again cow'ring shamefastly' an' hiding
His dire plight, & thus he 'his old companyon accosted.
'Noblest Deiphobus, great Teucer's intrepid offspring,   500
Who was it, inhuman, coveted so cruel a vengeance ?
Who can hav' adventur'd on thée ? That last terrible night
Thou wert said to hav' exceeded thy bravery, an' only
On thy faln enemies wert faln by weariness o'ercome.
Wherefor' upon the belov'd sea-shore thine empty sepulchral
Mound I erected, aloud on thy ghost tearfully calling.
Name and shield keep for⁻thee the place ; but thy body, dear
    friend,
Found I not, to commit to the land ere sadly' I left it.'
    Then the son of Priam ' 'I thought not, friend, to reproach
    thee :
Thou didst all to the full, ev'n my shade's service, accom-
    plish.   501
'Twas that uninterdicted adultress from Lacedæmon
Drave⁻me to doom, & planted in hell, her trophy triumphant.
On that night,—how vain a security and merrymaking
Then sullied us thou know'st, yea must too keenly re-
    member,—
When the ill-omened horse o'erleapt Troy's lofty defences,
Dragg'd in amidst our town pregnant with a burden of arm'd
    men.
She then, her Phrygian women in feign'd phrenzy collecting,
All with torches aflame, in wild Bacchic orgy paraded,
Flaring a signal aloft to her ambusht confederate Greeks.
I from a world of care had fled with weariful eyelids   520
Unto my unhappy chamber', an' lay fast lockt in oblivyon,

Sunk to the depth of rest as a child that nought will awaken.
Meanwhile that paragon helpmate had robb'd me of all arms,
E'en from aneath the pillow my blade of trust purloining ;—
Then to the gate ; wide flings she it op'n an' calls Menelaus.
Would not a so great service attach her faithful adorer ?
Might not it extinguish the repute of her earlier illdeeds ?
Brief-be the tale. Menelaus arrives : in company there came
His crime-counsellor Æolides. . So, and more also
Déal-ye', O Gods, to the Greeks ! an' if I call justly upon
    you.—   530
But thou ; what fortune hitherward, in turn prithy tell me,
Sent-thee alive, whether erring upon the bewildering Ocean,
Or high-prompted of heav'n, or by Fate wearily hunted,
That to the sunless abodes and dusky demesnes thou
    approachest ? '
  Ev'n as awhile they thus converse it is already mid-day
Unperceiv'd, but aloft earth's star had turn'd to declining.
And haply' Æneas his time in parley had outgone,
Had not then the Sibyl with word of warning avized him.
' Night hieth, Æneas ; in tears our journey delayeth.
See our road, that it here in twain disparteth asunder ; 540
This to the right, skirting by th' high city-fortresses of Dis,
Endeth in Elysium, our path ; but that to the leftward
Only receives their feet who wend to eternal affliction.'
Deiphobus then again, ' Speak not, great priestess, in anger ;
I will away to refill my number among th' unfortun'd.
Thou, my champyon, adieu ! Go where thy glory awaits
    thee ! '
When these words he 'had spok'n, he-turn'd and hastily was
    fled.
  Æneas then look'd where leftward, under a mountain,
Outspread a wide city lay, threefold with fortresses engirt,
Lickt by a Tartarean river of live fire, the torrentíal 550
Red Phlegethon, and huge boulders his roundy bubbles be :
Right i' the front stareth the columnar gate adamantine,
Such that no battering warfare of mén or immortals

E'er might shake; blank-faced to the cloud its bastion
upstands.
Tisiphone thereby in a bloodspotty robe sitteth alway
Night and day guarding sleeplessly the desperat entrance,
Wherefrom an awestirring groan-cry and fierce clamour
outburst,
Sharp lashes, insane yells, dragg'd chains and clanking of
iron.

   Æneas drew back, his heart by' his hearing affrighted:
'What manner of criminals, my guide, now tell⁻me,' he⁻
question'd,   560
'Or what their penalties? what this great wail that ariseth?'
Answering him the divine priestess, 'Brave hero of Ilîum,
O'er that guilty threshold no breath of purity may come:
But Hecate, who gave⁻me to rule i' the groves of Avernus,
Herself led me around, & taught heav'n's high retribution.
Here Cretan Rhadamanthus in unblest empery reigneth,
Secret crime to punish,—full surely he⁻wringeth avowal
Even of all that on earth, by vain impunity harden'd,
Men sinning have put away from thought till⁻impenitent
death.

On those convicted tremblers then leapeth avenging   570
Tisiphone with keen flesh-whips and vipery scourges,
And of her implacable sisters inviteth attendance.'
—Now sudden on screeching hinges that portal accursèd
Flung wide its barriers.—'In what dire custody, mark thou,
Is the threshold! guarded by how grim sentry the doorway!
More terrible than they the ravin'd insatiable Hydra
That sitteth angry within.   Know too that Tartarus itself
Dives sheer gaping aneath in gloomy profundity downward
Twice that height that a man looketh-up t'ward airy
Olympus.
Lowest there those children of Earth, Titanian elders,   580
In the abyss, where once they fell hurl'd, yet wallowing lie.
There the Alöīdæ saw I, th' ungainly rebel twins
Primæval, that assay'd to devastate th' Empyræan

With huge hands, and rob from Jove his kingdom immortal.
And there Salmoneus I saw, rend'ring heavy payment,
For that he idly' had mockt heav'n's fire and thunder
    electric ;
With chariot many-yoked and torches brandishing on high
Driving among 'his Graian folk in Olympian Elis ;
Exultant as a God he rode in blasphemy worshipt.   589
Fool, who th' unreckoning tempest and deadly dreaded bolt
Thought to mimic with brass and confus'd trample of horses !
But 'him th' Omnipotent, from amidst his cloudy pavilyon,
Blasted, an' eke his rattling car and smoky pretences
Extinguish'd at a stroke, scattering his dust to the whirlwind.
There too huge Tityos, whom Earth that gendereth all
    things
Once foster'd, spreadeth-out o'er nine full roods his immense
    limbs.
On him a wild vulture with hook-beak greedily gorgeth
His liver upsprouting quick as that Hell-chicken eateth.
Shé diggeth and dwelleth under the vast ribs, her bloody
    bare neck
Lifting anon : ne'er loathes˗she the food, ne'er fails the re-
    newal.   600
Where wer' an end their names to relate, their crimes and
    torments ?
Some o'er whom a hanging black rock, slipping at very
    point of
Falling, ever threateneth : Couches luxurious invite
Softly-cushion'd to repose : Tables for banqueting outlaid
Tempt them ever-famishing : hard by them a Fury regardeth,
And should théy but a hand uplift, trembling to the dainties,
She with live firebrand and direful yell springeth on them.
    Their crimes,—not to' hav lov'd a brother while love was
       allow'd them;
Or to' hav struck their father, or inveigled a dependant; 609
Or who chancing alone on wealth prey'd lustfully thereon,
Nor made share with others, no greater company than they :

Some for adultery slain; some their bright swords had
  offended
Drawn i' the wrong: or a master's trust with perfidy had met:
Dungeon'd their penalties they await. Look not to be
  answer'd
What that doom, nor th' end of these men think to determine.

Sóme aye roll heavy rocks, some whirl dizzy on the revolving
Spokes of a pendant wheel: sitteth and to eternity shall sit
Unfortun'd Theseus; while sad Phlegias saddeneth hell
With vain oyez to' all loud crying a tardy repentance,
"Walk, O man, i' the fear of Gód, and learn to be righteous!"
Here another, who sold for gold his country, promoting 621
Her tyrant; or annull'd for a base bribe th' inviolate law.
This one had unfather'd his blood with bestial incest:
All some fearful crime had dared & vaunted achievement.
What mind could harbour the offence of such recollection,
Or lend welcoming ear to the tale of iniquity and shame,
And to the pains wherewith such deeds are justly requited?
  Ev'n when thus she' had spok'n, the priestess dear to
    Apollo,
' But, ready, come let us ón, perform-we the order appointed!
Hast'n-we (saith-she), the wall forged on Cyclopian anvils
Now I see, an' th' archway in Ætna's furnace attemper'd, 631
Where my lore biddeth us to depose our high-privileg'd
    gift.'
  Then together they trace i' the drooping dimness a foot-
    path,
Whereby, faring across, they arrive at th' arches of iron.
Æneas stept into the porch, and duly besprinkling
His body with clear water affixt his bough to the lintel;
And, having all perform'd at length with ritual exact,
They came out on a lovely pleasance, that dream'd-of oasis,
Fortunate isle, the abode o' the blest, their fair Happy
    Woodland.
Here is an ampler sky, those meads ar' azur'd by a gentler

Sun than th' Earth, an' a new starworld their darkness
    adorneth.   641

    Some were matching afoot their speed on a grassy arena,
In playful combat some wrestling upon the yellow sand,
Part in a dance-rhythm or poetry's fine phantasy engage;
While full-toga'd anear their high-priest musical Orpheus
Bade his prime sev'n tones in varied harmony discourse,
Now with finger, anon sounding with an ivory plectrum.
And here Æneas met Teucer's fortunate offspring,
High-spirited heroes, fair-favor'd sons o' the morning,
Assarac and Ilos ¹ and Dardan founder of Ilĩum :   650
Their radiant chariots he' espied rank't empty afar off,
Their spears planted afield, their horses wandering at large,
Grazing around:—as on earth their joy had been, whether
    armour
Or chariot had charmed them, or if 'twer' good manage and
    care
Of the gallant warhorse, the delight liv'd here unabated:
Lo! then others, that about the meadow sat feasting in
    idless,
And chanting for joy a familyar pæan of old earth,
By fragrant laurel o'ercanopied, where 'twixt enamel'd banks
Bountiful Eridanus glides throu' their bosky retirement.
Here were men who bled for honour, their country defend-
    ing;   660
Priests, whose lives wer' a flame of chastity on God's altar;
Holy poets, content to await their crown of Apollo;
Discoverers, whose labour had aided life or ennobled;
Or who fair memories had left through kindly deserving.
On their brow a fillet pearl-white distinguisheth all these:
Whom the Sibyl, for they drew round, in question accosted,
And most Musæus, who tower'd noble among them,
Center of all that sea of bright faces looking upward.
' Tell, happy souls, and thou poet and high mystic illustrious,
Where dwelleth Anchises? what home hath he? for 'tis in
    his quest   670

We hither have made journey across Hell's watery marches.'
  Thertó with brief parley rejoin'd that mystic of old-time.
'In no certain abode we‑remain : by turn the forest glade
Haunt‑we, lilied stream-bank, sunny mead; and o'er valley
    and rock
At will rove‑we: but if ye aright your purpose arede me,
Mount‑ye the hill: myself will prove how easy the pathway.'
Speaking he léd: and come to the upland, sheweth a fair
    plain
Gleaming aneath; and they, with grateful adieu, the descent
    made.

  Now Lord Anchises was down i' the green valley musing,
Where the spirits confin'd that await mortal resurrection   680
While diligently he‑mark'd, his thought had turn'd to his
    own kin,
Whose numbers he‑reckon'd, an' of all their progeny foretold
Their fate and fortune, their ripen'd temper an' action.
He then, when he' espied Æneas t'ward him approaching
O'er the meadow, both hands uprais'd and ran to receive him,
Tears in his eyes, while thus his voice in high passion outbrake.
'Ah, thou'rt come, thou'rt come! at length thy dearly
    belov'd grace
Conquering all hath won‑tnee the way.   'Tis allow'd to
    behold thee,
O my son,—yea again the familyar raptur' of our speech.
Nay, I look't for 't thus, counting patiently the moments, 690
And ever expected; nor did fond fancy betray me.
From what lands, my son, from what life-dangering ocean
Art‑thou arrived? full mighty perils thy path hav' opposèd:
And how nearly the dark Libyan thy destiny o'erthrew!'
Then 'he, 'Thy spirit, O my sire, 'twas thy spirit often
Sadly appearing aroused‑me to seek thy thy far habitation
My fleet moors i' the blue Tyrrhene : all wíth‑me goeth well.
Grant‑me to touch thy hand as of old, and thy body embrace.'
Speaking, awhile in tears his feeling mutinied, and when
For the longing contact of mortal affection, he out-held 700

His strong arms, the figure sustain'd them not : 'twas as
    empty
E'en as a windworn cloud, or a phantom of irrelevant sleep.
    On the level bosom of this vale more thickly the tall trees
Grow, an' aneath quivering poplars and whispering alders
Lethe's dreamy river throu' peaceful scenery windeth.
Whereby now flitted in vast swarms many people of all lands,
As when in early summer 'honey-bees on a flowery pasture
Pill the blossoms, hurrying to' an' fro,—innumerous are they,
Revisiting the ravish'd lily cups, while all the meadow hums.
    Æneas was turn'd to the sight, and marvelling inquired, 710
' Say, sir, what the river that there i' the vale-bottom I see?
And who they that thickly along its bank have assembled ? '
    Then Lord Anchises, ' The spirits for whom a second life
And body are destined ar' arriving thirsty to Lethe,
And here drink th' unmindful draught from wells of oblivyon.
My heart greatly desired of this very thing to acquaint thee,
Yea, and show-thee the men to-be-born, our glory her'after,
So to gladden thine heart where now thy voyaging endeth.'
' Must it then be-believ'd, my sire, that a soul which attaineth
Elysium will again submit to her old body-burden ?   720
Is this well ? what hap can awake such dire longing in them ?'
' I will tell thee', O son, nor keep thy wonder awaiting,'
Answereth Anchises, and all expoundeth in order.
' Know first that the heavens, and th' Earth, and space fluid
    or void,
Night's pallid orb, day's Sun, and all his starry coævals,
Are by one spirit inly quickened, and, mingling in each part,
Mind informs the matter, nature's complexity ruling.
Thence the living creatures, man, brute, and ev'ry feather'd
    fowl,
And what breedeth in Ocean aneath her surface of argent :
Their seed knoweth a fiery vigour, 'tis of airy divine birth, 730
In so far as unimpeded by an alien evil,
Nor dull'd by the body's framework condemn'd to corruption.
Hence the desires and vain tremblings that assail them, unable

Darkly prison'd to arise to celestial exaltation ;
Nor when death summoneth them anon earth-life to
    relinquish,
Can they in all discard their stain, nor wholly away with
Mortality's plaguespots. It must¯be that, O, many wild graffs
Deeply at 'heart engrain'd have rooted strangely upon them :
Wherefore must suffering purge them, yea, Justice atone them
With penalties heavy as their guilt : some purify exposed 740
Hung to the viewless winds, or others long watery searchings
Low i' the deep wash clean, some bathe in fïery renewal :
Each cometh unto his own retribution,—if after in ample
Elysium we attain, but a few, to the fair Happy Woodland,
Yet slow time still worketh on us to remove the defilement,
Till it hath eaten away the acquir'd dross, leaving again free
That first fïery vigour, the celestîal virtue of our life.
All whom here thou seêst, hav' accomplished purification :
Unto the stream of Lethe a god their company calleth,
That forgetful of old failure, pain & disappointment,   750
They may again into' earthly bodies with glad courage enter.'

      *   *   *   *   *   **

Twín be the gates o' the house of sleep : as fable opineth 893
One is of horn, and thence for a true dream outlet is easy:
Fair the other, shining perfected of ivory carven ;
But false are the visions that thereby find passage upward.
Soon then as Anchises had spok'n, he¯led the Sibyl forth
And his son, and both dismisst from th' ivory portal.

21

PRIAM & ACHILLES

Line for line paraphrase of Homer
Iliad xxiv. 339–660

Thus sed⁻he, & Hermes hearing did not disobey him, 339
But stoop'd quickly to bind his wingèd shoon on his ankles
Gold-glittering, which bear him aloft whether over the ocean
Journeying, or whether over the broad earth, swift as a wild
  wind;
And his Rod, wherewith men's eyes he drowsily sealeth,
Whom that he list, or again from torpor awakeneth—his
  wand
Seiz'd he in hand, an' arose & sped forth, God's merry angel.
Till when soon he espied fair Troy & briny Hellespont,
Then he alighted on earth, to a young prince likening him-
  self
With first down on^his cheek in manhood's most loveable
  prime.
  They meantime onward past th' old tomb-tower of Ilos
Had driven, & were halting awhile their teams to refresh
  them   350
At the river: when now, as nightfall already darken'd,
Idaeus descried Hermes very near them approaching,
And turning to Priam, he in earnest whisper addrest him.
  'Haste to avise⁻thee, mў liege! an affair for discretion
  asketh:
I see a man, who I think very soon may annihilate us both.
Say now, will you we urge our steeds to 'escape from him,
  or stay
Friendly to deal, and humbly with all entreaty beseech him?'

  Thus sed⁻he, but th'old king lost heart & greatly affrighted
Felt his skin to be staring, an' all his limbs wer' atremble:
Dazed he stood: but anon Hermes coming up to him outheld

(461)

His right hand, and thus with frank enquiry accosted.   361
  ' Where ever, O father, farest thou with this equipment
In the hallow'd starlight, when mén are wont to be sleeping ?
Art thou not then afraid o' the slaughter-breathing Achaeans,
Those monsters of fury relentless lurking around thee ?
Haply an if one here espied thee, neath the flying night
Convoying such a prize, how then would thy business be ?
Thyself art not young, and th' old man here thy attendant
Scarce would serve to protect thee against whoso sh^d attack
      thee.   369
Ne'ertheless I'd not wrong thee a whit, would rather against all
Strive to defend ; for like mine own father thou appearest.'

  Him then in answer addrest god-like Priam, Ilyon's old king.
' Truly it is very much, my dear son, as thou opinest ;
Yet some god, 'tw^d appear, vouchsafes me a kindly protection,
Sending upon my journey to meet me so able a helper
As thyself, for in outward mien not comelier art thou
Than thou show'st in mind : blessed & happy are thy parents.'

  Then bespake him again God's angel, slayer of Argus.
' Nay and what thou say'st, sir, is all most rightfully spoken.
But now tell me, I pray, & speak thou truthfully plain words,
If thou'rt convoying thy wealth & costly-treasur'd store 381
Unto some outland folk to remain safe for thee in hiding,
Or whether all your warrior-folk are abandoning Ilyon
In dismay, since that their bravest champyon is undone,
Thy son, who was fearless afield to resist the Achaeans.'

  Him then in answer addrest god-like Priam, Ilyon's old king.
' Who then, valyant sir, may'st thou be, an' of what parents,
That to me such fair speech hast made of my unhappy son's
      death ?'

  Then bespake him again God's angel, slayer of Argus.
' Thou wouldst prove me, O king, in making question of
      Hector.   390

Him many times I have seen scattering with glorious onset
All the battle's nobley : then too when he drave the Achaeans
Back to the ships, & smote with trenchant blade the flying
    ranks.
That day stood we aloof wond'ring, for not yet Achilles
Would let us out to battle, since Atreïdes had aggriev'd him.
'Tis to him I give fealty ; the same good ship carried us both.
Myrmidon is my nation, a man of plenty, Polyctor,
Is my sire, in his age reverend & grey-headed as thou.
Six sons hath he beside myself, and I, the seventh son,
In the brothers' lotterie was cast for service against Troy.
Now I am come to the plain here scouting, for the Achaeans
Will sally forth at dawn in full puissance to attack you : 402
Long they chafe sitting idle, an' all their kings are unable
In their impacience any more from fight to withhold them.'

    Him then in answer addrest god-like Priam, Ilyon's old
      king.
' If that tho͞u indeed bĕ the squire of mighty Achilles,
Tell me the whole truth plainly, I pray, nor seek to delude
    me.
Lȳeth yet by the shipping my son's body, or hath Achilles
Rent and cast it away for beasts piecemeal to devour it ?'

    Then bespake him again God's angel, slayer of Argus.
' O good sire, not yet hath foul dog nor ravening bird   411
Made their prey of him : ev'n as he was, so lies he neglected
Hard by Achilles' ship i' the camp : and already twelve days
There hath lain, nor doth his flesh rot nor the corrupt worms
Touch him, that fatten on mankind nor spare the illustrious.
But when morning appears Achilles cometh & draggeth him
    forth
Trailing around the barrow builded to his old companyon.
Nor yet is injury done : thou mightest go thither and see
How dew-fresh he lieth, how free from death's blemish or
    stain :   419

His blood bathèd away, & healèd those heavy wounds all
Where many coward spears had pierc'd his fair body fallen.
Such care take the blessed gods for thy dearly belov'd son,
Yea, tho' he live no more; since they full heartily lov'd him.'

Thussed̄he, & th'old king reassured spake after in answer.
'See, lad, how good it is to offer due gifts in atonement
Unto the gods: for, sure as he liv'd, my son never injur'd,
Nay nor at home forgat, the pöwers that rule in Olympos:
Wherefore ev'n i' the grave have they his píety remember'd.
But come, an' at my hands this daintily-wrought flagon accept:
And thou guard & guide me, that I, if so be the gods' will,
Safe may arrive with these my goods to the tent of Achilles.'

Him then in answer addrest high Zeuses favouring angel.
'Tempt not a young man, sire! Thou wilt not lightly corrupt
    me,   433
Thus proffering me presents of worth unknown to Achilles;
Whom I fear, nor ever my heart for shame would allow me
So to defraud, lest haply some ill should come to me after.
But as a guide w^d I aid̄thee; yea, ev'n to illustrious Argos
Faithfully both by land and sea w^d accompany thy way;
And not a man for scorn of thine escort sh^d attack thee.'

Thus saying, on to the car high heav'n's merry fortuner
    upsprang,   440
And, with his either hand reins and whip seizing alertly,
Both mules and wearied horses with fresh vigour inspired.
Till to the fosse they came, & rampart, where the defenders
Chanc't to be off their guard, busilie with their supper engaged;
Whom Hermes drowz'd deeply, in senseless slumber immers-
    ing
Ev'ryone, and coming up to the gate & thrusting it open
Brought Priam into the camp, & Hector's ransom in his train.

So full soon they arriv'd at Achilles' lofty pavilyon,
That high house which for their king his folk had erected,
Hewing pines o' the hill for timbering, & for a roof-thatch

Harvesting the rushes that grew i' the lowland pastures ;
And had around the dwelling fenc't for their chieften a wide
    court   452
With thick stakes, & one huge bar clos'd its carriage-entry,
Made of a pine, which three men of his servants, pulling all
    three
All together, would shift back or forwards, so immense was
His gate-bar, but Peleïdes would handle it himself.
This gate for th' old king th' archfortuner easily open'd,
And brought in the treasures of Troy to the house of Achilles ;
And there standing awhile turn'd t'wards Priam, & bespake
    him.

'O sir, I that accost thee am in good truth the celestial
Hermes, whom great Zeus did charge to attend thee in
    escort :   461
But hence must I turn me again, nor now will I enter
Into Achilles' sight ; twould make good cause for his anger
Were an immortal god to befriend men so manifestly.
Enter thou, and as thou pray'st, in lowliness embrace
His knees, & by^his sire & fair heav'n-born mother implore
And by^his son, that thou may'st melt his soul with emotion.'

With these words Hermes sped away for lofty Olympos :
And Priam all fearlessly from off his chariot alighted,
Ordering Idaeus to remain i' the entry to keep watch   470
Over the beasts : th' old king meanwhile strode doughtily
    onward,
Where Achilles was then most wont to be, and sitting indoors
Found he him ; all his men sat apart ; for his only attendance
His squire Automedon and Alkimos in battle upgrown
Mov'd busilie to and fro serving, for late he had eaten,
And the supper-table disfurnish'd yet stood anigh him.
And Priam entering unperceiv'd til he well was among them,
Clasp'd his knees & seized his hands all humbly to kiss them,
Those dread murderous hands which his sons so many had
    slain.

As when a man whom spite of fate hath curs'd in his own
land   480
For homicide, that he fleeeth abroad & seeketh asylum
With some lord, and they that see^him are fill'd with
amazement,
Ev'n so now Achilles was amaz'd as he saw Priam enter,
And the men all wer' amaz'd, & lookt upon each other in turn.

But Priam (as Hermes had bade) bow'd down to beseech
him.
'O God-like Achilles, thy father call to remembrance,
How he is halting as I, i' the dark'ning doorway of old age,
And desolately liveth, while all they that dwell about him
Vex him, nor hath he one from their violence to defend
him :   489
Yet but an heareth he aught of thee, thy wellbeing in life,
Then he rejoiceth an' all his days are glad with a good hope
Soon to behold thee again, his son safe home from the
warfare.
But most hapless am I, for I had sons numerous and brave
In wide Troy ; where bē they now ? scarce is one o' them
left.
They were fifty the day ye arriv'd hither out of Achaia,
Nineteen royally born princes from one mother only,
While the others women of my house had borne me ; of all
these
Truly the greater part hath Ares in grim battle unstrung.
But hé, who was alone the city's lov'd guardian and stay,
Few days since thou slew'st him alas ! his country defending,
Hector, for whose sake am I‾come to the ships of Achaia
His body dear to redeem, offering thee a ransom abundant.
O God-like Achilles, have fear o' the gods, pity him too,
Thy sire also remember, having yet more pity on mé,   504
Who now stoop me beneath what dread deed mortal ever
dar'd,
Raising the hand that slew his son pitiably to kiss it.'

(466)

Then did Achilles yearn for thought of his ancient father
And from th' old king's seizure his own hand gently disen-
    gag'd.
And each brooded apart ; Priam o'er victorious Hector
Groan'd, low faln to the ground unnerved at feet of Achilles,
Who sat mourning awhile his sire, then turn'd to bewailing
Patroclus ; while loudly the house with their sobbing
    outrang.   512

But when Achilles now had sooth'd his soul in affection,
And all his bosom had disburden'd of passion extreme,
Swiftly from off his seat he arose, & old Priam uprais'd,
In pity & reverence for his age & silvery-blancht head,
And making full answer addrest him in airywingèd words.

' Unhappy man ! what mighty sorrows must thy spirit
    endure !   518
Nay, how durst thou come thus alone to the ships of Achaia,
Into the sight of him who thy sons so many and good
Spoil'd and sent to the grave ? Verilie thy heart is of iron.
But come, sit thee beside me upon my couch ; let us alwise
Now put away our griefs, sore tho' we be plagued with
    affliction.
Truly there is no gain in distressful lamentation,
Since the eternal gods have assign'd to us unhappy mortals
Hardship enough, while they enjoy bliss idly without end.
    Two jars, say they, await God's hand at th' entry of his court,
Stor'd ready with free gifts, of good things one, one of evil.
If mingling from both heav'n's thunderer equaly dispense,
Then will a man's fortune be chequer'd with both sorrow
    and joy ;   530
But to' whom Zeus giveth only of evil that man is outcast,
Hunger houndeth him on disconsolate over the brave earth,
Unrespected alike whether of mortals or immortals.
So my sire Peleus was dow'r'd with favour abounding,
And, from birth and cradle honour'd, all men living outshone

In wealth & happiness, king o'er his Myrmidon armies :
And tho' he was but a man, Zeus made him a fair goddess
    espouse.
But yet an' ev'n to him was an ill thrown in, that he hath
    not
Sons born into his house to retain its empery,—one son
Only he gat, one doom'd to a fate untimely, nor evn he
Comforts th' old man at home, since exiled far from him I
    bide   541
Here in Troy, thy sons' destruction compassing and thine.
Thou too, sir, we have heard enjoy'd'st good fortune afore-
    time ;
From Mytilene in Lesbos away to the boundary eastward
Of Phrygia's highlands, & north to the briny Hellespont.
Thou, sir, didst all men for wealth & progeny excel :
But when once th' high gods let loose this mischief anigh
    thee,
Thy city was compast with nought but fierce battle and blood.
Bear up, allow thy temper awhile some respite of anguish :
Thou wilt not benefit thy dear son vainly bewailing,   550
Nor restore him alive ere thou taste further affliction.'

    Him then in answer addrest god-like Priam, Ilyon's old
    king.
' Bid me not, O heav'nborn, to be seated, while ever Hector
Lyeth i' the camp dishonour'd, nay rather quickly with all
    speed
Fetch him here to my eyes ; & this great ransom apportion'd
Unto^his worth accept : may^it serve thy good pleasure, &thou
Safely return to thy home & sire, since now thou allow'st me
Still to renew my days i' the light o' the sun to behold it.'

    Then glancing full dourly bespake him swift-foot Achilles.
' O sir, vex me no more : myself I am already minded   560
Now to restore him. Awhile Zeus sent one here to command
    me,

My mother,—&* the wizard who hometh in Ocean is her sire.
Yea, an' I-know, Priam, also^of thee,—think not to deceive
    me—
That 'twas a god who brought-thee hither to the ships of
    Achaia,
Since no mortal alive would dare, nay not one in his prime,
Here to' intrude, neither c^d he pass our senteries unseen,
Nor the resistant bars of my doors easily undo.
Spare then again to provoke my soul o'erstrain'd in afflic-
    tion,
Lest, old king, I do-thee a wrong in thine enemy's camp,
Lest I in anger offend mine own honour &* sin against God.'

Thus he spake, and th' old king afeard in trembling
    obey'd him.   571
Peleïdes then arose, and sprang out over the doorway
Like a lion, nor alone; for with him two followers went,
Automedon the renown'd, and Alkimos, of many heroes
First in honour since Patroclus was lost to him in death.
They then quickly the beasts all from their harnessing
    unyoked,
And bidding into the house the herald in royal attendance,
Made him there to be seated: anon they from the wagon
    lift
Great Hector's body-ransom of ungrudg'd costliness untold:
Two rich mantles left they, a tunicle of linen also,   580
Comely to shroud his corpse when 'twas given-up to be
    borne home.
And the women were call'd who laved it an' after anointed
Laid in a chamber apart, lest if Priam 'haply beheld it
In his affliction he might restrain not his undying anger,
But break out and kindle the anguisht heart of Achilles,
Who might slay him an' in blind recklessness sin against
    God.
So the women-servants lav'd Hector's corpse an' anointed,
Shrouded it in the linen with broider'd mantle around it:

Then himself Achilles on a fair bier laid it, assisted   589
By his two followers, and on to Priam's wagon upraised,
Groaning deeply' and calling aloud on his old companyon.

   ' Be not aggriev'd, Patroclus, against me an' if thōu hearest,
Tho' i' the grave, that now I allow the surrender of Hector
Unto his sire, for surely he pays me full ample a ransom.
Thine is it all, as ever thou sharedst with me in all things.'
   With these words he return'd to his house, god-hearted
     Achilles,
Taking again his accustom'd seat whence late he had upris'n,
On one side opposite to Priam whom straight he addrest
   thus.

   'Thy son now, sir, is ev'n as thou hast pray'd to me restor'd.
His body lies on a bier, with dawn thou'rt free to behold
   him   600
And to depart with him home : take thought now but to
   refresh thee.
Nay nor was grand-tress'd Niobe disdainful of eating,
When her twelve children lay dead in her palace outstretch'd.
Six blossoming daughters had she 'and six lusty growing
   sons,
But her boys did Apollo^in silvery archery destroy
Wrathful against her, an' all her daughters Artemis o'erthrew,
For that against Leto the goddess their great mother had she
Vaunted, "thou'st two only, but I have borne many myself."
Then they, tho' but a pair, all her fair quantity fordid.
Nine days lay they on earth expos'd in butchery, no one
Could bury them, for men smitten in God's fury were as
   stones.   611
Then the 'high gods themselves came down & their burial
   made.
But Niobe took thought to renounce not food in affliction ;
And somewhere ev'n now, on a mountain pasture among
   rocks,
On Sipylus, where, as 'tis told, all-nightly the nymphs lie,

Who by day go dancing along splendent Achelous,
There in stone the mother sits brooding upon the goddes
  wrong.
But come, now let us also remember, most reverend guest,
Our food.   After again, at what time thou carry him home,
Thou may'st weep thy son ; heavy too will that sorrowing be.'

    Thus sed¯he, & forthwith went out, & seizing a white sheep
Kill'd it, an' his followers skinning & dismembering aptly
Into lesser portions cut it up, which fixing upon spits   623
Laid they anigh to the fire, & drew off daintily roasted.
Meanwhile Automedon set fine loaves out on a table
In baskets, but Achilles made the apportioning of flesh.

Then leapt forth their hands to the good cheer outspread
  afore them.
But when anon they^had ta'en their fill of drinking an' eating,
Then Priam in wonder sat mute as he gaz'd on Achilles,
In what prime, yea a man whom no god's beauty c^d excel ;
And Achilles on comely Priam look'd, marvelling also,
Considering his gracious addrèss and noble bearing :   632
Till their hearts wer' appeas'd gazing thus on each other
  intent.
When first broke silence god-like Priam, Ilyon's old king.

  ' Lead me to bed, heav'n-born, as soon as may be, let us
  both
In kind slumber awhile forgetfully drowse our senses :
For never hath sweet sleep seal'd mine eyelids for a moment
Since the sad hour when aneath thy hand mine unhappy son
  fell :
But ever o'erbrooding the deluge of my sorrow I lay
'Mong the cattle grovelling disgraced i' the mire o' the court-
  yard.   640
But now bread have I eaten again, & pour'd the mellow wine
Down my throat : but afore until now nought had I eaten.'

Thus sed⁻he, & Achilles bade his handmaids an' attendants
Place bedsteads i' the south corridor, with mattresses & rugs
Of fair scarlet dye, and counterpanes spread above them :
Also ther'on for night-apparel two warm woolly mantles.
So the women came torches in hand forth from the inner
    rooms,
And working busilie laid out very quickly the two beds.

Then laughingly to godly Priam spake swift-foot Achilles.
   'I must lodge⁻thee without, dear sir ; lest someone of our
     folk   650
Haply come in : 'tis ever some councillor asking an audience.
And ther' is old counsel when they sit with me debating.
If one of all that flock chanc'd here i' the swift-shadowing
    night
Thee to espy, 'twᵈ reach the shepherd, their great Agamemnon,
And there might be delay in accomplishing our agreement.
But come, tell thy mind to me nor make scruple about it,
How many days thou'rt fain to devote to the mourning of
    Hector,
That for so long a time I await & from battle abstain.'

  Whom answer'd then again god-like Priam, Ilyon's old
    king.
' If thou nobly desire me to bate my son's honour in nought,
Scarce, Achilles. couldst thou with a greater kindness attach
    me. . . .   661

OCTOBER

&

OTHER POEMS

*with occasional verses
on the war*

NOTE

POEM 3.—*As the metre or scansion of this poem was publicly discussed and wrongly analysed by some who admired its effects, it may be well to explain that it and the three other poems in similar measure, 'Flowering Tree', 'In der Fremde', 'The West Front', are strictly syllabic verse on the model left by Milton in 'Samson Agonistes'; except that his system, which depended on exclusion of extra-metrical syllables (that is, syllables which did not admit of resolution by 'elision' into a disyllabic scheme) from all places but the last, still admitted them in that place, thereby forbidding inversion of the last foot. It is natural to conclude that, had he pursued his inventions, his next step would have been to get rid of this anomaly; and if that is done, the result is the new rhythms that these poems exhibit. In this sort of prosody rhyme is admitted, like alliteration, as an ornament at will; it is not needed. My four experiments are confined to the twelve-syllable verse. It is probably agreed that there are possibilities in that long six-foot line which English poetry has not fully explored.*

OCTOBER

& OTHER POEMS

DEDICATED TO

GEN. THE RIGHT HON^{ble} JAN CHRISTIAAN SMUTS

I

OCTOBER

APRIL adance in play
  met with his lover May
  where she came garlanded.
The blossoming boughs o'erhead
  were thrill'd to bursting by
  the dazzle from the sky
  and the wild music there
  that shook the odorous air.

Each moment some new birth
  hasten'd to deck the earth
  in the gay sunbeams.
Between their kisses dreams :
  And dream and kiss were rife
  with laughter of mortal life.

But this late day of golden fall
  is still as a picture upon a wall
  or a poem in a book lying open unread.
  Or whatever else is shrined
when the Virgin hath vanishèd :
  Footsteps of eternal Mind
  on the path of the dead.

2

THE FLOWERING TREE

WHAT Fairy fann'd my dreams
   while I slept in the sun?
As if a flowering tree
   were standing over me:
Its young stem strong and lithe
   went branching overhead
And willowy sprays around
   fell tasseling to the ground
All with wild blossom gay
   as is the cherry in May
When her fresh flaunt of leaf
   gives crowns of golden green.

The sunlight was enmesh'd
   in the shifting splendour
And I saw through on high
   to soft lakes of blue sky:
Ne'er was mortal slumber
   so lapt in luxury.
Rather—Endymion—
   would I sleep in the sun
Neath the trees divinely
   with day's azure above
When my love of Beauty
   is met by beauty's love.

So I slept enchanted
   under my loving tree
Till from his late resting
   the sweet songster of night
Rousing awaken'd me:
   Then! this—the birdis note—
Was the voice of thy throat
   which thou gav'st me to kiss.

(476)

3
NOEL: CHRISTMAS EVE, 1913

Pax hominibus bonae voluntatis.

A FROSTY Christmas Eve
   when the stars were shining
Fared I forth alone
   where westward falls the hill,
And from many a village
   in the water'd valley
Distant music reach'd me
   peals of bells aringing:
The constellated sounds
   ran sprinkling on earth's floor
As the dark vault above
   with stars was spangled o'er.

Then sped my thought to keep
   that first Christmas of all
When the shepherds watching
   by their folds ere the dawn
Heard music in the fields
   and marveling could not tell
Whether it were angels
   or the bright stars singing.

Now blessed be the tow'rs
   that crown England so fair
That stand up strong in prayer
   unto God for our souls:
Blessed be their founders
   (said I) an' our country folk
Who are ringing for Christ
   in the belfries to-night
With arms lifted to clutch
   the rattling ropes that race

(477)

Into the dark above
   and the mad romping din.

But to me heard afar
   it was starry music
Angels' song, comforting
   as the comfort of Christ
When he spake tenderly
   to his sorrowful flock :
The old words came to me
   by the riches of time
Mellow'd and transfigured
   as I stood on the hill
Heark'ning in the aspect
   of th' eternal silence.

4

IN DER FREMDE

AH ! wild-hearted wand'rer
   far in the world away
Restless nor knowest why
   only thou canst not stay
And now turnest trembling
   hearing the wind to sigh :
'Twas thy lover calling
   whom thou didst leave forby.

So faint and yet so far
   so far and yet so fain—
' Return belov'd to me '
   but thou must onward strain :
Thy trembling is in vain
   as thy wand'ring shall be.
What so well thou lovest
   thou nevermore shalt see.

5

THE PHILOSOPHER AND HIS MISTRESS

WE watch'd the wintry moon
 Suffer her full eclipse
Riding at night's high noon
 Beyond the earth's ellipse.

The conquering shadow quell'd
 Her splendour in its robe:
And darkling we beheld
 A dim and lurid globe;

Yet felt thereat no dread,
 Nor waited we to see
The sullen dragon fled,
 The heav'nly Queen go free.

So if my heart of pain
 One hour o'ershadow thine,
I fear for thee no stain,
 Thou wilt come forth and shine:

And far my sorrowing shade
 Will slip to empty space
Invisible, but made
 Happier for that embrace.

6

NARCISSUS

ALMIGHTY wondrous everlasting
Whether in a cradle of astral whirlfire
Or globed in a piercing star thou slumb'rest
 The impassive body of God:

Thou deep i' the core of earth—Almighty !—
From numbing stress and gloom profound
Madest escape in life desirous
      To embroider her thin-spun robe.

'Twas down in a wood—they tell—
In a running water thou sawest thyself
Or leaning over a pool : The sedges
      Were twinn'd at the mirror's brim
The sky was there and the trees—Almighty !—
A bird of a bird and white clouds floating
And seeing thou knewest thine own image
      To love it beyond all else.

Then wondering didst thou speak
Of beauty and wisdom of art and worship
Didst build the fanes of Zeus and Apollo
      The high cathedrals of Christ :
All that we love is thine—Almighty !—
Heart-felt music and lyric song
Language the eager grasp of knowledge
      All that we think is thine.

But whence ?—Beauteous everlasting !—
Whence and whither ? Hast thou mistaken ?
Or dost forget ? Look again ! Thou seest
      A shadow and not thyself.

7

OUR LADY

I.

GODDESS azure-mantled and aureoled
That standing barefoot upon the moon
      Or throned as a Queen of the earth
      Tranquilly smilest to hold
      The Child-god in thine arms,

Whence thy glory?   Art not she
The country maiden of Galilee
Simple in dowerless poverty
Who from humble cradle to grave
     Hadst no thought of this wonder?

    When to man dull of heart
    Dawn'd at length graciously
    Thy might of Motherhood
The starry Truth beam'd on his home;
Then with insight exalted he gave thee
The trappings—Lady—wherewith his art
Delighteth to picture his spirit to sense
    And that grace is immortal.

    Fount of creative Love
    Mother of the Word eternal
    Atoning man with God:
Who set thee apart as a garden enclosed
From Nature's all-producing wilds
To rear the richest fruit o' the Life
Ever continuing out from Him
    Urgent since the beginning.

II.

Behold!   Man setteth thine image in the
    height of Heaven
And hallowing his untemper'd love
    Crowneth and throneth thee ador'd
    (Tranquilly joyous to hold
    The man-child in thine arms)
God-like apart from conflict to save thee
To guard thy weak caressive beauty
With incontaminate jewels of soul
Courage, patience, and self-devotion:
    All this glory he gave thee.

Secret and slow is Nature
Imperceptibly moving
With surely determinate aim :
To woman it fell to be early in prime
Ready to labour, mould, and cherish
The delicate head of all Production
The wistful late-maturing boy
Who made Knowing of Being.

Therefore art thou ador'd
Mother of God in man
Naturing nurse of power :
They who adore not thee shall perish
But thou shalt keep thy path of joy
Envied of Angels because the All-father
Call'd thee to mother his nascent Word
And complete the creation.

8

THE CURFEW TOWER

THRO' innocent eyes at the world awond'ring
Nothing spake to me more superbly
Than the round bastion of Windsor's wall

That warding the Castle's southern angle
An old inheritor of Norman prowess
Was call'd by the folk the Curfew Tow'r.

Above the masonry's rugged courses
A turreted clock of Caroline fashion
Told time to the town in black and gold.

It charmed the hearts of Henry's scholars
As kingly a mentor of English story
As Homer's poem is of Ilion :

(482)

Nor e'er in the landscape look'd it fairer
Than when we saw its white bulk halo'd
In a lattice of slender scaffoldings.

Month by month on the airy platforms
Workmen labour'd hacking and hoisting
Till again the tower was stript to the sun:

The old tow'r? Nay a new tow'r stood there
From footing to battlemented skyline
And topt with a cap the slice of a cone

Archæologic and counterfeited
The smoothest thing in all the high-street
As Eton scholars to-day may see:

They—wherever else they find their wonder
And feed their boyhood on Time's enchantment—
See never the Tow'r that spoke to me.

9

FLYCATCHERS

Sweet pretty fledgelings, perched on the rail arow,
Expectantly happy, where ye can watch below
Your parents a-hunting i' the meadow grasses
All the gay morning to feed you with flies;

Ye recall me a time sixty summers ago,
When, a young chubby chap, I sat just so
With others on a school-form rank'd in a row,
Not less eager and hungry than you, I trow,
With intelligences agape and eyes aglow,
While an authoritative old wise-acre
Stood over us and from a desk fed us with flies.

Dead flies—such as litter the library south-window,
That buzzed at the panes until they fell stiff-baked on the sill,
Or are roll'd up asleep i' the blinds at sunrise,
Or wafer'd flat in a shrunken folio.

A dry biped he was, nurtured likewise
On skins and skeletons, stale from top to toe
With all manner of rubbish and all manner of lies.

10

GHOSTS

MAZING around my mind like moths at a shaded candle.
 In my heart like lost bats in a cave fluttering,
Mock ye the charm whereby I thought reverently to lay you,
 When to the wall I nail'd your reticent effigys?

11

Ἐτώσιον ἄχθος ἀρούρης

WHO goes there? God knows. I'm nobody. How should
 I answer?
 Can't jump over a gate nor run across the meadow.
I'm but an old whitebeard of inane identity.   Pass on!
 What's left of me to-day will very soon be nothing.

12

HELL AND HATE

Two demons thrust their arms out over the world,
 Hell with a ruddy torch of fire,
  And Hate with gasping mouth,
 Striving to seize two children fair
Who play'd on the upper curve of the Earth.

Their shapes were vast as the thoughts of man,
 But the Earth was small
 As the moon's rim appeareth
 Scann'd through an optic glass.

The younger child stood erect on the Earth
 As a charioteer in a car
 Or a dancer with arm upraised;
 Her whole form—barely clad
 From feet to golden head—
Leapt brightly against the uttermost azure,
Whereon the stars were splashes of light
Dazed in the gulfing beds of space.

The elder might have been stell'd to show
The lady who led my boyish love;
But her face was graver than e'er to me
 When I look'd in her eyes long ago,
 And the hair on her shoulders fal'n
 Nested its luminous brown
 I' the downy spring of her wings:
Her figure aneath was screen'd by the Earth,
 Whereoff—so small that was
 No footing for her could be—
 She appeared to be sailing free
I' the glide and poise of her flight.

Then knew I the Angel Faith,
Who was guarding human Love.

Happy were both, of peaceful mien,
Contented as mankind longeth to be,
 Not merry as children are;
And show'd no fear of the Fiends' pursuit,
As ever those demons clutched in vain;

(485)

And I, who had fear'd awhile to see
Such gentleness in such jeopardy,
Lost fear myself; for I saw the foes
Were slipping aback and had no hold
On the round Earth that sped its course.

The painted figures never could move,
    But the artist's mind was there:
The longer I look'd the more I knew
They were falling, falling away below
    To the darkness out of sight.

This poem was written December 16, 1913. It is the description of a little picture hanging in my bedroom: it had been painted for me as a New Year's gift more than thirty years before, and I described it partly because I never exactly knew what it meant. When the war broke out I remembered my poem and sent it to ' The Times ', where it appeared in the ' Literary Supplement ', September 24, 1914.

13

ODE ON THE TERCENTENARY COM-MEMORATION OF SHAKESPEARE
1916

KIND dove-wing'd Peace, for whose green olive-crown
The noblest kings would give their diadems,
    Mother who hast ruled our home so long,
      How suddenly art thou fled !
    Leaving our cities astir with war;
    And yet on the fair fields deserted
    Lingerest, wherever the gaudy seasons
      Deck with excessive splendour
      The sorrow-stricken year,
    Where cornlands bask and high elms rustle gently,
And still the unweeting birds sing on by brae and bourn.

The trumpet blareth and calleth the true to be stern
Be then thy soft reposeful music dumb ;
   Yet shall thy lovers awhile give ear
     —Tho' in war's garb they come—
   To the praise of England's gentlest son ;
   Whom when she bore the Muses lov'd
   Above the best of eldest honour
     —Yea, save one without peer—
    And by great Homer set,
Not to impugn his undisputed throne,
The myriad-hearted by the mighty-hearted one.

For God of His gifts pour'd on him a full measure,
And gave him to know Nature and the ways of men :
   To dower with inexhaustible treasure
    A world-conquering speech,
   Which surg'd as a river high-descended
   That gathering tributaries of many lands
   Rolls through the plain a bounteous flood,
    Picturing towers and temples
    And ruin of bygone times,
And floateth the ships deep-laden with merchandise
Out on the windy seas to traffic in foreign climes.

Thee SHAKESPEARE to-day we honour ; and evermore,
Since England bore thee, the master of human song,
   Thy folk are we, children of thee,
    Who knitting in one her realm
   And strengthening with pride her sea-borne clans,
   Scorn'st in the grave the bruize of death.
   All thy later-laurel'd choir
    Laud thee in thy world-shrine :
    London's laughter is thine ;
One with thee is our temper in melancholy or might,
And in thy book Great-Britain's rule readeth her right.

Her chains are chains of Freedom, and her bright arms
Honour Justice and Truth and Love to man.
 Though first from a pirate ancestry
  She took her home on the wave,
 Her gentler spirit arose disdainful,
 And smiting the fetters of slavery
 Made the high seaways safe and free,
  In wisdom bidding aloud
  To world-wide brotherhood,
Till her flag was hail'd as the ensign of Liberty,
And the boom of her guns went round the earth in salvos
 of peace.

And thou, when Nature bow'd her mastering hand
To borrow an ecstasy of man's art from thee,
 Thou her poet secure as she
  Of the shows of eternity,
 Didst never fear thy work should fall
 To fashion's craze nor pedant's folly
 Nor devastator whose arrogant arms
  Murder and maim mankind;
  Who when in scorn of grace
He hath batter'd and burn'd some loveliest dearest shrine,
Laugheth in ire and boasteth aloud his brazen god.

 * * * * * *

I saw the Angel of Earth from strife aloof
Mounting the heavenly stair with Time on high,
 Growing ever younger in the brightening air
  Of the everlasting dawn:
 It was not terror in his eyes nor wonder,
 That glance of the intimate exaltation
 Which lieth as Power under all Being,
  And broodeth in Thought above,
  As a bird wingeth over the ocean,
Whether indolently the heavy water sleepeth
Or is dash'd in a million waves, chafing or lightly laughing.

(488)

I hear his voice in the music of lamentation,
In echoing chant and cadenced litany,
   In country song and pastoral piping
     And silvery dances of mirth:
   And oft, as the eyes of a lion in the brake,
   His presence hath startled me,
   In austere shapes of beauty lurking,
     Beautiful for Beauty's sake;
     As a lonely blade of life
Ariseth to flower whensoever the unseen Will
Stirreth with kindling aim the dark fecundity of Being.

Man knoweth but as in a dream of his own desire
The thing that is good for man, and he dreameth well:
   But the lot of the gentle heart is hard
     That is cast in an epoch of life,
   When evil is knotted and demons fight,
   Who know not, they, that the lowest lot
   Is treachery hate and trust in sin
     And perseverance in ill,
     Doom'd to oblivious Hell,
To pass with the shames unspoken of men away,
Wash'd out with their tombs by the grey unpitying tears of
      Heaven.

But ye, dear Youth, who lightly in the day of fury
Put on England's glory as a common coat,
   And in your stature of masking grace
     Stood forth warriors complete,
   No praise o'ershadoweth yours to-day,
   Walking out of the home of love
   To match the deeds of all the dead.—
     Alas! alas! fair Peace,
     These were thy blossoming roses.
Look on thy shame, fair Peace, thy tearful shame!
Turn to thine isle, fair Peace; return thou and guard it well!

14

THE CHIVALRY OF THE SEA

DEDICATED TO THE MEMORY OF CHARLES FISHER, LATE
STUDENT OF CHRIST CHURCH, OXFORD, LOST
IN THE 'INVINCIBLE'.

OVER the warring waters, beneath the wandering skies
The heart of Britain roameth, the Chivalry of the sea,
Where Spring never bringeth a flower, nor bird singeth in
    a tree ;
Far, afar, O beloved, beyond the sight of our eyes,
Over the warring waters, beneath the stormy skies.

Staunch and valiant-hearted, to whom our toil were play,
Ye man with armour'd patience the bulwarks night and day,
Or on your iron coursers plough shuddering through the
    Bay,
Or neath the deluge drive the skirmishing sharks of war :
Venturous boys who leapt on the pinnace and row'd from
    shore,
A mother's tear in the eye, a swift farewell to say,
And a great glory at heart that none can take away.

Seldom is your home-coming ; for aye your pennon flies
In unrecorded exploits on the tumultuous wave ;
Till, in the storm of battle, fast-thundering upon the foe,
Ye add your kindred names to the heroes of long-ago,
And mid the blasting wrack, in the glad sudden death of
    the brave,
Ye are gone to return no more.—Idly our tears arise ;
Too proud for praise as ye lie in your unvisited grave,
The wide-warring water, under the starry skies.

15

FOR 'PAGES INÉDITES', ETC.

April, 1916.

BY our dear sons' graves, fair France, thou'rt now to us
    endear'd ;
  Since no more as of old stand th' English against thee
    in fight,
But rallying to defend thee they die guarding thy beauty
  From blind envious Hate and Perfidy leagued with
    Might.

16

GHELUVELT

EPITAPH ON THE WORCESTERS. OCTOBER 31, 1914.

ASKEST thou of these graves? They'll tell thee, O stranger,
    in England
How we Worcesters lie where we redeem'd the battle.

17

THE WEST FRONT

AN ENGLISH MOTHER, ON LOOKING INTO MASEFIELD'S
'OLD FRONT LINE'.

  No country know I so well
    as this landscape of hell.
  Why bring you to my pain
    these shadow'd effigys
  Of barb'd wire, riven trees,
    the corpse-strewn blasted plain?

  And the names—Hebuterne
    Bethune and La Bassée—

(491)

I have nothing to learn—
    Contalmaison, Boisselle,
And one where night and day
    my heart would pray and dwell;

A desert sanctuary,
    where in holy vigil
Year-long I have held my faith
    against th' imaginings
Of horror and agony
    in an ordeal above

The tears of suffering
    and took aid of angels:
This was the temple of God:
    no mortuary of kings
Ever gathered the spoils
    of such chivalry and love:

No pilgrim shrine soe'er
    hath assembled such prayer—
With rich incense-wafted
    ritual and requiem
Not beauteous batter'd Rheims
    nor lorn Jerusalem.

18

TRAFALGAR SQUARE

September, 1917.

FOOL that I was: my heart was sore,
Yea sick for the myriad wounded men,
The maim'd in the war: I had grief for each one:
And I came in the gay September sun
To the open smile of Trafalgar Square;
Where many a lad with a limb fordone

Loll'd by the lion-guarded column
That holdeth Nelson statued thereon
Upright in the air.

The Parliament towers and the Abbey towers,
The white Horseguards and grey Whitehall,
He looketh on all,
Past Somerset House and the river's bend
To the pillar'd dome of St. Paul,
That slumbers confessing God's solemn blessing
On England's glory, to keep it ours—
While children true her prowess renew
And throng from the ends of the earth to defend
Freedom and honour—till Earth shall end.

The gentle unjealous Shakespeare, I trow,
In his country tomb of peaceful fame,
Must feel exiled from life and glow
If he think of this man with his warrior claim,
Who looketh o'er London as if 'twere his own,
As he standeth in stone, aloft and alone,
Sailing the sky with one arm and one eye.

19

CHRISTMAS EVE, 1917

MANY happy returns, sweet Babe, of the day!
Didst not thou sow good seed in the world, thy field?
Cam'st thou to save the poor? Thy poor yet pine.
Thousands to-day suffer death-pangs like thine;
Our jewels of life are spilt on the ground as dross;
Ten thousand mothers stand beneath the cross.
Peace to men of goodwill was the angels' song:
Now there is fiercer war, worse filth and wrong.
If thou didst sow good seed, is this the yield?
Shall not thy folk be quell'd in dead dismay?

Nay, with a larger hope we are fed and heal'd
Than e'er was reveal'd to the saints who died so strong;
For while men slept the seed had quicken'd unseen.
England is as a field whereon the corn is green.

Of trial and dark tribulation this vision is born—
Britain as a field green with the springing corn.
While we slumber'd the seed was growing unseen.
Happy returns of the day, dear Babe, we say.

ENGLAND has buried her sins with her fathers' bones.
Thou shalt be throned on the ruin of kingly thrones.
The wish of thine heart is rooted in carnal mind;
For good seed didst thou sow in the world thy field:
It shall ripen in gold and harvest an hundredfold.
Peace shall come as a flood upon all mankind;
Love shall comfort and succour the poor that are pined.

Wherever our gentle children are wander'd and sped,
Simple apostles thine of the world to come,
They carried the living seed of the living Bread,
The angel-song and the gospel of Christendom,
That while the nation slept was springing unseen.

So tho' we be sorely stricken we feel no dread:
Our thousand sons suffer death-pangs like thine:
It shall ripen in gold and harvest an hundredfold:
Peace and Love shall hallow our care and teen,
Shall bind in fellowship all the folk of the earth
To kneel at thy cradle, Babe, and bless thy birth.

Ring we the bells up and down in country and town,
And keep the old feast unholpen of preacher or priest,
Wishing thee happy returns, and thy Mother May,
Ever happier and happier returns, dear CHRIST, of thy day!

20

THE EXCELLENT WAY

MAN's mind that hath this earth for home
Hath too its far-spread starry dome
Where thought is lost in going free,
Prison'd but by infinity.
He first in slumbrous babyhood
Took conscience of his heavenly good;
Then with his sins grown up to youth
Wept at the vision of God's truth.

Soon in his heart new hopes awoke
As poet sang or prophet spoke:
Temples arose and stone he taught
To stand agaze in trancèd thought:
He won the trembling air to tell
Of far passions ineffable,
Feeding the hungry things of sense
With instincts of omniscience,
Immortal modes that should abide
Cherish'd by love and pious pride,
That unborn children might inherit
The triumph of his holy spirit,
Outbidding Nature, to entice
Her soul from her own Paradise,
Till her wild face had fallen to shame
Had he not praised her in God's name.

Alas! poor man, what blockish curse
Would violate thy universe,
To enchain thy freedom and entomb
Thy pleasance in devouring gloom?
Behold thy savage foes of yore

With woes of pestilence and war,
Siva and Moloch, Odin and Thor,
Rise from their graves to greet amain
The deeds that give them life again.

Poor man, sunk deeper than thy slime
In blood and hate, in terror and crime,
Thou who wert lifted on the wings
Of thy desire, the king of kings,
In promise beyond ken sublime:
O thou man-soul, who mightest climb
To heavenly happiness, whereof
Thine easy path were Mirth and Love!

October, 1918.

21

ENGLAND TO INDIA

Christmas, 1918.

BEAUTIFUL is man's home: how fair,
Wrapt in her robe of azurous air,
The Earth thro' stress of ice and fire
Came on the path of God's desire,
Redeeming Chaos, to compose
Exquisite forms of lily and rose,
With every creature a design
Of loveliness or craft divine
Searchable and unsearchable,
And each insect a miracle!

Truth is as Beauty unconfined:
Various as Nature is man's Mind:
Each race and tribe is as a flower
Set in God's garden with its dower
Of special instinct; and man's grace
Compact of all must all embrace.

China and Ind, Hellas or France,
Each hath its own inheritance;
And each to Truth's rich market brings
Its bright divine imaginings,
In rival tribute to surprise
The world with native merchandise.

  Nor least in worth nor last in years
Of artists, poets, saints and seers,
England, in her far northern sea,
Fashion'd the jewel of Liberty,
Fetch'd from the shore of Palestine
(Land of the Lily and mystic Vine).
Where once in the everlasting dawn
Christ's Love-star flamed, that heavenly sign
Whereto all nations shall be drawn,
Unfabled Magi, and uplift
Each to Love's cradle his own gift.

  Thou who canst dream and understand,
Dost thou not dream for thine own land
This dream of Truth, and contemplate
That happier world, Love's free Estate?
  Say, didst thou dream, O Sister fair,
How hand in hand we entered there?

22

BRITANNIA VICTRIX

CARELESS wast thou in thy pride,
Queen of seas and countries wide,
Glorying on thy peaceful throne :—
Can thy love thy sins atone?
What shall dreams of glory serve,
If thy sloth thy doom deserve,
When the strong relentless foe
Storm thy gates to lay thee low?

K k

Careless, ah ! he saw thee leap
Mighty from thy startled sleep,
Heard afar thy challenge ring :
'Twas the world's awakening.

Welcome to thy children all
Rallying to thee without call
Oversea, the sportive sons
From thy vast dominions !
Stern in onset or defence,
Terrible in their confidence.

Dauntless wast thou, fair goddess,
'Neath the cloud of thy distress ;
Fierce and mirthful wast thou seen
In thy toil and in thy teen ;
While the nations looked to thee,
Spent in worldwide agony.

Oft, throughout that long ordeal
Dark with horror-stricken duty,
Nature on thy heart would steal
Beckoning thee with heavenly beauty,
Heightening ever on thine isle
All her seasons' tranquil smile ;
Till thy soul anew converted,
Roaming o'er the fields deserted,
By thy sorrow sanctified,
Found a place wherein to hide.

Soon fresh beauty lit thy face,
Then thou stood'st in Heaven's high grace :
Sudden in air on land and sea
Swell'd the voice of victory.

Now when jubilant bells resound
And thy sons come laurel-crown'd,

After all thy years of woe
Thou no longer canst forgo,
Now thy tears are loos'd to flow.

    Land, dear land, whose sea-built shore
Nurseth warriors evermore,
Land, whence Freedom far and lone
Round the earth her speech has thrown
Like a planet's luminous zone,—
In thy strength and calm defiance
Hold mankind in love's alliance!

    Beauteous art thou, but the foes
Of thy beauty are not those
Who lie tangled and dismay'd
Fearless one, be yet afraid
Lest thyself thyself condemn
In the wrong that ruin'd them.

    God, who chose thee and upraised
'Mong the folk (His name be praised!),
Proved thee then by chastisement
Worthy of His high intent,
Who, because thou could'st endure,
Saved thee free and purged thee pure,
Won thee thus His grace to win,
For thy love forgave thy sin,
For thy truth forgave thy pride;
Queen of seas and countries wide,—
He who led thee still will guide.

    Hark! thy sons, those spirits fresh
Dearly housed in dazzling flesh,
Thy full brightening buds of strength
Ere their day had any length
Crush'd, and fallen in torment sorest,
Hark! the sons whom thou deplorest

Call—I hear one call; he saith:
'Mother, weep not for my death:
'Twas to guard our home from hell,
'Twas to make thy joy I fell
Praising God, and all is well.
What if now thy heart should quail
And in peace our victory fail!
If low greed in guise of right
Should consume thy gather'd might,
And thy power mankind to save
Fall and perish on our grave!
On my grave, whose legend be
Fought with the brave and joyfully
Died in faith of victory.
Follow on the way we won!
Thou hast found, not lost thy son.'

November 23, 1918.

23

POOR CHILD

On a mournful day
   When my heart was lonely,
O'er and o'er my thought
   Conned but one thing only,

Thinking how I lost
   Wand'ring in the wild-wood
The companion self
   Of my careless childhood.

How, poor child, it was
   I shall ne'er discover,
But 'twas just when he
   Grew to be thy lover,

With thine eyes of trust
   And thy mirth, whereunder
All the world's hope lay
   In thy heart of wonder.

Now, beyond regrets
   And faint memories of thee,
Saddest is, poor child,
   That I cannot love thee.

24

TO PERCY BUCK

Folk alien to the Muse have hemm'd us round
And fiends have suck'd our blood: our best delight
Is poison'd, and the year's infective blight
Hath made almost a silence of sweet sound.
   But you, what fortune, Percy, have you found
At Harrow? doth fair hope your toil requite?
Doth beauty win her praise and truth her right,
Or hath the good seed fal'n on stony ground?

   Ply the art ever nobly, single-soul'd
Like Brahms, or as you ruled in Wells erewhile,
—Nor yet the memory of that zeal is cold—
Where lately I, who love the purer style,
Enter'd, and felt your spirit as of old
Beside me, listening in the chancel-aisle.

1904.

25

TO HARRY ELLIS WOOLDRIDGE

Love and the Muse have left their home, now bare
Of memorable beauty, all is gone,
The dedicated charm of Yattendon,
Which thou wert apt, dear Hal, to build and share.

(501)

What noble shades are flitting, who while-ere
Haunted the ivy'd walls, where time ran on
In sanctities of joy by reverence won,
Music and choral grace and studies fair !

These on some kindlier field may Fate restore,
And may the old house prosper, dispossest
Of her whose equal it can nevermore
    Hold till it crumble : O nay ! and the door
Will moulder ere it open on a guest
To match thee in thy wisdom and thy jest.

October, 1905.

26

FORTUNATUS NIMIUM

I HAVE lain in the sun
I have toil'd as I might
I have thought as I would
And now it is night.

My bed full of sleep
My heart of content
For friends that I met
The way that I went.

I welcome fatigue
While frenzy and care
Like thin summer clouds
Go melting in air.

To dream as I may
And awake when I will
With the song of the birds
And the sun on the hill.

(502)

Or death—were it death—
To what should I wake
Who loved in my home
All life for its sake?

What good have I wrought?
I laugh to have learned
That joy cannot come
Unless it be earned;

For a happier lot
Than God giveth me
It never hath been
Nor ever shall be.

27

DEMOCRITUS

Joy of your opulent atoms! wouldst thou dare
Say that Thought also of atoms self-became,
Waving to soul as light had the eye in aim;
And so with things of bodily sense compare
Those native notions that the heavens declare,
Space and Time, Beauty and God—Praise we his name!—
Real ideas, that on tongues of flame
From out mind's cooling paste leapt unaware?

Thy spirit, Democritus, orb'd in the eterne
Illimitable galaxy of night
Shineth undimm'd where greater splendours burn
Of sage and poet: by their influence bright
We are held; and pouring from his quenchless urn
Christ with immortal love-beams laves the height.

1919.

New Verse

written in
1921
with the other poems of that year
& a few earlier pieces

PREVIOUS PUBLICATIONS

1. *In an illustrated Album. 1924.*
2. *On a 4to sheet with Preface, notes, and references, for private circulation. June 1923.*
6. *The Queen; 'Elizabethan' number, July 1923.*
7. *London Mercury, Nov. 1924.*
8. *London Mercury, July 1923.*
10. *Yale Review, July 1923; and contemporaneously, with a translation into Greek Elegiacs by Francis Pember, in the Nineteenth Century.*
11. *London Mercury, June 1923.*
13. *Cornhill, August 1923.*
18. *Some War Album.*
25. *Subscribed to a Keats memorial volume.*
1–7. THE TAPESTRY. *Privately printed by F. W. and S. M. Nov. 1925.*
1–25. NEW VERSE. *Clarendon Press, Oxford, 1926. See Preface to that book.*

All the poems not specially dated at the foot were written in 1921.

NEW VERSE

CHEDDAR PINKS

MID the squander'd colour
   idling as I lay
Reading the Odyssey
   in my rock-garden
I espied the cluster'd
   tufts of Cheddar pinks
Burgeoning with promise
   of their scented bloom
All the modish motley
   of their bloom to-be
Thrust up in narrow buds
   on the slender stalks
Thronging springing urgent
   hasting (so I thought)
As if they feared to be
   too late for summer—
Like schoolgirls overslept
   waken'd by the bell
Leaping from bed to don
   their muslin dresses
      On a May morning:

Then felt I like to one
   indulging in sin
(Whereto Nature is oft
   a blind accomplice)

(507)

Because my aged bones
    so enjoyed the sun
There as I lay along
    idling with my thoughts
Reading an old poet
    while the busy world
Toil'd moil'd fuss'd and scurried
    worried bought and sold
Plotted stole and quarrel'd
    fought and God knows what.
I had forgotten Homer
    dallying with my thoughts
Till I fell to making
    these little verses
Communing with the flowers
    in my rock-garden
        On a May morning.

2

POOR POLL

I saw it all, Polly, how when you had call'd for sop
and your good friend the cook came & fill'd up your pan
you yerk'd it out deftly by beakfuls scattering it
away far as you might upon the sunny lawn
then summon'd with loud cry the little garden birds
to take their feast. Quickly came they flustering around
Ruddock & Merle & Finch squabbling among themselves
nor gave you thanks nor heed while you sat silently
watching, and I beside you in perplexity
lost in the maze of all mystery and all knowledge   10
felt how deep lieth the fount of man's benevolence
if a bird can share it & take pleasure in it.
    If you, my bird, I thought, had a philosophy
it might be a sounder scheme than what our moralists

propound : because thou, Poll, livest ín the darkness
which human Reason searching from outside would pierce,
but, being of so feeble a candle-power, can only
show up to view the cloud that it illuminates.
Thus reason'd I : then marvell'd how you can adapt
your wild bird-mood to endure your tame environment   20
the domesticities of English household life
and your small brass-wire cabin, who sh^{dst} live on wing
harrying the tropical branch-flowering wilderness :
Yet Nature gave you a gift of easy mimicry
whereby you have come to win uncanny sympathies
and morsell'd utterance of our Germanic talk
as schoolmasters in Greek will flaunt their hackney'd tags
φωνᾶντα συνετοῖσιν and κτῆμα ἐς ἀεὶ,
ἡ γλῶσσ' ὀμώμοχ', ἡ δὲ φρὴν ἀνώμοτος
tho' you with a better ear copy ús more perfectly   30
nor without connotation as when you call'd for sop
all with that stumpy wooden tongue & vicious beak
that dry whistling shrieking tearing cutting pincer
now eagerly subservient to your cautious claws
exploring all varieties of attitude
in irrepressible blind groping for escape
—a very figure & image of man's soul on earth
the almighty cosmic Will fidgeting in a trap—
in your quenchless unknown desire for the unknown life
of which some homely British sailor robb'd you, alas !   40
'Tis all that doth your silly thoughts so busy keep
the while you sit moping like Patience on a perch
——*Wie viele Tag' und Nächte bist du geblieben!*
La possa delle gambe posta in tregue—
the impeccable spruceness of your grey-feather'd pôll
a model in hairdressing for the dandiest old Duke
enough to qualify you for the House of Lords
or the Athenaeum Club, to poke among the nobs
great intellectual nobs and literary nobs
scientific nobs and Bishops *ex officio* :   50

nor lack you simulation of profoundest wisdom
such as men's features oft acquire in very old age
by mere cooling of passion & decay of muscle
by faint renunciation even of untold regrets;
who seeing themselves a picture of that wh: man should-be
learn almost what it were to be what they are-not.
But you can never have cherish'd a determined hope
consciously to renounce or lose it, you will live
your threescore years & ten idle and puzzle-headed
as any mumping monk in his unfurnish'd cell   60
in peace that, poor Polly, passeth Understanding—
merely because you lack what we men understand
by Understanding.   Well! well! that's the difference
C'est la seule différence, mais c'est important.
Ah! your pale sedentary life! but would you change?
exchange it for one crowded hour of glorious life,
one blind furious tussle with a madden'd monkey
who would throttle you and throw your crude fragments away
shreds unintelligible of an unmeaning act
dans la profonde horreur de l'éternelle nuit?   70
Why ask? You cannot know. 'Twas by no choice of yours
that you mischanged for monkeys' man's society,
'twas that British sailor drove you from Paradise—
Εἴθ' ὤφελ' Ἀργοῦς μὴ διαπτάσθαι σκάφος!
I'd hold embargoes on such a ghastly traffic.

  I am writing verses to you & grieve that you shᵈ be
absolument incapable de les comprendre,
Tu, Polle, nescis ista nec potes scire :—
Alas! Iambic, scazon and alexandrine,
spondee or choriamb, all is alike to you—   80
my well-continued fanciful experiment
wherein so many strange verses amalgamate
on the secure bedrock of Milton's prosody:
not but that when I speak you will incline an ear
in critical attention lest by chánce I míght
póssibly say sómething that was worth repeating:

I am adding (do you think?) pages to literature
that gouty excrement of human intellect
accumulating slowly & everlastingly
depositing, like guano on the Peruvian shore,   90
to be perhaps exhumed in some remotest age
(*piis secunda, vate me, detur fuga*)
to fertilize the scanty dwarf'd intelligence
of a new race of beings the unhallow'd offspring
of them who shall have quite dismember'd & destroy'd
our temple of Christian faith & fair Hellenic art
just as that monkey would, poor Polly, have done for you.

3

THE TAPESTRY

' Sequel to the foregoing' W. W.

' THESE tapestries have hung fading around my hall
centuries long ; their old-fashion'd mythology
infects the fresh and young with blighting influence
like Abram there with knife and faggot standing stark
to slay his son. I'm vow'd I'll have no more of them.
Turn me them outside-in, their faces to the wall,
so shall we have more colour and less solemnity.'—
 Thus the young heir & lord enjoin'd his wondering steward
who obey'd, and many a guest was bidden, and at the feast
the wine flow'd free with fine hubbub and merriment. 10

 My tale is but a fable of God's fair tapestry
the decorated room wherein my spirit hath dwelt
from infancy a nursling of great Nature's beauty
which keepeth fresh my wonder as when I was a child.
Such is the joy of the eye, that dark conduit whereby

the swift creative ray, offspring of heavenly fire,
steals to the mind, wakening in her secret chamber
vast potencies of thought which there lie slumbering
in the image of God.   Ah! had I not heard and seen
today, when at my window a meryl sat fluting   20
his happy canticle to hail the sun's uprise?
Then looked I forth and lo! The Elysian fields of Dawn!
and there in naked peace my dumb expectancy
mirror'd above the hills, a pageant like music
heard in imagination or the silence of dreams.
What if I had not seen the cloths of Night take hue
soft-tinged as of brown bear-skin on green opal spredd
which still persisting through shift imperceptible
grew to an incandescent copper on a pale light-blue!
Then one flame-yellow streak pierced thru' the molten
          bronze   30
with lilac freak'd above, where fiëry in red mist
the orb with slow surprise surged, till his whole blank blaze
dispell'd from out his path all colour—and Day began.

    Thus ever at every season in every hour and place
visions await the soul on wide ocean or shore
mountain forest or garden in wind and floating cloud
in busy murmur of bees or blithe carol of birds:
nor is it memoried thought only nor pleasured sense
that holds us, nor whate'er Reason sits puzzling out
of light or atom, as if—say, the Rainbow's beauty   40
lay in our skill to fray the Sun's white-tissued ray
to unravel and measure-off the gaudy threads thereof:
It is a deeper thrill, the joy that lovers learn
taking divine instruction from each other's eyes,
the Truth that all men feel gazing upon the skies
in constellated Night—𝕺 𝕲𝖔𝖉 𝖙𝖍𝖊 𝕱𝖆𝖙𝖍𝖊𝖗 𝖔𝖋 𝕳𝖊𝖆𝖛𝖊𝖓!
'When I arose and saw the dawn, I sighed for Thee.'

    Reckon the backward stretch of Mankind's pedigree
should it be fifteen thousand generations told
were that so long to climb from dim selfconsciousness   50

up to the eagle aëry of high philosophy?
to escape from his wild-beast cave in the wilderness
to till'd plains and safe homes, farms and mansion'd gardens,
populous wall'd cities, temples and pillar'd schools,
to dwell in grace, gravity, amity and good manners?
Was then the first dawning of his savage wonder
a vain terror to scare him from his aim astray?
all his prophetic seers, poets, enthusiasts,
dreamers, artists, adorners, whose meditation
won to purity of soul in the visions of God,   60
have guided him on securely and taught him wisely;
their soul's desire came with man's Reason from Nature,
transfiguring his sorrows in heroic grace;
their temples even in ruin reproach his follies
his science is consecrated by their beauty.

    I prop so far my slight fable with argument
to lay malison and ban on the upstart leprous clan
who wrong Nature's beauty turning her face about:
for, certes, hath the goddess also her hinder parts
which men of all ages have kindly thought to hide: 70
But as a man, owning a fine cloth of Arras,
in reverence for his heirloom will examine it all
inside and out, and learn whether of white wool or silk
the high-warp, what of silver and gold, how fine the thread,
what number of graded tints in hatching of the woof;
so we study Nature, wrong side as well as right
and in the eternal mystery of God's working find
full many unsightly a token of beauty's trouble;
and gain knowledge of Nature and much wisdom thereby:
but these making no part of beauty's welcome face,   80
these we turn to the wall, hiding away the mean
ugly brutish obscene clumsy irrelevances
which Honesty will own to with baffling humour
and in heightening the paradox can find pleasure;
since without such full knowledge can no man have faith
nor will his thought or picture of life be worth a bean.

L l

Now, bean, button, or boterfly, pray accept of me
for my parrot verses this after apology:
making experiments in versification
I wrote them as they came in the mood of the day   90
whether for good or ill—it was them or nothing.

4

KATE'S MOTHER

PERCH'D on the upland wheatfields beyond the village end
a red-brick Windmill stood with black bonnet of wood
that trimm'd the whirling cross of its great arms around
upon the wind, pumping up water night and day
from the deep Kentish chalk to feed a little town
where miniatured afar it huddled on the coast
its glistening roofs and thrust its short pier in the sea.
Erewhile beside the Mill I had often come and gazed
across the golden cornland to the purple main
and distant town, so distant that I could not hear   10
the barrack bugles but might spy the castle-flag
a speck of bunting held against the foam-fleck'd waves:
and luggers in black rank on the high shingle-bank
drawn up beside the tarr'd huts of the fishermen
(those channel boatmen famous for courage and skill)
and ships that in the offing their scatter'd courses fetch'd
with sunlit sails, or bare-masted outrode the tide:
'Twas such a scene of bright perspective and brave hues
as no painter can forge, brushing his greys and blues,
his madder, vermilion, chrome and ultramarine,   2c
'Twas very England herself as I grew to love her
—as any manchild loveth looking on beauty—
England in the peace and delight of her glory,
beneath the summer sun in the wild-roving wind
the mighty fans hurtling steadily above me as there
Nature flooded my heart in unseizable dream:

Long ago—when as yet the house where I was born
was the only home I knew and I no bigger then
than a mastiff-dog may be, and little of clothing wore
but shirt and trews and shoes and holland pinafore : 30
then was my father's garden a fairy realm of tree-
worship, mimic warfare and ritual savagery
and past its gates a land of peril and venture lay
my field of romance the steep beach of the wild sea
whither might I go wander on high-days for long hours
tended at every step by a saint, a nurse and mate
of such loving devotion patience and full trust
that of all Catharines she hath been my only Kate.

But inland past the Windmill lay a country unknown,
so that upon the day when I was grown so strong 40
(to my great pride 'twas told) that I might walk with Kate
on her half-holiday's accustomed pilgrimage
to see her old mother who lived across the downs
in the next combe, it happ'd that I so stirred must be
that after seventy years I can revive the day.

A blazing afternoon in splendor of mid-July
Kate and my elder sister and I trudged down the street
past village pond and church, and up the winding lane
came out beside the windmill on the high cornland 49
where my new world began.   A wheel-worn sunken track
parted the tilth, deep rugged ruts patch'd here and there
with broken flints raked in from strewage of the ground,
baked clay fissured by drought, as splinter'd rock unkind
to a child's tread, and on either hand the full-grown corn
rose up a wall above me, where no breeze might come
nor any more sight thence of the undulating sweep
of the yellow acres nor of the blue main below.

For difficulty and roughness and scorch of the way
then a great Bible-thought came on me : I was going
like the Israelites of old in the desert of Sin, 60
where forty years long they journey'd in punishment :
'twas such a treeless plain as this whereon they went,

this torrid afternoon under the fiery sun
might be the forty years ; but I forgat them soon
picking my way to run on the low skirting banks
that shelved the fields, anon foraging mid the ranks
fending the spikey awns off from my cheeks and eyes
wherever I might espy the larger flowers, and pull'd
blue Cockle and scarlet Poppy and yellow Marigold
whose idle blazonry persists to decorate   70
the mantle of green and gold which man toileth to weave
for his old grandmother Earth :—with such posies in hand
we ran bragging to Kate who plodded on the track
and now with skilful words beguiled us in her train
warning how far off yet the promised land, and how
journey so great required our full strength husbanded
for the return : 'twere wise today to prove our strength
and walk like men. Whereat we wished most to be wise
and keeping near beside her heeded closely our steps
so that our thoughts now wander'd no more from the way
(O how interminable to me seem'd that way !)   81
till it fell sloping downwards and we saw the green
of great elms that uplifted their heads in the combe :
when for joy of the shade racing ahead we sat
till Kate again came up with us and led us on
by shelter'd nooks where among apple and cherry trees
many a straw-thatcht cottage nestled back from the road.
A warp'd wicket hidden in a flowery Privet-hedge
admitted to her mother's along a pebbled path
between two little squares of crowded garden framed   90
in high clipt Box, that blent its faint pervading scent
with fragrant Black-currant, gay Sweet-william and Mint,
and white Jasmin that hung drooping over the door.
A bobbin sprang the latch and following Kate we stood
in shade of a low room with one small window, and there
facing the meagre light of its lace-curtain'd panes
a bland silver-hair'd dame clad in a cotton frock
sat in a rocking chair by an open hearth, whereon

(516)

a few wood embers smouldering kept a kettle at steam.
She did not rise, but speaking with soft courtesy   100
and full respectful pride of her daughter's charges
gave us kind welcome, bade us sit and be rested
while Kate prepared the tea. Many strange things the while
allured me : a lofty clock with loud insistent tick
beguiled the solemn moments as it doled them out
picturing upon its face a full-rigg'd ship that rocked
tossing behind an unmoved billow to and fro :
beside it a huge batter'd copper warming-pan
with burnish'd bowl fit for Goliath's giant spoon,
and crockery whimsies ranged on the high mantel-shelf :
'twas a storeroom of wonders, but my eyes returned   111
still to the old dame, she was the greatest wonder of all,
the wrinkles innumerable of her sallow skin
her thin voice and the trembling of her patient face
as there she swayed incessantly on her rocking-chair
like the ship in the clock : she had sprung into my ken
wholly to enthrall me, a fresh nucleus of life-surprise
such as I knew must hold mystery and could reveal :
for I had observed strange movement of her cotton skirt
and as she sat with one knee across the other, I saw   120
how her right foot in the air was all a-tremble and jerked
in little restless kicks : so when we sat to feast
about the table spredd with tea and cottage cakes
whenever her eye was off me I watched her furtively
to make myself assured of all the manner and truth
of this new thing, and ere we were sent out to play
(that so Kate might awhile chat with her mother alone)
I knew the SHAKING PALSY. What follow'd is lost,
how I chew'd mint-leaves waiting there in the garden
is my latest remembrance of that July day,   130
all after is blank, the time like a yesterday's loaf
is sliced as with a knife, or like as where the sea
in some diluvian rage swallowing a part of the earth
left a sheer cliff where erst the unbroken height ran on,

and by the rupture has built a landmark seen afar
—as 'tis at the South Foreland or St. Margaret's bay—
so memory being broken may stand out more clearly
as that day's happenings live so freshly by me, and most
the old widow with her great courtesy and affliction :
and I love to remember it was to her I made   140
the first visit of compliment that ever I paid.

5

THE COLLEGE GARDEN

IN 1917

The infinitude of Life is in the heart of man,
a fount surging to fill a lake that mirrors heav'n,
and now to himself he seemeth stream to be and now pool
as he acteth his impulse or stayeth brooding thereon.
    There is no beauty of love or peace, no joy nor mirth
but by kindred artistry of contemplation enhanc'd
decketh his sovranty with immortalities.
Jewels of imagination hath he, purities
and sanctities whereby he dareth approach God
plenishing his temples with incense of music   10
in praise and lyric litanies that call on Christ :
his Destiny is one with the eternal skies : he lieth
a dream in the elemental far vistas of Truth
inhaling life to his soul as the ambient azurous air
that he draweth into his mortal body unconscious
to fire the dutiful-desperate pulse of his blood.
    And yet again there is neither any evil nor mischief
sprung from teeming chaos to assault his mind, but he
will harbour it—he will be goodfellow in turn with Sin.
Hark to him how cheerily he windeth his hunting-horn   20
whipping-in his wolf-pack to their pasture of blood !
See his comforting mastery of Nature's forces

how he skilleth it to his own ruin, ev'n to mimic
cosmic catastrophe in her hideous destructions !
He will have surfeit of passion and revel in wrong
till like a shameless prodigal at death's door he find
his one nobility is but to suffer bravely
in the lazar-house of souls his self-betrayal.

   Surely I know there is none that hath not taint at heart :
Yet drink I of heav'nly hope and faith in God's dealing 30
basking this summer day under the stately limes
by the immemorial beauty of this gothic college,
a place more peaceful now than even sweet peace should be
hush'd in spiritual vacancy of desolation
by sad desertion of throng'd study and gay merriment—
since all the gamesome boys are fled with their glory
light-hearted in far lands making fierce sport with Hell
and to save home from the spoiler have despoil'd their homes
leaving nought in their trace but empty expectancy
of their return, Alas ! for how few shall return !   40
what love-names write we daily in the long roll of death !
And yet some shall return, and others with them come :
life will renew ; tho' now none cometh here all day
but a pensive philosopher from his dark room
pacing the terrace, slow as his earth-burden'd thought,
and the agèd gardener with scythe wheelbarrow and broom
loitering in expert parcimony of skill and time
while on the grassy slope of the old city-rampart
I watch his idleness and hearken to the clocks
in punctual dispute clanging the quarter-hours—   50
dull preaching calendars ticking upon their wheels
punctilious subdivisions of infinity
and reckoning now as usual all the monstrous hours
these monstrous heartless hours that pass and yet must pass
till this mischief shall pass and England's foe be o'erthrown—
and shall be o'erthrown—'tis for this thing her dear boys die
and this at each full hour the chimes from Magdalen tow'r
proclaim with dominant gay cloze hurl'd to the sky.

Thus hour draggeth on hour, and I feel every thrill
of time's eternal stream that passeth over me   60
the dream-stream of God's Will that made things as they be
and me as I am, as unreluctant in the stream
I lie, like one who hath wander'd all his summer morn
among the heathery hills and hath come down at noon
in a breathless valley upon a mountain-brook
and for animal recreation of hot fatigue
hath stripp'd his body naked to lie down and taste
the play of the cool water on all his limbs and flesh
and lying in a pebbly shallow beneath the sky
supine and motionless feeleth each ripple pass   70
until his thought is merged in the flow of the stream
as it cometh upon him and lappeth him there
stark as a white corpse that stranded upon the stones
blocketh and for a moment delayeth the current
ere it can pass to pay its thin tribute of salt
into the choking storage of the quenchless sea.

6

THE PSALM

While Northward the hot sun was sinking o'er the trees
as we sat pleasantly talking in the meadow,
the swell of a rich music suddenly on our ears
gush'd thru' the wide-flung doors, where village-folk in church
stood to their evening psalm praising God together—
and when it came to cloze, paused, and broke forth anew.

A great Huguenot psalm it trod forth on the air
with full slow notes moving as a goddess stepping
through the responsive figures of a stately dance
conscious of beauty and of her fair-flowing array   10
in the severe perfection of an habitual grace,
then stooping to its cloze, paused to dance forth anew;

To unfold its bud of melody everlastingly
fresh as in springtime when, four centuries agone,
it wing'd the souls of martyrs on their way to heav'n
chain'd at the barbarous stake, mid the burning faggots
standing with tongues cut out, all singing in the flames—
O evermore, sweet Psalm, shalt thou break forth anew.

Thou, when in France that self-idolatrous idol reign'd
that starv'd his folk to fatten his priests and concubines, 20
thou wast the unconquerable paean of resolute men
who fell in coward massacre or with Freedom fled
from the palatial horror into far lands away,
and England learnt to voice thy deathless strain anew.

Ah! they endured beyond worst pangs of fire and steel
torturings invisible of tenderness and untold;
No Muse may name them, nay, no man will whisper them;
sitting alone he dare not think of them—and wail
of babes and mothers' wail flouted in ribald song.   29
Draw to thy cloze, sweet Psalm, pause and break forth anew!

Thy minstrels were no more, yet thy triumphing plaint
haunted their homes, as once in a deserted house
in Orthes, as 'twas told, the madden'd soldiery
burst in and search'd but found nor living man nor maid
only the sound flow'd round them and desisted not
but when it wound to cloze, paused, and broke forth anew.

And oft again in some lone valley of the Cevennes
where unabsolvèd crime yet calleth plagues on France
thy heavenly voice would lure the bloodhounds on, astray,
hunting their fancied prey afar in the dark night   40
and with its ghostly music mock'd their oaths and knives.
O evermore great Psalm spring forth! spring forth anew!

7

COME SE QUANDO

How thickly the far fields of heaven are strewn with stars!
Tho' the open eye of day shendeth them with its glare
yet, if no cloudy wind curtain them nor low mist
of earth blindfold us, soon as Night in grey mantle
wrappeth all else, they appear in their optimacy
from under the ocean or behind the high mountains
climbing in spacious ranks upon the stark-black void:
Ev'n so in our mind's night burn far beacons of thought
and the infinite architecture of our darkness,
the dim essence and being of our mortalities,   10
is sparkled with fair fire-flecks of eternity
whose measure we know not nor the wealth of their rays.

  It happ'd to me sleeping in the Autumn night, what time
Sirius was uplifting his great lamp o'er the hills,
I saw him not—my sight was astray, my wonder
held by the epiphany of a seraphic figure
that was walking on earth—in my visions it was—
I saw one in the full form and delight of man,
the signature of godhead in his motion'd grace,   19
and the aureole of his head was not dimm'd to my view;
the shekinah of azure floating o'er him in the air
seem'd the glow of a fire that burn'd steadfast within
prison'd to feed the radiance of his countenance;
as a lighthouse flasheth over broken waters
a far resistless beam from its strong tower: it was
as if Nature had deign'd to take back from man's hand
some work of her own as art had refashion'd it
—when Giorgione (it might be) portraying the face
of one who hath left no memory but that picture
and watching well the features at their play to find   30
some truth worthy of his skill, caught them for a moment
transfigured by a phantom visitation of spirit

which seizing he drew forth and fix'd on the canvas
as thence it hath gazed out for ever, and once on me:
Even such immanent beauty had that heroic face
and all that look'd on it loved and many worshipp'd.

For me, comfort possess'd me, the intimate comfort
of Beauty that is the soul's familiar angel
who bringeth me alway such joy as a man feeleth
returning to the accustom'd homeliness of home   40
after long absence or exile among strange things,
and my heart in me was laughing for happiness—
when I saw a great fear fell on the worshippers,
The fear of God: I saw its smoky shadow of dread;
and as a vast Plutonian mountain that burieth
its feet in molten lava and its high peak in heaven,
whenever it hath decoy'd some dark voyaging storm
to lave its granite shoulders, dischargeth the flood
in a thousand torrents o'er its flanks to the plain
and all the land is vocal with the swirl and gush   50
of the hurrying waters, so suddenly in this folk
a flood of troublous passion arose and mock'd control.

Then saw I the light vanities and follies of man
put on dragonish faces and glour with Gorgon eyes
disowning Shame and Reason, and one poët I saw
who from the interdependence and rivalry of men
loathing his kind had fled into the wilderness
to wander among the beasts and make home of their caves:
like to those Asian hermits color'd by their clime
who drank the infatuation of the wide torrid sand   60
the whelming tyranny of the lonely sun by day
the boundless nomadry of the stars by night, who sought
primeval brotherhood with things unbegotten;
who for ultimate comfort clothing them i' the skin
of nakedness wrapt nothingness closely about them
choosing want for wealth and shapeless terrors for friends,
in the embrace of desolation and wearied silence
to lie babe-like on the bosom of unpitying power.

But he found not rest nor peace for his soul : I read
his turbulent passion, the blasphemy of his heart   70
as I stood among the rocks that chuckled the cry
wherewith he upcast reproach into the face of heaven.

' UNVEIL thine eyes, O THEMIS ! Stand, unveil thine eyes !
from the high zenith hang thy balance in the skies !
In one scale set thy Codes of Justice Duty and Awe
thy penal interdicts the tables of thy Law
and in the other the postulant plea of Mercy and Love :
then thine unbandaged sight shall know thy cause how light
and see thy thankless pan fly back to thee above.

' Or wilt thou deeplier wager, an if thou hast the key   80
to unlock the cryptic storehouse of futurity,
fetch the mint-treasure forth, unpack the Final Cause
whose prime alweighty metal must give Reason pause ;
or if 'tis of such stuff as man's wit cannot gauge
scale thou the seal'd deposit in its iron-bound cage
Nay, lengthen out the beam of the balance on thy side
unequal as thou wilt, so that on mine the pan
to hold the thoughts of man be deep enough and wide.

' What Providence is this that maketh sport with Chance
blindly staking against things of no ordinance ?   90
Must the innocent dear birds that singing in the shaw
with motherly instinct wove their nest of twisted straw
see in some icy hail-gust their loved mansion drown'd
and all their callow nurslings batter'd on the ground ?
Even so a many-generation'd city of men
the storied temple of their endeavour and amorous ken
is toss'd back into rubbish by a shudder of the earth's crust :
Nor even the eternal stars have any sanction'd trust
that, like ships in dark night ill-fatedly on their course,   99
they shall not meet and crash together, and all their force

be churn'd back to the vapory magma whence they grew
age-long to plod henceforth their frustrate path anew.

   ' From this blind wreckage then hath Wisdom no escape
but limitless production of every living shape?
How shall man honour this Demiurge and yet keep
in due honour the gift that he rateth so cheap?
Myriad seeds perfected that one seed may survive—
Millions of men, that Reason in a scant few may thrive,
Multiplication alike of good bad strong and weak
and the overflow of life more wasteful than the leak.   110

   ' And what this treasure, of which, so prodigal of the whole,
he granteth unto each pensioner in such niggard dole?
its short lease on such terms as only can be enjoy'd
against some equal title invaded or destroy'd?
What is this banquet where the guests are served for meat?
What hospitality?   What kind of host is he
the bill of whose purveyance is *Kill ye each other and eat?*

   'Or why, if the excellence of conscient Reason is such,
the accomplishment so high, that it renounce all touch
of kindness with its kin and humbler parentage   120
—building the slaughter-house beside the pasturage—
Why must this last best most miraculous flower of all
be canker'd at the core, prey to the spawn and spawl
of meanest motes? must stoop from its divine degree
to learn the spire and spilth of every insensate filth
that swarmeth in the chaos of obscenity?

   ' And if the formless ferment of life's primal slime
bred without stint, and came through plant and beast in time
to elaborate the higher appurtenance of sex
Why should this low-born urgency persist to vex   130
man's growth in grace? for sure the procreant multitude
would riot to outcrowd the earth wer't not for lack of food,
and thus the common welfare serveth but to swell
the common woe, whereat the starvelings more rebel.

See, never hungry horde of savage raiders slipp'd
from Tartary's parching steppes so for destruction equipp'd
as midst our crowded luxury now the sneaking swarm
that pilfereth intelligence from Science to storm
Civilization in her well-order'd citadel.
Thus Culture doeth herself to death reinforcing hell   140
& seeth no hope but this, that what she hath wrought in vain
since it was wrought before, may yet be wrought again
and fall to a like destruction again and evermore.

'And what Man's Mind? since even withoutthisfouloffence
it breedeth its own poison of its own excellence:
it riseth but to fall deeper, it cannot endure.
Attainment stayeth pursuit and being itself impure
dispiriteth the soul.   All power engendereth pride
and poor vainglory seeing its image magnified
upon the ignoble mirror of common thought, will trust   150
the enticements of self-love and the flattery thereof
and call on fame to enthrone ambition and mortal lust.

'Wherefore, since Reason assureth neither final term
nor substantive foundations impeccable and firm
as brutish instincts are—and Virtue in default
goeth down before the passions crowding to the assault;
Nothing being justified all things are ill or well
are justifiable alike or unjustifiable
till, whether in mocking laughter or mere melancholy,
Philosophy will turn to vindicate folly: 160
and if thru' thought it came that man first learnt his woe,
his Memory accumulating the recorded sum
his Prescience anticipating fresh ills to come,
How could it be otherwise? Why should it not be so?

'And last, O worst! for surely all wrongs had else been nought
had never Imagination exalted human thought
with spiritual affection of tenderness intense

beyond all finest delicacy of bodily sense;
so that the gift of tears, that is the fount of song
maketh intolerable agony of Nature's wrong.   170

    Ask her that taught man filial love, what she hath done
the mother of all mothers, she unto her own dear son?
him innocently desirous to love her well
by unmotherly cruelty she hath driven to rebel,
hath cast out in the night homeless and to his last cry
for guidance on his way hath deign'd him no reply.

    'And thou that in symbolic mockery feign'st to seal
thine eyes from horrors that thou hast no heart to feel,
Thou, THEMIS, wilt suspect not the celestial weight
of the small parcels that I now pile on the plate.   180
    These are love's bereavements and the blightings of bloom
the tears of mourners inconsolable at the tomb
of promise wither'd and fond hope blasted in prime:
These, the torrential commiserations of all time
These, the crime-shrieks of war, plague-groans & famine-cries
These, the slow-standing tears in children's questioning eyes
These, profuse tears of fools, These, coy tears of the wise
in solitude bewailing and in sad silence
the perishing record of hard-won experience
Ruin of accomplishment that no toil can restore   190
Heroic Will chain'd down on Fate's cold dungeon-floor.
See here the tears of prophets, confessors of faith
the tears of beauty-lovers, merchants of the unpriced
in calumny and reproach, in want, wanhope and death
persecuted betray'd imprison'd sacrificed;
All tears from Adam's tears unto the tears of Christ.

    'Look to thy balance, THEMIS; Should thy scale descend
bind up thine eyes again, I shall no more contend;
for if the Final Cause vindicate Nature's laws
her universal plan giveth no heed to man   200
No place; for him Confusion is his Final Cause.'

THUS threw he to the wilderness and silent sky
his outrageous despair the self-pity of mankind
and the disburdenment of his great heaviness
left his heart suddenly so shaken and unsteadied
he seem'd like one who fording a rapid river
and poising on his head a huge stone that its weight
may plant his footing firmly and stiffen his body upright
against the rushing water, hath midway let it fall   209
and with his burden hath lost his balance, and staggering
into the bubbling eddy is borne helpless away.
Even so a stream of natural feeling o'erwhelm'd him
whether of home maybe and childhood or of lovers' eyes
of fond friendship and service, or perchance he felt
himself a rebel untaught who had pilfer'd Wisdom's arms
to work disorder and havoc in the city of God :
For suddenly he was dumbstruck and with humbled step
of unwitting repentance he stole back to his cave
and wrapping his poor rags about him took his way
again to his own people and the city whence he had fled.
There in the market-place a wild haggard figure   221
I saw him anon where high above a surging crowd
he stood waving his hands like some prophet of old
dream-sent to warn God's people ; but them the strong words
of his chasten'd humanity inflame but the more ;
forwhy they cannot suffer mention of holiness
nor the sound of the names that convince them of sin
If there be any virtue, if there be any praise,
'tis not for them to hear of or think on those things.
I saw what he spake to them tho' I heard it not   230
only at the sting thereof the loud wrath that arose.
  As a wild herd of cattle on the prairie pasturing
if they are aware of one amongst them sick or maim'd
or in some part freak-hued differently from themselves
will be moved by instinct of danger and set on him
and bowing all their heads drive him out with their horns
as enemy to their selfwill'd community ;

even such brutish instinct impell'd that human herd   238
and some had stoop'd to gather loose stones from the ground
and were hurling at him : he crouch'd with both his arms
covering his head and would have hid himself from them
in fear more of their crime than of his own peril
Then with a plunge of terror he turn'd and fled for life
and they in wild joy of the chase with hue and cry
broke after him and away and bent on sport to kill
hunted their startled game before them down the streets.

    Awhile he escaped and ran apart, but soon I saw
the leaders closing on him—I was hiding my eyes
lest I should see him taken and torn in blood, when, lo !
the street whereon they ran was block'd across his way   250
by a white-robed throng that came moving with solemn pace
waving banners and incense and high chant on the air,
and bearing 'neath a rich canopy of reverence
their object of devotion—as oft in papal Rome
was seen vying with pomps of earthly majesty
or now on Corpus Christi day thro' Westminster
in babylonish exile paradeth our roads—
and as I looked in wonder on the apparition, I saw
the hunted man into their midst dash'd wildly and fell.

    'Twas like as when a fox that long with speed and guile
hath resolutely outstay'd the yelling murderous pack   261
if when at last his limbs fail him and he knoweth
the hounds hot on his trail and himself quite outworn
will in desperation forgo his native fear
and run for refuge into some hamlet of men
and there will enter a cotter's confined cabin and plead
panting with half-closed eyes to the heart of his foe,
altho' he knoweth nought of the Divinity
of that Nature to whom he pleadeth, nor knoweth
ev'n that he pleadeth, yet he pleadeth not in vain   270
—so great is Nature—for the good wife hath pity,
will suffer him to hide there under settle or bed
until the hunt be pass'd, will cheer him and give him

milk of her children's share until he be restor'd
when she will let him forth to his roguish freedom again—
   So now this choral convoy of heavenly pasture
gave ready succour and harbour to the hunted man
and silencing their music broke their bright-robed ranks
to admit him, and again closed round him where fordone
he fell down in their midst : and hands I saw outstretch'd
to upraise him, but when he neither rose up nor stirr'd 281
they knelt aghast, and one, who in solemn haste came up
and for the splendour of his apparel an elder seem'd,
bent over him there and whisper'd sacred words, whereat
he motion'd and gave sign, and offering his dumb mouth
took from the priestly fingers such food as is dealt
unto the dying, and when the priest stood up I knew
by the gesture of his silence that the man was dead.

   Then feet and head his body in fair linen winding
they raised and bore along with dirge and shriving prayer
such as they use when one of their own brotherhood 291
after mortal probation has enter'd into rest
and they will bury his bones where Christ at his coming
shall bid them all arise from their tombs in the church;
Whereto their long procession now went filing back
threading the streets, and dwarfed beneath the bright façade
crept with its head to climb the wide steps to the porch
whereunder, as ever there they arrived, the dark doorway
swallowed them out of sight : and still the train came on
with lurching bannerets and tottering canopy 300
threading the streets and mounting to the shadowy porch
arriving entering disappearing without end
when I awoke, the dirge still sounding in my ears
the night wind blowing thro' the open window upon me
as I lay marvelling at the riddle of my strange dream.

8

TO FRANCIS JAMMES

'Tɪs April again in my garden, again the grey stone-wall
   Is prankt with yellow alyssum and lilac aubrey-cresses ;
   Half-hidden the mavis caroleth in the tassely birchen
      tresses
And awhile on the sunny air a cuckoo tuneth his call :
Now cometh to mind a singer whom country joys enthral,
   Francis Jammes, so grippeth him Nature in her caresses
   She hath steep'd his throat in the honey'd air of her
      wildernesses
With beauty that countervails the Lutetian therewithal.

You are here in spirit, dear poet, and bring a motley group,
   Your friends, afore you sat stitching your heavenly trous-
      seau—
   The courteous old road-mender, the queer Jean Jacques
      Rousseau,
Columbus, Confucius, all to my English garden they troop,
   Under his goatskin umbrella the provident Robinson
      Crusoe,
And the ancestor dead long ago in Domingo or Guadaloupe.

9

MELANCHOLY

'Twᴀs mid of the moon but the night was dark with rain,
Drops lashed the pane, the wind howl'd under the door ;
For me, my heart heard nought but the cannon-roar

(531)

On fields of war, where Hell was raging amain :
My heart was sore for the slain :—
As when on an Autumn plain the storm lays low the wheat,
So fell the flower of England, her golden grain,
Her harvesting hope trodden under the feet
Of Moloch, Woden and Thor,
And the lovingkindness of Christ held in disdain.   10

    My heart gave way to the strain, renouncing more & more ;
Its bloodstream fainted down to the slothful weary beat
Of the age-long moment, that swelleth where ages meet,
Marking time 'twixt dark Hereafter and Long-before ;
Which greet awhile and awhile, again to retreat ;
The Never-the-same repeating again and again,
Completing itself in monotony incomplete,
A wash of beauty and horror in shadows that fleet,
Always the Never-the-same still to repeat,
The devouring glide of a dream that keepeth no store.   20

    Meseem'd I stood on the flats of a waveless shore,
Where MELANCHOLY unrobed of her earthly weeds,
Haunteth in naked beauty without stain ;
In reconcilement of Death, and Vanity of all needs ;
A melting of life in oblivion of all deeds ;
No other beauty nor passion nor love nor lore ;
No other goddess abideth for man to adore ;
All things remaining nowhere with nought to remain ;
The consummation of thought in nought to attain.

    I had come myself to that ultimate Ocean-shore,   30
Like Labourer Love when his life-day is o'er,
Who home returning fatigued is fain to regain
The house where he was unconsciously born of yore ;
Stumbling on the threshold he sinketh down on the floor ;
Half-hearteth a prayer as he lieth, and nothing heeds,
If only he sleep and sleep and have rest for evermore.

New Verse

10

BUCH DER LIEDER

Be these the selfsame verses
　　That once when I was young
Charm'd me with dancing magic
　　To love their foreign tongue,

Delicate buds of passion,
　　Gems of a master's art,
That broke forth rivalling Nature
　　In love-songs of the heart;

Like fresh leaves of the woodland
　　Whose trembling screens would house
The wanton birdies courting
　　Upon the springing boughs?

Alas, how now they are wither'd!
　　And fallen from the skies
In yellowy tawny crumple
　　Their tender wreckage lies,

And all their ravisht beauty
　　Strewn 'neath my feet to-day
Rustles as I go striding
　　Upon my wintry way.

II

EMILY BRONTË

'Du hast Diamanten'

THOU hadst all Passion's splendor,
  Thou hadst abounding store
Of heaven's eternal jewels,
  Belovèd; what wouldst thou more?

Thine was the frolic freedom
  Of creatures coy and wild,
The melancholy of wisdom,
  The innocence of a child,

The mail'd will of the warrior,
  That buckled in thy breast
Humility as of Francis,
  The self-surrender of Christ;

And of God's cup thou drankest
  The unmingled wine of Love,
Which makes poor mortals giddy
  When they but sip thereof.

What was't to thee thy pathway
  So rugged mean and hard,
Whereon when Death surprised thee
  Thou gav'st him no regard?

What was't to thee, enamour'd
  As a red rose of the sun,
If of thy myriad lovers
  Thou never sawest one?

Nor if of all thy lovers
  That are and were to be
None ever had their vision,
  O belovèd, of thee,

Until thy silent glory
    Went forth from earth alone,
Where like a star thou gleamest
    From thine immortal throne.

12

THE TRAMPS

A SCHOOLBOY lay one night a-bed
    Under his window wide,
When dusk is lovelier than day
    In the high summertide ;

The jasmin neath the casement throng'd
    Its ivory stars abloom ;
With freaking peas and mignonette
    Their perfume fill'd the room :

Across the garden and beyond
    He look'd out on the skies,
And through black elmen boughs afar
    Watch'd where the moon should rise :

A warm rain fed the thirsty earth,
    Drops patter'd from the eaves
And from the tall trees as the shower
    Fell lisping on their leaves :

His heart was full, and pleasant thoughts
    Made music in his mind,
Like separate songs of birds, that are
    By general joy combined.

It seem'd the hour had gather'd up
    For every sense a bliss
To crown the faith of all desire
    With one assuaging kiss ;

So that he fought with sleep to hold
    The rapture while he might,
Lest it should sink and drowning die
    Into the blank of night;

Nor kenn'd it was no passing thing
    Nor ever should be pass'd
But with him bide a joy to be
    As long as Life should last.

For though young thoughts be quite forgone,
    The pleasure of their dream
Can mesh them in its living mood
    And draw them in the stream:

So I can fancy when I will
    That there I lie intent
To hear the gentle whispering rain
    And drink the jasmin scent:

And then there sounds a distant tread
    Of men, that night who strode
Along the highway step by step
    Approaching down the road,

A company of three or four
    That hastening home again
After a Sabbath holiday
    Came talking in the rain:

Aloof from all my world and me
    They pass aneath the wall,
Till voice and footstep die away
    And into silence fall:

Into the maze of my delight
    Those blind intruders walk;
And ever I wonder who they be
    And of what things they talk.

13
THE GREAT ELM

FROM a friend's house had I gone forth,
    And wandering at will
O'er a wide country West and North
    Without or vale or hill,
I came beneath the broken edge
    Of higher sloping ground,
Where an old Giant from the ledge
    O'erlook'd the landscape round:

A towering Elm that stood alone,
    Last of an ancient rank,
And had great barky roots out-thrown
    To buttress up the bank;
His rough trunk of two hundred years
    In girth a pillar gave
As massive as the Norman piers
    That rise in Durham's nave;

But this for stony roof and wall
    Upliving timber held,
Where never in its forest tall
    Had woodman lopp'd or fell'd:
Above its crown no wind so fierce
    Had warp'd the shapely green,
And scarce with bated breath might pierce
    Its caves of leafy screen.

It seem'd in that dark foliage laid
    Suspended thought must dwell;
As in those boughs that overshade
    The river-sides of Hell,
That fabled Elm of Acheron,
    Within the gates of death,

(537)

Which once Æneas look'd upon—
    As Virgil witnesseth—
Whose leafage the last refuge was
    And haven of mortal dreams,
That clustering clung thereto because
    They might not pass the streams.

Now suddenly was I aware
    That on the grassy shelf
A spirit was waiting for me there,
    A coy seraphic elf—
My other half-self, whom I miss
    In life's familiar moods,
And ken of only by his kiss
    In sacred solitudes;
And for that rare embrace have borne
    With Fate and things distraught,
The wanhope of my days forlorn,
    My sins, have counted nought.

He is of such immortal kind,
    His inwit is so clean,
So conscient with the eternal Mind—
    The self of things unseen,
That when within his world I win,
    Nor suffer mortal change,
I am of such immortal kin
    No dream is half so strange.

Alas, I have done myself great wrong
    Truckling to human care,
Am shamed to ken myself so strong
    And nobler than I dare:
And yet so seldom doth he grant
    The comfort of his grace,
So fickle is he and inconstant
    To any time or place,

That since he chose that place and time
 To come again to me,
I'd hold him fast by magic rhyme
 Forever to that tree:
As there in lavish self-delight,
 Godlike and single-souled,
I lay until the dusk of night
 Came creeping o'er the wold.

14

THE SLEEPING MANSION

As our car rustled swiftly
 along the village lane,
we caught sight for a moment
 of the old house again,

Which once I made my home in—
 ev'n as a soul may dwell
enamouring the body
 that she loveth so well:

But I long since had left it;
 what fortune now befals
finds me on other meadows
 by other trees and walls.

The place look'd blank and empty,
 a sleeper's witless face
which to his mind's enchantment
 is numb, and gives no trace.

And to that slumbering mansion
 was I come as a dream,
to cheer her in her stupor
 and loneliness extreme.

(539)

I knew what sudden wonder
    I brought her in my flight;
what rapturous joy possess'd her,
    what peace and soft delight.

15

VISION

How should I be to Love unjust
    Since Love hath been so kind to me?
O how forget thy tender trust
    Or slight the bond that set me free?
How should thy spirit's blithe embrace,
    Thy loyalty, have been given in vain,
From the first beckoning of thy grace
    That made a child of me again,
And since hath still my manhood led
    Through scathe and trouble hour by hour,
And in probation perfected
    The explicit fruit of such a flower?

Not ev'n the Apostles, in the days
    They walked with Christ, lov'd him so well
As we may now, who ken his praise
    Reading the story that they tell,
Writ by them when their vision grew
    And he, who fled and thrice denied
Christ to his face, was proven true
    And gladly for His memory died:
So strong the Vision, there was none
    O'er whom the Fisher's net was cast,
Ev'n of the fearfullest not one
    Who would have left Him at the last.

So 'tis with me; the time hath clear'd
    Not dull'd my loving: I can see

Love's passing ecstasies endear'd
   In aspects of eternity:
I am like a miser—I can say
   That having hoarded all my gold
I must grow richer every day
   And die possess'd of wealth untold.

16

LOW BAROMETER

THE south-wind strengthens to a gale,
Across the moon the clouds fly fast,
The house is smitten as with a flail,
The chimney shudders to the blast.

On such a night, when Air has loosed
Its guardian grasp on blood and brain,
Old terrors then of god or ghost
Creep from their caves to life again;

And Reason kens he herits in
A haunted house. Tenants unknown
Assert their squalid lease of sin
With earlier title than his own.

Unbodied presences, the pack'd
Pollution and remorse of Time,
Slipp'd from oblivion reënact
The horrors of unhouseld crime.

Some men would quell the thing with prayer
Whose sightless footsteps pad the floor,
Whose fearful trespass mounts the stair
Or bursts the lock'd forbidden door.

Some have seen corpses long interr'd
Escape from hallowing control,
Pale charnel forms—nay ev'n have heard
The shrilling of a troubled soul,

That wanders till the dawn hath cross'd
The dolorous dark, or Earth hath wound
Closer her storm-spredd cloke, and thrust
The baleful phantoms underground

17

A DREAM

I HAD come in front of a building and knew
    I should enter : the gates were barr'd,
but a postern was open, and I push'd through
    and stood in a wide courtyard.

'Twas built, as colleges are, four-square,
    though arch and colonnade
all here were of wood and out of repair,
    timeworn but undecay'd.

Great carven portals in Gothic style,
    when building could save man's soul :
doors worthy to face a cathedral aisle,
    or where men-at-arms patrol.

But whether 'twere some old abbey of monks
    with cloister, chapel and cell,
or a farmstead with pens and stalls and bunks
    for cattle, I could not tell.

There neither were cattle nor men about,
    no cock nor clock gave steven ;
and I in my dream had never a doubt
    'twas the entry-court of heaven.

An old man then appear'd from a door
  and silently moved around;
his beard was grisled and thick, and he wore
  a cassock that reach'd the ground;

Stately his figure and lofty his mien,
  solemn and slow his tread:
'twas Peter the Saint; I had often seen
  in pictures his noble head,

Which truly in Guido's painting is shown
  sadden'd and full of force,
as unconvinced he sits on a stone
  suffering Paul's discourse.

Like any night-watchman he walked along
  peering about on his rounds,
attentive to see that nothing is wrong,
  no smoke nor thief within bounds;

Or like a merchant who checks his stores,
  sorting his trusty keys,
he unlock'd and anon relock'd the doors,
  visiting now those, now these.

Quiet I stood sans hope or fear,
  nor moved to catch his eye,
nor felt annoy'd when he came quite near
  and pass'd me unnoticed by:

I knew he must know I was there; the scheme
  of eternity gave us time;
so I took whatever might hap in my dream
  as easy as now in my rhyme.

When, as to a prodigal son, from afar
  he approach'd—he had been remiss
through kindness—he said 'I know who you are:
  you won't get further than this:

'You needn't be bash'd nor mortified,
   nor fancy you're laid on the shelf:
things ain't as they used to be inside;
   I don't go in much myself.'

Then passing away he turn'd again,
   as if to relieve his mind,
and spoke—if partly he wished to explain,
   I'm sure he will'd to be kind:—

He look'd full glum—it may be a sin
   to repeat his words, as I know it's
bad taste—but he said—(He'll square me the sin):
   'Why! what d'you think? We've just took in
     a batch of those French poets.'

18

TO HIS EXCELLENCY

ONE of all our brave commanders,
   Near of kin and dear my friend,
Led his men in France and Flanders
   From the first brush to the end:

Peril lov'd he, and undaunted
   Sought it out, and thanked his stars
That to him a place was granted
   In the worst of all the wars.

He brought Uhlans in from Soignies,
   Where the first blood was let out—
With his remnant from Andregnies
   Saved St. Quentin's desperate rout.

Stiffly fought he through the onset
   Undishearten'd by defeat;
Held the rear from dawn to sunset
   Through the long days of retreat.

Times were, to retake the trenches
   He dismounted his dragoons,
Suck'd his share of gas and stenches
   With lieutenants of platoons.

Hit by howitzers and snipers
   He in his five years campaign
Rode the land from Reims to Wipers,
   On the Marne and on the Aisne.

Many deeds would be to blazon,
   Many fights, to tell them all;
Niewport, Witchet, Contalmaison,
   La Boiselle and Passendaal.

Nothing in his clean vocation
   Vex'd his soul or came amiss,
From the hurried embarcation
   To the fateful armistice:

But when terms of truce were bruited,
   Then his cheery countenance fell
In confession undisputed
   That things were not going well:

'Nay (he said), my hope was larger;
   'Twas not thus I look'd to win:
I had vow'd to rein my charger
   In the streets of proud Berlin.'

19

*Spoken by Sir Johnston Forbes-Robertson
at the opening of the Theatre
of the Royal Academy of Dramatic Art
by H.R.H. the Prince of Wales,
May 27, 1921.*

ENGLAND will keep her dearest jewel bright,
   And see her sons like to their sires renown'd;
   Whose Shakespeare is with deathless Homer crown'd,
Her freedom the world's hope throned in the height.
All gifts of spirit are of such airy flight
   That if their fire be spent they fall to ground;
   Their virtue must with newborn life abound,
And by young birth renew their old birthright.

   We workers therefore in this troublous age
Would keep our beauty of language from misfeature,
     Presenting manners noble, and mirth unblamed:
So Truth shall walk majestic on our stage,
And when we hold the mirror up to Nature,
     She, seeing her face therein, shall not be ashamed.

20

HODGE

After reading Maurice Hewlett's ' Song of the Plow'

COUNTRYMAN HODGE has gone to fight;
   The girls must help to raise the grain,
Must fag in the workshops day and night,
   Till Hodge come back to his home again.

His life was ever a life of toil
   In snow and frost, in drought or rain ;
But he is heir and son of the soil
   And Hodge shall come to his own again.

The Norman oppressed him long ago,
   But nought reck'd he of pity or pain,
He stuck to his work and lay full low
   Till he should come to his own again.

Then Commerce swelled and drove him down ;
   Little he got from all her gain ;
His boys went off and made the town,
   But Hodge shall come to his own again.

He has waited long and foughten well
   That Peace should smile and Plenty reign ;
And now, as bygone riddlers tell,
   Hodge shall come to his own again.

'The day when folk shall fly in the air
   And skim like birds above the plain,
Then shall the plowman have his share
   And Hodge will come to his own again.'

                             1917.

21

SORROW and joy, two sisters coy,
   Aye for our hearts are fighting :
The half our years are teen and tears,
   And half are mere delighting.

So when joy's cup is brimm'd full up,
  Take no thought o' the morrow:
So fine 's your bliss, ye shall not miss
  To have your turn wi' sorrow.

And she with ruth will teach you truth,
  She is man's very med'cin:
She'll drive us straight to heav'n's high gate,
  Ay, she can stuff our heads in.

Blush not nor blench with either wench,
  Make neither brag nor pother:
God send you, son, enough of one
  And not too much o' t'other.

22

SIMPKIN

They tell me Simpkin is a saint
  I've often wish'd he wasn't,
If 'tis a note of that complaint
  To look so d—d unpleasant.

The world 's no doubt a sorry place
  For Simpkin; and, by Jabez,
The merest glimpsing of his face
  Will wring and writhe a baby's.

A lout he is, a kill-joy loon
  Where wit and mirth forgather;
In company I'd just as soon
  Sit by an old bell-wether.

But Simpkin, I have heard men state,
  Is kindly and well-meaning;
'Tis that his goodness is so great
  It takes so much o' screening.

I would the fiend, that made his skin
  So yellow dry and scurvy,
Had turn'd the creature outside-in
  Or set him topsy-turvy.

And yet since nothing's made in vain,
  And we must judge our brother
Unfitted for this world, 'tis plain
  He's fitted for another;

Where angels glorious to behold
  Shall come, as he supposes,
To lead him through the streets o' gold
  And crown his head with roses.

And if to Simpkin it befal
  Just as he thinks, so be it!
I would not grudge the man at all,
  But should not press to see it.

23

TO CATULLUS

WOULD that you were alive today, Catullus!
Truth 'tis, there is a filthy skunk amongst us,
A rank musk-idiot, the filthiest skunk,
Of no least sorry use on earth, but only
Fit in fancy to justify the outlay
Of your most horrible vocabulary.

My Muse, all innocent as Eve in Eden,
Would yet wear any skins of old pollution
Rather than celebrate the name detested.
Ev'n now might he rejoice at our attention,
Guess'd he this little ode were aiming at him.

O! were you but alive again, Catullus!

For see, not one among the bards of our time
With their flimsy tackle was out to strike him;
Not those two pretty Laureates of England,
Not Alfred Tennyson nor Alfred Austin.

1902.

24

TO SIR THOS. BARLOW, P.R.C.P.

IT's all up I may tell you, good Thomas Barlow,
The new medicine is wholly broken and done for:
You must give up Profession and College, Barlow.

Your fine *Address*, man, *on the basis of treatment*,
So practical so blindly hopeful of progress,
'Tis but delusion; all is ended and done for.

For lately Stephen Coleridge in a current Monthly
Has wittily in a few words the system exploded.
Better retire and leave the stage, my dear Barlow.

  You've been accustom'd in matters of importance
To look to me to give you earliest tidings;
So I devote a penful of little scazons
To write the dirge of medicine and modern science.

The wonder is how nearly both of us miss'd it:
Nor would any whisper'd hint of it have ever reach'd me,
Had not the well-deserving excellent author
Most kindly frank'd me a copy of his dissertation.

Oct. 1902.

25

ΠΟΙΚΙΛΟΘΡΟΝ᾽

Translated from Sappho

ALL-ADOR'D, all glorious Aphrodita,
Heav'n's goddess mysterious, I beseech thee
With thy anguish and terror overwhelm not
    My spirit, O queen:

But hither come thou, as, if e'er, aforetime
Thou to my crying from afar attentive
Harkenedst, an' out o' the golden archways
    Unto me camest,

Harnessing thy fair flutterers, that earthward
Swiftly drew thee down to the dusky mountains
Multitudinously winging from unseen
    Heights o' the wide air,

And arrivèd, thrice-blessed, I beheld thee
Smiling on me beautiful and triumphant,
Heard thee asking of me what had befal'n me,
    Why had I call'd thee,

And what I desir'd above all to comfort
My madden'd heart :—Who is it hath deny'd thee?
Shall not I subdue the rebel to thy love,
    Sapph', an' avenge thee?

      .   .   .   .

Come then, O queen : come to me and release me
From bitter woe. Stand my ally. The thing that
My spirit most longs for, accomplish, and win
    Victory with me.

1910.

Two Pieces
written after the war

*not included
in any of the foregoing publications*

PREVIOUS PUBLICATIONS

1. *Oxford: at the Clarendon Press. 1932, in facsimile.*
2. *The Legion Book. Privately printed, 1929.*

I

VERSES
WRITTEN FOR MRS. DANIEL

TO

EMILY DANIEL

In memory of the War-work done in the Provost's Lodgings at Worcester College, Oxford, during the last two years of the War under the presidency of Mrs. Daniel, her fellow-workers beg to offer her with their homage this copy of William Blake's Lyrical Poems as a token of their gratitude for the very pleasant conditions which she provided for their meeting and to record their appreciation of her perpetual kindness and courtesy and cheerful hospitality throughout that sad time, and hereto they sign their names.

[Here followed 51 signatures.] [1]

AND I am asked for mere variety
To join my name with this society ;
For tho' I wasn't rightly in't
I too hav pasted at a splint
And after wash'd my hands beslubber'd
Half-way downstairs i' the' housemaid's cupboard,
And follow'd others of the meinie
To sit around the steaming cheney,
Chatting with apostolic souls
Noel or Hack or Stuckey Coles,   10
The soft aroma and effulgence
Of afternones merged in th' indulgence

---

[1] [The above dedication and the signatures of the 51 donors followed by the MS. of R. B.'s verses, were bound up with the copy of Blake's Poems which was presented to Mrs. Daniel, April 1919.]

(555)

Of a spiritual kindly hostess
(which is what butter on hot toast is),
In friendship that began maybe
In eighteen eighty two or three,
When Daniel printed my PROMETHEVS
—a thing that others judged beneath use—,
He living then in Worcester House
Along with many a rat and mouse,   20
Which multiplying as their manner is
Had overswarm'd the neighb'ring granaries.

    On winter eves when Bodley's bell
Drove every reader from his cell,
Betwixt my book and railway-station
Time found with place accommodation
There, by his study fire where he
Mid bursary bills was wont to be ;
And other friends would end their walk,
Ere they went home, with tea and talk,   30
Which, if 'twas bookish, Toby Watson
Had he stol'n in could put the dots on,
Half-buried in an easy chair,
With gentle murmur and modest air
Fetching out learning with demurrage
As fearful to disturb his storage.
    Or if 'twas summer and tea was laid
By wicker seats beneath the shade,
I must pass where in the garden entry
A monstrous effigy stood sentry,   40
One of those column-heads which Wren
Contracted for at two-pound-ten
To top the wall he built between
Theatre and road his work to screen,
Figuring those metaphysic sages
Whose lucubrations cross the ages ;

For tho' they mistook heat-condition
Of matter for its composition
(in which not one of all the lot'll
seem more at sea than Aristotle),   50
We've now-a-days no boss so swagger as
Empedocles or Anaxagoras;
While th' intuitions of Democritus
Transcend whatever Hume or Locke writ us.

But jealous Time, who was unwilling
To suffer those poor fifty-shilling
Presentments of the brows of Hellas,
Snubb'd them as readily and as well as
His frost and rain make scald and sorry
Th'ashlar of our suburban quarry.   60

So 'twas in my day that the thirteen [1]
Left all who look'd on them uncertain
Whether the comical old fossils
Were sages Kaisers or Apostles,
Or studied types of such impostors
As any seat of learning fosters;
Prehaps, said some malicious guessers,
Old Heads of Houses or Professors
In days when scholars all were topers,
After Charles sack'd the interlopers,   70
And every don and dean was able
To drink a Dutchman neath the table.

Faced with this scandal the Curators
Would to their trust hav been but traitors,
Had they allow'd the wrecks to worsen;
Nor 'mong them was a single person,
Master of Arts or scarlet D.D.
So void of scruple and unheedy

---

[1] There had been originally 14 on the segment. One was cut out when the Clarendon printing house invaded the site. Those on the straight wall to the west are a spurious addition neglected in this description.

As not to deem it an iniquity
That genuine objects of antiquity,   80
Howe'er incongruous or rumbustuous,
Should thro' neglect be wholly lost to us:
Wherefor in '68 the Board
Decreed the heads should be restored
Before the most decay'd and choppiest
Should quite defy a faithful copyist.

Lo! then, whate'er the first designer
Had dream'd of earthlier or diviner,
His little effort quite went under
And we possess'd the world's tenth wonder.   90
Thank heaven I saw them at their smartest
As they were turn'd out by the artist,
And recognised that there were things
Unknown to prophets and to kings,
Whether or no they had desired them,
However much their faith inspired them.
Daring incompetence had master'd
Th' impossible and gotten a bastard,
Which tower'd in strength without relation
To human thought or God's creation,   100
And made what still in travellers' eyes is
One of old England's great surprises.

But Time again, who all things stomachs,
Soon brought them to their pristine flummux;
And that especial mullion-scullion,
Second in rank from th' old Ashmolean
(whose prototype at trifling expense
Daniel secured for three and sixpence)
And, 'mong the intellectual progeny, 's
Intended doubtless for Diogenes,   110
Is moulder'd down until his noddle
Well represents its quondam model:
Indeed the stone may hav been weaker
Of which they fashioned the replica,

(558)

for Mrs. Daniel

(so Madan says with perfect fitness)
For all the set—as I can witness,
Oft as I visit Henry Bradley
To suck his brains, who suffers gladly,
Stuffing the words into their pigeonholes—
Are rotted worse than the originals.   120

   This of the bust in Daniel's garden:
Tho' stone will soften ink may harden
To save a memory else abolish'd
Of Worcester House long since demolish'd,
When the townfolk to disentangle
The traffic, rounded off the angle
By which the carts and cabs must always
Crowd from north-Oxford to the railways.

   Long live the bust, a festering relic
Of days perhaps not quite angelic,   130
Those changeful days that pass'd between,
say, Verdant Green and T. H. Green,
With th' eighteenth century still fruiting,
The nineteenth rooting and uprooting:
But since all things the while they germinate
Are undefined and indeterminate,
I'll not set up to be historian
Of th' era now yclept Victorian,
Full tho' it was of strength and colour
Nor emptier of delite nor duller   140
Than days which with their customs ántique
Seen from afar look more romantic.

   Not then to theorise or speculate,—
When '63 saw me matriculate
There still wer fights 'twixt Town and Gown,
Nor Bouncer's type was yet liv'd down.
I knew one fellow, a handsome scout
Of Corpus, had an eye put out
Following as Bull-dog with the Proctor;
And 'twas an earl who paid his doctor.   150

If Tommy Case then bought a new cur,
He dealt perforce with Filthy Luker:
But if men hunted or drove tandem
The Proctor did not reprimand 'em.
At crowded wines ' with songs and clatter
Freshmen wer taught their brains to scatter,
Yet still within the college compass
Monkish seclusion lurk'd in rumpus;
A pore scoler might sport his oak
Nor fear to hav his windows broke,   160
Nor was there any intrusion feminine,
The porter let not dogs or women in:
But now—even tho' no college ball's on—
Girls are about, and if one calls on
A nephew, ten to one the blade is
Giving a teaparty to ladies,
His room with cigarette-smoke stuffy;
Wherat he spends, on tea and coffee
And butter'd buns, so sober-minded,
As much as we on beer and wine did.   170
No don survives now whom it vexes
To see this ease between the sexes,
And we'd some dons dead as those dummies
Carven on tombs to look like mummies
Waiting until the resurrection
To put their trowsers and their neck-tie on.[1]
    As for the boys, tho' our *juventus*
Was not perhaps all as God meant us,
Too eager in th' exploit of pastime,
Yet on our books we spent no less time,   180
Pronouncing Latin quite as oddly
As A. C. Clark or A. D. Godley,
And sportively intent on getting
A first in Greats against the betting:
For teachers know examination

[1] Consonantia obsoleta imaginis vetustati liberrime congruens.

To be the crown of education:
Since minds cannot like plants be trusted
To keep their rootlets well-adjusted,
They who would rear them must examine 'em
To gauge th' effect of what they cram in 'em.   190
True, in our gamesome gay ideal
Comfort bulk'd somewhat large and real,
Plus aequo operati in cute
Curanda, yet 'twas not so footy;
We liv'd a life of joy unchequer'd;
We lov'd and laugh'd and beat the record.

   Delivering well-pitch'd balls no worse is
Than turning out neat Latin verses;
Or, if the latter trick surpasses
The former, 'tis in making asses.   200
Within the church, which sadly suffers
From blinkerdom of classic duffers,
To hav been a batsman does not weaken
The reverence paid to an archdeacon,
And every bishop knows it biasses
The public favour in his diocese;
While if he has only stroked the eight-oar
He curules it like a dictator.

   And certain 'tis that nature ossifies
In students who too much philosophize;   210
No man can brood on abstract Unity
Or abstract Being with impunity;
And some I knew that haunted whilom
The schools who died in an asylum.

   There was malaise in the defiance
With which the gown regarded science;
As now it wounds whom it astounds
To hear that speech is made of sounds,
Phonetical,—O word of fear
Unpleasing to a marrèd ear!   220
   Awkwardness shyness and selfconsciousness

(561)   o o

Were but the garment of pretentiousness;
'Twixt younger don and undergraduate
There's freer commerce now, and, had you it
Complete, 'twould lubricate the wheel
Which otherwise must stick or squeal.

    Who'd now believe that wisdom's pith
Was wrapp'd from sight in Goldwin Smith?
Ah! if some scornful future Timon
Should know the names that I coud ryme on,   230
And judge those men by what they built,
Will he distinguish folly and guilt
In him who rear'd that gothic fustian
On Christ Church meadows for a bastion?
In them whose taste it was to shunt
Butterfield's box on Merton front?
Or, seeing Balliol as we know it,
Will he suppose that Master Jowett
More light and sweetness suck'd from Plato
Than a man might from a potato?   240
Nay! Pin each name to its memorial;
'Twas the high fellowship of Oriel,
On such a site, in such a seat,
Perpetrated King Edward Street!

    The boys meanwhile clear of these shames
Added on music to their games;
And, freelier so their legs to use,
Above the knee cut short their trews,
And did not for ill-manners take it
To run upon the street half-naked.   250

    And then the WAR . . . . . .
. . . . . . I thought not, when
I laid hand on this skittish pen
To carry me cantering across country,
The jade would show so much effront'ry,
And lurching with a vice inveterate

for Mrs. Daniel

Refuse the last fence that I set her at.
She does.—And since my run is ended
I'll plead 'least said is soonest mended',
And shove the rest back in my storeroom:
So make the most of this culorum.   260

THE WIDOW

WHENEVER I pass that house
   my heart is in prayer
for reverence of the angels
   who are watching there ;
where a widow reareth
   the child that she bore
after her young lover
   was kill'd in the war.

A bird torn by the hawk
   hath pangs bodily
and a birth of wonder
   in its agony :
'Tis man's Gethsemane
   to know his soul riven
and feel the bleeding roots
   being torn out from heaven.

God speed thee with comfort,
   thou sorrowing one,
may God give thee great joy
   and pride in thy son !
Thy hope's haunted ruin
   is not to rebuild :
How shall the broken cup
   with wine be refill'd ?

Keep thou bravely for him
   thought of thy morrow,
and thy beauty for grace
   of thy life's sorrow,
like a wreathing rainbow
   over thy way thrown,
sanctifying thy presence
   while thou walkest alone.

1921.

FINIS

INDEX OF TITLES AND FIRST LINES

Index of Titles and First Lines

Index of Titles and First Lines

Index of Titles and First Lines

Index of Titles and First Lines

Index of Titles and First Lines

Index of Titles and First Lines

Index of Titles and First Lines

Index of Titles and First Lines

Index of Titles and First Lines

Index of Titles and First Lines

(575)

Index of Titles and First Lines